In the expanding field of feminist literary studies of the Bible, this work represents a shift in the paradigm of biblical study. While scholars have traditionally privileged the Bible and isolated it from ideological scrutiny, this readable study applies cultural perspectives to a group of biblical texts revolving around the "wicked" literary figures in the Bible – the wife of Potiphar, Bathsheba, Delilah, Salomé – and suggests what it is that makes them different from biblical heroines who kill – Esther and Judith.

Alice Bach has designed an approach to these texts that is kaleidoscopic – its function is to find new arrangements, ones that allow the reader to move outside the self-referential loop of reading the Bible only against itself. Most importantly, Bach argues that biblical characters have a "life" in the mind of the reader independent of the stories in which they were created. Thus, the reader becomes the site at which the texts and the cultures that produced them come together. In her final chapter, Bach follows the cultural history of the biblical figure Salomé, using visual representations as well as films, in order to explain the fluctuations of interest in, and the varieties of interpretation of, this biblical character.

WOMEN, SEDUCTION, AND BETRAYAL IN BIBLICAL NARRATIVE

WOMEN, SEDUCTION, AND BETRAYAL IN BIBLICAL NARRATIVE

ALICE BACH

Stanford University

CAMBRIDGE
UNIVERSITY PRESS

Barnard

PUBLISHED BY THE PRESS SYNDICATE OF THE UNIVERSITY OF CAMBRIDGE
The Pitt Building, Trumpington Street, Cambridge CB2 1RP, United Kingdom

CAMBRIDGE UNIVERSITY PRESS
The Edinburgh Building, Cambridge CB2 2RU, United Kingdom
40 West 20th Street, New York, NY 10011-4211, USA
10 Stamford Road, Oakleigh, Melbourne 3166, Australia

© Cambridge University Press 1997

First published 1997

Printed in the United Kingdom at the University Press, Cambridge

Typeset in Baskerville $11/12\frac{1}{2}$ pt

A catalogue record for this book is available from the British Library

Library of Congress cataloguing in publication data
Bach, Alice.
Women, seduction, and betrayal in biblical narrative / Alice Bach.
p.   cm.
Includes bibliographical references and index.
ISBN 0 521 47532 5 (hardcover). – ISBN 0 521 47560 0 (paperback)
1. Women in the Bible.   2. Bible – Feminist criticism.   I. Title.
BS575.B24   1997
221.9'22'082 – dc21   97–8912 CIP

ISBN 0 521 47532 5 hardback
ISBN 0 521 47560 0 paperback

For Mieke Bal and Ed Greenstein

Contents

Illustrations

[Illustrations 3, 4, 5, and 6 are screen shots from *Salomé* (1953) directed by William Dieterle, written by Harry Kleiner and Jesse Lasky Jr., produced by Buddy Adler, Columbia Pictures.]

Acknowledgments

There is no way to thank everybody who inspired this book. Some like George Eliot, Anna Magnani, Elizabeth Bowen, and Martin Scorsese would be surprised anyway. Closer to home, Cheryl Exum has listened to the stories, argued with me and supported me in equal measure, and urged me to get busy. Rudy Busto helped me to rearrange my study – about a dozen times. Generous and wise colleagues poured out their time and care lavishly upon these pages. Mary Callaway, Cheryl Exum, Jennifer Glancy, Bernard Faure have flavored my thinking, although of course they are not responsible for the finished product. Equally precious to me and important to my work are the email cohort, without which I would indeed be working without a Net: Athalya Brenner, A. J. Levine, Jane Schaberg, Philip Davies, Francis Landy, Irena Makarushka. They remind me daily what fun this business of reading texts can be.

I would like to thank the Marcos Foundation for the Violet Andrews Wright Fellowship that made it possible for me to spend an unmatchable year at the Stanford Humanities Center. The Director Keith Baker and the staff treated me far better than anyone deserves. My lunchtime colleagues at the Center will find themselves hidden in descriptions of ancient banquets and strong-willed women.

The Feminist Faculty Group has been a source of exuberance and excellence for my years at Stanford. The support and friendship of Jane Collier, Estelle Freedman, and Sylvia Yanagisako have made institutional life far less institutional. Michelle Scott proved that editorial and research assistants can be friends as well as library mavens.

xiii

During the time of working with these biblical characters and narratives, some friends helped by not offering opinions. For all the other wisdom and kindness they throw my way, I hope Nancy Dyer Babb, Carl Bielefeldt, Lou Martyn, Judy Buck, Kassie Temple, Elizabeth Janeway, and Mollie Rosenhan know that I am grateful. Peter Minichiello deserves a sentence to himself.

My aunt Ellen Bach offered much needed support during a difficult time. Peerless copy-editor Susan Beer combed the manuscript clean of tangles, and providential plant maven Susie Mader kept the surroundings very green.

Professor Edward Greenstein has my gratitude for taking me on as a graduate student and training me in biblical studies with care and precision. Fortunately, his wisdom and readerly insights continue to shape my scholarly musings. Professor Mieke Bal has a generosity of spirit that is remarkable. Her work has provided the foundation for this study; her explorations in both literary and cultural analysis have raised questions that continually challenge my perceptions and assumptions. As a feminist she has shown me how to tear down the master's house and still live quite well.

Note

Transliterations from Hebrew and Greek are not scientific in order to make them more accessible to the general reader.

CHAPTER I

Signs of the flesh

To arrest the meanings of words once and for all, that is what
Terror wants.
Jean-François Lyotard, *Rudiments Paiens*

The use of the biblical icon is widespread in our culture. We are
named Sarah, Leah, Jacob, Joseph. We live in towns called
Canaan, Bethlehem, Jericho. We refer to a deceiving cheating
woman as a Jezebel; a man is strong as Samson. On a recent
best-selling CD-ROM Charlton Heston gives a sonorous reading of
the book of Exodus from a craggy vista somewhere on Mt. Sinai.
We are so accustomed to being addressed by these images that we
scarcely notice their total impact. Indeed the tropes and figures of
the Bible reside in the collective unconscious of Western culture as
well as in the conscious streams of moralizing that drench our
popular media.

Mostly we interpret biblical narratives in terms of binary
oppositions: divine and human, male and female, Israelite and
gentile. It is the intention of this study to use a variety of reading
strategies to shake loose the habit of binary interpretations that
have been bound by a central interpretive unity or logic. This logic
springs from two mouths: either condemning or protecting women
from the seemingly "clear" interpretations of biblical narratives. A
central cause of women bearing the weight of patriarchy is to be
found in the biblical portraits of women. If women want to
extricate themselves from the androcentric logic of the roots of
Western culture, they need to analyze the strategies, conscious and
latent, that have been used to make all areas of life conform to the

old androcentric biblical logic – or what we take it to be – that
woman thwarted the divine plan. A majority of feminist intellec-
tuals have freed themselves from the religious biases first planted in
the Garden that continue to teach androcentrism as God's law. But
this is not enough to change a culture.

As historians, anthropologists, and literary critics have all
recently argued, the social construction of reality does not produce
a clear and coherent world view. As any reader of a novel knows, to
find one's way through a book is not the same as to make one's way
through life. Yet the parallel can be instructive. A persuasive
version of the process of reading has been developed by French
philosopher Michel de Certeau, who understands reading as the
appropriation of texts, or as he termed it, "poaching" texts. He
argued that ordinary people are not helpless passive victims of
texts, but rather they take what they want from mass media,
regardless of the intention of the author. De Certeau was primarily
concerned with the readerly connection between the characters of
soap operas and life depicted within tabloids, the texts of those at
the bottom of the social order, but he could have included the Bible
as a text that everyone freely poaches.

Most important for de Certeau's argument is that readers use
the same tactics in their everyday lives as they do in their reading
process, snatching whatever advantage they can to survive within a
hostile environment (de Certeau 1984: 168–70). De Certeau and
others acknowledge that ordinary readers award life to the
characters who dwell in their minds. Janice Radway's *Reading the
Romance: Women, Patriarchy, and Popular Literature* (1984) analyzes the
way working-class women in contemporary America read Harle-
quin Romances, identifying with some female characters, judging
others. Too often scholarly analyses of literary figures deprive the
characters of the juiciness of life. While I agree with scholarly
conclusions that the gap between the lives of real and imagined
women can be large, the process through which ordinary readers
identify with literary characters has largely been ignored. Similarly
the route that a reader takes through texts is largely unknown.

The question of what are the significant categories in the study of
a literary character is twofold. First, the study of character in the
Bible has too often attempted to produce a theory that is unitary,

homogenized. I suggest that readings need to incorporate the arena of contradictions: to acknowledge the endless conflict and negotiation that goes on within the mind of the reader, a matter of drawing lines, contesting boundaries, reinterpreting symbols, and rearranging experience into constantly shifting categories – an effort which corresponds to the efforts of readers to make sense of narratives and the characters who live within them. Second, it is important to realize and to take into account that characters exist in our consciousness independently of the stories in which the characters were originally encountered. This is how it is relevant to speak of a biblical culture today. But such a culture, then or now, can not be conceived of as pure and homogeneous. Assuming the ongoing "life" of characters, one can identify counter voices and forge links with other noncanonical literary figures. Again, emphasizing contradictions allows the reader to perceive the differences between culturally valued elements, such as rationality, language, masculinity, whiteness, over against that which is outside the white, male order. In biblical narratives, a major otherness is created between the chosen of YHWH and followers of other gods. In reading the dominant elements against the other, the effect of the literary text can be both to release and repress the other. Since repression never succeeds completely, the reader functions like a psychiatrist who asks questions of the resisting text, which nevertheless gives its unconscious away in slips of the tongue.

When female literary figures within biblical narratives are analyzed solely against each other, too much cultural otherness is dropped out and a self-referential loop is created. In order to break free of that loop, I present readings of biblical literary figures, in particular the so-called wicked women, against various extrabiblical narratives. In focusing upon the life of characters within biblical narratives I remain an oppositional critic: that is, I do not attempt to harmonize, to set a fixed horizon line for a particular group of readers. Instead, I have tried to design an approach that is kaleidoscopic – its function is to find new arrangements, ones that emphasize cultural connections that move between scholarly disciplines. One advantage to this method is that it decreases the reader's fascination with a hypostasized notion of literary theory. Too often such toying with metatheory leads one to believe she has carved out the road to some grand universal truth. Thus, the reader can explore how conflicts within the biblical text become transferred in varied narrative expansions into critical conflicts about the biblical text and doxic traditions. By doxa I mean one's idea of a narrative plot point or character or place from some remembered version of it, such as thinking that Delilah cut off Samson's hair, or that Herod's luscious step-daughter Salomé is named in the Bible. Often the doxic version becomes cultural baggage for the reader, setting up assumptions that blind one to what appears in the actual text.

Reading Second Temple narratives and rabbinic midrashim lets the reader in on the ancient doxa as well as the process of canonization. The biblical expansions provide the interpreter with prime examples of the efficacy of using extracanonical narratives to highlight and resolve textual irritants in the canonical version. One thus rattles the keystone of the edifice of canon in which the texts are viewed as blocks of a unified object. This is a first interdisciplinary move: from biblical to literary studies. By ignoring the artificial barriers of canon, I can enable previously unthinkable readings.

While scholars of biblical studies have traditionally been resistant to subjecting biblical texts to the same critical border-crossings as those who study secular texts, the paradigm of privileging the Bible, isolating it from ideological scrutiny, is shifting. Concomitant with this move is the acknowledgment that the weight of the doxa must be figured into the readerly equation. Following the move toward cultural readings of literary texts, I have applied cultural perspectives to a group of biblical narrative units centered upon female figures: Judith, Esther, and Jael, each celebrated as a heroine of Israel for seducing men with wine and food and then cutting off their heads (or in the book of Esther, causing Haman to be impaled) and two other biblical vixens, Delilah and Salomé, who used the same weapons – wine and food and sexuality – to bring down their enemies.

Reading through the binary code of good and evil results in the first group of female literary figures being judged as good and the second group as evil. Such dichotomous reading reproduces essentialism by assuming that texts have a fixed identity and that literary value can inhere only in the unchanging properties of the text, such as imaginative and linguistic. An analysis of the plot structure in each narrative indicates that each of these women has performed similarly in plotting the demise of an enemy and caused the same dis-ease among the members of the male audience. The basic move, however, is to attach more labels to plot structures.

Part of the ideological effect of the text is to splinter the power of women, and the most efficient way of accomplishing this effect literarily is to isolate women from each other within textual units and commentaries. Moving outside the boundaries of individual texts allows me to break through the isolation of character portraits of individual female characters. One way to negotiate this comparison is through intrabiblical interpretations: to bring biblical characters together who have been isolated by the storyteller. A second strategy is to compare the portrait of a biblical character with the expansion of her role in postbiblical literature and other uses of a figurative motif in a variety of modern literatures. By extending my palette, I present a chiaroscuro of character. Vibrant portraits can be painted when the reader views a character from more than one angle. The wider the reader's gaze, the more vivid the portrait. A deeper point here is that criticism of the Bible is oddly capable of keeping everybody engaged. Moralists and Marxists, Freudians and Feminists, semioticians and deconstructionists – all find a literary banquet in biblical narratives. And for every generation of critics, and readers, the Bible is effortlessly renewed.

As has proved evident even in feminist readings conscious of gender biases, remaining within the biblical canon as a closed universe presents problems. To seek a coherent pattern in biblical portraits of women is bound to marginalize women unless one lays bare the social and cultural codes as well as the gender codes that are reflected in the texts of the society that produced them. The first character to be analyzed in this study is the wife of Potiphar (Genesis 39), whom I call Mut-em-enet, following Thomas Mann in his novel *Joseph and his Brothers* (1934). In chapter 3, I read the biblical narrator's story. In order to see how his bias has been incorporated into the text, I perform a rhetorical analysis of both his interpretive frame and the narrative unit it encloses. This strategic move allows me to peel a particular ideology away from the story. I then juxtapose the traditional portrait of Mut-em-enet with that of Susanna, often considered to be the female counterpart of Joseph, a pious Jew falsely accused of sexual activity. An alternative reading that brings Susanna together with Mut-em-enet allows both female characters a measure of subjectivity in contrast to the doxic versions in which they are objects of male stories. A reading of the gender code links Mut-em-enet and Susanna, as female objects dependent on male characters to resolve each story.

Once I have established a subjective position for Mut-em-enet through a suspicious analysis of the male story, I can turn a deaf ear to the narrator's voice. Then I can substitute my own voice as I read *her* story against the first-century Greek expansion, the *Testaments of the Twelve Patriarchs* (T12P), in which a dying Joseph tells his sons his version of his life's struggles, especially his sexual encounters with that predatory Egyptian virago. The *Testament of Joseph* (*TJos*), usually read as a moral and ethical portrait of Joseph, has considerable literary interest for this study, since it is a detailed first-person account of "what happened" between him and his master's wife. The Joseph of the biblical account is curiously silent after her accusations; this later story is focalized through the hero Joseph. Thus, I shall set up within the reader's mind two stories: the narrator's version in the biblical account and Joseph's version (a second narration) in *TJos*. In neither version does Joseph's character move beyond the opaque consciousness of a man wronged, pursued. In order to subjectivize the story, I have read these male versions against a third, imagined narration, recounted in the voice of Mut-em-enet. Thus, reading a biblical text against its later Jewish expansions awards the female character a measure of subjectivity.

One can identify throughout T12P the beginnings of the conflict that became apparent in literary as well as religious works of late antiquity, when people embraced asceticism and penitence as protection against the seductions of physical pleasure. An important interpretive shift has occurred from the confidence of the biblical writers, who assumed divine protection against erotic evil to the fears of the writers in the Second Temple period of the serious threat of Eros. In Proverbs the believer is certain of his own immunity, while in T12P the evil spirit Beliar threatens the believer, both as protagonist and as reader, who "feels his soul torn asunder." In the *Testament of Levi*, the patriarch warns his sons, "Choose for yourselves light or darkness, the Law of the Lord, or the works of Beliar" (19:1). In the expansion of the biblical tale, the transformation of the character of Joseph as well as the fuller portrait of his female seducer can be seen in terms of this shift. Joseph takes refuge in penitent behavior, as protection against the sensuality of his master's wife.

In chapter 4 I explore the wickedness traditionally allocated to Mut-em-enet with the virtue of another Egyptian female figure, the wife of Joseph. Because Aseneth is mentioned only one time in the Bible (Gen. 41:45), I have imported the fuller portrait of Aseneth from the novella *Joseph and Aseneth* (*JosAsen*) a first century CE Greek romance composed during the same period as the Testaments. In sharp contrast with the sinful Mut-em-enet is the portrait of the ascetic Aseneth, who controls her desire for Joseph and transforms wantonness into wifeliness. In neither version do the sensual woman and virginal wife interact. That meeting takes place in the mind of the reader.

Like Aseneth, Bathsheba might also be considered as a biblical character committed to protecting Jewish tradition by plotting to have her son Solomon anointed king. Instead Bathsheba is traditionally considered a temptress who has seduced David, by intentionally bathing in the chill evening air in Jerusalem to catch the monarch's eye. In chapter 5 I examine the objectified Bathsheba in the same order as the biblical narrator presents her, originally as an object of male sexual fantasy, seen and not heard, and in I Kings 1–2, finally, as a good mother, heard and not seen. My reading results in a portrait of a female biblical figure who is not as wicked as traditional interpretations have drawn her.

Jezebel is another biblical figure who has become a stock character representing seduction and betrayal. Unlike the case of Bathsheba there is no mention of sexual attraction in the narratives of Jezebel. She is a political queen, attempting to gain the extra land that her husband Ahab desires. Her narrative is the reverse of Bathsheba's. Jezebel moves from being heard to being seen; painted, her body adorned as though for a celebration, she is thrown from a window, the usual site for a woman to observe male activity. Thrown to the ground, in death, Jezebel becomes the object of a contemptuous male gaze.

Objectified female characters, especially when used to promote masculine sexual fantasies, are not confined to the domain of the canonical texts. By interpreting popular fictive portraits of Bathsheba, I begin a second disciplinary move from literary to cultural studies. Leaving the limited literary canon for a wider cultural one permits the reader/spectator to explore first-hand the construction of female sexuality not only in the ancient culture that produced the foundational biblical text, but also today, in the widely diffused media, including advertising, music-videos, journalism, and television, that continue to produce a heavily gendered rhetoric of sexuality and provide the ineluctable cultural context in which the biblical story is and will be read.

One example of cultural poaching or appropriation can be found amid the fragments of popularized Freudian analysis that decorate and direct contemporary literary readings. Most literary critics accept that the study of biblical literature, or any canon for that matter, is not a matter of imposing order on a corpus of texts, but rather is a function of readers making sense of symbols. Such a process can not operate independently of the influence of the reader's unconscious. In a post-Freudian culture such as ours, it is impossible to escape saturation with Freudianism, which operates in our culture in unconscious as much as conscious modalities, so that even so-called "neutral" or "apolitical" or "mainstream" readings work from unspoken assumptions colored by post-Freudian cultures, which speak through us, whether we acknowledge such activity or not. Thus, it is necessary to foreground such cultural mediation, rather than to pretend that there is a possible pre-Freudian access to the Bible. Ironically, since the days of the Viennese master, the specifics of sexuality may have changed, but the essential use to which the images of the evil woman are put has not changed. Women are depicted in a significantly different way from men – not because the feminine is different from the masculine – but because the "ideal" spectator has always been assumed to be male and the image of the woman is designed to flatter him.

The woman consciously displaying herself for male pleasure is a motif that has only recently begun to be explored. The trope of the woman on display returns us in chapter 6 to the biblical figures whose sensuous beauty trapped the men who could not turn away from them. Traditionally the difference has been one of ethnic or theological triumph. Jael, Judith, and Esther killed the right men, while Delilah and Salomé are represented as viraginous vixens for destroying men whom the ideal community had identified as heroes. Underneath the songs of praise are warnings about women connected to the sublime delights of wine, food, and sex. Expecting platters of pleasure and celebration, the male reader sees his own death as the main course. Through analyzing the cultural connections between food and sexuality, and comparing the function of banquets and sexuality in other peri-Mediterranean texts, I argue that all women are potentially deadly seducers to the extent that they reflect male fears of castration. Reading through a psychoanalytic lens, then, allows one to enumerate the nuanced differences between a seemingly unified group of female biblical literary figures: those who occupy a traditional position of valorized heroine, like Esther and Judith, and those who have been devalorized. My mode of reading demonstrates that these narratives signify the success or failure of the cultural effort to repress the knowledge of sexual danger in the first instance and to close it down in the second.

Thus, interweaving cultural and literary questions suggests additional possibilities in understanding the motivation of character. Cultural studies offers the reader a blueprint for negotiating the challenge of evoking the past while being rooted in a world that is totally different. By imagining oneself as an ethnographer of the biblical corpus, one is able to read across the barriers of time and space without being trapped in universalistic thought. When I refer to a peri-Mediterranean world, I am not required to halt before ethnic or nationalistic borders. I can simultaneously slip the bonds of area or discipline (religious studies) and moralistic interpretation (theology).

While the great proportion of scholarly investigation of the term *banquet* in biblical texts has been philological, the same concentration on philology has kept cultural analysis of the occasion to a minimum. If the Bible can be considered a compressed record of some two thousand years of struggles, then the ethnographer's

interpretive project is one of decompression. Such a cultural study
is actually a representation not of the ancient culture itself, but of
the dynamics among a culture, an interpreter, and the institutions
of study and discourse. It is within the space of a decoding process
that expands meaning that the subjectivities and the discursive
practices of the interpretive community assert themselves.
Through looking at the cultural context of food, sexuality, and
death, one can connect figures who have been separated by
theological readings, Old and New Testament locations, and even
wider disciplinary distances of the cultures of the ancient Mediterranean world.

The reader becomes the site at which the texts and the cultures
that produced them come together. Thus, comparative analysis of
the symbolic connections that various Mediterranean cultures
made among ritual and social celebrations, sexuality, and death
decompresses or fills the gap of understanding between the
function of banquets in one narrative and the function of banquet
in the other. Considering the signs connected to the narrative
detailing of aromatic fragrances and food adds depth to the
reader's appreciation of the story. While banquets have not
everywhere signified the same thing, there are relationships
between eating and nurturing identified with women as locus of
food, sexuality, and death that form a basis of comparison. The
food becomes a crucial trope in this complex: it poisons, intoxi-
cates, or causes delusions of grandeur or pleasure. The food either
represents sexual pleasure or accompanies it. The Persian banquets of Ahasuerus and Herod's birthday banquet were products of
the same cultural understandings as the Greek symposia attended
by Socrates and his students. Each was understood as a major
event of homosocial solidarity among men, attended or served by
women. One reading examines how that affinity is reversed when
the woman severs the man's head from his body rather than
serving his bodily desire. Another reading connects the temporal
nature of perfume and tastes with the moment of action in which a
female literary figure uses her fragrant sensuality to entrap a man.

The seventh chapter deals with the figure of Salomé, one of the
characters who shares a variety of tropes with the female literary
figures examined in the preceding chapters. To make the case for a

cultural reading that integrates visual poetics, I have used both films and paintings as lenses through which to examine the relations between narrative versions of Salomé and iconographic interpretations. Like the verbal analysis it has stimulated, visual theory assumes that both readers and viewers bring to texts and images their own cultural assumptions. When viewed together, images provide testimony to the lack of coherence in this sweep of cultural images of Salomé. The so-called "sword and sandal" films of Hollywood give a Technicolor testament to the absence of a universal story of Salomé. More than stamping out similar interpretations, film shows how each cultural production makes of the biblical icon a reflection of its own values, not of the ancient culture in which the story was rooted. Each of the Hollywood Bible films proclaims itself as a recitation of shared cultural history, but also accedes to the strong current of belief in its intended Christian audience.

Both academic and ordinary readers have been accustomed to coherent readings, readings that progress in a linear fashion to a payoff, a bottom line, a result. Traditional commentaries on biblical texts emphasize a unity of reading, a single viewpoint, a pronouncement of moral or theological truth. In analyzing the roles and assumptions of biblical criticism, I have tried to separate each text from its interpretive frames in an attempt to shatter the stereotypes that have held most interpreters within the confines of traditional interpretations. A first frame is binary thought. Whether theological or literary, the majority of interpretive strategies have reflected the dichotomy of good and evil. But dichotomy as a mode of thinking entails decisions of method. My interest in analyzing dichotomies has developed from Bal's concerns leveled in *Murder and Difference*:

dichotomies have two inevitable consequences: They subsume all relevant phenomena under only two categories, thus restricting the possibilities and paralyzing the imagination, their centripetal quality. And they turn hierarchical, shedding off one pole as negative in favor of the other which needs to establish its value, their centrifugal quality. (1988:9)

A method suspicious of binary opposition, therefore, one that tries to increase the interpretive possibilities, offers the reader weary of wandering in the perfection of the biblical garden of good and evil a different landscape, where no category can claim hegemony. There is no fence to protect the garden of narratives into which I would transplant the biblical narratives. Rather they will be intertwined with other narratives that grew in the cultural soil of the ancient Mediterranean world and thrived in the cultural unconscious of Western literature.

A second frame is the unification of the readership. Resistant readers are acutely aware of the politics of language, of the need to examine that troublesome "we," which often has not included us. The biblical interpretive tradition has a variety of subjectivities, or "we" identities that includes belief positions as well as those that revolve around ethnic or cultural views. For the reader of biblical texts it is essential to include the gender code among the strategic choices – in order to cut through the patriarchal hegemony of the text. But, since gender is not the only difference among people, probably not even the essential difference, I will propose readings that incorporate gender but are not relegated to this single interpretive slot. Only then will I be able to create readings that play across codes, rather than identify the world of readers exclusively on the basis of anatomy.

One way to avoid such a trap consists of shedding a third confining frame, the unification of methods within disciplines. A transdisciplinary method, I suggest, enables the reader to free her/ or him/self from such ideology. By examining the interaction of codes, including the gender code, the reader of biblical narratives becomes aware, as Bal has shown us, of the partial nature of each code. The primary goal of this study, then, is to devise a way of telling "her" story in a literature that has been interested foremost in "his" story.

When I began pursuing that end, I first worked within traditional methods of literary analysis, as well as newer methods developed by rabbinic midrashists, literary critics, and feminists concerned with alternative readings of biblical texts. Throughout my efforts, however, new questions continued to plague me: why have these methods not led to readings that reveal *her* story, or in narratological terms, the embedded story of the woman? An answer suggested itself: I had not yet contended with the biblical narrator.

CHAPTER 2

Contending with the narrator

> So many different men – and learned men among them –
> have been and are so inclined to express both in speaking and
> in their treatises and writings so many wicked insults about
> women and their behavior . . . judging from the treatises of all
> philosophers and poets, it seems that they all speak from one
> and the same mouth. They all concur in one conclusion: that
> the behavior of women is inclined to and full of every vice.
>
> Christine de Pisan, *The Book of the City of Ladies*

Every story needs a storyteller. And storytellers are by definition
biased. The act of imagining both a reader and a narrator is central
to the reading of fiction. I am occupying two subjectivities in this
analysis: that of literary scholar and ordinary reader. Because the
Bible is a text that has occupied a central place in the unconscious
of Western culture, its characters survive in the minds of readers.
The biblical narrator can be considered as one of those voices who
lives on in the mind. Jonathan Culler has written about the relation
of the narrator to the fiction-making process.

> Making narrators is not an analytical operation that lies outside the
> domain of fiction but very much a continuation of fiction making: dealing
> with details by imagining a narrator, telling a story about a narrator and
> his/her responses so as to make sense of them. (1982: 34)

Within the Bible, the importance of recognizing the biblical
narrator as a figure telling a slanted story has been undervalued.
Indeed there have been concerted efforts to protect the biblical
narrator from his status as ordinary storyteller. For example, the
literary critic Robert Alter has described the biblical narrator as
"impassive and authoritative" (1989: 176). While he acknowledges

that ancient narratives may switch momentarily from the narrator's point of view to a character's angle of vision, he is content to describe prenovelistic narrative as containing "a high degree of uniformity of perspective maintained by an authoritative overviewing narrator"(1989: 176). Not troubled by awarding exclusive and absolute authority to the narrator, Alter allows no room for iconoclastic readers. Gayatri Spivak would be such a reader. She describes her task as "to read it and run with it and go somewhere else. To see where in that grid there are the spaces where, in fact, woman oozes away" (1993: 145).

I have found one method of running with it, and that is to run away from or at least to stand firm against such a self-serving authoritative vision. The method I have developed in this study, is to present a mode of reading which accepts the naturalizing presumption, that is, I imagine the biblical narrator as a storyteller with whom the reader must contend, as s/he does with characters within the story. Instead of blindly obeying, I argue with this narrator. And instead of being seduced by the narrator's version, I endorse a strategy that allows the reader to step outside the reader's appointed place in order to defy the fixed gaze of the male narrator. Instead of believing the narrator, I imagine him as a combination of dual subjectivities, as presenter of Israel's oral and theological position, and as the one whose version of the stories we are hearing. I realize the difficulty in conferring upon the narrator, or indeed upon any character in the story, more "reality" or verisimilitude than the text itself would offer. Therefore, I am not suggesting a "true" or historical identity for the narrator, but rather a fictive one based upon his agenda and upon his role as storyteller. Following literary theorist Barbara Herrnstein Smith, I argue that to understand fictive discourse, one needs to treat it as if it were a representation of a real person performing a natural discursive act (Smith 1989: 27–29). If one challenges the notion of the omnipotent voice of an impassive narrator, female biblical characters will not be in so much danger of oozing away.

According to the cultural perspective proposed in this study, the narrator shares with the characters a narrative life in the reader's consciousness. The reader imagines a person behind the voice that she reads. I will take that projection seriously as a heuristic device.

A tension is thus set up between the reader's desire to form narrative conclusions concerning characters and the narrator's attempts to control the reader's understanding of figures within the story. By fleshing out the narrator, we flush out his intentions. By refusing to award him the transparency he seeks as omniscient voice of truth, the reader will be aware of the narrator's motives, what he's up to in fashioning his story. Because the redactors have spliced the biblical narrator's voice with that of the author and of God himself, one task of a literary critic who is suspicious of the narrator's identity as the authoritative voice of truth is to separate the role of the narrator as self-interested agent from the narrator as the teller of the tale. To make the narrator visible, and thus his agenda more identifiable to the reader, one needs to regard his version of the story as a self-conscious telling of the tale, intended to convince us that he has provided the true account of what happened.

One way to figure out the narrator is to shift our readerly identity from that of ideal reader, an individual who would believe, understand, and appreciate every word and device of the text, to that of suspicious narratee. In using the term narratee, a construction of a reader with particular interests connected to those of the narrator, I evoke Gerald Prince's concept of narratee-character as the fictive one addressed by the narrator. The signals that he sends out within the text to the narratee are then read by the reader to smoke him out. Prince theorizes that interpreting the signals sent to this narratee-character, a construct created by the author, allows one to categorize the narration *according to the type of narratee to whom it is addressed* (Prince 1982: 15). Even if the narratee is not explicitly addressed, as he is not in the majority of biblical narratives, when the narrator lavishes his opinions upon him, the narratee "becomes as clearly defined as any character" (1982: 18). Thus, constructing a narratee within the biblical text is a technique that may help the biblical critic figure out the narrator's game. For the narratee "constitutes a relay between narrator and reader, he helps to establish the narrative framework, and he serves to characterize the narrator" (1982: 23).

A second strategy of reading characters, connected to the first, is to retrieve or reconstruct characters from the structuralist cosmol-

ogy in which they are actants, performers of the plot. By looking at
sights not within the narrator's gaze, for instance, a reader may be
able to "see" characters who are not primary agents of the plot.
Literary techniques focus the delineation of character within the
insight of the reader rather than within the fixed gaze of the
narrator. Shifting the gaze from the narrator's eye to the reader's
"I" is especially important for feminist readers since the elements
of structural analysis applied to character often deflate female
biblical characters, who are not usually the focal point of narration.

Only recently has biblical criticism moved past the positivistic
formalist arena in which one assumes that there is *one* correct
interpretation of story and characters that can be adduced from a
proper analysis of form. Among the most totalizing of the presuppositions that underlie such a formalist reading of the text is that
language has a stabilizing force, that it means what it says and says
what it means. The New Critic looks for a balanced order, and not
surprisingly, finds one. Literary studies at this point claimed that
texts were by nature unified. In contrast, the Russian critic Mikhail
Bakhtin, eager to diversify the strengths of discourse from which
any text is made up like a patchwork or collage, finds limitless
textual diversity, arguably because he is looking for diversity rather
than singularity. Language for Bakhtin is at any given moment of
its historical existence heteroglot from top to bottom: "it represents
the co-existence of socioideological contradictions between the
past and present, between differing epochs of the past, between
different socioideological groups in the present, between tendencies, schools, circles and so forth, all given a bodily form" (1981:
291). This view has been recently taken up by biblical scholars. As
Ilana Pardes' study, *Countertraditions in the Bible*, suggests, the Bible is
just such a text of many tongues.

In a view continuous with the formalist denial of the effect of a
reader on the text, many interpreters have continued to ignore the
effect of a female reader upon the text. As I shall argue in this study,
too often biblical critics have cast themselves as ideal readers, allied
with the patriarchal narrator, and have not sufficiently recognized
that he was telling his view of things. This kind of reader does the
work laid out for him or her. They comprise the audience
presupposed by the narrative itself – and as such readers define

themselves. The ideal reader, a fictive character constructed by the literary critic, is the creator and protector of the canon. A bumptious reader, on the other hand, will challenge the privileged role of the narrator and recast him as the fictive henchman of the author. Such a reader desires to slip across the borders of canon. This act is sometimes termed reading as a woman, a reference to Jonathan Culler's analysis in *On Deconstruction* (1982: 42–62).

Critics have commonly figured the narrator as omniscient and entwined with the divine voice without questioning his reliability as a narrator. Indeed the biblical narrator has a privileged position within the text, possessing the ability to move outside time and space. Since there is no textual distinction between the implied author and the public narrator, readers have equated the two voices, while considering themselves part of a universal audience. As Bakhtin has indicated, authorial discourse is "directed toward its own straightforward referential meaning," and authorial narrators possess a stronger voice than that of characters who are contained within the events of the story (1981: 187). Clearly the biblical narrator, not being content merely to tell his tale, has made himself such a significant literary presence. Or so it seems.

Literary critic Meir Sternberg has described the biblical narrator's function in these terms:

the narrator enjoys free movement in time (among narrative past, present, and future) and in space (enabling him to follow secret conversations, shuttle between simultaneous happenings or between heaven and earth). These two establish an unlimited range of information to draw upon or, from the reader's side, a supernatural principle of coherence and intelligibility. (1985: 84)

This, clearly, is too convenient to be true. It is a literary rephrasing of a religious belief, a formulation of the narratological function of narrator in conformity with a major theme of biblical narrative as well as a recognition of the narrator's apparent omniscience. When divine omnipotence is transfered to narrative omniscience, or when the authorial voice is equated with that of the deity, as it is in the biblical narratives, the plot thickens.

So far I have been assuming that the biblical narrator is male, like the community (ideal reader) he represents. Recently Harold

Bloom has hypothesized a female author for the J material in the Torah. Since I understand the narrator to be a figure in the biblical text, one whose authority is never questioned within the text, and I recognize the control the patriarchal society exerted upon woman, I find it hard to imagine a female in antiquity who would be credited with omniscience. I am surprised that Bloom did not use the occasion of his presumption of a female author to confront the politics of reading, exploring the convention generally assumed "that the voice of authority is male, albeit a comprehensive male voice in which sexual distinctiveness is to some extent neutralized" (Culler 1982: 205). Certainly in the ancient peri-Mediterranean cultures, a female voice was rarely heard, and thus the issue of gender and authorship has not been often raised. Well known for his understanding of the artist as male figure struggling against the father while courting the female muse, Bloom is suggesting an even more remarkable argument, then, when he characterizes J as a female writer. The reaction by the reading public underscores the idea of a female as writer of a portion of the Bible as a novelty: *The Book of J* became a momentary bestseller. Clearly the general assumption of both scholar and reader is that a male persona rests behind the creation of these texts. A similar situation of social and ideological surprise at attribution of a work of art to a female artist is described by feminist art historians Parker and Pollock.

She is being presented to us as an exception – unusual as an artist by virtue of her sex. As such she is being evaluated by special criteria reserved for women, for it is only her sex and novelty that can merit her an otherwise undeserved place in Renaissance art history. (Parker 1988: 41)

Given the stake involved here, the narrator's power to bend the reader, let me for the moment continue to contend with a male narrator or at least a male authority who controls the power to define both female and male characters in the narratives of the Bible. The omniscient biblical narrator has a task of the utmost significance: he is the prophet of prophets. His most privileged job is to relate the word of the Lord, thus proving that the narrator's authority is secondary only to that of the deity, to whom he is scribe. The ultimate evidence of his omniscience is that he is privy to God's "feelings." His audience believes his explanations, that waters flooded the earth because the Lord repented of making human beings and "it grieved God in his heart" (Gen. 6:6), and that Saul lost his kingship because God repented making Saul king (1 Sam. 15:11). There is no episode in which the narrator's voice represents or supports a point of view different from that of the Bible's doxic ideology. In fact the choice of omniscient narrator strengthens the biblical view of an omnipotent deity and "serves the purpose of staging and glorifying an omniscient God" (Sternberg 1985: 87–89). To smooth out the wrinkles in quirky characters, who sometimes do not reflect the divine message, Sternberg eliminates incongruities by arguing that the recipient of the divine point of view is the narrator and not the other characters (1985: 85–87). When the narrator engages in extrarepresentational acts – "judgments, generalizations about the world, directly addressed to the narratee" – he renders the textual events (as well as characters' behaviors) more plausible (Lanser 1992: 16–17).

Sternberg does not resist the narrator's version, but rather describes how the text functions to preserve the only "correct" account by silencing "alien and erroneous viewpoints (not excluding criticisms of God or appeals to idols)." These voices that are not compatible with the norms of the implied author occur on the surface of the text, or on the level of story, but the narrator discredits these errant discourses, silences them. Sternberg does not allow a dissonant voice even a momentary breath of life, brooking no competition to his storyteller, who would then become "a maker rather than a shaper of plot" (1985: 128). By viewing the narrator as teller of the tale rather than the creator of the tale, Sternberg fuses the identity of the fictive narrator with the "real" author and thus avoids the morass of untangling sighs and whispers of voices other than the narrator/author. He cannot allow the narrator to become one of several possible narratorial voices directed to the narratee, because that would sever the indivisible authoritative troika: deity, author, narrator. The voice of the narrator is the "voice of the one and indivisible truth" (1985: 128).

This statement of Sternberg furnishes an important clue about such strategies of reading. By privileging or foregrounding rhetorical or structuralist techniques – e.g. persuasion, sound patterns, syntactical structures, narrative or thematic structures, repetitions, and motifs – and thrusting into the background the question of reading, as Sternberg does, one ignores many questions of interpretation (see Suleiman 1990: 2–45). In such a view the critics see no ambiguities related to the identity or loyalties of the narrator, and certainly no possibilities of multiple or indeterminate readings engendered by the reader's suspicions of the narrator's version. Hence, such critics endorse the ideology of the biblical narratives, seeing the rhetorical conventions as expressions of ideology and, quite properly from his perspective, a unified biblical theology controlling the forms and structures within the text. Sternberg calls this the "ideology of narration" (1985: 84–128).

But form, I contend, *is* meaning. This literary view of the narrator is in fact already a theological position. For, it would seem, as Freud suggested in *Moses and Monotheism,* that the establishment of patriarchal power in the Bible is linked to the preference for an invisible God. In the biblical text the narrator who is everywhere present and nowhere visible relates the story of the omnipotent God of the Patriarchs. A similar process can be observed in traditional interpretations of biblical texts, whenever the role of the author and narrator are conceived as paternal and when the allegiance of the reader rests with this paternal pair, to whose credit everything in the text accrues: in other words, the female reader loses the power of subjectivity. Theology, thus, becomes gendered. For this is a simple case of literary seduction. The seduction is so strong that the loyal reader has continued to defend the male author and narrator as though the duo might not survive even the echo of another interpretive voice. Reading with the canon assures the continued pleasure of the unchallenged paternal voice of the narrator. This study, introducing dissonance, demands divorce from the canon.

The pleasure of filial obedience seems considerable, if the attitude of even the most disenchanted literary critics is anything to go by. Like Sternberg, Alter, for example, seems eager to please the father narrator and allows only for an ideal reader, one who believes that the events portrayed are "true." His observation that the role of the narrator helps the biblical authors express God's will to the community reveals his interpretive alliance with the author, projecting a straight line from author to narrator to reader. Alter is certainly not alone in combining the narrative and authorial audiences. Even so august a charter of readers' maps as Iser does not acknowledge a duality in the construction of reader – the one implied in the narrative and the one who is actually reading the text – until the final chapter of *The Implied Reader*. Prince's distinction between real readers, virtual readers, ideal readers, and narratees leads to a more subtle analysis of readerly roles. Put another way, Alter does not leave room for a fictive or implied narratee except for the complicit one who accepts the convention that the omniscient voice serves the pivotal function of reporting "God's assessments and intentions, or even what He says to Himself" (1981: 157). Instead, it seems more relevant to disunify the narratee. One technique for adjusting the tension between narrator and narratee is to posit that the narratee occupies a position similar to that of a fictive character and thus is "immanent to the text" (Leitch 1983: 254). Imagining various types of narratees gives us a glimpse at the cards the narrator is holding. For example, the portrait of the fumbling pharaoh in the account of the plagues in Exodus might tell us that the narrator expected an anti-pharaonic attitude in his narratees and played to that audience. Although the narrator doesn't like to show that he casts his shadow across the biblical narratives, one instance of his performing alongside a character is to be found in the book of Deuteronomy, when he overshadows the persona of Moses preaching directly to the community of Israel. In *Moses and the Deuteronomist* Polzin offers a compelling reading of this passage in which the narrator is presented as dominant and Moses as his subordinate. The narratee, then, like the actual reader, identifies with the audience listening to Moses on the plains of Moab. Usually, however, in biblical narratives the narratee maintains a more elusive presence.

Although authors generally try to create the illusion that the gap between the narrator and the reader is narrow, the narrative audience is firmly planted within the elements of the fiction. Thus, an irritable or suspicious narratee could question the story told through the narrator's fixed gaze, and surreptitiously glance around the fictive landscape to pick up clues about the story ignored by the narrator. In the biblical narrative, irritable voices, like Miriam questioning Moses' power as sole prophet of Israel, are quickly silenced. Their cause must be taken up by an equally suspicious or irritable reader. To read with suspicion, I construct just such a restive audience, very far from the ideal one projected by biblical critics who imagine only an audience harmonious with the agenda of the implied author. Such an audience is fictive, neither more nor less than the faithful audience projected by traditional biblical scholarship.

Such a description of a fictive audience presupposes an acceptance on the part of that audience of the text as fiction, making the double-level aesthetic of true/not true possible. For some interpreters of biblical texts, it is not within the scope of their inquiry to imagine a fictive biblical text, an implied reader or audience, and an unreliable narrator. But fictionality can be a heuristic mode rather than a textual essence. For example, Alter and Sternberg have acknowledged that the biblical author has designed his work rhetorically for a specific hypothetical audience, but neither critic addresses the question of a narrative audience or an implied narrator at variance with the author. In order to peel the ideology of the interpretive tradition away from the story, a necessary task for the feminist critic – the hypothesis of a volatile narrative audience is helpful. This hypothesis would be a parallel to the hypothesis of a female reader reading male-authored texts suggested by Elaine Showalter in her pivotal article, "Feminist Criticism in the Wilderness." Showalter contends that the hypothesis of a female reader changes our understanding or vision of a text. In other words, shifting the gaze of the reader/viewer creates another story. Without focusing upon "what happened," fictionality can help to get at another kind of "truth." The "real" issue is that Alter and Sternberg believe there is a code of conventions *in* the literary text, a code which must be obeyed by the reader. Since the (posited) code includes an omniscient and reliable narrator, Sternberg and Alter cannot accept a reading that refuses to respect that convention. In contrast my mode of reading is similar to Showalter's in that the conventions of reading are those of the reader.

Let me rephrase in this context what I suggested earlier on the congruence between literary form and theological allegiance. Alter does not question the biblical convention of describing God's intentions with precision. Alter's view of the narrator does,

nonetheless, offer a valuable observation in comparing the anonymity of the narrator to the more historically designed "characters" who interpret and mediate God's will to the reader, the
biblical prophets. The lack of information about the personal
history of the narrator "assumes for the scope of his narrative a
godlike comprehensiveness of knowledge that can encompass even
God Himself" (Alter 1981: 157). This epistemological result is not
inevitable. The more blurred the portrait of the narrator, the easier
it is for the reader to "forget" the narrator's alliances. Thus, the
narrator's anonymity or blurred identity is used as a strategy of
manipulation of the reader – to hide narratorial bias. I would add
to Alter's theory, then, that the more invisible the narrator, the less
likely he is to raise the hackles of dissident readers.

The reader's conformity to narrative form is in turn open to
analysis. Faithful readers share the narrator's theological code,
male readers the gender code, and those whose political stripe
matches that of the narrator the political code. Suspicions arise
when the reader does not share the social, political, and gender
codes of the narrator. The more codes one does not share with the
narrator, the more incongruent the reading (Bal 1988: 5). Thus, the
narrator, like the characters in the text, will come to exist as a figure
possessing various attitudes in the consciousness of the reader.
Inspired by Bal, a renewed feminist approach in biblical studies
focuses the main areas of attention upon the author/narrator being
understood as a gendered author/narrator and upon the signified,
that is, the images of women and men represented within a text.

This "existence" of figures gives a more concrete meaning to
such literary terms. Theorists focusing upon modern literature
have been concerned with questions of how the reader "sees" what
the narrator describes. The French literary theorist Gérard Genette attempted to fine-tune the concept of point of view or
narratorial voice by distinguishing "focalization," or the consciousness that absorbs a narrative (the reader), from "voice," the
discourse that tells the narrative (the narrator) (Genette 1972b, esp.
mode, voix). As Bal points out in her response to Genette, to identify
narrative point of view one must not only make a distinction
between the vision through which the elements are presented and
the identity of the voice that is narrating that vision, but take these

acts as the products of separate narrative agents. To put it succinctly one must distinguish between "the one who sees and the one who speaks" (see Bal 1985: 101, 110–14). The discrepancy between the two comes to the fore in the reader's production of meaning. When the reader's squint reveals something other than what the biblical narrator expresses, the reader can conclude only that the narrator is not omniscient. The story that he tells can thus be read as a version or modified retelling of a previous story, rather than the "one and only" story. Literary readings of this two-tiered model point inevitably to a narratorial perspective that is limited, not omniscient. As Bal has demonstrated, the technique of focalization can re-view female biblical characters, while at the same time making the reader conscious of the narrator's role in shaping a version of the autonomous story (Bal 1988). As I shall argue in chapter 5, for example, the narratorial focalization of Bathsheba as a female figure seen and not heard has been central to traditional interpretations of the first encounter between her and David. Hence, the decision to contend with instead of obeying the narrator, necessitates a nonunified view of narrative representation. Taking focalization as a meaning-producing aspect, then, enables me to *see* characters in a different way.

CHARACTERS SEEN

The status of characters as mental constructs has led me to consider their visual status in a more literal sense. In biblical texts a crucial ambiguity for the feminist reader revolves around the narrator's text providing one version of how female characters behave within the situations in which they have been placed, and another *imagined* version that might be provided by the female figure – if one could reconstruct her story. I seek to find strategies for retrieving the female character who may have been flattened or suppressed by the weight of the story that is not hers. Structuralist attempts to analyze character as a function of plot-types, termed by Culler "the grammar of narrative," entice the reader away from connecting one's thinking about literary figures in a way similar to one's reading of people in real life. A necessary first step to rejoin the character of the figure and the person is to move past the Proppian idea that the characters are of no interest in themselves, but rather are agents of the plot, secondary elements necessary to the enactment of the story. In a male-driven plot, the functions of female agents are going to be limited. In the process of constructing character out of the text, the reader reads her own experience into the text, giving expression to the counter female voices which attempt to put forth other truths (Pardes 1992: 4).

As I have suggested above, one way to shake off the strictures of the literary structuralists and to identify these countervoices is to acknowledge that characters exist in our consciousness as figures independent of the story in which the character was originally discovered. In a literary or nonliterary narrative work, a sequence of events can lend itself to various interpretations depending upon the perspective or context in which the reader/spectator places the material. A story is more than a detailing of events. In the sphere of the reader's mind, character is not reduced to minimal functions as it is in the semiological schema that has drawn such attention away from the emotional "living" qualities of the character. In the reader's mind, a character is understood and remembered as a person.

In his study of the dynamic "existence" of characters, Hochman argues that a work of literature is an entity made up of these imagined things not there, "a conjuring of absent nonexistent parts" (1985: 33, 54, 73, 111). Thus, within the process of reading either literary or visual narratives, we do not respond passively to characters as they have been presented within the story, but rather our own baggage, including previously encountered and absorbed stories, interacts with the characters, even appropriates them. In the case of the Bible, the reader is encouraged to model the characters, to use them as moral guides. Therefore, traditional interpretations, especially classical and medieval ones, often flatten each character into a monotonal representation of good or evil, laudable or condemnable. The classical interpretation of Rachel stealing the *teraphim* is a good act, stamping out idolatry, but some also judge it as appropriation of idols and thievery. Generally, in the case of biblical wives, good mothers nurture the tradition, and evil types show their erotic natures to tempt the central male characters away from the preservation of

the tradition through obedience to the Law. All female literary
figures have the potential to use their sexuality as the tool of a
destructive game; the wicked ones are explicit in displaying their
sexuality.

Because of the lack of explicit narratorial interest in nuanced
characters, both male and female, in biblical stories, there are two
ways to thicken these moral representatives into human form. One
is by seeing them in a variety of situations, at various times in their
lives, interacting with a variety of other characters. Rarely do the
female characters appear in such a variety of roles. Some contemporary biblical critics accept the biblical narrator's agenda as a
moral one, in which he is not concerned with depicting people
juggling nuanced moral issues. The narrator wants choices to
appear simple. Obedience will bring rewards. Many other biblical
critics, however, believe it is up to the reader to provide other stages
on which the characters can perform. And readers do by definition.
They read as they live: in a culture that is not unified. Thus, the
stages upon which readers set characters, as I shall show in this
study, can be extrabiblical, even extraliterary. The stages cross
ethnic and cultural barriers as easily as the reader does. To keep
literary texts separated by canon is an artificial act of sifting that no
real reader can readily live up to.

When one responds to the narrator by rejecting his neatly
ordered sequence of codes, it becomes possible to reject his story
without rejecting the narrative. Similarly, a biblical character from
one story may live on in the reader's mind, linked with another
character, in spite of the biblical narrator's desire for simplicity.
The details of Miriam's outrage at Moses in the Wilderness that
result in her being isolated from the community for seven days may
blur, the reader may reject the alliance between God and prophet
that results in punishment of Miriam, but the figure of Miriam,
contentious in speech and vulnerable in illness, can live on in the
reader's consciousness. Her willingness to object to YHWH about
divine preference for Moses can be compared with other stories of
female figures who question authority: the goddess in Ugaritic epic
literature Anat demands a better house for her brother Baal from
El and the house is built. The father god does not punish her for the
request nor does he think it odd that she, as a female, should make

such a request. This comparison suddenly makes Miriam's reaction less unexpected, hence, less outrageous.

Another example is Michal. She loses her husband David twice: after she saves David from Saul's men and when Saul gives her to Palti. She is shamed by these explicit rejections that result in her losing wifely status. Her only weapon is to speak contemptuously to her husband. She is punished with barrenness and narratorial exile. I have read that story before. When Ishtar is shamed by Gilgamesh, who refuses her offer of marriage, she wages war in two worlds to get her revenge. She does not lose her status as goddess – at best she loses the battle but never the war. One may immediately argue that Anat and Ishtar are divine, and that makes them incomparable to the mortal Miriam and Michal. But is there really a difference in the mind of the reader, for whom all four are literary figures from religious texts produced by Near Eastern cultures?

Similarly national allegiances are not necessarily decisive for narrative processing. Although scholars are trained to canonize or separate the characters from these stories, it is as difficult to nationalize characters in the mind as it is to separate competing aromas in the kitchen. An analysis of the process of reading shows that the disciplinary separation is an artificial one maintained to protect the territory of the interpreter, not the fictive world of the story. I can compare Miriam with Anat and Michal with Ishtar and then snap them back into their own stories without destroying the symmetry of the narrative. What I have gained is other perspectives from which to read each isolated woman's story. I have allowed myself to create a community of women figures, rejecting the narrator's ploy of keeping women in the biblical texts isolated from each other. In the biblical narratives of David's court, the cowives – Abigail, Michal, and Bathsheba – never meet narratively. They share neither plot features nor dialogic moments. Abigail and Michal do not keen for Bathsheba's dead baby son. But in my mind they do.

A GOOD WOMAN IS HARD TO FIND

The literary figures in this study have been linked by the storytellers, who have relied on the stereotyping of the sensual

woman as the *ishah zarah*. The term *ishah zarah* has been translated
by Claudia Camp as Woman Stranger, which emphasizes the
double alien nature, or otherness, of the character: she is both
woman and strange. A great deal of scholarly debate has centered
upon whether the term strange or foreign woman refers to an
ethnic, legal, or social status, emphasizing one category of otherness over another, which denies gender as a crucial *otherness*, female
from male. In a male-centered narrative the woman is frequently
figured as the limit or borderline of that otherness. "From a
phallocentric point of view, women will then come to represent the
necessary frontier between man and chaos; but because of their
very marginality they will also always seem to recede into and
merge with the chaos of the outside" (Moi 1986: 167). The Woman
Stranger of Proverbs 7 beckons the young man to cross boundaries
away from the tidy world invoked by his father to her landscape of
chaos. The narrator reminds us that her path leads to Sheol.

The book of Proverbs provides a sharp contrast to Woman
Stranger by presenting her *Döppelganger*, Woman Wisdom. One
assumes she is only once removed from the male author; she might
even be the fictive wife of the father-narrator. She certainly appears
to be the ideal woman of the narrator, who wants his son to set his
sights on this woman, from whose lips will come what is right (8:6).
A good woman, like the wife in Proverbs 31, stays at home and is
chaste; she thus does not threaten the stability of the society that
depends on her compliance. Through her, the husband will even
improve his position; he will have no lack of gain (31:11). In social
terms, women are put under the control of men, having been
assigned a specific space within male culture and society where
they can give birth, weave, and cook, while being excluded from
economic and political spheres.

Unlike her sedentary sister, the Strange Woman is restless. Her
feet do not stay at home. Now in the street, now in the market, and
at every corner she lies in wait (7:12). She must cross her boundaries
to get to her victim. She pulls men inside her, into a place of
darkness and chaos, like Lilith or Delilah. The Good Woman is a
representative of a higher and purer nature, venerated as an
asexual companion. They rule opposite realms: Wisdom is presented as a divine figure in Proverbs 8, positioning herself at the

gates of the house where the Lord lives, the counterpart of the Woman Stranger, the adulterer of Proverbs 7, through whom men slip down into Sheol.

And what of the speech of the two competing woman? We have already spoken of the sly smooth words of the Strange Woman, "loud and wayward, her feet do not stay at home" (7:10). But the speech of the Wise Woman soothes and speaks noble things. All the words of her mouth are righteous (8:8). Watching at her gates will profit the man, for "he who finds me finds life and obtains favor from the Lord" (8:35). With the cards stacked so heavily against the Strange Woman, it is a testament to the power of her dark house that even the occasional son wandered into her path. Like the Sirens, she utters words that hypnotize those foolish men who would listen.

When Abigail, the consummate good wife, left her house and spoke eloquent, prophetic words to the outlaw David, she ceased to be a good wife to Nabal. Instead she offered herself as well as her husband's larder to the other man. Once betrothed to the future king, Abigail returned to goodness, she retreated inside the house to chastity and silence. Michal, another of David's wives, is punished with barrenness after coming out of her house to speak against her husband. Like Abigail, she is silenced by the biblical author after her outburst. Thus, regardless of the content of the speech, one that saves David from blood guilt or one that mocks him, resolution of the narrative dictates that women be enclosed within their houses, enclosed in silence.

Yee has noticed the same narrative judgment placed upon seemingly opposite types of women in Proverbs. "The greatest seduction to evil consists in inviting the foolish [young man] with the same words that summon one to good" (Yee 1989: 62). The female characters' limited moments of narrative power heighten and express more starkly the cultural beliefs that define the ways in which the female threatens social structures, and therefore the place she is supposed to occupy according to male desire. Ambiguity is eliminated from the text as female characters are suppressed. Only a silent woman presents no risk. While the Good Woman values quietness, the Strange Woman seduces with words. Repeatedly the author of Proverbs warns that the *ishah zarah* seduces with words; she is noisy (7:11) and it is her smooth speech that turns the young man (7:21). In Proverbs 6:25 the Strange Woman's beauty is considered the cause of her sexual sorcery. Reading with the ideology of the text, one might, therefore, attach to the paradigm of this strange women the Orientalized women, the foreign women like Delilah and Salomé, whose beauty and barbarous acts trap "our" heroes. If immorality drove these models of Strange Women, it is powerlessness that surrounds the figure of Tamar. Perhaps her beauty drove Amnon to his sexual attack upon her, but she was not Other. In spite of her best efforts, she is unable to maintain her status: suffering the humiliation of rape and the further humiliation of rejection by her rapist brother and rejection by her father.

The young man, to whom the narrator in Proverbs directs his warnings, is not portrayed as a sexually promiscuous or irresponsible man like Amnon. But he is also not an articulate partner for the Strange Woman, whose verbal artistry is met with silence. If he approaches her dark house, he is, still silent, on the way to Sheol, a victim of the woman of words. He bears a resemblance to Joseph, who remains silent throughout the accusations and retellings of Mut-em-enet's story to the servants and to Potiphar. He has taken the road to her house (Prov. 7:8) and has been caught by the Strange Woman. His punishment is proof of her power. But his power is greater; his ally, the narrator, punishes her, and all the female figures who are her literary legatees, through the force of the narrative.

The circumstances in Genesis 39 are the same as those in Proverbs 7. In both episodes the husband is not at home and the wife attempts her seduction with much smooth talk. The two accounts complement each other. In Proverbs the scene is set: the woman has decked her couch with coverings, colored spreads of Egyptian linen. She has perfumed her bed with myrrh, aloes, cinnamon (7:16–17). Mut-em-enet exerts her sexuality with her opening words, "Lie with me." Instead of being chaste and silent within her house, she opens her house when she opens her mouth. Like her archetype, at every corner she lies in wait to seize and kiss the young hero (Prov. 7: 12–13). On the surface it might seem ironic that Mut-em-enet, the only character with extensive dialogue, is convicted by her own words of accusation. But her creator's judgment is perfectly in keeping with the description of her kind in Proverbs: "The lips of *ishah zarah* drip honey and her tongue is smoother than oil." As she speaks, she opens herself and her house to desire. Having been rejected, it is little wonder that she attempts to portray herself as victim since the law will consider her husband the victim because the crime occurred within her house. When her mouth is closed by the biblical narrator, the social order is no longer threatened. As soon as the woman emerges as carnal, her language and her activity are curtailed. A feminist reader may well be struck with how little the powerless (in this case a woman) had to use against those who could use narrative against them. Shut up in her house again, she is shut out of the narrative.

Although she has remained chaste, through no fault of her own, her failure to remain silent has cost her her virtue. Even though ancient rabbis imagined a situation in which God warned Joseph that his vanity would cost him, that the deity would stir up Mut-em-enet against him, in reality it is the woman who has paid the price. If she had stayed where she belonged, passive and docile, we would never have known of her existence. Refusing invisibility, rejecting the submissive role her society has reserved for her, Mut-em-enet is doomed to reflect the stereotype of the *ishah zarah*, whose lips unleash lies.

The other characters in this study are also remarkable for their desirability, their ability to hold the male gaze. The lissome widow Judith leaves her house, covers herself with silks and perfumes, and invades the male's tent. But rather than being labeled a viraginous woman, Judith is revered. Yet her clever lips unleashed lies – or at least *doubles entendres*. Holofernes heard what he wanted to hear when the beautiful widow referred to her unwavering obedience to *'adonai*, "my Lord." Delilah also used food and wine to ensnare a man who heard what he wanted to hear. Although she told only the truth, Delilah is accused in layers of Jewish tradition of lying to Samson. A dangerous *ishah zarah*, she is soundly punished by the storyteller and his sympathetic readers. Esther and Salomé were each offered half a kingdom by a besotted monarch. Later in this study I shall explore the reasons why Esther is considered a heroine and Salomé a harridan. A major difference, of course, is whether the woman is using her wiles to serve the interests of Israel, which is laudable, or using sexuality in her own interest, which is deplorable. The traditional readings have concentrated on the political/ethnic/theological codes, while my own mode of reading seeks to replace this calculus with a feminist/humanist mode of reading. What is at stake, in my view, is ethos rather than ethnos, or as Greenstein has put it, "not pro or con Israel, but pro or con person, especially with respect to woman."

To rescue a sensual women from the caricature of *ishah zarah* who resides in the male imagination, the feminist critic must put words in her mouth. As I illustrate in my analysis of Genesis 39 (see chapter 3), it is not enough to decry phallocentric literature nor to run rhetorical fingers over the surfaces of a text to uncover its contours. While these strategies have certainly been applied to biblical texts by feminist scholars seeking surface patterns, they too often remain patriarchal readings, that is, they do not disturb the underlying structures of biblical authority. Critics, both male and female, who want to dilute the phallogocentric concern with its unity of meaning and certainty of origin, need to knit together the reading of the text with a reading of its reception, past and present, in all cultural sectors.

As a point of departure we can incorporate into our readings an investigation of the procedures, assumptions, and goals of current criticism to determine whether they are in complicity with the preservation of male authority. We can pose different questions:

> What could she say in her own defense?
> What did her creators fear that she might say?

The following chapters will offer defenses of some biblical figures who too often showed signs of the flesh. My interpretations reflect what happens when a woman reading stories of women stubbornly reads them like any reader reads, recreating, assembling, connecting figures, freeing them from the prison house of language and tradition that isolated them artificially. Altering the landscape, playing with the texts, permits the hypothesis of an unreliable narrator, one who is not the mouthpiece for the omnipotent deity, one whose version of the story may be challenged. This game offers the player one way around the ideological old-boy network that has held the Bible in thrall. To imagine a female reader whose otherness has not been obliterated by layers of traditional interpretation is another possibility. Another alteration of the landscape involves transporting characters to a place where women are not thought strange for acknowledging their sexual desire. The mind of a feminist reader is such a place.

CHAPTER 3

A story of reading the story of Genesis 39

Someone must have been telling lies about Joseph K., for without having done anything wrong, he was arrested one fine morning.

Franz Kafka, The Trial

On land it's much preferred for ladies not to say a word and she who holds her tongue will get her man.

Song lyric, The Little Mermaid (1989)

When attempting to extract a woman's story from a male-authored literary text, it is often necessary to read between the lines. That is, the most interesting elements of the narrative for feminist critics have been the suggestions of a character's story which can be collected through a combination of literary criticism and hermeneutical strategies. In this chapter I have begun with a close reading of the text, the primary method in which biblicists such as myself are trained to read. As a second stage, I have pushed my reading process past an analysis of the surface text to examine the theoretical consequences of reading as a woman upon the biblical text, in which "she" is an object of male controlled narratives. One of the most interesting aspects for a feminist literary critic of examining characters in the Bible is that their imaginative lives continue after their narrative life has been concluded. Once one ceases to view a female character as a fixed identity existing prior to all social modeling and devoid of ideological function, then one's attention can encompass the historical circumstance of certain representations. Reading as a woman, like reading as a man, seduces the reader into finding a unity, a stability *at least* of the character within the work one is reading.

A primary undisputed unity has been the dual nature of sexuality and gender: male and female, God created them. Assumptions about what is natural and normal have directed much of the traditional biblical interpretation of gender and sexuality. Male and female have been the fundamental duality of human nature in the time of the biblical authors and in the time of Freud and are still largely regarded as such today. Just as the evolving ideas of gendered readings have challenged the "normality" or "objectivity" of what we now acknowledge is a male reading, so have other questions related to the dichotomizing of sexuality and gender challenged me to rethink the assumptions inherent in a classification system, be it a biological or social system that reduces or essentializes the reading process into the balanced dichotomy of reading as a woman or reading as a man. The emphasis on the constructedness of gender that initially drew me to this investigation has now led me to recognize the fluidity of gender itself, which can best be accounted for through an acknowledgment of culture as a factor in construction of gender and to deal with the anomalous nature of gender, especially, as Gilbert Herdt argues, "to identify persons whose minds or bodies or actions seemed to defy sexual dimorphism" (15). Transcending traditional or coherent characterizations of gender is essential if the reader is going to transcend conventional representations and readings.

If coherence is in the eye of the reader, and not inherent to the text or the author's intention or the editor's expertise, or indeed of a constructed "woman," then a character does not have to function as a role model or an interpreter of the biblical ideology. Two heuristic positions help the reader avoid the temptation of a coherent reading. First, the historicization of women by cultural historians is a necessary development in the study of women in the Bible. Not until bits of the lives of actual women had been described by recent feminist scholars of the modern period could one separate the lives of real women of the Enlightenment and later periods from the idealized lives of female literary figures. Classical archeologists as well as biblicists are currently engaged in research that will give us more nuanced understandings of material culture, and such models as the women inside the house versus the man out in the world. Second, literary theorists have analyzed the erasure or attempted

erasure of female characters as subjects of biblical narrative. Such
strategies of the biblical authors can be compared with the
subjectivity given to the biblical figure through later literary and
cultural representations of the same figure. One of the most striking
differences in characterization can be seen through a comparison of
Thomas Mann's memorable figure Mut-em-enet and the biblical
author's figuring of the wife of Potiphar in Genesis 39.

In *Joseph in Egypt* Mann shifts the focus of his earlier novel *The
Young Joseph* to the lover of the Israelite hero. In his treatment of
Mut-em-enet Mann goes completely against biblical tradition. In
most versions of the Joseph stories, as will be shown in this study,
Mut-em-enet is a nameless shrew, tempting the virtuous hero with
all the wiles of a foreign woman. Having given her a name and a
heart, Mann never disgraces her. Instead Mann portrays the
Jewish hero Joseph as a somewhat dim-witted figure and makes
even his beloved Mut's "god intoxication" more vivid than
Joseph's. The idiosyncratic rewriting of a biblical text may reach
its apogee with Mann's glorious Mut-em-enet, who parodies her
own lovestruck predicament by recognizing that Joseph is merely
average; there are thousands like him. As Mann defines Jacob as
the maternal figure in Joseph's life, so love masculinizes Mut-em-
enet. Her breasts "once so tender and maidenly" become asym-
metrically abundant, her thighs develop "illicitly," becoming
vigorous enough to grip a broomstick between them.[1] Certainly the
most developed and nuanced of Mann's female literary figures,
Mut was a paean to the intense emotions of youth, and a
recognition of Mann's own "frantic oscillation between exultation
and despair when he was thirty-four years younger" (Hayman
1995: 412). The critic Marquis Childs was lavish in his praise of
Mann's creation. In 1939, when *Life* magazine ran a story on
"Germany's foremost literary exile," Childs called Mut's "an-

---

[1] The question of why Mann figures Mut-em-enet as a heroine is outside the scope of this
study. Heilbut suggests that "the narrative of Mut's passion is Proustian in its slow-paced
itinerary of desire, and its attention to the manic phases, excess that Mann had previously
denied his German lovers. Thus, it is the love affair itself that is fascinating and its leisurely
exposition provides part of the attraction for Mann" (1938: 555). I would push Heilbut a bit
further and suggest that lingering over sexual obsession with a young boy day after day
would be safer for Mann to explore when the obsessive gaze originated in a female biblical
figure than a contemporary European male.

guished and frustrated love . . . one of the most superb accounts of passion in all literature."

While my intention is not to provide an in-depth analysis of Mann's characterization of Mut-em-enet, his perceptions are vital to prevent the reader forming a unified characterization of Mut-em-enet as provided by readings of the doxa and rereadings of the biblical text. If one studies the question of characterization of a biblical figure across time and space, the pitfalls of remaining within the biblical arena and its cultural and historical boundaries are avoided. This strategy allows the contemporary reader to identify female literary figures outside of the roles and expressions provided to them by the theology/ideology that drove their biblical creators. Thus, Mann's passionate Mut-em-enet afforded the author "the pleasure of looking for human impulses that were invisible on the surface" (Hayman 1995: 75). On reflecting upon the novelist's ability to measure time within one's mind, Mann understood his work to be concerned with beginnings, writing as if each human experience were unprecedented. Neider catches the essence of the creation of modern midrash.

But this dominant originality is at the same time repetition, reflection, image, the result of rotation of the spheres which brings the upper, the starlike, into the lower regions, carries in turn the worldly into the realm of the divine so that the gods become men, men in turn become gods. The worldly finds itself pre-created in the realm of the stars, and the individual character seeks its dignity by tracing itself back to the timeless mythical pattern giving it presence. (Neider 1948: 197)

I will struggle against the equally tempting desire to argue as though there were a unified poetics of biblical narrative. Part of the difficulty with formulating such a poetics of ancient texts is that as modern critics we are displaced persons, a long way from home. Writing about the necessity for the modern critic to employ critical flexibility, Terry Eagleton has refused to view the literary work as a stable object of study.

You can discuss the poet's asthmatic childhood or examine her peculiar use of syntax, you can detect the rustling of silk in the hissing of the s's, explore the phenomenology of reading, relate the literary work to the state of class-struggle or find out how many copies it sold. These methods have nothing whatsoever of significance in common. (1983: 197)

While traditional methods of literary analysis have wanted to disclose the personality behind the narrative, the author within the text, I shall move directly from the reader's imagination to the work itself, in order to create an immediate connection between the reader and the characters. This strategic move, as the reader will realize, allows me to separate myself from any claims made by the ideological agenda of the biblical author. Struggling against a sense of solidarity with such an author, the reader will not necessarily share the storytellers' views of the victim and the hero, as I hope to show in my analysis of Mut-em-enet and Joseph. As I stated in the introduction, most biblical figures, certainly the female ones, function in traditional interpretation more as commodity than character, more as solid blocks of black and white than chiaroscuro, more as single note than symphony. It is the modern reader's task to insert the melody, the lighting, the multiple possibilities of reading.

LOCKED IN THE FRAME

The storyteller ordinarily uses a narratorial frame to slant the story in a particular direction: this frame may serve a dual purpose. First, the frame contains the ideological motor that drives a particular version. Since ideology is a matter of interaction between the work and the reader, the reader can be resistant to becoming engaged within the frame. Second, for the ideal reader, the frame and the story can work together on one level as a chain of narrative voices. The reader hears the story from the narrator, who presumably has heard the story earlier. Thus the reader and the narrator are drawn into the story: as members of a circle "enclosing inside the story what is usually outside; its own reader" (Felman 1981: 123). But at the same time, the frame does the very opposite, pulling the inside outside. Culler expresses this convoluted theory with great clarity:

An external frame may function as the most intrinsic element of a work, folding itself in; conversely, what seems the most inner or central aspect of a work will acquire this role through qualities that fold it back outside of and against the work. The secret center that appears to explain everything folds back on the work, incorporating an external position from which to elucidate the whole in which it also figures. (Culler 1982: 198)[2]

The narrator in telling someone else's story is essentially alienated from it; story and narratorial frame split, and as happens in Genesis 39, the woman who might have been the subject of the story is expelled from the narrator's frame. The intrusion of the female into a male story of power and wealth parallels her intrusion into the well-ordered world of male institutions, where both the Egyptian courtier Potiphar and the Israelite slave Joseph know their place. Thus, in examining the two basic units of the narrative, the frame and the story, the reader jumps from the world of male power in the frame into the world of female seduction and betrayal in the story. At the conclusion of the story the narrator has returned the reader to the safe prison-house of male privilege after the far more dangerous escapade in the dark house of the woman. At the same time the narrator has been more successful at seducing the reader than Mut-em-enet was at seducing Joseph. We hear his voice, we overhear hers.

In order to offer a resistant reading of the story of Mut-em-enet in Genesis 39, I have put to one side the ideological interference of the frame. The reading strategies employed by the majority of biblical interpreters have shared the ideology of the storyteller. Only recently has biblical criticism moved past the New Critical arena in which one assumes the correct interpretation can be adduced from the correct analysis of form and content. Among the most totalizing of the presuppositions that underlie a formalist reading of the text is that language has a stabilizing force, that it means what it says and says what it means.[3] This strictly formalist method gave way in biblical studies to the formulation of rhetorical

---

[2] Culler finds a similar distinction between literature and criticism as the relation between the inside/outside arrangement present in a framing device. "The distinction between criticism and literature opposes a framing discourse to what it frames, or divides an external metalanguage from the work it describes" (1982: 199). Culler's distinction is helpful in mapping the relationship of the critic to the text, a relation that underscores the critic's involvement in the work (inside) in spite of an attempt to remain outside or above the text one is reading.

[3] John Crow Ransom's view indicates the extent to which the identity of the reader is locked out of a New Critical reading: "The first law to be prescribed to criticism, if we may assume such authority, is that it shall be objective, shall cite the nature of the object rather than its effect on the subject" (Freund 1987: 40).

criticism, a perspective argued by James Muilenburg and refined
and reified by his students, notably Phyllis Trible. Muilenburg
recognized one of the shortcomings of formalist theory, that it
fragmented the text, concentrating on small narrative units,
without regard to historic, psychologic, or biographic elements. "It
neglects the individual, personal, unique, particular, distinctive,
precise, versatile, and fluid features of the text. Muilenburg used all
these adjectives to set the stage for his proposed supplement. It lifts
up the words "artistry," "aesthetics," and "stylistics" (Trible 1994:
26). A faithful reader who taught Old Testament at Union
Theological Seminary in New York, Muilenburg devised a critical
method that added to form criticism a context developed from the
features of classical Hebrew literature. Because his focus was
directed upon biblical studies, the method reflected Muilenburg's
concern with Hebrew composition, "discerning structural patterns, verbal sequences, and stylistics that make a coherent whole"
(ibid.).

One can create a literary map in which Muilenburg and his
followers occupy a site of reader-response criticism, with the
reading community agreeing to a well-demarcated boundary that
protects and reflects their literary work of interest: the Bible. The
most important element for an understanding of the place of
rhetorical criticism within recent literary theories is that the
interpreter tries to uncover authorial intent through an affinity
with the imagined author. Described by Muilenburg as "the
proper articulation of form yields a proper articulation of meaning,"[4] there is no doubt that the proper interpreter will reveal the

---

[4] This quote from Muilenburg has become a statement of recognition invoked by his
followers, usually orally. When I was in graduate school, Phyllis Trible augmented the
statement: "The proper articulation of form *and content* yields the proper articulation of
meaning," indicating a desire on the part of Trible to connect a surface reading more to its
contextual scaffolding than classical rhetorical criticism had. Trible's own work does not
consider the term *context* to suggest synchronic readings of similar tropes, characters, in
either other biblical or extrabiblical texts. A thorough explication of the method of
rhetorical criticism and Trible's memorable application to the book of Jonah is found in
Rhetorical Criticism: Context, Method, and the Book of Jonah. Chapter 2 provides a lucid and
complete recounting of the development of the method by its primary practitioner.
    For a demonstration of Muilenburg's use of rhetorical analysis, and a parade example
of the beauty of his prose style, see his commentary on Isaiah 40–66, in *The Interpreter's Bible*,
ed. G. A. Buttrick et al. (New York: Abingdon Press, 1956) 381–419; 422–773. A collection
and bibliography of Muilenburg's work appears in T. F. Best, ed., *Hearing and Speaking the*

text's secrets – through a legerdemain of chiasmas and parallel-isms. Emphasizing coherence of the biblical text through form and language, Muilenburg concentrated on syntactic and syntagmatic differences that would yield the correct meaning. Muilenburg and Trible's emphases on precise or true meaning residing within chiastic structures, parallel inversions, and other biblical Hebrew conventions demonstrater both the positivistic and the dichotomizing tendencies of the method. In a remarkable statement, Trible appears to argue otherwise.

rhetorical analysis itself characterizes deconstructionist activity. In dis-mantling texts, it investigates the persuasive power of language (as well as the lack thereof), delineates tropes and figures, and pursues close reading with focus on the particularities (rather than the similarities) of texts. (1994: 72)

What she has not acknowledged in this passage, but has argued elsewhere in her book, is that the persuasive power of language in the Bible is used in service to its ideology or theology. A structural or a deconstructive reading would insist on laying bare the codes that point to the ideology embedded within the text. If one acknowledges that literary meaning is a form of ideology, that is, meaning originates not in an individual mind but intersubjective-ly, then it becomes clear why the rhetorical method in biblical studies never challenged the text's ideology – its loyal readers were preserving that ideology all the way. Such iconic reading produced the following statements emblematic of the Muilenburg school: "Whichever orientation prevails, meaning always con-tains a theological dimension. Scripture as artistic composition engages the ultimate questions of life. Art serves faith" (Trible 1994: 27).

Leaving aside the concentration on the theological code in the analysis of biblical texts, a more general problem inherent to the formalist concentration on *form*, is that form is not separate from content. In his article on the work of Vladimir Propp, Lévi-Strauss, sums up the problem succinctly: "Formalism destroys its

Word: Selections from the Works of James Muilenburg (Chicago: Scholars Press, 1984). The breadth of applications of rhetorical criticism within biblical studies is found in D. F. Watson and A. J. Hauser, *Rhetorical Criticism of the Bible: A Comprehensive Bibliography with Notes on History and Method* (Leiden: E. J. Brill, 1994).

object" (1966: 132). What concerns Lévi-Strauss and literary structuralists is two-fold:[5] (1) a formalist claim that structure inherent in the text is actually an accident of reading; (2) when one concentrates upon specific forms (grammar) and leaves aside the subtleties of content (vocabulary), stripping the narrative of its "naturing nature" (143), one separates content from the morphological analysis central to formalism. Further, formalism has compared narratives with similar structures, but the method does not allow an arena to examine the differences that appear in the narratives. In a view related to the formalist ignoring of the effect of a reader on the text, or the rhetorical critic's focus upon faithful readers, structuralist interpreters of the same period, acknowledging the variety of possible hermeneutic positions, continued to ignore the effect of a *female* reader upon the text. In Genesis 39 a crucial ambiguity revolves around the narrator's text providing one version of what happened and the female figure providing a contrasting one. Interpreters have concluded that the proper interpretation reveals that she (the female character) means what he (the narrator) says she means.[6] It is the interpretive instructions of the narrator, contained within the frame, that have led critics, new and old, to be deafened to her story, because they were listening to his story.

FRAMING WOMEN

A primary struggle for feminist scholars who deal with the ancient world is that we have no direct means of access to ancient women; we have only literary sources written by men. Thus, a close reading of rhetorical features will never bring us closer than the outer suburbs of the woman's story enclosed in Genesis 39. One must,

---

[5] In this seminal article on the differences between Russian formalism and subsequent structural analysis, Lévi-Strauss takes care to note the historical role of the Russian school and its intrinsic importance. A major difference between the methods, which Lévi-Strauss lays out in great detail, is that a Proppian imagines folktales to come from myths, as a substrata, and for a structuralist, the myth and the folktale coexist. See "Reflections on a Work by Vladimir Propp," 1976.

[6] Of course one can use rhetorical design to aid either side. In a subversive reading one can note that the preponderance of the woman's dialogue claims that she has been sexually assaulted: "He came into [the house] to have sex with me and I cried out in a loud voice." Only her opening suggestion *sekab immi*, "Lie with me," supports the narrator's version.

therefore, disrupt some of the cultural and ideological codes in order to extract a voice for the woman identified in Genesis 39 merely as "wife of Potiphar." Most modern interpreters of Genesis 39 view Potiphar's wife as an illustration that reinforces wisdom ideology: the faithful Israelite hero is rewarded for choosing propriety over the tempting foreign woman, *ishah zarah*. The Egyptian wife is the embodiment of the much-repeated warning from the book of Proverbs: "Watch out for the *ishah zarah* with her smooth words. Her house is the way to Sheol." Exegetes and commentators habitually wag a punitive finger at the Egyptian woman who would dare to toy with God's chosen boy. According to *Bereshit Rabbah*, God used Mrs. Potiphar to teach Joseph humility and the dangers of vanity.

Free from anxieties, he turned his attention to his external appearance. He painted his eyes, dressed his hair, and aimed to be elegant in his walk. But God spoke to him. "Your father is mourning in sackcloth and ashes, while you eat, drink, and dress your hair. Therefore, I will stir up thy mistress against thee. (*Bereshit Rabbah* 87.3–4. Also *Tanhuma Wa-Yeseb* 8)

While this midrash makes the callow youth responsible for the woman's attraction and advances toward him, another rabbinic tradition, found in tractate Sotah of the Babylonian Talmud, explains that Joseph demanded this trial of YHWH since Abraham, Isaac, and Jacob had been tested (T. B. Sotah 36B). *Midrash Tanhuma* states that Joseph, Boaz, and Palti were the three men in the Bible who were able to control their passion in the sight of God (*Tanhuma* 56). The common thread among these varied midrashim is the connection between the statement that Joseph is "beautiful in form and appearance" and the ensuing struggle between self-control and sexuality, represented in Genesis 39 by male and female figures. In spite of his beauty and his youth, elements that contribute to temptation, Joseph ultimately exercises self-control. In no version of the Potiphar's Wife motif[7] does the myth of seduction become a story about anybody's sexual pleasure. In spite of the suggestion that the wife had ungovernable sexual desire because her husband was a eunuch (from an interpretation of the

---

[7] Stith Thompson (1955–57) has so identified the motif. For extrabiblical and classical versions of the motif, see Y. D. Yohanan (1968).

term *saris* in the opening verse of Genesis 39),[8] there is no suggestion that this situation might offer a mitigating factor in the woman's conduct.[9]

Ancient societies did not regard the marriage bed as the locus of eroticism. Marriage in the peri-Mediterranean world did not raise questions as far as the ethics of pleasure was concerned, since the wife was restricted by status, law, and custom. Marriage was under male control, being arranged between heads of households. A wife's sexual activity had to be within the conjugal relationship; and her husband had to be her exclusive partner. A woman's sexuality was viewed in relation to the man's sexual desires or to the woman's desire for children.[10] Demosthenes reminded his audi-

[8] The term *saris* in some biblical passages refers to a position or rank in the king's entourage (1 Sam. 8:15; Jer. 34:19, 41:16; 1 Kgs. 22:9; 2 Kgs. 8:6, 9:32). However, the word, which is customarily translated as "eunuch," has that sense in Isa. 56:3–5; Sir. 30:20 and perhaps 2 Kgs. 20:18, Esther 1–2, *passim*; Dan. 1 *passim*. Translation of the term in Genesis 39 has caused much consternation among interpreters since one level of the story turns on sexual matters. The word itself is borrowed from Akkadian, transcribed *sha-reshi*, "he at the head," [de Vaux 121]. This meaning seems widely accepted by scholars, except for Albright, who prefers Haupt's etymology from the Arabic, *siresu*, "beer," which receives its name from the preparation of malt. Albright (1918: 127–28, n. 15) connects the term with a cup-bearer, meaning one who precedes the king, one of his confidants. In Aramaic the word is *sarisa*, from which it probably passed into the Egyptian during the fifth century BCE as *srs*. For further etymologic explanations, see Redford (1970: 51 *passim*). For certain tasks in the royal household, such as supervising the harem or overseeing the education of the children, eunuchs probably were chosen. Thus, the later understanding of the term as "eunuch," refers to a trusted highly placed court official. Since Potiphar has a wife, the understanding seems likely that of "Egyptian official." Philo (*De Josepho*: 8) remarks that in Potiphar's house Joseph was given the opportunity to acquire the knowledge necessary for a statesman; for the management of a house is the management of a state in miniature. Such an understanding would add weight to political rather than sexual interpretation of the term in the first century.

Rabbinic literature is filled with speculations about Potiphar as *saris*. For some sages the term sparked sly humor and provided a ready-made denigration of the Egyptian. For others the term did not indicate the absence of sexual relations between Potiphar and his wife. The term *saris* may have meant that Potiphar was capable of sexual performance, but sterile (Kugel 1990: 76). For an altered but similar connection between the *saris* and the servant, see *b. Sotah* 13b. In this Talmudic aggadah the Egyptian's designs on Joseph were thwarted when the angel Gabriel mutilated Potiphar and made him a eunuch. For similar interpretation see Jerome on Genesis 37:36.

[9] There is at least one tradition in which Potiphar does possess the physical ability to beget children. Thus, in T Jos, Potiphar had children when he purchased Joseph, "for he was third in rank with Pharaoh, head of all the eunuchs, having a wife and children and concubines" (T Jos 13.6). But see also T Jos 3:6–7, where the text states that it took Joseph's prayers to the deity for the wife of Potiphar to give birth to a male child. For the traditional Jewish texts in which the lineage of Aseneth is debated, and the questions of Potiphar's sterility and his wife's barrenness are resolved, see Aptowitzer (1924: 243–56).

ence of the law that guaranteed married women take seriously the power of the house that had been built around them: "The law has declared that our women may be inspired with a fear sufficient to make them live soberly (*sophronein*) and avoid all vice (*meden hamartanein*) and, as their duty is, to keep to their household tasks" (*Against Neaera*, 122). The seducer of a married woman violated the husband's authority. When the wife of Potiphar opened her house to Joseph, it was her husband's property and reputation that were in danger. Some rabbinic authorities claim that Potiphar had not believed his wife's story. "I know that you are innocent," Potiphar is said to have told Joseph, "but I must do this lest a stigma fall upon my children" (*Bereshit Rabbah*, 87.9). If that stigma is the fact that their mother is a liar, the rabbis have inscribed that truth within their counterversion of her story.

As I shall show in this chapter, the male/female struggle is also played out rhetorically between the frame and the story. A close reading of the narrative frame reveals that repetition of certain motifs and words inscribes a world of male prosperity and trust, while the story the frame encircles presents a picture of female destruction and perfidy. Specifically the *Leitwörter* remind us of the slippery nature of words: *bayit* can be an estate or prison; *yad* can be the male hand that clutches power or the female hand that clutches an empty garment. Our ears attuned to play, we follow the actions of *adonai* and *adonaiv*, the characters who control the fate of the hero. Thus, rhetorical devices preserve the victory of one set of each binary pair: the estate is better than the prison, the male hand is refilled with wealth; the divine master triumphs over the Egyptian courtier. The frame removes the story's sting.

Another important convention related to that of narrative frame is that of the identity of the narrator. As I have already explained, I

[10] Setel sums up the predominant view of female sexuality in biblical Israel: "Female sexual activity that diminished the property value of a woman's body was discouraged; that which challenged the paternity of a husband was strongly prohibited. Sexual activity that did not disrupt the paternity system was tolerated" (Setel 1985). Clearly a woman's adulterous liaison would cast doubts on the paternity of her children, her major contribution to the household. For a discussion of the woman's primary function within the Israelite family unit as her ability to produce children, see Ardener (1978); Appignanesi (1993); Bal (1988a & b); Bird (1974; 1989); Brown (1988); Bynum (1984); Canto (1986); Carson (1990); Duby (1988); Eron; (1987); Frymer-Kensky (1981); Fuchs (1988); Grosz (1989); Keuls; Kraemer (1992); Lerner (1986); Meyers (1983, 1988, 1989).

think that the narrator functions as a character in the mind of the reader. Unless consciously acknowledging the bias of the narrator, the reader will accept the narrator's version as true and authoritative. Regardless of a current critical antipathy toward delineating authorial intention, I suspect that until the fall from grace of readerly identification of authorial intention, most people did read texts at least "*as if* they were trying to extract the author's meaning" (Rabinowitz 1987: 194). Thus, the literary interpreters of Genesis 39 followed the instructions of the text by accepting the narrator's version of the story and the ideology it espouses. In order to offer a different reading of the story of Mut-em-enet, we will have to unmask the narrator and examine his credentials.

THE FRAME AND THE STORY

Another rhetorical technique that allows the narrator to control the story is the use of a narrator's frame in which the narrator can remind the reader of the social and ethnic tensions in the enclosed story. The limits of the frame are not absolute. Alter has divided Genesis 39 into a story and a frame, consisting of two basic units: verses 1–6 and 21–23, the frame of the story; and verses 7–20, the story itself (Alter 1981: 107–08). While I also see a narrative frame enclosing the story, I divide the text slightly differently. My reading assigns the second unit "Joseph was handsome in figure and appearance," to the story, since the young hero's beauty is what connects him to the woman in the story.[11] In the frame of Genesis 39, that is verses 1–6a and verses 20–23, there is no mention of a woman, of seduction or sexual desire, of trouble for Joseph. Beginning the story with verse 6b allows one to recognize a shift in the narrative and hints at the sexual reversal to follow. The unit containing the actor who has seen/focalized Joseph's form and

[11] Sura 12 in the Qur'an also emphasizes Yusef's physical beauty – the women connect Yusef's dazzling appearance with his semidivine status. The beauty of the male hero is found in other parallel tales: Bata and Bellerephon were both awarded great beauty. As Speiser has noted (1964: 303) the same phrase that describes the wife of Potiphar's gaze fixed upon Joseph is used to describe Ishtar's designs on the equally beautiful Gilgamesh. *Bereshit Rabbah* 87 states that two-thirds of the beauty of mankind was granted to Joseph, the same percentage used to describe Gilgamesh as being two-thirds divine and one-third human.

appearance is different from the previous unit, "He placed all that he had into Joseph's hands and, with him [Joseph] there, he thought of nothing except for the food that he ate" which has been narrated. Hierarchy and social position are emphasized in the beginning of the frame with the recitation of Potiphar's titles, placing him within the social and political structure.[12] The mention of the pharaoh in connection with Potiphar as well as the extensive list of civil titles of Potiphar informs the reader that Joseph has turned up in an aristocratic household, certainly a better fate than the pit or the caravan of Midianites/Ishmaelites.

The attention of the reader is caught at the mention of Joseph's beauty.[13] One moves from the frame's cool collation of the elements of social status into the story of heated sexual tension. Like Joseph entering the house of Mut-em-enet, we are now in a different world: one bare of recitations of wealth, one bold with recitations of wanting. But we are the narrator's guests in this world, not Mut-em-enet's. Thus, we are reminded that Joseph's display of self-control and rejection of desire are our path away from this house, back to a world of exemplary behavior where we (and Joseph) belong.

Sternberg, who defines the framing device as the places in the text where the narrator's voice comes through the level of the story, argues that the biblical narrator transfers the incongruous elements from his central episode to his framework in order to set the stage for a bifocal reading: one from his own point of view and one from the central character's viewpoint. "Since the narrator does not

[12] The name Potiphar is an Egyptian theophoric name, an exact transcription of *Pedephre*, "He whom the Sun God gives" (Skinner 1930: 457; Westermann 1986: 61). According to Redford (1970: 136), the original text did not include the personal name of Potiphar, since the name is missing from the rest of the chapter. He argues that the verse has been expanded by the inclusion of "Potiphar, the officer of Pharaoh," as well as "who had brought him there," an addition Redford calls a midrash supplied by P, the same redactor who had inserted 37:36. In the strongest terms Redford insists that this verse in its present form "cannot be treated as an integral part of the chapter," but his argument, the absence of the personal name Potiphar in the rest of the chapter, seems weak.

[13] "Handsome in appearance," *yefeh to'ar* is used of eight women and three men in the Bible. But the complete phrase *vayhi yosef yefeh to'ar vifeh mar'eh* is used only of Rachel and Joseph (Gen. 29:17). Thus, the ancient aggadists concluded that Joseph inherited his mother's beauty and both resembled her and was her equal in beauty (*Bereshit Rabbah* 86.6). Some contemporary interpreters have understood the association of mother and son as a textual feminizing of Joseph, a reading reinforced by the coat worn only by Joseph and David's daughter Tamar.

change from telling to retelling," Sternberg claims, "something else must: the angle, object, focus, or point of his narration" (1985: 415). In my analysis both frame and story of Genesis 39 reflect the narrator's ideological perspective. While the wife of Potiphar seems to be the subject of the story, it is not told from her viewpoint. It is not her story. Instead of containing incongruous elements, the frame exerts the power of order and smothers any hint of fire that might be ignited by a story of a woman's sexual desire. In other words by demonstrating self-control *sophrosyne* the frame keeps the story in its place.

Our proper place is the frame to which we are returned. The final unit (verses 20–23) mirrors the top of the frame in describing Joseph's situation as prisoner to another master. Verse 1 begins "Joseph was taken to Egypt"; verse 20 "the master of Joseph took him." Verse 21 echoes verse 2: YHWH was with Joseph (verses 2/21).

v 2   he became a *successful man*
v 21   he extended *hesed* to him and *gave him favor*
v 2   lived in the *house* of his Egyptian master
v 21   in the eyes of the captain of the *prison*

The final two verses (22 and 23) contain many semantic elements of verses 3 and 4. There is one interesting omission. Potiphar recognized that YHWH made Joseph prosper and thus the Egyptian had wisely decided to put everything under his charge. Later Potiphar forgets or ignores Joseph's divine connection when he tosses him into prison. The captain of the prison is not awarded even partial perception since he never recognizes YHWH as Joseph's protector.

The framework of Genesis 39 is indeed about men, success, position, and power. Safety resides in the house of men. Even the prison house is safer than the domain of the woman. The initial phrases of both pieces of the frame indicate Joseph's enforced obedience to the social structure. Silent, unprotesting, he is taken to Egypt; silent and without struggle, he is taken to prison. Having responded correctly to the overtures of Mut-em-enet, the boy with the Midas touch now continues his ascent into the world of political power.

The repetition of the Tetragrammaton within the frame points to its frequent use of wordplay and hierarchical pairs. These are the only times in the Joseph cycle where the Tetragrammaton appears. The term appears only in the frame, not within the story of the encounter between Joseph and his master's wife, verses 7–20. Joseph does invoke God at the end of verse 9, where the word is *'elohim,* the term used when God is mentioned in direct speech.[14] Only the narrator uses YHWH; and only in the frame of this story about Joseph's first experiences in Egypt.[15]

Theologically oriented readers have pondered this change in terms of the deity. Westermann concludes that the repeated use of the Tetragrammaton emphasizes the link between God's presence with Joseph and the divine presence with all the patriarchs, "by taking over the fixed formula of YHWH's assistance which is firmly rooted in the Isaac–Jacob tradition" (Westermann 1986: 63). Von Rad does not agree, arguing that God has only "mediated significance." The narrator prefers to focus on a portrait of Joseph, as modest, clever, pleasing, like the portrait of the young David (1 Sam. 16:18) (von Rad 1959: 364).[16] Von Rad implies the same presence of God, I believe, since clearly God's responsibility for David's rise to power parallels that of Joseph. Redford contends that the use of YHWH exclusively in Genesis 39 indicates that "someone wished to insert a pre-existent tale of Potiphar's wife, embellished it first with his own theological commentary (a reference to the frame of the story) and then slipped it into its present context" (Redford 1970: 130).[17] Put in narratologic terms,

[14] In 40:8 Joseph uses *'elohim* in speaking to the prisoners; in 41:16 in speaking to Pharaoh; in 41:51,52 Joseph to himself; 42:18 Joseph to his brothers; 43:29 Joseph to Benjamin; 45:5,7,8,9 Joseph to his brothers; and 50:19,20 Joseph to his brothers.

[15] There are frequent instances of other characters' use of *'elohim* in direct speech in the Joseph cycle; Gen. 41:25, 28, 32, 38, 39; 42:28; 43:14,23; 44:16; 50:17. The name is invoked eight times in ch.41, twice as many in the next most frequent usage, ch. 45. Joseph calls upon *'elohim* 13 times; the other characters 10 times. Thus, the commonly cited observation that God is mentioned only in ch. 39 of the Joseph cycle refers only to the Tetragrammaton, used by the narrator, since *'elohim* is quite common in direct speech, fairly evenly distributed between the central character and the secondary characters.

[16] Von Rad has sentimentalized Joseph, who is neither modest nor pleasing to his brothers. Rabbinic tradition, often grittier than modern readings, considers him so vain that God presented Mrs. Potiphar as a trial/test for him (see verse 6).

[17] Unlike other source analysts who divide the work according to the Documentary Hypothesis, in which the use of the name YHWH would reflect only the J source, Redford (1970) argues for a complex layer of redaction. For classical source-critical descriptions based on internal textual inconsistencies, see Budde (1906: 61ff); Eissfeldt, *Einleitung in das*

the reader Redford is responding to the power of the narrator's frame, allowing the theological codes to saturate the story they enclose.

The use of the divine name *'adonai* is balanced or joined with that of the Egyptian master, called *'adonav* in verses 2, 3 (twice), 5 (twice), 21, 23 (twice). This use of *'adonav* could be heard as a sonorous play on *'adonai*, which from the time of the Second Temple would probably have been substituted for the divine name. The Greek text uses *kurios* for both terms; the Vulgate uses *dominus*. Thus in those versions the play is clear. Stratified parties are established; God is with Joseph in the house of Joseph's Egyptian master, now referred to simply as "his master, the Egyptian." This anonymity, a stylistic feature common to stock characters in *Märchen*, emphasizes the unimportance of the Egyptian courtier compared with the power of the Israelite deity.

This verse (2) also introduces variants of *bayit* "house," a word that has several nuances in this chapter. This first instance, *bebeit 'adonav* "in the house of his master," probably serves to define Joseph as a servant of the house, not of the field, connecting Joseph to the *anshei habayit* "men of the house," referred to in verses 11, 14. By working in the house, Joseph has the opportunity to display his talents to the master and to win his favor. As Sarna notes, it also puts Joseph into "close and constant contact with his master's wife" (*JPS* 271).

The phrase also embraces a second understanding of *bayit* as the wealth of the Egyptian in both verses 4 and 5. In verse 5,

---

Alte Testament 36ff; Holscher, *Geschichtsschreibung in Israel: Untersuchungen zum Jahvisten und Elohisten* 179ff; Gunkel (1967: 126); Smend, *Die Erzalung des Hexateuch auf ihre Quellen Untersucht* 99f.

Redford (1970: 141) has devised his own system of assigning sources for the Joseph material, referring to them as Judah source and Reuben source, rather than the conventional J/E. Similar to the accepted source-critical designations, he separates the sources of the Joseph cycle into a Southern Judah source and a northern Reuben source. The appellations come from the widely noted source-critical observation that in the J source, it is Judah and in the E version it is Reuben who acts as the conscience and/or spokesman for the brothers regarding the fate of Joseph. Redford has determined that the Judah source is dependent upon the Reuben source, "an expansion of a pre-existent version in which Reuben was the sole protagonist."

For a recent Bloomian literary reading that also plays with defining northern and southern traditions in Genesis, see Brisman (1900). His imagined biblical authors are the contentious brothers (J)acob and (E)issac. Jacob rewrites some of his brother's material.

everything in the house is put under Joseph's care; then "God blessed everything in the house(hold) of the Egyptian on account of Joseph," and in a repeated phrase, "the blessing of God was upon everything (belonging to Potiphar) in the house and the field." Presumably one of those belonging inside the house of Potiphar who received God's blessing (at least at this stage of the story) is the wife of Potiphar. At the end of verse 5, house is differentiated from field,[18] a distinction which will be important in the unfolding of the story, where the nuance of *bayit* changes from safe to dangerous. In the frame house is used metonymically for the rise, advancement, and success of Joseph. *Bayit* refers to the wealth of the master. However, in the story, when he enters the woman's house, he is put into danger, and loses all he has gained in the male domain.

In verse 6a Strus has identified an important wordplay between the name *yosef* (*ysf*, add increase) and the imperfect verb *ya'zob* (*'zb*, leave, forsake, abandon) used repeatedly and with different nuances in this chapter. According to Strus,

The verb *ya'zob* is similar to a proper noun according to the QT L type with the metathesis of the phoneme O, thus [the verb] assumes the role of leitmotif in the narration of Joseph and the woman seducer. It is repeated four times, verses 12, 13, 15, 18 in the context, narrated two times by the author, verses 12 and 13, and spoken finally twice by the woman, verses 15 and 18, except in verse 13, which reads *ki y'azab*, it is always the same: *ya'zob*. (Strus 1978: 139–52, translation mine)[19]

Strus's observation emphasizes the narrator's use of wordplay to demarcate the difference between life inside and outside the frame, since *ya'zob* functions as a positive trait, when it is Potiphar leaving everything he has in the hands of Joseph (verse 6) and in the verb's usage in the story, where Joseph leaves his garment in the hands of the wife of Potiphar. In the story the verb is used twice by the narrator describing the action (verses 12 and 13) and twice by Mrs. Potiphar in her retellings of the event. The one who adds, Joseph,

---

[18] Sarna reads the phrase as a merism, acknowledging the contrast, but emphasizing the totality of the blessing, "house *and* field," rather than a distinction between house and field. *JPS* 272.

[19] Strus's (1978) tracing of "motif sonore" is far more elegant than this brief example implies. Strus follows phonomic plays connected to the name Joseph throughout Gen. 37–50, but for the purposes of this study his identification of the *leitwort ya'zob* is sufficient.

yosef, is connected in his ability to increase honor and prestige for his master Potiphar. He increases only frustration and guilt for the wife of Potiphar. Mut-em-enet is not able to add to her pleasure; she can only be abandoned by the one who increases. The anthropologic coded pair of honor/shame actually applies only to the males in the story. It is Potiphar's shame that would be enacted if Joseph did not exercise his own honor. The men share this code, whereas the female character is shamed only in relation to her shaming her husband.

Another of the *Leitwörter* used in Genesis 39 is *yad*. The phrase "in his hand" *beyado* is found only in the frame, which emphasizes the narrator's concern with the male codes of position and power. The frame, actually a doublet of Joseph's initial ascent to power in Egypt, focuses on the wealth which accumulates in Joseph's hand. In the story (verses 7–20), however, the suffix changes. In verses 12 and 13 the narrator uses *beyadah* to focus upon the garment left in female hands, the snatching of power and position from Joseph's hands.[20] Her quoted retelling of the incident with Joseph allows the reader to see how she twists the young man's words. Repetition of *beyadah* adds to the reader's understanding of the result of her action upon his fortunes – from the husband's wealth in Joseph's hands to the incriminating garment in her hands.[21]

Skirting the question of whether a rapist has the time to undress leisurely, Alter allows for no other possible interpretation of *beyadah*, which he construes as implicating Mut-em-enet as the

---

[20] Note also verse 8, where *beyadi* is used in direct speech by Joseph to emphasize his power within the master's household. In verse 15 if one amends the Hebrew text to agree with the Samaritan version which reads *beyadi*, instead of *'etzli*, the text continues the repetition of the root *yad* from verses 12 and 13. The amended reading allows a subtle echo in the words of Mut-em-enet of Joseph's own statement in verse 8.

[21] *Bereshit Rabbah* supplies two possible interpretations of *'etzlah* (verse 10) that the invitation is literally (1) "to lie beside the woman, not to have sexual relations"; or (2) if he lies beside her in this world, Joseph will not have to lie beside her in Gehanna (87:6). In verse 16 when the garments are *'etzlah*, the rabbis imagine that she is hugging them to her, as a remembrance of Joseph.

The MT reading, *'etzli*, also allows for echoes, since the narrator uses *'etzlah* (verses 10 and 16) to emphasize the intimacy of the invitation to lie "beside her, with her" and then, after the flight of Joseph, to describe the empty garment which lay "beside her," as a poor substitute for the person she wanted *'etzlah*. Without considering the echoes produced by either reading, Alter reads *'etzli* with the MT, interpreting the change from *beyadah* as a "quiet transformation," that permits Joseph to appear to have undressed "quite voluntarily as a preliminary to rape" (Alter 1981: 110).

actor, the undresser.[22] It seems quite reasonable that the woman could have picked up the shirt after it had been removed by Joseph and held it *beyadah*. Another contemporary reading interpreting along the traditional lines of the ancient rabbis ignores the possibility of rape and supports the notion of Joseph voluntarily undressing and succumbing to seduction – nearly. Kugel contends that if Joseph had not been tempted, he would have been outside "the range of normal human emotions." In order to make him a model of ethical conduct, the storyteller must present "an example of sudden repentance others might seek to emulate" (Kugel 1990: 98). This reading acknowledges Joseph's approach to the house, when all others were away, as an intentional act, one that might result in sexual play with Mut-em-enet. What is lacking in this interpretation is a recognition that the "sudden repentance" might actually be a fearful reaction to the woman initiating sexual action.

By opening her house and opening her mouth, the woman has upset the social order. She notices Joseph (sees him) and within another breath, she has delivered the shortest seduction line in the Bible: *shikvah immi*.[23] Lie with me. An emphatic command.[24] In handling handsome Joseph's shirt, Mut-em-enet crosses boundaries of status as well as sexuality. The moment of physical contact with Joseph is the crisis of the story; crisis that would become chaos had Joseph allowed himself to remain in that foreign country: the woman's house. Only when he is an active subject, only when he enters her house, does the situation prove dangerous for Joseph. The sole words in Genesis 39 from the hero are his rejection of

---

[22] *Midrash Tanhuma* assumes that Joseph willingly undressed. After she seized him by his garment, Joseph "went into bed with her." *Vayyeshev* 9. *Aggadot ha-Talmud* also heats up the biblical account: "the two of them went naked into bed." See E. Z. Melamed (1988: 478).

[23] Mut-em-enet's unadorned command has a rare Masoretic cantillation mark which indicates sustained deliberation. For the Masoretes deliberation emphasizes the refusal, the probity and self-control of Joseph, the Israelite hero. Even the visual markings of the text must take note of the hero spurning the foreign woman. Read another way, the "sustained deliberation" could indicate the hero's flickering temptation. For further discussion see Lowenthal (1973). Another interpretation of the deliberation or hesitation in the woman's discourse was her struggle against uttering the words of desire.

[24] The use of the verb *s-k-b* has crass sexual nuances in other biblical narrative contexts. It appears in the stories of incest and rape (Gen. 19:32,34,35; Gen. 34:2,7; 2 Sam. 13:11,14) and a variety of other illicit sexual relationships (Lev. 20:11,12,13,18,20). Niditch has suggested that *sekab* in the scene in which Leah buys conjugal rites to Jacob from her sister Rachel (Gen. 30:15–16) implies that Jacob is the hired lover, "told with whom he will lie" (Niditch 1989: 49).

Mut-em-enet. In his speech Joseph refers to Potiphar as "my master," rather than "your husband." His words focus upon the connection of wealth and prosperity, "everything in *his* house he put into *my* hands." From Potiphar to Joseph, man to man.[25] His next phrase, "no one in the household is greater than I" reminds us of a familiar side of Joseph, the *baal hahalomot*. "Nothing is held back from me – except you because you are his wife" (rather than "he is your husband"), the ownership phrase "his wife" reinforcing the ancient understanding that the victim of adultery is the offended husband (Kornfeld 1950: 92).

Having begun by invoking Joseph's allegiance to the social order, the storyteller concludes with proof of his hero's piety. In sharp contrast with her two words, *shikvah immi*, Joseph presents a three-point refusal. First he would be abusing the trust and violating the husband's proprietary rights over his wife; second, on the level of pagan morality, adultery is an affront to the injured husband;[26] third, on the level of Israelite morality, it would be a sin against God.[27] Joseph's discourse is permeated with possessive pronouns. "My master has no worry about anything in *his* house[28]; he has put everything[29] of *his* in *my* hand," emphasizing his connection to Potiphar. The phrase *beyadi* is central to the entire story (it has already been introduced in verse 6 by the narrator *beyado*) and will be altered to ultimate effect in verse 13, "she saw that he had left his garment in *her* hands." That statement, the only one to focalize the narrative through the woman Mut-em-enet, becomes a refrain in each of the woman's retellings of the event, first to the male servants and then to her

---

[25] One rabbinic tradition claimed that the connection between Potiphar and his Israelite servant was a sexual one as well. Interpreting the word *seris* with the traditional meaning of eunuch, the rabbis understood that God punished the Egyptian Potiphar with castration for his lugubrious sexual designs. "[He] purchased him [Joseph] for the purpose of sodomy, whereupon the Holy One, blessed be He, emasculated him." 86.3.

[26] For documents relating to adultery in the ANE: The Code of Hammurabi, *ANET* 171, nos. 129, 131, 132; Middle Assyrian Laws, *ANET* 181, nos. 14–16; Hittite Laws, *ANET* 196, no. 198.

[27] See Deut. 22:14ff, 23ff; Exod. 20:15; Lev. 18:20. See also Lev. 18:3 "You shall not do as they do in Egypt."

[28] I would add to the MT with the Greek, Samaritan, Syriac, and Vulgate, *bebeito*, a further emphasis to the phrase *in the house* emphasizing the focus in Joseph's mind upon his male counterpart: *in his house*.

[29] Reading with the Samaritan version.

husband.[30] All the wealth entrusted in Joseph's hands is contrasted with the telltale tunic grabbed by the greedy woman.

Examining Joseph's entire speech, it is remarkable how little of it is directed toward the wife of Potiphar.

> everything in his house he put into my hands
> no one in (his) household is greater than I
> nothing is held back from me   except you . . . his wife
> I would not do this great evil
> I would not sin against God.

As I have arranged the speech, in the first pair of lines, the movement is from Potiphar to Joseph, master to servant, male to male. The central phrase contains the prohibition against contact with the female. The second pair of lines focuses upon Joseph's faithfulness to his divine master.

His loyalties having been established, Joseph flees without responding directly to the lusty invitation of Mut-em-enet. Rather he has refused to transgress the territory of Potiphar. Since the narrative never leaves the hands of its male creator, grabbing hold of Joseph's shirt does not result in Mut-em-enet grabbing hold of the story. Even her audacious sexual advance does not result in a shift of point of view to the woman. Her desperate bid for attention is rejected not only by Joseph, but also by the narrator. Later interpreters have praised Joseph's rejection as "sudden repentance," a great moral resurgence in the hero. In doing so, the sexual tension between the man and woman becomes a singular predatory act on the part of the woman. The narrator transmits to the reader his relief at Joseph's escape.

Verse 12 reflects the narrative tug of war: Mut-em-enet snatches the garment and Joseph pulls away and flees. Her amorous advance is met with refusal and retreat. The virtuous young man eludes her grasp, his empty shirt lifeless in her hands. In verse 13 she moves into action, momentarily winning the tug of war. She sees that she holds in her hands the evidence that will convict Joseph. She sets her devious plan into motion with the only power available

---

[30] Alter (1981: 148) and Sternberg (1985: 424) have both noted the *Leitworter yad* and *bayit*. The term *Leitworter*, coined by Buber and Rosenzweig, refers to a convention governed by thematic key words that function as binding devices within the narrative. Also Humphreys (1988: 94).

to her, the power of words. She who could not seduce Joseph with words succeeds in seducing her Egyptian servants. She even seduces her husband into believing her. But she is ultimately powerless in her scheme to discredit Joseph because the reader has already been seduced by the narrator. In spite of the repeated attempts of Mut-em-enet to speak, to scream, to tell and retell her story, the reader's inner ear has already been filled with the voice of the narrator. He drowns out the diversionary attempt at female assertion of sexuality and restores control to his story of power and position. Two chapters later the pharaoh will give Joseph a finer garment (41:42) and the daughter of Potiphera, a finer woman (41:45).

PLOTTING AGAINST THE PLOTTING WOMAN

One of the most insidious literary deaths attached to Mut-em-enet is the "stereotype" wasteland of the noncharacter, as she is considered by Formalist critics, who remain sympathetic to the narrator's version of the story. In her biblical poetics, Berlin identifies types as "flat characters who are built around a single quality or trait" (Berlin 1983: 23).[31] Similarly Brenner flattens the Egyptian wife as a negative temptress (Brenner 1985: 111). Following the poetics of Berlin, Humphreys calls the wife of Potiphar a type of lusty wife (1988: 68), then proceeds to analyze her in a way that one might argue makes her not a type, but an individual. It is the reader's choice to fill the gaps in the narrative, reducing to flatness Mut-em-enet or any other character. One has only to turn to Mann with his prodigious gap filling to see how effective a reader can be at developing multifaceted characters. Following the narrator's lead, reductionist interpreters have read with the

---

[31] Berlin does not mention the wife of Potiphar, but in her analyses of David's wives, she assigns the category *agent* to Bathsheba (2 Sam. 11–12), "a complete nonperson," who thus is not judged guilty of adultery, but "only the means whereby it was achieved" (27). She reduces Abigail to a *type*: "fair maiden freed from the wicked ogre to marry Prince Charming" (31). Using Berlin's delineation of flat characters, one would assign the appelation to most biblical female figures. More vigorous gap-filling would permit the reader to assign a rounder shape to these female characters, imagining Bathsheba's grief over the death of her infant, Abigail's courage in confronting the outlaw David, and with even more gap-filling, imagining the dialogue among all David's wives. For a fuller discussion of these texts, see chapter 5.

ideology presented in the text.[32] They have, perhaps unintention-
ally, aligned themselves with the biblical storyteller by supplying a
sense of unity in analyzing biblical characters, by consigning
Mut-em-enet to the epithet "wife of Potiphar," the prototypic
Strange Woman.

Genesis 39 applauds and preserves the cultural ideology reflected in three basic systems of exchange: financial, sexual, and
linguistic, from which women must be excluded – or at the very
least controlled. Unless the reader slips underneath the surface of
the text, he will remain walled in by the narrator's ideology. As
those who offer subversive readings have found, literary texts not
only represent ideology, but also in circular fashion, support it as
well. "For they can make what *is* seem like *has to be,* can make that
which is constructed and artificial appear "natural" and "necessary" (Rabinowitz 1987: 127). Clearly *what happens* in Genesis 39
empowers men and reaffirms their authority by celebrating
relationships of wealth and position, relations between men, while
at the same time abjectifying women. Traditionally scholars have
interpreted the story told in Genesis 39 as centering on Joseph, the
hero who must deflect the advances of the out-of-bounds woman.
Mut-em-enet has her own program, gratifying her sexual desires,
which runs counter to that of Joseph, who must remain faithful to
his masters.[33] As each of these actors aspires toward a goal, action is
generated.

Let us first follow the actions of Joseph's story. Peter Brooks
offers a succinct description of narrative: "an adventure is a piece
of action in which beginnings are chosen by and for ends" (Brooks
1984: 93). At the beginning of the narrative, the storyteller creates
the plot element, the temptation, that awakes desire within the
reader: what will happen to Joseph taken to Egypt and sold into
slavery? Immediately following this information, we are told that
God supports Joseph. Expectation quickens the reader's desire;

[32] Standard commentaries on the book of Genesis including Speiser (1964), von Rad (1972),
Westermann (1986) read the story of Joseph in Egypt through its theological code, as the
rise of the Israelite hero Joseph against foreign complications and threats because God
was with Joseph. Similar literary analyses in monographs devoted to the Joseph story
read the narrator's version: Coats (1976); Humphreys (1988); Redford (1970).
[33] For a discussion of distinguishing among actants and classes of actors, see Bal (1985:
26–34).

that God is with Joseph presupposes a satisfactory conclusion.[34] The end suggests a return to the beginning, Joseph is again in trouble, under the thumb of a new master. But in Brooks' scheme the end also points to a new beginning: a rereading (Brooks 1984: 109). With the strong voice of the narrator in the reader's ear, how different will that rereading be?[35]

My analysis of the text of Genesis 39 has shown the ways in which the story is controlled by its framework, directing the reader toward an adventure about men. To further my goal of narrating a new story of reading, after peeling the narrative frame from the story, I shall examine the plot structure to show how it functions to control the reader's responses to the story. The role of the plot is central in shaping the reader's understanding of the text and conversely in uncovering ways in which the text itself represents and reflects upon the plot. Brooks has observed in *Reading for the Plot* that works of literature generally tell the reader something about how they are to be read, guiding one toward the conditions of their interpretation through the structure of the plot (1984: xii–xv). The reader then can choose to be swept along by the textual tide or to turn and swim against the current of narrated evidence, the choice of the resistant reader. On its surface the plot of Genesis 39 concerns itself with temptation: an upper-class Egyptian woman engaged in the seduction of her Hebrew servant. Clearly the triple lines of tension, denoting class, ethnicity, and gender, point to the way the storyteller wants the story resolved. The hero's refusal of the woman's invitation makes the situation grist for a parenetic tale. After reading the story, almost any reader will get the narrator's point: a warning of the danger of shattering conventional codes and patterns. By presenting a case of what happens when a woman overflows her boundaries, the plot reflects and confirms the narrator's pieties.

---

[34] The sense of Joseph as *matsliah* is emphasized in commentaries ancient and modern. "R. Berekiah said: This means that he rushed away from moral danger," *Bereshit Rabbah* 86.4; "God's assistance extends to the political domain of a distant land" (Westermann 1986: 62); "God ensures his [Joseph's] success. Like his father before him, he turns to profit all he puts a hand to." (Humphreys 1988: 38).

[35] Commentators like von Rad, reading with the ideology of the text, reflect the narrator's theology: "The narrator is very expansive in unfolding this matter; several times he emphasizes the reason for this surprising preferred status, namely YHWH" (1972: 364).

Reading with the plot, thus, reveals its complicity with social
values, in this case the unthinkable treachery of the woman who
ignores her status as wife and scorns the authority of her husband
by desiring a forbidden male.

The most apparent narrative technique used to further the plot
of the story is repetition.[36] In Genesis 39 the effect of the repetitive
dialogue, the various versions of what happens, takes us back again
over the same ground. The central event of the story, the encounter
between Joseph and Mut-em-enet, gains meaning by its repetition
which both recalls the earlier moment and supplies variations of it.
Within the text comes a system of repetitive statements that
confound the forward movement of the story. Listening to the
narrator's version, then to Mut-em-enet's multiple versions of what
happened (or did not happen) between her and Joseph, the reader
oscillates between suspicion and belief. One effect of the repetition
is to create a return in the text, a doubling back. Joseph moves
from safety to danger; Potiphar moves from honor to shame. When
the woman Mut-em-enet kicks over the traces and attempts to
open her house, she moves from concealment to revelation. She
becomes Brenner's negative temptress (Brenner 1985: n. 72).[37] In
such an unsympathetic reading she becomes an articulate woman
threatening the society. Inside and silent, she lives a proper life of
concealment.

Let us look closely at the character of this woman so universally
condemned by the traditional audience. The biblical text tells us
nothing about her, except that she is the wife of Potiphar. He has a
string of titles that place him within the social hierarchy. She is the
wife of the man with the titles. In spite of the declaration by
folklorically oriented readers that she is the older "evil stepmother"[38] seducing the chaste hero (Thompson 1992: 4:471), an

---

[36] The technique of multiple repetitions in this chapter is so striking that both Alter (1981:
107–13) and Sternberg (1982: 423–28) have used Genesis 39 as their parade examples of
narrative repetition in biblical prose.

[37] For a similar categorization see Williams (1985: 88–92).

[38] The older female figure who seduces the younger hero is so identified in a recent feminist
study by Hollis (1989: 38). As Bal (1987b: 57–59) has noted, both the lustfulness of the
stepmother and the innocence of the young hero Joseph are assumptions that do not
appear in the biblical account, but rather have been appended by interpreters. Moreover,
the characterization of stepmother does not fit the relationship between Mut-em-enet
and Joseph.

assumption born out of an identified parallel of the Egyptian "Tale of Two Brothers,"[39] the biblical text provides no information about her age, her parentage, or background. The episode between the goddess Ishtar who invites Gilgamesh to a sexual tryst and is angered when he refuses her (Tablet VI) is similarly connected to the K2111 Motif in folklore studies. What all these stories share, according to those who would find a unifying structure in them, is their depiction of the viraginous woman.[40] Barthes' warning to those who practice comparative myth criticism, "myth is a value; nothing prevents it from being a perpetual alibi," challenges the reader to shake herself loose from such a rigid fixed structure: to turn the text and fill the gaps (Barthes 1975: 123). Perhaps such suspicion caused the ancient sages to envision a narcissistic Joseph who has angered God (*Bereshit Rabbah* 87.3–4, n. 1); or as Mann did with a "moon-nun who not only desires sexual initiation, but also fears it" (Bal 1987b).

In the biblical version of the tale Mut-em-enet is isolated, never pictured in her own sphere, with other women. The biblical story is expanded in Surah 12 of the Qur'an and in later Jewish midrashim: from one woman gone wrong to a universal statement about women unable to control desire. In the version preserved in the Qur'an, the other women of the city are scornful of Mut-em-enet's obvious infatuation with her slave Joseph. Clearly she is guilty of disorderly conduct. Aware of their judgmental attitudes, Mut-em-enet invites them to a party. When Joseph serves the fruit,

[39] "The Tale of the Two Brothers" is written in hieratic in the New Egyptian dialect, found in Papyrus d'Orbiney, BM 10183. For English translations, see *ANET* 23–25; Lichtheim, vol. 2, 200–11. For a history of scholarship relating to this story and its parallels, see Hollis (1982: ch. 1). The first episode is the only one that even suggests a parallel with the biblical story in Genesis 39:6b–20. In "The Tale of Two Brothers" the older brother Anubis is married and plays the role of father to his younger brother Bata. The event which parallels the biblical story is Anubis' wife attempting to seduce Bata. Like the biblical hero Joseph, Bata is morally outraged at female sexual aggression. Anubis, informed by his wife that Bata has tried to seduce her, becomes enraged and sets off to kill his brother. A major problem with the oft-cited comparison is that the older brother/younger brother relationship is not the same as master/servant.

[40] I take issue with Hollis (1982: 28–42), who argues that the motif of the "apparently destructive woman" is ameliorated by the "long-term positive results that affect not only her male target but also his people" (38). By reading with the traditional view that these women are destructive, Hollis can only give the women the role of fulcrum. Since Joseph returns to hero status, the woman wasn't *that* destructive, she didn't irrevocably rattle society's order. Thus, as I read Hollis's reading, Mut-em-enet is only a little wicked.

the other women are so dazzled by his beauty that they slice their fingers with their fruit knives.[41] Their bloody skirts are blatant symbols of the danger of female desire. Commenting upon Mann's version of this episode, Bal characterizes Mut-em-enet's reaction ("My loves, what ever has happened to you all? What are you doing? Your blood is flowing.") as the response of "a plotting lovesick virgin . . . She wants her friends to *understand* her love at the very same moment they *know* it; the difference is identification" (Bal 1987c: 70).

In the biblical story, the reader is warned of the impending sexual reversal when Joseph is described as beautiful of face and figure. He has a body. Like the lissome Bathsheba seen bathing from David's roof, Joseph has been seen. The one who gazes carves a path from inside to outside, from concealment to revelation. The reader's gaze also rests upon the sexual object. In Genesis 39 the sexual inversion is confirmed by Mut-em-enet's bold invitation. Emotion propels Mut-em-enet to invade boundaries, to touch the forbidden body. Having revealed herself by her sexuality and her speech, she is as exposed as Joseph's bare back, fleeing from inside to outside.

My intention in this section has been to present a literary study that reveals the effect of a suspicious reader upon the text. Its primary result has been to counteract traditional studies which have in reality presented men's views of women. Interpreters, both ancient and modern, have not thought about the wife of Potiphar except as she has threatened the life of the hero Joseph and brought shame to her husband. I have retold the story, focalizing it through the character of Mut-em-enet. By challenging the dictum of remaining within the boundaries of the narrator's version, my retelling provides a theoretical explanation of the *how* and the *why* of the biblical narrative. What happens when we reverse the narrative power of male and female, and read Genesis 39 against the story that precedes it? – the story of a righteous woman who uses her sexuality for a purpose other than pleasure, Genesis 38.

[41] To make the women's giddy response even more dramatic, Muslim commentator Wahhab ibn Munabbih related that there were forty women at this party and that seven of them died of longing for Joseph (Goldman 1986: 105). For the way the episode is used by Thomas Mann, see Mann (1938: 803).

A WOMAN ON TOP OF THE SITUATION:
THE APPROPRIATE SEDUCTION IN GENESIS 38

Rarely are Genesis 38 and 39, contiguous stories of Tamar and Mut-em-enet, compared as stories of women married to brothers. The stories of these two foreign women seem strikingly parallel[42]: one the story of the older brother and his sexual encounter with his dead son's wife; the other the story of the younger brother and his sexual encounter with his master's wife. In both stories the woman is the sexual aggressor; Genesis 38 relates an acceptable sexually aggressive act initiated by a woman; Genesis 39 describes an unacceptable one. Judah, the eldest son of Jacob, the eldest brother of Joseph, the object of Tamar's sexual duplicity, is himself a master of duplicity. In the episode in which the brothers plan to kill Joseph (Gen. 37:18–36), Judah argues that selling the troublesome boy rather than killing him will relieve Jacob's sons of bloodguilt, while accomplishing their purpose of getting rid of the favored brother of their own flesh (verse 27). The earlier episode in which Judah toys with the law, pushing to its extreme in order to serve his own ends, is reflected back upon him, where Tamar uses the force of the law to restore her position in Judah's family.

Genesis 38, the next chapter, appears to leave a gap as deep as the pit from which the Midianites pulled Joseph in order to sell him to Potiphar. The narrative unit begins with a story focused around the character Tamar, the Canaanite widow of the son of Judah. Wrapped in a veil of ambiguity, Tamar conceals her desire to achieve her goal: to give birth to a male heir. As the story unwinds, the reader learns that the narrator and Judah have judged Tamar to be more righteous than Joseph's brother Judah (Gen. 38:26); she has remained within appropriate boundaries. Her identity concealed, she has tried to hold on to her status as wife. Desire has

---

[42] *Contra* Westermann (1986), where he states, "ch. 38 is a self-contained individual narrative; there is no place where it can be fitted into the patriarchal story." (Holzinger). As already indicated, the narrative of Judah and Tamer has not been inserted into the Joseph story; it has nothing to do with it, but rather is an insertion into the Jacob story." See for similar views, Emerton (1975: 338–61); von Rad (1972: 356–57). Gunkel's understanding varies slightly, claiming the redaction is "*nicht ungeschickt*" (1901: 371), but rather forms an interlude to fill the elapsed time period in the Joseph narrative.

stripped Mut-em-enet of her protected status as wife. Unlike the widow Tamar, Mut-em-enet resists being bound too tightly to social custom. Corrupted by desire Mut-em-enet has abandoned her position as wife. She has threatened the stability of the culture. Like others of her kind, Medusa, Circe, Kali, Delilah, and Lilith, Mut-em-enet has stolen male generative energy. Tamar, conversely, has used male generative energy to get herself a son, an appropriate ambition.[43]

From the time of the first retellings in the Second Temple period, authors and interpreters have been puzzled by the question of where to place Genesis 38. In *Jubilees* the story is inserted after the narration of Joseph in Egypt, which may reflect the second-century BCE author's idea that since Judah had been forgiven for the sin of having sexual relations with his daughter-in-law (*Jub.* 41:23–28), he would similarly be forgiven for having sold the young Joseph, who had just been awarded second chariot status in Egypt (Goldin 1977: 122). Philo ignores the story of Tamar and Judah in *De Josepho*, but does use her character in highly allegorized form in other treatises.[44] Most noteworthy is *De Virtutibus* in which Tamar is presented as the example of a free-born foreign woman, who is an ideal female proselyte (219). She "kept her own life stainless and was able to win the good report which belongs to the good and to become the original source to which the nobility of all who followed her can be traced" (221). But the story of Tamar's seduction of Judah is not used by Philo, who may be more concerned with justifying Tamar's place as the mother of the twins Perez and Zerah, two clans of Judah (Num. 26:19–22) in the royal lineage of Israel (Sly 1990: 176).

In *Bereshit Rabbah* the rabbis also want to know "what is the chapter [focusing upon Judah] doing here?" The answer they offer clearly unites the stories of Tamar and Mut-em-enet.

Samuel b. Nahan said: In order to bring the stories of Tamar and Potiphar's wife into proximity, thus teaching that as the former was

---

[43] For a discussion of the proper role of a married woman specifically related to Tamar's socioliterary function in Gen. 38, se Niditch (1979: 143–48).

[44] Tamar is mentioned in *LA* 3.74; *Deus* 136f; *Cong.* 124; *Fug.* 149–156; *Mut.* 134; *Som.* ii.44, and *Virt.* 221. In no instance does Philo discuss the morality of Tamar's actions. She is allegorized in most of the discussions.

actuated by a pure motive so was the latter. For R. Joshua b. Levi said: She [Potiphar's wife] saw by her astrological arts that she was to produce a child by him [Joseph] but she did not know whether it was to be from her or from her daughter. Thus it is written, "Let now . . . the monthly prognosticators stand up and save thee from some of the things that shall come upon thee" (Isa. 47:13), whereon R. Abin commented: from *some of the things* but not all the things. (*Bereshit Rabbah* 85.2)[45]

Thus, from the earliest times some readers have heard connections between the stories of Tamar and Mut-em-enet. Among the most interesting of the recent interpretations is that of Nelly Furman. Connecting the female figures through the cloaks of the two brothers, she views the garments as "visual markers of a father (or master) and son relationship" (Furman 1989: 145). Both women use the cloaks to further their own interests or program: for Tamar, Judah's cloak will legitimize the birth of her sons. For Mut-em-enet, Joseph's cloak will legitimize her version of what happened in the house.[46] Since both women function as outsiders in the patriarchal system, the garments serve as a bridge or mediating device that "breaks up the exclusive father–son dialogue and forces recognition of [the female] presence" (Furman 1989: 147). As such, the garments become means of communication between the sexes. For Tamar the cloak is a symbol of the paternity of her children; it assures her future. For the wife of Potiphar the coat conceals her sexual desire. Joseph and the narrator see the coat as proof of Joseph's innocence; for the woman it is the reminder of her frustrated desire.[47]

The majority of scholars in connecting the stories look for the

[45] Note that the ancient rabbis considered that "Potiphar is identical with Potiphera." *Bereshit Rabbah* 86.3. Thus, the daughter mentioned here is Aseneth.

[46] There is a third woman for whom the cloak is a primary marker. Tamar, the daughter of David, is raped while wearing *cetoneth hapassim*, echoing Joseph's fine garment from Genesis 37 (2 Sam. 13:18). Like her namesake Tamar, she is desperate to maintain social status – even after the rape, Tamar wants to do the right thing and marry Amnon, her rapist. Similarly Tamar wants to bear the child of her father-in-law Judah in order to preserve the family's inheritance lines. Like Mut-em-enet, a veil of sexual disaster surrounds Tamar's story. As Mut spent the rest of her life inside her husband's house, Tamar receives shelter inside her brother Absalom's house (2 Sam. 13:20).

[47] The cloak is also the evidence of Joseph's guilt for Potiphar, according to Furman (1989: 149). I would argue that Potiphar's judgment is intentionally ambiguous, since acceptance of his wife's version of the story would have resulted in the death penalty for Joseph. His reaction seems to be as passive as the rest of his inaction in the story.

Judah/Joseph connection,[48] and argue along the lines of Judah Goldin, that the connection is the fraternal rivalry, the triumph of the younger brother over the older one. Thus, the stories are read as stories about men. The only way for Mut-em-enet to return to a safe sphere is to close all her openings: she must turn her back on revelation and return to concealment. She constructs a garment of lies, a cleverly concocted couture that conceals her initiatory act and reveals Joseph as the sexual aggressor. Of course her attempt at covering herself fails, because she has neglected to sew up all her openings. It remains for the narrator to close that final opening – to stop sounds from slipping out of the woman's mouth. Once the sighs and screams and accusations have been silenced, Mut-em-enet is put in her place. But the narrative revelation of her kind redraws the contours of her world. There is no way for her to return to her place. She is placed into the permanent prison of the narrator's retribution, while Joseph's sojourn in prison is temporary.

SUSANNA SPEAKING FOR HERSELF

There is another kind of silencing of women within the stories of men: the situation when a woman is forced into a position in which she cannot speak for herself. A literary example from the Second Temple period of such a situation is the tale of Susanna from the Greek additions to the book of Daniel.[49] A reading of this story allows me to inject a jarring, inconsistent note to the ideological unity of canonical comparisons while illuminating further developments of the character of Mut-em-enet. Another exception to the happily ever after love stories, the story of Susanna inverts the roles of the predatory woman and the passive youth. Biblical exegetes have occasionally compared the pious Susanna with Joseph, since both stories bear motifs of a chaste hero falsely accused of sexual

[48] See Alter (1981: 10–11), who interprets the goat/kid episode as the connecting symbols of the Judah and Joseph narratives.

[49] The tale of Susanna is found both in the LXX and the Theodotion versions. I have used the longer Theodotion version. For the differences in the two versions, see Moore (1977: 78–80). The story is not found in Josephus or in the Qumran scrolls. Moore and other scholars posit a Semetic *Vorlage*, but the earliest edition of the Old Latin are based upon the Theodotion version. For argument about why the early church preferred the Theodotion version with its greater emphasis on Daniel, see Moore (1977: 92).

activity.[50] Recent feminist analyses have begun to look at Susanna as object of the masculine gaze (Levine 1995). The traditional reader admires the piety of the woman, and may draw consolation from her behavior, but does not focus upon the woman immobilized by the engines of patriarchy. Levine, in his gendered readings, demonstrates how saturated the text of Susanna is with the theology or ideology of its author.

While Thompson's *Motif-Index* (Thompson 1992: 4:471) assigns the tale of Susanna to the category of "chaste wife falsely accused and repudiated, generally on the word of a rejected suitor" (K2112), thus connecting it as a specular reflection to the Stepmother and Chaste Hero motif (K2111) immediately preceding it, interpreters generally have not compared the two female figures: Mut-em-enet and Susanna. Yet their stories have a common dramatic element: each woman is powerless to act for herself. Each woman must depend on men for the resolution of her story. Mut-em-enet cannot achieve revenge upon Joseph directly. Her husband must put Joseph into prison. Susanna cannot defend herself against the elders. Daniel must reverse the condemnation of the community. My reading of the story of Susanna focuses upon a second commonality between the figures of Susanna and Mut-em-enet: each one is trapped in men's lies about her sexual activity. The Jewish storytellers have rescued the pious Susanna through the young Jewish hero who rescues her by speaking the truth. There was no such sympathetic plot twist devised for the Egyptian woman – until Mann's most touching portrait.

The story of Susanna is set in Babylon. Wealthy, well-respected Joakim is married to Susanna, a very beautiful pious woman. Elders of the Babylonian Jewish community meet frequently to decide community disputes at Joakim's house. Unseen by Susanna or Joakim, day after day, two lecherous elders watch Susanna stroll in the garden. "They lusted for her. So they perverted their own minds and averted their eyes, not looking to Heaven or rendering just decisions" (verses 5–8). One day they admit their passion to each other and hide themselves in Susanna's lush garden. When

---

[50] The use of Genesis 39 by the author of "Susanna" has been observed by Nickelsburg (1984: 38). An echo of the biblical story is noted but not developed by Moore (1977: 98, n. 23).

her servants leave her alone in the garden to bathe, the men lock the garden gates and approach her. "Look," they said, "the garden gates are shut and nobody can see us; and we desire you. So let us have you" (verse 20). Susanna realizes that she is in a bind, but her piety forbids an adulterous act. Thus, she must risk the threat of the men's accusation against her. She must take her chances with the judgment of the community. Reading from a feminist perspective, one recognizes the sexual trap into which the woman has been placed.

In this opening scene there are elements which have distinct parallels with the story of Joseph and the wife of Potiphar. The narrator characterizes the elders with derogatory phrases: they perverted their own minds, they did not worship God, nor did they invoke just decisions (verse 8). This narratorial determination of who is good and who is bad is reminiscent of *TJos*, in which the narrator Joseph delivers descriptions of Mut-em-enet's actions wrapped in a negative frame. The "day after day" motif of the men watching the young woman is similar to the close observation under which Mut-em-enet held Joseph. The servants leave Susanna alone in her garden, just as Mut-em-enet is left alone in her house. In both instances the women dismiss the servants who might have served as witnesses to subsequent actions. Clearly each plot turns on the unsubstantiated words of women, requiring that there be no witnesses.

Susanna's "I would rather not do it and so fall into your hands than sin in the Lord's sight," (verse 23) is a restatement of Joseph's "How can I do this great wickedness and sin against God?" (Gen. 39:9). The two elders "assent to us" (*dio sugkatathou emin*) parallels Mut-em-enet's desire for Joseph "to be with her" (*tou suggenesthai aute*) (Moore 1977: 98, n.20). Both women groan and scream, bringing the servants on the run. In Genesis 39, the silence of the servants weakens Mut-em-enet's credibility. Where the male servants do not respond to Mut-em-enet's story, the female servants of Susanna are shocked "for nothing of this sort had ever before been said about Susanna" (verse 27). Thus, the narrator, emphasizing the piety of the Jewish heroine, is anxious to fill the silence that might allow the reader to doubt the veracity of Susanna's story. The use of female servants also emphasizes the impotence of women in the story. Susanna speaks only with them or to God in her prayer. Although the women are loyal to Susanna, their convictions about her piety are no match for the elders. Only Daniel has the narrative power to resolve the conflict and restore Susanna's good name.

The elders have thought out their plan far better than Mut-em-enet had thought out hers. They offer Susanna the choice: "Have intercourse with us or we will testify against you, saying that a young man was with you, and that is why you had dismissed your maids" (verse 21). Mut-em-enet appears not to have thought out a revenge strategy until she holds Joseph's warm empty shirt in her hands after Joseph has fled (Gen. 39:13). In the second scene the people of the town are gathered at Joakim's house when the elders arrive to accuse Susanna. In front of these witnesses, they order that Susanna be unveiled (evoking the prescribed ritual of Sotah), thus implying her guilt and publicly shaming her. The elders provide their tainted witness.

As we were strolling by ourselves in the garden this woman came in with two maids. She shut the doors and dismissed the maids. Then a young man, who had been hiding, went over to her and lay down with her. But being in a corner of the garden, we saw this wicked thing and so ran toward them. Though we saw them having sexual intercourse, we could not hold the man because he was too strong for us; and he opened the gates and took off. But we grabbed this one here and asked who the young man was. But she would not tell us. These things do we testify. (verses 36–41)

The people of the town believe the elders' story, in spite of Susanna's reputation, and condemn the woman to death. Susanna provides no testimony, nor is she, a woman, asked to bear witness. Since the elders were the two witnesses necessary in a capital crime, the ritual of Sotah, based on the husband's suspicion of adultery, gives way to the biblical law condemning both adulterers to death stated in Lev. 20:10. God answers Susanna's prayer and "rouses the holy spirit" (verse 45). The motif parallels the "I was in trouble and you rescued me," of Joseph's prayer in T Jos 1. However, unlike Joseph's prayer which frames his story, Susanna's prayer occurs in its expected chronological position. Thus, it neither prescribes the reading nor erases the suspense as Joseph's prayer does. That perfect literary example of female virtue and passivity, Susanna waits for God to enact vengeance upon her enemies.[51]

Once her prayer has been answered, however, Susanna drops out of the narrative. The spirit whom God sends is the young prophet Daniel, who unmasks the wicked twosome. Susanna becomes the "pretext for Daniel's ascendancy." The feckless crowd of witnesses cheers and "blesses God, who saves those who trust in him" (verse 60). The familiar measure for measure principle is invoked, reminiscent of the Sotah (Num. 5:11–31), in which the shame the woman has inflicted upon her husband is inflicted upon her. "So they punished the elders the way the elders had intended to afflict their neighbor. Acting in accordance with the Law of Moses, they put them to death" (verses 61–62).[52] The neighbor is Joakim, who would have been deprived of his wife and shamed publicly had she been put to death as an adulterer.

A feminist reader might well identify with Susanna as object of the gaze, rather than the "intended" masculinized voyeuristic view of sharing the gaze of the Elders. It is a struggle to re-present the figure of the objectified woman as the subject of her narrative. Further, the female reader who takes pleasure in viewing Susanna as object, as one may identify with the Hollywood beauty queen, imagines herself as the object of male desire and attention.[53] Each divine rescue emphasizes the active and passive gender roles attributed to male and female characters, and underscores the "naturalness" of such dichotomized constructions.

Susanna is unable to save herself; Joseph saves himself through

---

[51] As Pervo points out in his fine study *Profit with Delight*, Susanna fits the model of the romantic heroine in the Greek novel – not only in depending on "vengeance from Most High" but also in undergoing accusation and trial (42–50). I am not aware of a Greek novel providing the gritty detail found in LXX v. 32 of Susanna, in which she is stripped for the voyeuristic pleasure of the judges. Such a picture echoes the Sotah, in which the effect of the poison upon a guilty woman's body is specifically recounted.

[52] The law concerning false witness is Deut. 19:18–21: "If the witness is a false witness and has accused his brother falsely, then you shall do to him as he had meant to do to his brother. It shall be life for life, eye for eye, tooth for tooth." The perjured elders' crime then is treated with the same severity as if they had both born witness against another man. Perhaps this is because they had shamed Joakim in unjustly accusing his wife of adultery.

[53] Women as spectators have become a major concern for feminist film theorists. See de Lauretis, Doane, Kaplan, Mulvey, for discussions of female spectators and women's pleasure.

his ability to interpret dreams. While God grants that everything prosper under Joseph's hand, no such remarkable divine assistance is given to Susanna. What Susanna gets is a man of God to rescue her. God rewards the hero Joseph by allowing him to rise to be second chariot to Pharaoh. Susanna is rewarded by returning to her life inside the house of a husband who did not even try to defend her. Levine raises the warning of feminist glorification of the victim in the text. If the plot is to have credibility, Susanna must be a figure of desire to the reader as well as to the elders. "Once we see her as desirable," argues Levine, "we are trapped; either we are guilty of lust, or she is guilty of seduction" (1995: 313). Certainly the picture presented at the opening of the tale of the wealthy and pious woman walking in the garden of her husband is a "pretty picture," one which would tempt the gaze. While I concur in Levine's discomfort with the all-too facile designation of victim, I think it comes from reading without suspicion the gendered constructions of female characters: either we avert the gaze (to a good woman) or we gaze with lust (a bad woman). Being caught in this dichotomous trap illustrates the problem with reading "stock" characters without taking into account either the reader's empirical or intuitive reactions. This is precisely the reading process that engages Levine, who is unimpressed with the luxury in which Susanna and Joakim find themselves in Babylon. "Representing the threatened covenant community, she is already a warning to those who would enjoy social privileges in foreign settings: no garden is safe" (312).[54] By looking at social codes of luxury, wealth, and covenant, as well as the sexual codes, Levine complicates her reading and presents us with the image of a spoiled Jewish exile, who has nothing better to do than walk in her Edenic garden each day. Of course a sharp irony comes from the recognition of the exile, who as Levine notes, is hardly weeping by the waters of Babylon. She is not walking in Eden; she is in danger, in exile.

The oddest element in this story in my view is the deafening silence of Joakim, the wealthy husband of Susanna. He has no discourse nor does he perform any action in the story. The powerful elder of the community has less literary life than the

[54] One of the most interesting elements of Levine's analysis of the book of Susanna is her association of Susanna, *shoshanna*, with the sexually engaged woman in Song of Songs.

female servants who attend his wife. Never does he question the veracity of the accusation of the elders, never does he try to defend his wife. Lest the reader conclude he has died of a stroke upon hearing of the elders' accusation (as Nabal died upon hearing of Abigail's consorting with his enemy David, 1 Sam. 25:10), the narrator returns the mute man to the story in the coda. Joakim and "all [her] relatives bless God because Susanna was found innocent of any impropriety" (verse 63). Potiphar, the foolish Egyptian, at least on the surface does more to support his wife's accusations than the greatest of the elders of the Babylonian Jewish community (verse 4) does to defend his innocent wife. However, this distinction is minimal. Both husbands are portrayed as powerless and silent in the world of women. Neither speaks in the story; neither commits an act commensurate with his powerful status in the community. While Potiphar puts Joseph in prison, that act is turned by the deity into another opportunity for Joseph to solidify his position in the court of Egypt. Although the most respected of the elders in his community, Joakim is entirely absent from the scene in which the duplicitous elders accuse his wife and she is condemned to death. It appears, then, that Joakim cannot trust a woman even as pious and good as Susanna. For it takes the young Daniel to exonerate even a good wife of the charges of adultery.

Thus, in spite of the fact that Susanna has been falsely accused, the possibility of her committing adultery is very real in the minds of the storytellers of the Second Temple period. The role of a beautiful woman like Susanna is defined by her sexual identity. She is expected to entice men.

The clever elders have picked a credible lie. They are condemned for bearing false witness against her; nothing is said of their lascivious designs on her. Mut-em-enet, in contrast, is twice condemned by the storytellers: for wanting Joseph and for falsely accusing him of rape. The deity in each instance can reach out and rescue the good woman and punish the evil one.

The status of paternal authority is more of an issue than the dangers of unrepressed female sexuality in both stories. The elders have cheapened and corrupted their authority by breaking the law, by delivering false judgments, and by not looking to God for their authority. Thus, their punishment restores the legitimized power structure. Retelling the story serves to warn other men who would misuse their power and give in to their passions. Mut-em-enet, the figure who represents unrepressed female sexuality, also serves to warn men of the danger of passionate women. Both stories stand as reminders of chastity as a code for female value. The deliberate strategy of bringing these two female characters together in the reader's mind has resulted in destabilizing the reader's perception of female characters as flat or unresisting commodities within the text. Insistence upon the inconsistency of character also allows the reader to subvert narrative closure. The characters, if not their stories, live on in the reader's imagination.

JEWISH HELLENISTIC EXPANSIONS OF GENESIS 39

The Second Temple period expansions of the biblical narratives self-consciously transformed and expanded the earlier work of Genesis 39 into a combination of the genres of romance and epic, which are basically the same genre, each being produced by a different type of society (Perry 1967: 44–95). Thus the classical "national warrior-epic" like the *Iliad* or the Deuteronomistic History[55] is characterized by the cultural homogeneity of a small, closed world. Within this genre, the hero is idealized as unshakably brave.[56] His experiences are generalized as symbols of the fate of humanity. The cultural unity of the ideal audience is revealed by reading the ethical and religious codes of the epic, which "teach" history and impart the state of knowledge in various fields (Hägg 1983: 88). Even though the genres of comedy and romance differed

---

[55] This study is not the place to debate the dating or historicity of biblical narratives as examples of continuous historiography, or as a redacted collection of histories. However, I am more drawn to the views of Lemche (1991) and Thompson (1992) than the views of traditional biblical historians that our inability to understand ancient historiography coupled with our theological reading of the narratives has led to scholars deciding in advance what was present in the epic literature. It is the same situation with historical texts: if one believes that they provide evidence of something external (the so-called real history), and think that they reflect religious practices and beliefs, than one is projecting history onto these texts. Lemche and Thompson argue that these literary texts cannot be used to describe or verify historical occurrences.

[56] In the religious epic history of Israel, the role of the unshakable hero belongs to God. The human characters are flawed in order to give the greater glory to God, a *Heilsgeschichte* mythologization of history. For a discussion of the religious character of Israel's treatment of history, the *religionsmorphologischer Hintergrund* (Krecher and Muller 1975: 30–44).

from the genres of epic and tragedy of the classical era, the new genres popular in the Hellenistic period continued to rely upon stereotyped plots and stock characters. This is not surprising since literary originality was not valued in antiquity as it is in modern times. A text's value came from the reworking of common mythic past of the audience. Since a major concern of this literature was to regulate the conduct of the reader, authors would shore up their cases by appealing to "the worthies who had already been accepted as teachers of previous generations."[57] The presentation of character had little to do with the inwardness or consciousness of the figure, but rather the mechanical working out of time, event, and divine intervention.

In Jewish Hellenistic literature, the appeal was to Moses, the patriarchs, and other biblical heroes. The authors had no need to authenticate the tales since the Jewish audience was familiar with the genre of biblical stories and expected the narratorial voice to carry divine authority. A familiar narratorial voice continued to relate *tales* of authority, even when the narratorial voice did not make explicit claim to a divine connection. The three versions of the story of Joseph and the wife of Potiphar found in the biblical account, *Testaments of the 12 Patriarchs*, and Josephus' *Jewish Antiquities* are "the only ancient subject matter which offers an opportunity to compare the different phases of development from novella (Genesis 39) to romantic presentation (T12P) to full-blown romance (Josephus) (Braun 1938: 89–90).[58] Braun's view that the Potiphar legend is the only ancient material that offers the critic such an opportunity overstates the situation. As should be evident from this study, literary analysis of any biblical narrative can be enriched through an examination of postbiblical expansions of its source text.

I suspect a major reason for the extensive expansions of the

---

[57] Bickerman, "New Literature," in *Jews in the Greek Age*.

[58] Braun's argument is that the Genesis novella becomes a "cycle of episodes" in the Testament of Joseph, which exhibits a number of literary qualities generally attributed to the romance. Finally, in the hands of Josephus the novella becomes "a copy of the rhetorical Greek romance down to the smallest detail" (Braun 1938: 90). It is not my intention to debate Braun's generic categories. I am surprised, however, that Braun's study lacks any mention of *Joseph and Aseneth*, a Jewish Hellenistic romance of the same period with roots in the Joseph *Märchen*.

episode concerning Joseph and the wife of Potiphar is the erotic potential in the seduction of the chaste hero by the wicked woman. Ancient authors, surrounded by Greek literary erotica, were either attracted or repulsed by the idea of female sexual desire. Scenes of erotic love were frequently reworked in the Hellenistic New Comedy plays, romances, and Apocryphal Acts, where major issues are temptation and adultery. By emphasizing the danger in the figure of female seducer, the Jewish writers were building up a wall against Hellenization or paganization of biblical tales.

The cast of central characters in the biblical expansions of the Second Temple period was familiar to the audience. Like their Greek counterparts, the Jewish Hellenistic authors added to the *what* happened of the earlier plots, filling in narrative gaps, and bringing the young heroes into old age. Even more important these Hellenistic Jewish authors saturated the texts in *how* it happened, the moral and social pressures that fell upon the hero, forcing him to commit devastating acts. Thus, emotion was added to the stock scene-types, producing the forerunners of the ancient novel, the elements of which are found in Hellenistic narratives before the actual novel form. While the romance may be a deliberate literary creation,[59] then, as Braun has argued, its embryonic roots stretch deep into literary time, at least as far back as the narrative units of the *Odyssey* or Genesis. Herodotus' history has short fictive narratives embedded in it.[60] Melodramatic historiography and travel tales were also common in the Hellenistic period. Direct literary filiation is not apparent, but there are fictive constructs, such as the

[59] "The first romance was deliberately planned by an individual author, its inventor. He conceived it on a Tuesday afternoon in July" (Perry 1967: 175).

[60] I consider historiography to be another form of storytelling. As Hayden White has argued, it is this beginning-middle-endness that provides the metagenre of history its plot (White 1980). Some scholars place the beginning of the metanarrative of Western historiography at a precise point: Herodotus' account of Persia and its empire (completed toward the end of the fifth century BCE), and Thucydides' narration of the war between Athens and the major Dorian city-states (unfinished at the author's death around 400 BCE). That Thucydides considered himself superior to Herodotus as a historian is clear from the beginning of his Work, "Perhaps the absence of story-telling will be displeasing," (1.22) he remarks while clearly believing the opposite. The ancients seemed to prefer Thucydides to Herodotus, "as the more sober scientific historian. In the second century AD Plutarch wrote an essay protesting Herodotus malevolence, as though he were no more than a gossip, the Antony Trollope, as it were, of historians, an opinion that survived the ages" (Beye 1987: 200–01). For an analysis of historiography as it directly encounters the biblical "histories," see Rosenberg (1986): 100–12.

ones noted above, that gave rise to the genre known as the novel or romance.

In the new Hellenized society, the fixed norms were broken down and replaced by a syncretistic outlook. The motifs of the earlier epic flourished in the form of novelistic prose.[61] Classical views on romance's basic structure remain unknown to us, but the genre appears to have been an open one, "not regulated by any authoritative prescriptions" (Hägg 1971: 109). Instead of the air-brushed stock characters of the classical epics, the characters in New Comedy and the romances are individuals portrayed with all their blemishes. Braggarts and boors abound. Young lovers plot clandestine moonlight meetings. Although these characters are stereotypical, they are drawn from the world of commoners, replacing the aristocratic or semi-divine characters from the classical era.

When considering the literary productions of the Jewish Hellenistic writers, the reader must keep in mind what was at stake for the Jewish writers. The eroticism of Greek culture reflected in these delicious romances was clouding the fixed surety of their belief system. The text of 1 Maccabees sets out the conflict between the Jews attracted by the temptations of their Greek rulers and those who were strict observers of the Law, set on preserving their own tradition. Lawless men from Israel [said],

"Let us go and make a covenant with the Gentiles, round about us, for since we separated from them many evils have come upon us." This proposal pleased them, and some of the people eagerly went to the king. He authorized them to observe the ordinances of the Gentiles. So they built a gymnasium in Jerusalem, according to Gentile custom and removed the marks of circumcision, and abandoned the holy covenant. They joined with the Gentiles and sold themselves to do evil. (1 Macc. 1:11–15)

Under the leadership of the High Priest Jason, the so-called paganizing program progressed, including the most astounding

---

[61] Reardon (1989: 8; 1991: chap. 1) suggests that the first novels were written under the influence of Egyptian demotic stories circulating in Greek translations. These works provided the Greeks with the impetus to write fictive narrative in prose, the literary medium previously used for "factual," or informational writing.

merging of symbols: the building of a gymnasium directly underneath the citadel. As the Maccabean historian elaborates,

Despising the sanctuary and neglecting the sacrifices, they hastened to
take part in the unlawful proceedings in the wrestling arena after the call
to the discus, disdaining the honors prized by their fathers and putting the
highest value upon Greek forms of prestige. (2 Macc. 4:14–15)

The sanctuary became desolate as a desert, the feasts were
turned into funerals, and the sabbath became a reproach (1 Macc.
1:39). It seems likely that the people were also being attracted to
Gentile literary amusements. Archaism, or historicized fiction, was
a reaction of the societies of the ancient Near East to "their
barbarian masters."[62] Jewish literature from this period, then,
revolved around the founders of Israel, direct ancestors of the
audience and did not draw upon historical traditions outside the
Bible, except for the recounting of events within the Maccabean
period itself. Thus, the historiography of the period, tended to
approximate the conditions of romance.[63] As the polyglot Hellenistic society grew bigger and more stratified, the individual's place
became smaller. Reading stories particularized to one's heritage
helped to retain one's identity. For the Jewish audience the only
source of historical information about the past was the Bible.

While the Jews of the Hellenistic age could still obtain some information
concerning the last Babylonian king, Nabonidus, who is not mentioned in
the Scripture, they apparently preserved no written oral memory, for
example, about the fall of Jerusalem, except the brief and dry report in
the Bible. (Bickerman 1988: 179)

And the single-mindedness of interpreting only the religious
codes has prevented these literary works from being read as literary
responses to the Greek works produced during the same period. In
the hands of religious writers, social control of women was

[62] Bickerman explains further, "The books about or ascribed to men of ancient renown
  compensated the native intelligentsia for the inferiority of its present status; even the
  Greeks ascribed profundity and wisdom to the spiritual ancestors of these modern writers
  in Jerusalem and Memphis." Bickerman, "New Literature," 202–03, in *Jews in the Greek
  Age.*
[63] Reardon (1991: 142–43) sees the same romantic tendency within the Greek writers, in
  particular Dio Cassius and Herodian. Similar features are found in both Jewish and
  Greek historiographers: a biographical nature and "world events seen in their aspect as
  personal history."

achieved through literary control of the works that exhorted women to sexual adventure. The religiously oriented romance, exemplified by *The Testaments of the Twelve Patriarchs* and *Joseph and Aseneth*, can be read as a late Hellenistic *mythos*, a fictive embellishment of actual occurrences,[64] in which the hero in his wisdom turns from the threatening sexually infused other to the security in God and is rewarded by the "right" wife (Reardon 1971: 309–403).[65] The young man hopelessly in love with a courtesan was a stock figure in Hellenistic comedy, so that in the *The Testaments of the Twelve Patriarchs* when the aged patriarch Judah recalls being drawn in by the courtesan-attired Tamar many years earlier, the audience recognized the familiar predicament of the young man drunk with wine. "For wine turns the mind away from the truth and throws in [it] the passion of lust and leads the eyes into error" (*T Jud* 14:1). By building a bridge between then and now, the Jewish authors of the Second Temple period could travel back to the biblical past of Israel, fusing the myths with the erotic themes of Hellenistic literature. However, in the strict moralizing eyes of these interpreters, the erotic themes have been transformed from invitations to warnings.

Testaments of the Twelve Patriarchs is a prime example of such a Jewish response to Hellenization. In spite of commentators' insistence upon categorizing this collection of narratives as "testamentary literature," I believe that the reader interested in challenging established assumptions needs to resist genre stereotyping as it leads to one-note readings, intellectual inertia. While parts of the work contain the themes and motifs of Greek romance, it is possible to read *T Jos* as a warning *against* those seductive tales. The contrast between the trysting romances of the Greek New Comedy and the anti-erotic deportment of the good Jewish hero is played out in *T Jos*. Instead of the hero agreeing to a moonlight meeting, or any idyllic encounter with the woman who professes love for him, he

---

[64] Bickerman extends the view that the ideological concepts of a society are made visible in their myths to the Jewish writings of the Second Temple period, particularly the parabiblical books, "Their heroes are the founders of Israel and, for the most part, the direct ancestors of the readers of these books." "New Literature" 204.

[65] For a succinct presentation of Reardon's views of the ancient novels within their literary context, see Reardon (1969: 291–309) and his most recent revised theory in (Reardon 1989: 1–15; 1991: chap. 5).

flees her presence. In this un-romance, the theological and social codes have smothered the sexual code. Passion has curdled into revenge within the volatile Mut-em-enet. The true romance, *Joseph and Aseneth,* transforms female sexual desire into Jewish piety. The literary proof of Aseneth's trustworthiness is that she is identified as a city of refuge, a woman understood to be a safe mooring in whom a fleeing hero can find solace, not one like the wife of Potiphar, from whom he must flee.

EARLY AUDIENCE RECEPTION OF GENESIS 39

During the Second Temple period[66] in which the texts under consideration in the next chapter were written there was no canonical corpus, not even a canonical or fixed Torah. The final form of the text grew out of various strands of interpretations reflecting conflicts arising during the Second Temple period. Thus, the biblical interpretation found in *Jubilees, The Testaments of the Twelve Patriarchs,* and in Josephus' *Antiquities* mixes Scriptural quotation and interpretation. Later, the Qumran *pesherim*[67] and rabbinic exegesis replaced this rather loose narrative form with more precise structures of quotation and commentary, attesting to the growing authority of a canonical Scripture.[68] As we shall see in considering these expansions of the story of Joseph and Mut-em-enet, each writer reflects his own community's interests and agenda through the narratorial voice. The early interpreters as well as those modern scholars who have studied these texts have struc-

---

[66] I understand this period to span the period from the fourth century BCE to the middle of the second century CE, from the time of the building of the Second Temple, until the Jewish and Christian responses to the destruction of the Temple in 70 CE.

[67] Many scholars argue that the interpretive genre found in the Qumran scrolls is neither commentary nor midrash, but a new genre, *pesher.* For a review of the arguments about the degree of blending of the two literary forms, see Wright (1966: 418–22) analyzing views leading to his conclusion that "*pesharim* are *haggadic midrash*" (422); and the closely connected neologism, "midrash pesher" coined by Brownlee (1979).

[68] *Pesharim* are formally tighter than rabbinic *midrashim.* The *pesharim* quote the biblical text in regular blocks and introduce the interpretations with regular formulaic expressions, such as (1) *pesher had-davar 'al* ("the prophetic meaning of the passage concerns"); (2) *pisro 'al* ("its prophetic meaning concerns"); (3) *pisro 'asher* ("its prophetic meaning is that"). While rabbinic *midrashim* may use formulaic expressions to introduce interpretive text, they are not consistently employed. For full-length discussion about philosophical distinctions between Qumran and rabbinic hermeneutic, see Bickerman (1988); Boyarin (1990 a and b, 1993); Bruns (1987, 1990); Patte (1975); Handleman (1982).

tured the meaning of the texts through an interpretation of the theological code. As Bal has demonstrated, the religious code is often at work within the text itself. Thus, the theological code can lead the interpreter to enhance the religious aspect of the text (Bal 1988: 37–38). In order to find the suppressed female story, we must get beyond the narratorial version of the story. Another method of enhancing the theological code was through the uses of particular genres familiar to the Second Temple audience. The genres create expectation in the mind of the reader. *Testaments* not only tell what happened to an individual Patriarch after the story related in the biblical account, but they also create "an appetite in the mind of the auditor, and the adequate satisfying of that appetite." The use of the Testamentary genre, therefore, simultaneously reinforces the authority of the biblical version and extends that doxa text further into the consciousness of its readers.

Among the writers adding authoritative power to the biblical narratives are Josephus and Philo. In his works concerning the patriarchs, Philo follows the form of Greek aretalogy, presenting Abraham and Joseph as heroic models of behavior. Unlike his contemporary Flavius Josephus, Philo is not so concerned with expanding narrative in these works as he is with presenting biblical figures as ethical paradigms, illuminating the biblical theological code. *Joseph and Aseneth*, a Hellenistic romance, can be read as almost totally parenetic expansion of the biblical mention that Joseph married Aseneth, the daughter of Potiphera, priest of On (Gen. 41:45).[69] In *TJos*, the hero tells us that he even took as his wife the daughter of his masters (18:3). The early sages continued to emphasize the connection between Genesis 39 and 41:45 as the connection between the two women: Joseph was in essence

---

[69] Commentators have been consistent in their readings of this novel through the theological/religious code. Burchard (1978: 88) is the most succinct: "By design, the theological importance of a religious book is in its message." One of Philonenko's allegorical interpretations claims that Aseneth is the wisdom figure gone wrong, and Joseph, the divine Logos, rescues her. Through her union with the hero, she is saved from her erroneous ways. Aptowitzer (1924: 256, n. 43) traces another tradition, in which Aseneth is the rescuer of Joseph. According to *Mid. Abchir* in *Yalkut Genesis*, par. 146, Potiphar wished to kill Joseph for his crime against Potiphar's wife. Aseneth went to her father and told him "the truth," thus saving Joseph. Then God spoke to her as follows, "By thy life, because you have defended him, the tribes which I wish to have originate from him will descend from you."

recompensed for the sufferings which he had undergone at the hands of the wife of Potiphar by marrying her beautiful daughter (*Bereshit Rabbah* 89.2).

Testament of Joseph, a section of *The Testaments of the Twelve Patriarchs* (T12P), represents another popular Hellenistic genre, testamentary literature.[70] This genre gives an "attested" validity to the narratives and deathbed confessions. Within T12P, the Second Temple reader would be presented with a series of these confessional stories that extend and give authority to the versions of the patriarchal narratives related in the book of Genesis. Most modern scholars agree that the first ten chapters of *TJos*, which relate Joseph's version of his dire circumstances in the house of Potiphar, are in the form of homiletic *aggadah*, and have read T12P without much concern for its reception by an early audience. I would like to suggest a reading, one in which *TJos* becomes as much a warning to its Jewish audience against a Greek genre as it is against the female gender. At a time when the Jewish population was becoming alarmingly Hellenized, disporting in the gymnasia, the values of love and romance played out in Menander's comedies and in the Greek novels were popular forms of entertainment.

All the texts under consideration in the following chapter share one generic element: they all propose to be recounting "history," whether the overt form be testament, romance, or historicization.

The historical narrative, as against the chronicle, reveals to us a world that is putatively "finished," done with, over, and yet not dissolved, not falling apart. In this world, reality wears the mask of a meaning, the completeness and fullness of which we can only *imagine*, never experience. Insofar as historical stories can be completed, can be given narrative closure, can be shown to have had a *plot* all along, they give to reality the odor of the *ideal*. This is why the plot of a historical narrative is always an embarrassment and has to be presented as "found" in the events rather than put there by narrative techniques. (White 1980: 24)

Since the reader's expectations can be exploited through the rules of configuration, authors make use of these genres – testament, aretalogy, and romance – not only to create a sense of

---

[70] For an overview of the category or genre of testamentary literature in the Second Temple Period, see G. W. E. Nickelsburg, "Stories of Biblical and Early Postbiblical Times," and "The Bible Rewritten and Expanded" (1984).

resolution, by completing the patterns that the reader expects, but also to initiate surprise, by failing to fulfill a pattern in an expected manner (Rabinowitz 1986: 111). In the biblical expansions of the Second Temple period, most of the authors follow the former, predictable pattern. One exception to the rule is the expansion of Genesis 39 found in *TJos*. As Joseph relates the alarming and unpredictable sexual advances of the wife of Potiphar threatening his chastity for one entire year, the reader hears hollow echoes of a romance in which love might have been eagerly received.

My purpose in analyzing these Second Temple texts is not to review the traditional parenetic interpretations. Rather I want to read against the predictable patterns, to recover the suppressed story of the woman amid the strident moral warnings against her kind. In order to release the woman from the codes that have imprisoned her in his story, I shall first need to explore the ways in which the theological code has been effectively exploited within the texts under investigation. Within my reading in the next chapter, I shall present two different readings: one is his story, accepting that Joseph is part of the dominant group, the Jewish male hero, who shares all codes with the narrator. The alternate or oppositional reading is her story, revealing traces of Mut-em-enet, an Egyptian non-Jewish woman, who shares none of the codes of the narrator.

CHAPTER 4

"I shall stir up thy mistress against thee"

I had the feeling that Pandora's box contained the mystery of women's sensuality, so different from man's, and for which man's language was inadequate. The language of sex had yet to be invented.

Anais Nin

One can find everything in a text, provided one is irrespectful toward it.

Umberto Eco

GENRE AND GENDER

As should be apparent by this point, in my view an emphasis on genre runs the risk of a universalistic or totalizing reading. Frederic Jameson considers a genre to be a social contract "between a writer and a specific public, whose function is to specify the proper use of a particular cultural artifact" (106). Through the leavening of gender, I hope to break through the classification system that would imply (as genre does) that identifying the genre of a text determines its meaning. The interpretive mention of "stock" characters, such as the young heroine in distress, suggests that characters are universal, and have a standard role to play within society. Such assumptions not only indicate a predictability both to the narrative and to life, but also instruct the reader in how to fill the gaps of the narrative in the most conventional fashion. Reading as a woman insists that one fill the gaps with a mix of suspicion and empirical knowledge. Reading as a woman alerts one to the ideological or parenetic codes that often guide the plot of an ancient novel, and thus refuse to accept the semblance of completeness that the form can imply.

Warnings about genre having been given, I shall now examine some interpretive views that have accompanied the resurgence of interest in the genre of the ancient Greek novel. As scholars of the ancient novel have noted, romance is above all else a love story that offers a particular vision of life. The stock romance portrays what happens to people in love; it includes "a dangerous journey in life, a resolution that is physically and spiritually a homecoming" (Reardon 1991: 102). As a reflection of its social world, romance is usually "acutely fashionable, cast in the exact mould of an age's sensibility" (Beer 1970: 12). Perry and Reardon have argued that the Greek romances pointed toward an open society that produced the love-and-adventure story on a very human scale, allowing what the reader wants to happen to happen, the satisfying if sentimental element of happily ever after,[1] Frye constructed a similar pattern for the romance in which a questing hero was restored to his rightful identity.[2] Suspicious of the picture of a Hellenistic "reading" middle class eager for entertainment romances, Stephens warns against applying the analysis of Watt's *The Rise of the Novel* to the ancient form. It is not difficult to see how the modern reader might connect romance with a lower or popular form of culture. Even the descriptions of the star-crossed lovers struggling to find each other against all odds, both societal and villainous, sound similar to the shiny-covered paperback bodice-rippers that beckon from airport book racks. However, the feverish female victim and the heated scenes of passion belong not to the romance but to the subgenre of eros tale. Thus, if the romance detailed the period between the initial love at first to the final marriage of the lovers, then the eros tale inscribes the situation of passion overcoming propriety, ending in despair (Stephens 1995).

---

[1] Other proponents of this view are Egger, Hägg, as well as Perry and Reardon. There has been slight movement away from the desire to designate a "popular audience" by E. L. Bowie in "The Greek Novel," in *The Cambridge History of Classical Literature*, vol. 1, *Greek Literature*, ed. P. E. Easterling and B. M. W. Knox (Cambridge 1985) 683–99; see also B. Wesseling, "The Audience of the Ancient Novels," in *Groningen Colloquia on the Novel*, vol. 1, ed. H. Hofman (Groningen 1988) 67–79.

[2] Frye uses the language of religion in his description of the genre: "at the bottom of the mythological universe is a death and rebirth process . . . at the top is the individual's regained identity" (Frye 1976: 183).

The romantic pattern of danger and salvation, quest and identity[3] is often stitched together by a female figure. One crucial element of the ancient Greek love-romance has been observed by Reardon: "the heroine is likely to be if anything more deeply affected by 'circumstance' than the hero (who is sometimes a consort rather than an equal partner). Thus, the adventurous quest of the hero that brings trials and complication is resolved by love. With the entrance of a female, and the type scene of love at first sight, came the expected plot elements of peril and danger that signaled the genre of romance. There are two different types of romances, however.[4] The happily-ever-after romances focus on marriage and often exhibit the fairy-tale elements of meeting at a religious festival, love at first sight, many obstacles to overcome, either of parents or other suitors, and finally the reunited romantic ending (Egger 1993: 264–65). The unhappy eros tales ended in death rather than marriage, the ratio being about fifty to one. A force destructive to marriage, eros signaled a warning of bad times to come, often a wish for suicide as the only solution to a life saturated with eros (Stephens 1995: 32–34).

The Jewish writers of the Maccabean era, struggling against Hellenization and its resultant permissiveness, were threatened both by the genre of romance and by its tempting picture of the eroticized female character. Expansion of the biblical story of the wife of Potiphar by both the authors of *Jubilees* and the *Testaments of the Twelve Patriarchs* reinforced and extended the religious community's fear of contact with the Hellenistic culture, as typified by the foreign woman, who would seduce the pious Jewish hero from his proper life. This fear of female sexuality and its resultant attack on male power created stories in which the female voice was suppressed. Thus, the Jewish narrative of Mut-em-enet ended in silence and misery of the female character, almost a Greek eros tale, with its deadly ending.

---

[3] The pattern of romance is generally viewed as quest/identity by Frye and danger/salvation by Reardon/Perry. These are basically similar patterns with different terminology, as has recently been noted by Reardon (1991: 74).

[4] For other investigations of the pattern of ancient romance, see C. Ruiz-Montero, "The Structural Pattern of the Ancient Greek Romance and the Morphology of the Folktale of V. Propp," *Fabula* 22 (1981) 228–38; I. Nolting-Hauff, "*Märchenromane mit leidendem Helden*," *Poetica* 6 (1974) 129–78 and 418–55; Hägg (1983); Pervo (1987).

Recognizing that narrative is inherently fluid allows each reader an escape away from repetition; narrative aspires to "a narrative redescription of reality," to a "new story" (Brooks 1984: 235, 285).[5] The literary text is the place where writer and reader, narrator and narratee engage in the dialogue that produces the new literary work. Comparing the version of Genesis 39 with its altered version in T Jos provides an opportunity to examine the literary effect of this new story created from the skeleton of the old. The interpretive strategy I shall employ follows in part the narrativity model of Genette (1972a),[6] further developed by Rimmon[7] and Bal (1981: 41–59). Few interpreters of the biblical expansions have read beyond the first narrative level of the story, the one focalized through the narratorial voice, which predominates within the text. However, if one moves to a second level, the one accounted for in the narrative technique known as embedding (Bal 1981: 57), one can discover the story that might have been told by the woman. Bits and pieces of her story have come through the narrator's text through moments of focalization. In this chapter I shall attempt to uncover Mut-em-enet's story, her version of what happened, in part by determining what she as a focalizer saw and the significance of the focalized object. In order to reveal her story, the reader needs to speak out against the narrator's voice. One strategy is to read beyond the ending, beyond the telos of romance and its regimen of

---

[5] See also Roy Schafer, "Narration in the Psychoanalytic Dialogue," in Mitchell (1981: 25–49) for a discussion of "narrative redescription."

[6] Also Genette (1972b) for text subsequently critiqued by Rimmon and Bal. For collection of essays which contain both the method and application of Genette's narratological method to works of Stendahl, Flaubert, and Proust, see Genette (1982). Genette's most recent reconsideration of point of view, voice, and focalization and his response to his critics of these subjects can be found in Genette (1988).

[7] In her study of the major distinctions made by structuralist narratologists, Rimmon alters Genette's concept of focalization by arguing that "focalization depends on the narrator and on the amount of information imparted to the reader by the narrator" (59). The difficulty with this observation is that the reader will always be controlled by the narrator's version of the story. Bal (1985: 101) has offered another way of understanding the difference between the focalizer and the narrator by her observation that one needs to distinguish between "the vision through which the elements are presented and on the other hand, the identity of the voice that is verbalizing the vision." Bal's method of distinguishing between the dominant narratorial voice and the suppressed voice of the other is invaluable to those who wish to offer readings that give voice to the story of the silenced characters in a literary text.

resolutions.[8] The reader can thus create a story beyond the one told by the narrator in which Mut-em-enet reacts to Joseph's imprisonment (*TJos*), to one in which she becomes his mother-in-law (*JosAsen*), one in which her pain is palpably and sympathetically expressed (Mann) or adding any other narrative episode. While this sort of expansion of the source text is often disparaged as midrash, empirical gap-filling can be understood as the result of the character "living on" in the reader's mind. The story does not end – until it has no more readers.[9]

Just who were the readers of ancient romances? Stephens argues that the readers of romance were the elite literate readers of other contemporary literatures, that there were no ancient bourgeois middle-class consumers of this genre. While she may be overstating the prevailing argument that this "popular" literature was read by a different audience than the philosophic or other "high culture literature" of the Hellenistic period, she does present an interesting point about the difficulty of identifying ancient audiences. Viewing the readership of the ancient novel as limited to the small percentage of educated readers, Stephens argues that Hägg, Reardon, Egger, and others who argue in favor of the popular audience mode may be looking to the rise of the eighteenth-century novel in England for their model. While Stephens' view, that the literate population represented about one per cent of the largely agrarian nonliterate peri-Mediterranean world, added the dimensions of gender to the determination of "popular."[10] While we know that more males than females were educated, we do not

---

[8] See Rachel DuPlessis (1985), who analyzes women's fiction of the twentieth century in this manner.

[9] For the full scholarly arguments, see Susan A. Stephens, "Who Read Ancient Novels," in *The Search for the Ancient Novel*, ed. J. Tatum (Baltimore and London: Johns Hopkins University Press, 1994), 405–18. Also Brigitte Egger, "Women and Marriage in the Greek Novels," in Tatum 1994: 260–80. On the education of women, see Cole, "Could Greek Women Read and Write?" in *Reflections on Women in Antiquity*, ed. H. Foley (London: 1981) 219–45; Sarah Pomeroy, "Technikai kai Mousikai: The Education of Women in the Fourth Century and in the Hellenistic Period," *American Journal of Ancient History* 2 (1977), 51–68.

[10] Stephens does not consider *Joseph and Aseneth* in her survey of Greek novels, but I wonder if adding the observation that the Greek in which *Joseph and Aseneth* is written is a simplified almost koine style of Greek, might indicate that this Jewish Hellenistic novel would be more accessible to a popular readership.

know of the number of girls and women who may have been privately educated and may have read these romances. Egger suggests that the main female characters in the Greek novels know how to read and write, thus indicating that reading and writing were not beyond actual contemporary women's reach. More important to her argument, and important to my own as well, is that the content and "rendering of women and of female interest within the romances – features that invite female identification" provide the modern reader with an opportunity for gender analysis of these romances.

Women's alienation from the literary canon can be attributed partially to the fact that the literary works of male authors reflect a male view of life which is not necessarily women's experience and second, social restrictions have shaped women's lives but kept women's voices muted within literary works. The Greek romances, however, do evidence a more liberal attitude toward women than the laws that governed upper-class women in the classical era – although the novelists sentimentalized the good old days of once upon a time (Egger 1993: 265–68). Although paternal *potestas* (over daughters as well as sons) looms large in the background, it seems to be more a matter of economic and social pressure than an expression of legal control. In the romances the adult women do not usually have a legal guardian in the classical sense. Indications of shared matrimonial property are found in several couples' agreements, usually in favor of the bride. On the other hand, there are strong patriarchal shadows cast over the romances, most notably that the heroine's marriage arrangements are at the exclusive discretion of the father (the mother is left out of the arrangements), the girl's opinion is not sought. This patriarchal power of deciding family connections strengthens the male voice within the text and subdues the female voice, so that the happily-ever-after-ending is more of a lucky coincidence than an act the girl had the power to influence. As Egger notes, in the romance, the good father just happens to give, "by his exclusive decision, to his daughter the husband whom she would select herself if she could, that is, if she is a positive female figure who deserves poetic happiness" (1993: 269). Clearly in the genre of romance the good

ne would appeal to the hero only if she reflected the
of the social order.

eters who refuse to read the gender code, and thus
male shaping to a text that may exhibit a female
ьпist, have maintained the narrator's dependence upon
predictable social situations, in other words, interpretations rife
with genre stereotyping. Turning to the Jewish Hellenistic narratives, one finds the same dependence on genre without gendered
interpretation. By prefacing and suffusing their interpretations of
The Testaments of the Twelve Patriarchs with the description of a
testament as a combination of parenetic and apocalyptic genres,
scholars and critics have guaranteed the meaning of the literary
work. Such prescription insures a one-note reading for texts based
on shared similarities of form and language as well as assumed
gender unity. Reading a work within the confining category of
genre conveys the values of the social system which it reflects,
supports, and encompasses. There is also an element of elitism in
genre stereotyping, in which the theorist preserves this patriarchal
authority over the text and over its less expert readers. In contrast
to the traditional interpreters, I shall consider *TJos* as a narrative
within its ideological or moral agenda, and within the additional
encoding of gender. By making explicit its moral code, the one that
extols the pious Jewish hero for turning away from the sexual
advances of the woman, while at the same time condemning the
woman's sexual desire, a feminist reading challenges the normative
devaluing of the other. Most interpreters, both ancient and
modern, have been influenced by fear of the gender code to
suppress the woman's story by "structuring the differences according to the division between men and women on which the thematic
network is based" (Bal 1987c: 111).

JOSEPH'S STORY: A STUDY IN PERFECTION

In literature the idea of what makes a particular personality
probable or realistic differs for every society and for every era of
Western society. A literary personage is always a construction in
language of a network of relations and associations. It is an element
in a text, or in semiotic terms, a signifier analagous functionally to

other signifying elements in the text (Genette 1972a: 49–69). In Genette's terms the behavior of both Joseph and Mut-em-enet seen though the lens of the ancient world is "realistically" portrayed. Realism, seen as verisimilitude, is political; only morally acceptable behavior looks convincingly real. He embraces all the characteristics of the hero: loyal and pious, strong enough to resist the temptations of the female. She is the out-of-control female, slave to her passions. Read through the conventions of the moral code, his story is one of honor, hers one of shame. On the other hand, as I shall argue in the final section of this chapter, a literary character is more than an abstract literary function. Inevitably as readers we endow characters with three-dimensional lives of thoughts and feelings similar to our own. When one reads like a woman, therefore, one needs to resist the conventions of vraisemblance of motivation that assure the reader, "this is the only way the story could have happened." Thus, one goal of my reading is "to destroy the myth inside and outside ourselves" (Wittig 1981: 50–51).

The character of Joseph held particular appeal for a Hellenistic audience since he is the Jewish hero struggling for power and position in the foreign/gentile court. This model was one with which Flavius Josephus, a Jewish official on the fringes of the Roman court, connected himself. Philo, an Alexandrian, could make use of the popularity of Joseph as a biblical figure living and succeeding at the Egyptian court. A second aspect of Joseph's character that became important during the postbiblical period, a time when erotic themes were being played out dramatically in the works of New Comedy authors and in Greek romantic novels, was his God-assisted ability to hold the line against sexual temptation. In each retelling of Joseph's encounter with a woman (except for the romance *Joseph and Aseneth*) the key issue is adultery, the moral struggle between the good (male) and the wicked (female), between the self (Jewish hero) and the other (foreign/Gentile woman). *Joseph and Aseneth* also has the dichotomy of chastity/pleasure as the primary focus: it is a version of self and other, as in our adultery texts, but in this novel the resolution is marriage, since the foreign/wicked woman converts/is transformed into the self, thus absorbing or eradicating evil. In the adultery texts the good hero triumphs over the wicked, but the dichotomy of good/evil remains – defeated temporarily. In postbiblical associations with the biblical Joseph, according to Kugel's interpretation, Joseph's piety was connected specifically with his refusal to succumb to the sexual overtures of the Egyptian woman. "There can be little doubt," Kugel writes, "that this name [*yosef hassadiq*] was based on this incident with Potiphar's wife" (25).

In the traditional interpretation of the *Testaments of the Twelve Patriarchs*, Joseph is the "ethical model par excellence" (Hollander 1981: 16). In his own story, *T Jos*, the hero refers to himself at the beginning of his story as the beloved of Israel (1:2), an ambiguous appellation that refers both to his father and to his nation. Young Joseph, as we will learn in *T Jos* 3–9, is beloved of a woman, one who is obsessed with him and approaches him time after time for seven years (3:4). Because she is married, and dalliance with a married woman is a capital crime, Joseph sees her love as a threat, raw sexual desire as an overture to death. "Beloved of Israel" allies Joseph with his father rather than his mother, with whom the biblical text connects him. The father–son alliance signals the reader that this is a story about an all-powerful father who is able to rescue the hero from brothers who want what he has[11] and a woman who wants him. In his recounting of the ten temptations that prove Joseph validated by the symbolic Father "in ten temptations he showed that I was approved, and in all of them I endured; for endurance is a mighty remedy, and patience gives many good things" (verse 2:7), Joseph describes the tangle with the woman at great length before he describes in an incidental way the perfidy of his brothers that made him a martyr slave.[12] Thus, the danger from the Egyptian woman is so threatening that Joseph steps outside the chronology of his story in order to emphasize the primary danger of female sexual desire. In fact, in the second

---

[11] The fact that Joseph was beloved of his father clearly disturbs the brothers. Joseph's special status is mentioned in TSim 2:6; TDan 1:5, TGas 1:5, and at T Jos 10:5, where Joseph reminds us again that "my brothers know how my father loved me, and yet I did not exalt myself in my heart." One advantage of the monologue is, of course, the lack of response to self-aggrandizing statements. Aware of the biblical Joseph's arrogant nature, the reader may smile at his unwitting reminder that old age has not shriveled his ego.

[12] Kugel (1990: 23) recognizes that in T12P "the incident with Potiphar's wife is the main – virtually the only – item on the agenda: Joseph narrates it in some detail, then returns to it again afterwards with more particulars."

sequence of the *TJos* narrative, the narrator hero returns again to his purchase by Pentephres, which was engineered by the Egyptian woman.

About that time the Memphian woman passed by in a chariot

the wife of Pentephres, with great pomp and she cast her eyes upon me;
for the eunuchs had told her concerning me.
Now therefore, try him and set the youth free to be your steward,
and the God of the Hebrews will bless you,
for grace from heaven is upon him.　　　　　　　*(TJos* 12:1,3)

Thus, in Joseph's version, in spite of the moral code which refers the interpretation to the ultimate victory of society's demands over individual erotic desire, the woman is his rescuer. The wife of Pentephres is the one who saves him from the Ishmaelite merchant who has enslaved him, a detail that does not appear in the biblical version, Josephus, Philo, or *Jubilees*. However, Joseph is so threatened by her pursuit of him, and so involved in defending his boundaries from her invasion, he never experiences her act as one of rescue.

Much like the martyrs of Maccabean literature, Joseph feels threatened with death from several sides, although the most severe threat comes from the woman who would take his honor as well as his life.[13] The brothers set out to kill him, but as Joseph reminds us,

they let me down into a pit, and the Most High brought me up again. I was sold as a slave and the Lord made me free; I was taken into captivity and His strong hand protected me; I was beset with hunger and the Lord himself nourished me. *(TJos* 1:4–5)[14]

Having referred to the brothers' dastardly deed, although in no detail, Joseph focuses his extensive narrative upon the greater trouble with the Egyptian woman. Returning to the testamentary

---

[13]　The motif of transgression, a challenge to commit *paranomia* is also frequent in martyr traditions. See 4 Macc. 5:13, 17, 20, 27; 8:14; 9:3ff.; also Philo, *Somn.* II.124. Hollander and de Jonge (1985: 370) note that in T12P "both aspects seem to be combined; like the tyrant, the woman wants to bring the pious man to transgress the law."

[14]　It is interesting to note a similarity between the testimony Joseph gives of God's rescuing him from captivity, hunger, loneliness, sickness, and prison with the works of mercy as described in Isa. 58:7 and Jesus' statement to the disciples in Mt. 25:35–36, which recounts the same combination of trials as Trito-Isaiah and T12P. Hollander (1981: 19–20) notes the influence of Psalms of individual thanksgiving in both style and terminology.

frame of the narrative, it becomes apparent that all these years later, what Joseph the patriarch wants his sons to remember as the focus of his life story is his successful struggle against sexual desire. The central figure of *TJos*, then, is the primary adversary who threatened the hero with death, "the shameless woman, *he porne*, urging me to transgress with her; but the God of Israel my father guarded me from the burning flame" (*TJos* 2:2). Thus, God, the symbolic father, rescues Joseph from the predatory woman, much as Israel the father had rescued the child Joseph from his jealous siblings.

The language of the psalm of thanksgiving,[15] in which Joseph frames his story, sets the conditions for reading the story. Joseph is the hero; his adversaries the evil characters against whom God protects him. Thus, the psalm, found at the opening of the work, acts to suppress the story of the woman, by structuring the story as the rescue of the hero by the deity. God is on the side of Joseph. The traditional reader joins this elite "we" against the adversarial female "she."

The psalm pattern "I was in trouble and God rescued me," familiar to the readers of T12P, compresses the plot line and reveals the outcome of the story. Referring to *he porne* without name, adds to the effect of locking her out of his story. Later, we shall examine the hero's framing of the woman's dialogue, another way of prescribing the reader's interpretation of her words and intentions, a powerful narrative device in turning fragments of her story back into the fabric of his story.

The idea of the hero's fervent struggle (*agon*) against sexual passions is commonly found in Hellenistic moral philosophy as well as in Philo and Josephus. The picture of the heroic Joseph struggling (*agonisasthai*) against the Egyptian woman parallels Josephus' portrait of a hero who does not give in to the woman's temptations and threats (*tais apeilais*).[16] Philo's version, in contrast,

---

[15] See Hollander and de Jonge (1985: 367–68) for structure and analysis of TJos 1:4–26 as psalm of individual thanksgiving. Their argument is that the psalm in TJos indicates a later development of the type of psalm found in Dan. 2:20–23; Sir. 51:1–12; PssSol. 2, 13, 15.

[16] The woman's ethnicity is emphasized in Joseph's story much as his foreignness is emphasized in her story (Gen. 39:14,17). Joseph refers to the woman as *he aiguptia* five times: TJos 3:6; 4:3, 8:1,5; 16:5.

presents a not-so-heroic Joseph, a young man lacking strength to contend (*agonisasthai*) (*Leg All.* III.242), one who runs away from temptation instead of struggling hand to hand. In the Alexandrian's portrait of Joseph in *Leg. All.*, he implies that Joseph will grow into hero status. However, Joseph's ability to struggle against the woman is displaced because of his youth. The emphasis on Joseph's youth and concomitant naivete is implicitly paralleled with the passionate *porne*. The universal story is termed the Stepmother and the Chaste Youth, although the age of the woman is never explicitly mentioned in either the biblical story or any of its expansions.

The first words that open Joseph's story about the woman emphasize the persistent nature of her behavior,

How often (*posakis*) did the Egyptian woman threaten me with death! How often did she give me over to punishment . . . and threaten me . . . How often did she flatter me with words as a holy man.   (*TJos* 4:1)

In the eyes of the storyteller and of the commentators of this passage, Joseph's multiple refusals emphasize his piety and his *sophrosyne*. Another text from this period evidences a similar reading with an emphasis on the salvific element contained within *sophrosyne*. In 4 Macc. 2:1, Joseph is referred to as *ho sophron Ioseph*.

It is for this reason, surely, that the righteous Joseph [*ho sophron Ioseph*] has been praised, because by his mental effort he did overcome sexual desire. For when he was young and in his prime, by his reasons he nullified the frenzy of his passions. Not only is reason proved to rule over the frenzied urge of sexual desire, but also over every desire. (4 Macc. 2:1–4)

Thus, for the ancient exegetes, what distinguishes Joseph from the other patriarchs is not his treatment at the hands of his brothers, his ability to interpret dreams, nor his ability to negotiate the politics of the Egyptian court, but rather his power to resist sexual temptation. The "time after time" emphasis of the repetition of the woman's actions underscores the hero's righteousness. To my knowledge no ancient or modern commentator, with the exception of Thomas Mann, suggests that the woman's impassioned pleas indicate that her love for Joseph is genuine. As I read my blended narrative, the woman's feelings indicate a long-standing passion, not a thing of the moment. Her attempts at persuasion to seduce the beloved would be expected if the gender roles were reversed. Focusing on Mut's love for Joseph requires an effort to read the woman in the text, listening for her story. This sort of reading was monumentally achieved by Mann, who heard her voice and imagined the possibilities of her story.

Kugel emphasizes the ancient readers' propensity to concentrate on the adulterous proposal of the wife of Potiphar, but I would add that modern commentators have not moved far from that traditional reading.[17] Von Rad understands Joseph, the paradigmatic wisdom figure, to have heeded the warnings against the strange woman found in Prov. 2:16; 5:3, 20; 6:24; 22:14; 23:37ff. "Thus, the temptation story in chapter 39 reads like a story composed ad hoc to illustrate these admonitions of wisdom" (von Rad 1959: 436). Sarna equates Joseph's resistance to sexual temptation with his selection as the "instrument of God's providence." Arguing that the reader is so sympathetic to the hero's "nobility of character, we forget those displeasing traits that alienated us at the outset," Sarna (JPS: 272) envisions a reader who prefers a hero who exhibits sexual continence to a tale-bearing braggadocio.

Bloom understands the episode as "great comic writing in J, comedy for its own sake" (1990: 230). Again the commentator makes an assumption about the reader. If one is reading for the woman's story, a narrative that locks her into a position of permanent scorn and characterizes her as a manipulative predatory liar is not an example of great comedic writing. Whether the narrative of Genesis 39, with its negative portrait of a female figure, bears the hallmark of female authorship is an intriguing question, one that Bloom has sidestepped by characterizing it merely as "one of J's most delicious episodes" (1990: 230).[18] Bloom clearly reads

---

[17] One example is Louis Ginzberg (1911: 5:325) who states the position unequivocally. "There can be no doubt that this title was conferred on Joseph on account of his virtuous victory over the wiles of his master's wife."

[18] One of the most devastating critiques of Bloom's quirky assumptions in *The Book of J* comes from Alter, who begins with an attack on the Rosenberg translation of the Hebrew text on which Bloom depends. "It is baffling that a man of Harold Bloom's intelligence should be guilty of so extreme a lapse in taste, even without the ability to judge the philological issues, as to endorse this translation" (1992: 157). Alter seems to agree with Bloom's attempt to shake readers "out of their preconceptions about the Bible and that is all to the good" (1992: 161). But Alter, like Bloom, supports the fantasy of one individual

the episode as though it has only one reading, that of the wicked woman getting her just desserts. Bloom is reading like a man, although he presents his reading as *the* reading, leaving no room for those who might read from a different perspective. Bloom, the literary critic, does not read this text very differently from the theologian von Rad, who also "knows" how this text is to be understood. "In the description of Joseph's innocence," von Rad assures the reader, "only the person who is capable of listening sensitively really feels himself addressed" (von Rad 1972: 46).

Kugel reads the story solely from the perspective of Joseph the righteous. In spite of the univocal reading, Kugel provides important insights about the centrality of the episode between Joseph and his master's wife (1990: chap. 1) As I mentioned above, Kugel connects Joseph's appellation as *hassaddiq* directly with his rejection of the wife of Potiphar. Further, Kugel argues, Joseph's righteousness, his "meritorious behavior with Mrs. Potiphar," is rewarded by the "double portion" in his father's inheritance (Kugel 1990: 127). Pressing this insight further, I think there is a connection between the refusal of Joseph to commit adultery and the reward of double patrimony. The ancient world understood a married woman's sexuality to be the property of her husband. The laws related to marriage and adultery were constructed to protect patrimony. Thus, turning away from sexual desire brought Joseph a greater reward than he could have achieved simply by cashing in on his birthright. There is an added irony in that the "double portion" sons, Ephraim and Manasseh, are traditionally understood as the offspring of Aseneth, the daughter of Potiphar. So the hero's proper refusal of a sexual union with another man's wife and the proper execution of a husband's sexual duties with that man's daughter worked together in this story to provide a double reward for sexual restraint.

Joseph is figured in the biblical text, its expansions, and in the

author of genius who lived in a specific place and wrote at a specific time. Alter's major disagreement with the identity of this figure is connected to Bloom's "inaccurate" assumptions about dating and provenance drawn from a clumsy translation. However, Alter is relieved that Bloom fights the death of the author. Like Alter himself, Bloom "has remained resolutely attached to the idea of individual personalities willfully asserting themselves in the act of writing, struggling with other personalities who are their predecessors" (1992: 165).

responses to it as the primary male character in the
here are other male figures in the biblical text: Potiphar
nale servants. In *TJos*, as well as the versions found in
, Philo, and *Jubilees*, there are no male servants. In my
view the function of the Egyptian male servants in the biblical
version needs to be examined briefly so that their role may be
contrasted with that of the Egyptian women of the court who are
added to the tradition in the Talmudic and medieval periods.

It is interesting that the unnamed male servants who hear the
story from Mut-em-enet (Gen. 39:14–15) have not fired the reader's
imagination. They are servants like Joseph; they are Egyptian
unlike Joseph. Much has been made of Mut-em-enet's clever way
of manipulating them, by fanning the flames of ethnic competition,
referring to Joseph as *'ish 'ibri* "the Hebrew." But nothing has been
made of the effect of their silence and inaction in the light of their
mistress's accusation of rape. In the mind of the reader the silence
of the servants can be placed anywhere along a continuum from a
dour, accusatory silence to a parodic silence, in which the servants
make fun of the screaming female behind her back.

The biblical text does not provide even a glimmer of their
response to the woman. She has screamed out *beqol gadol* "in a loud
voice," and the men have responded with silence. However, their
backgrounded presence serves a narrative function. Since the
reader is given no response from these characters, one is left a gap
commodious enough to accommodate many possibilities: (1) The
male servants had been similarly propositioned by their mistress
and were relieved to see another man caught in her vice. (2) The
male servants were embarrassed at her prevarication, having
glimpsed the frightened fleeing Joseph. (3) The male servants were
delighted to see the much privileged Hebrew servant in trouble.
The one suggestion that seems unlikely, at least to this reader, is
that the servants' silence implies sympathy with the woman who is
claiming rape.

The total lack of reaction of the male servants to the woman's
startling accusation keeps them from any interaction with her
within the story. One can imagine that her frustration over
Joseph's rejection was enlarged by the silence of the servants. In
the biblical version, then, the woman presents her case to these

servants, who exhibit no reaction. Stepping outside the story, rising
to the level of readerly imagination, the men could be constrained
from exhibiting their true skepticism by their lower social status. As
men, however, the servants reflect the uncompromising silence,
lack of sympathy, that the male audience has shown to Mut. The
biblical and the Hellenistic story in which its characters arrive at
little awareness of what is going on with them and an audience that
arrives at very little more is common in ancient literature,
particularly the genre of romance (Hochman 1985: 156). Mut-em-
enet does not seem to confront the events in her life as an
individual, due to the lack of inward description, but rather she
appears to respond as a type, an *ishah zarah*, in an expected
predictable fashion. It is of course not possible for the reader to
supply the circumstances or particularities of Mut's life, without
writing another story, such as Mann has done. But any modern
reader, affected by reading of novels that emphasize the elusiveness
of experience, or the intrusion of past events into a character's
present life, is likely to inscribe consciousness, even intermittent
consciousness, to its characters.[19]

An attentive reader can imagine that Mut's frustration must be
multiplied when she presents a second slightly altered version of the
story to her husband (Gen. 39:17), an alteration that contains her
hopes of bringing the male (husband, servants, narrator, readers) to
her side. Her story does elicit action this time, although not a direct
verbal response. The narrator informs the reader that Potiphar's
"anger was ignited" (verse 19). But Potiphar does not articulate his
anger; he does not match Mut-em-enet's direct speech with an
outraged one of his own. Rather he shows his loyalty to his wife
through his action, putting the offensive Joseph in jail. For a
second time Mut-em-enet's voluble accusation is met by male im-
passivity. The combination of the male servants' lack of response
with Potiphar's tepid one suggests a tightly structured society with
strong male bonding, in which the female character is unsupported
against a range of men. This male solidarity asserts the powerful
patriarchal order arrayed against the female dissimulator: the

---

[19] Once again Chatman's concept of a paradigm of traits can be useful in this respect:
however, problematically, it legitimates the tendency to abstract, schematize, and
stabilize – indeed, to render static – the dynamic process of experience.

shame of Joseph in being imprisoned on the word of a woman is eradicated by the honor of his loyalty to his God and to his master. By not speaking against him, the male servants have increased the display of honor among men. Their silence is similar to the explanation Joseph presents of his own silence in prison, "I wanted to weep, but I restrained myself that I should not put my brothers to shame" (*TJos* 15:3).

The expected reaction, if Potiphar had believed her story, would have been to have Joseph put to death since adultery was a capital crime. However, the silence of the servants prefigures the luke-warm reception the story gets from the husband. The fact that the men did not rush off to defend their mistress indicates that they did not believe her story or did not feel impelled to feign outrage. Certainly the narrator omitting their response indicates that their behavior was not remarkable. Nor were they at risk by not supporting the accusations of the master's wife. What we do learn from their silence is that men do not genuinely ignite at the accusation of a sexual crime against another man, even a Hebrew servant. This numb response to a woman's accusation of a man is in sharp contrast with the Sotah, where a husband on the suspicion of his wife's possible sexual guilt, can have her publicly humiliated (at best) and killed (if the potion is poison).

Josephus has expanded the role of Potiphar, providing the reader with a description of courtly erudite character who behaves as an Egyptian mentor to the statesman-in-training.

> This man held him in the highest esteem, gave him a liberal education, accorded him better far than falls the lot of a slave, and committed the charge of his household into his hands. Yet, while enjoying these privileges, he [Joseph] even under this change of fortune abandoned not that virtue that enveloped him, but displayed how a noble spirit can surmount the trials of life, where it is genuine and does not simply accommodate itself to passing prosperity. (JA II.4.1.)

According to Josephus' version, even the largesse and easy life provided by the Egyptian did not spoil or corrupt *ho sophron*. Potiphar is a flat figure in the other versions, casting into sharper relief the female figure of villainy. In *TJos*, the most expansive of the Second Temple versions of the story, the narrator Joseph fashions a tale for his sons in which there are two poles of activity: himself and the erotic evil woman. In order to emphasize the tug of power between them, there are no extraneous characters to distract the reader's attention from the male/female struggle. In structuralist terms, the decrease in the number of actors within a fabula indicates the degree to which the fabula is subjective (Bal 1985: 32).

TESTAMENTS OF THE TWELVE PATRIARCHS (TESTAMENT OF JOSEPH)[20]

The genre of Testament followed a general form: the introduction to the dying patriarch, who summons his sons for final advice, narrative from the patriarch's life illustrating a virtue or vice; ethical exhortation, prediction of the future, possibly more parenesis, death and burial of patriarch. Thus, the tradition has affinity with wisdom literature and homiletic aggadah. In the *Testaments of the Twelve Patriarchs* the author fills in the all-important "what happened," completing the patriarchal stories of Jacob's sons. These stories in *Testaments of the Twelve Patriarchs* are built around Joseph as the ethical model of *sophrosyne*, or self-control, a key motif in the work, and his brothers' treatment of him.[21] Thus, Joseph becomes an Abrahamic model of suffering hero, undergoing trials with great *hupomone*, a second key motif. In the next chapter I shall

---

[20] The *Testament* has been preserved in Greek and in a number of versions dependent on the Greek text. The earliest Greek witness for the text is MS b dating from the tenth century. For a history of the textual transmission and a list of Greek manuscripts see Hollander and de Jonge (1985: 10–28). A history of interpretation is to be found in H. Dixon Slingerland (1977). For this study I have used M. de Jonge (1978) as well as the earlier critical edition of R. H. Charles (1908).

[21] *Contra* J. Becker (1970), who argues that *T Jos* 1:1o:4, the story of Joseph and the sexual advances of his master's wife, is a later interpolation because it resembles Hellenistic romance and emphasizes *sophrosyne*, unlike the rest of the *Testaments of the Twelve Patriarchs*. While I agree with Becker that elements of romance exist in the first unit of *T Jos*, it is because this unit exemplifies a *märchen*, not a full-blown romance. I think the focus upon *sophrosyne* is a fundamental Greek element of the entire *Testaments of the Twelve Patriarchs*, reflecting the Greek origin of the work. Thus, I prefer Pervo's reading of his story (Pervo 1976: 15–28). Pervo argues that the first part of *Testament of Joseph* (chs. 1–10:4) presents an aretalogy of Joseph, a model of exemplary piety rather than a romantic narrative about female deceit and male chastity, like *Joseph and Aseneth*, a genuine romance. Hence, if the genre of this literary work is more parenetic than romantic, one is not faced with Becker's problems of explaining the fragmentary nature of the narrative in *Testament of Joseph*.

look at the handling of the first story in *Testament of Joseph*, the *sophrosyne* of Joseph against the wiles of the wicked foreign woman. Joseph survives ten temptations or ten trials at the hands [sic] of Potiphar's wife. Since the story is told by Joseph in first-person, the focus is more markedly through his eyes than the other accounts. In a well-constructed narrative the first-person usually adds an element of suspense, but in this story the emphasis is so clearly parenetic, and the characters so clearly represent virtue and vice that the reader knows she/he is being taught, not entertained. *Joseph and Aseneth* is geared more toward entertainment; like Apuleius' *Metamorphoses* and other romances of the Hellenistic period.

Joseph's endurance is a model of what the Jewish community must undergo under Greek domination. The way for them to succeed is the way Joseph did, through following the Law and through prayer and fasting and directing all one's thoughts to God. Thus, even though one may undergo unfair punishment, even imprisonment, one will triumph eventually. Even the Egyptian woman praises Joseph's *sophrosyne* to her husband, although she then becomes the embodiment of its opposite axolasia when the husband is away. Throughout the *Testaments of the Twelve Patriarchs* the author reminds us that God loves the one who turns from darkness/wickedness/temptation and remains in prayer.

While a narratological analysis of Euripides' Hippolytus is outside the scope of this study, it will increase our mental picture of the wicked biblical woman to note briefly the parallel between the Jewish story of Joseph and Mut-em-enet and its Greek parallel. Braun's extensive analysis of the parallels in the two texts provides strong evidence for the connection between the two interpretations of the motif. Not surprisingly Braun's work does not focus upon the female figures in either work. His concern is to define the development of the genre of romance and not to provide character analyses. A close narrative analysis of *TJos* appears in the following chapter. But, following Braun's lead, I shall comment briefly on the remarkable similarities between Hippolytus and *Testament of Joseph*.

Ultimately *sophrosyne* saved the most proper Hippolytus from the sexual desire of his stepmother, the unhappy Phaedra. The chastity of the young hero Hippolytus is a reflection of the power of the goddess Artemis, and his *sophrosyne* is understood as a gift from the gods.[22] We will compare this tragic drama with the biblical story to show how both versions reflect the fundamental impossibility of ancient women being drawn as heroes of their own stories. Both stories, although in quite different portraits of their female protagonists, confirm the view that women's words wreak havoc on an orderly world.

Examining Euripides' version of the Potiphar's wife motif allows us to understand the fundamental impossibility of ancient women being drawn as subsects of their own stories. Reading like a man, Winnington-Ingram writes, "if honor is everything, what is the point of virtuous action, if it be known to none" (Winnington-Ingram 1958: 79–80). The private sphere, where the good woman dwells, is hidden from the agora of glory, the focus of male concern. Thus, the interpretation participates in keeping women of the narrative silent. Re-imagining the narrative, focusing upon the women of the text, allows me to create a story in which woman's subjectivity is not overlooked.

Comparing Phaedra's reactions to Hippolytus provides another perspective on the behavior of Mut-em-enet, another mode of analyzing this female literary figure, who is without parallel in the Hebrew Bible. Before we see Phaedra, we hear that she is suffering silently (40), has taken to her bed, keeps herself inside the house (*entos oikou*), covers up her head, and has not eaten for days (131–40). She confirms this version of her behavior when she makes her apologia to the chorus; first she tried to be silent (394), then to conquer her desire (399), then to commit suicide (401). As Rabinowitz has noted, death by starvation is particularly appropriate for one who feels the shame of the body (Rabinowitz 1986: 127–40). "At the same time, starvation as a means of death shows her poverty (she has only herself as a material) and indicates passive resistance." She will not push forward in life, but does not yet take an active step against her life. As Rabinowitz concludes, "by abstaining from the physicality of sexual desire and food, at the same time that she determines not to speak, she makes sure that if

---

[22] Note the similarity of theme in *Medea*, in which the Chorus sings, "May *sophrosyne*, the fairest gift of the gods, cherish me" (635–36).

nind sins, her mouth will not" (1986: 130). But she does, in the and all goes awry.

_n contrast, the biblical Mut-em-enet does not willingly retreat from an assertive stance; she does not accept what her culture says is appropriate behavior for a woman. When Joseph prudently refuses her sexual advances, she appears not to be shamed like Phaedra, but rather seeks retribution against Joseph. Where Phaedra purifies herself by fasting, closing herself to food as well as speech, Mut-em-enet spits out words of derision and accusation. Phaedra embraces the "dark inner chambers, silence and depriva-tion" (Rabinowitz 1986: 131). Mut-em-enet must be put in her place by the narrator's pen. And this is accomplished in *TJos*, where the Egyptian wife's wickedness is exaggerated and extended. The distraught woman tries everything from pretending interest in conversion (4:4) to enticing Joseph with magical food (6:1–8). If it is adultery that is the sticking point for the pious Joseph, she will kill her husband so that she and Joseph can be married (5:1). She even tries to bribe the stolid hero in prison. "Acquiesce in fulfilling my desire, and I will release you from the fetters and free you from the darkness" (9:1).

Of course this is Joseph's story, and he does not acquiesce. But how do we get at the suppressed story of Mut-em-enet, who is so in love with Joseph that she offers to commit murder, to convert to his faith, anything to get the object of her desire? Since the authors of the *Testaments* and of the rabbinic midrash related to Genesis 39 tell Joseph's story, perhaps it is the lack of a woman reader filling the gaps in the biblical story that have prevented us from hear-ing the woman's version. Perhaps if there had been women rabbis in the ancient world or in the biblical interpretive tradition, we might have heard the story of Mut-em-enet.

LITERARY IMAGES OF WOMEN IN HELLENISTIC TIMES

Generally in the archaic Greek epics women, like the male heroes who fought for them, were portrayed in a more idealized light than in subsequent literary texts, although the idealization is exactly that. It did not reflect social freedom of actual women of the time.

In the Odyssey Andromache and Helen walk freely through the streets of Troy (though they are usually not alone) and women are pictured on the shield of Achilles helping to defend the city's walls. Since the hearth was the center of the home, Homeric queens Penelope, Helen, and Arete demonstrated by sitting by the hearth that the ideal woman was involved in whatever occurred in the household. As good women, they defended and protected the hearth, while their hero husbands were outside defending the nation. Arthur points out that Helen is "notoriously free from the disgrace which later attaches to adulterous women," an observation central to understanding that the moral code encompassed men in the Homeric times. Not until the literature of the classical period did literary works reflect a social climate that regulated women's behavior morally as well as legally (Arthur 1984: 16).

Josephus and Philo, in their recountings of the ancestral period presented idealized portraits of the matriarchs.[23] In contrast to some of his stories recalling the exploits of Hasmonean and Herodian women, Josephus used the biblical matriarchs as examples of moral excellence to be admired by the Greek audience, who could connect them with the loyal and lofty Penelope.[24] Josephus uses two foreign women as the paradigms of villainry: the Midianite woman and the wife of Potiphar, whose sexual passion is seen by Josephus as a "desperate, base quality which directly or indirectly leads to betrayal" (Amaru 1988: 153).[25]

In Hellenistic times upper-class women's roles altered in major

---

[23] An example of the Jewish writers flattening the matriarchs into a proper Hellenistic wifely role can be found in a comparison of Gen. 16:2 in the LXX and in its subsequent treatment in Philo and Josephus. The LXX text of Gen. 16:2 states that Sarah wants to claim the child for herself. Philo's retelling in *Congr.* 1 states that Sarah encourages Abraham to have sex with Hagar so that *he* might have children from the Egyptian. In Josephus' rendition of this verse Sarah gets the idea to send Hagar to Abraham from the deity, removing even the initial motivation from the matriarch.

[24] For discussion of Josephus' hellenization of the matriarchal figures, see Bailey (1987: 154–79); see Amaru (1988: 143–70) for a literary analysis of Josephus' good and bad women.

[25] While Amaru (1988) does a neat job of schematizing the matriarchs and their wicked counterparts, she does not raise questions about why Josephus fills the gaps of the biblical stories about women by tamping down the fires of the biblical matriarchs, making them passive and deferential to their husbands. It is interesting to note, as Amaru does, that neither Sarah nor Rebekah have direct contact with the deity in Josephus' versions. Indeed, for him, good women are silent and unassertive.

ways.[26] When the city-states lost political autonomy, the power that men had wielded under a familial political structure waned. Under the domination of Hellenistic monarchs, for most men the center of power was somewhere else. The gap in privileges between men and women narrowed. Locked out of the elite public sphere, man's world included daily contact with ordinary women. Rather than attempting to hoard their shrinking store of privileges, men were more willing to share the "less valued privileges" they had (Pomeroy 1984: 126).

The social change experienced by nonroyal but upper-class Hellenistic women was connected to their acquisition of economic power. The stirrings of power felt by women were magnified in the lives of female imperial royalty, who wielded power as wives and mothers, primarily as the ambitious consorts of weak kings and as regents for very young sons and absent husbands (Pomeroy 1984: 125). These women enjoyed greater power as the mother of rulers than as the wives of rulers, reinforcing the power and status of mother over that of wife. Many of these stories of historical women bear the drama and sexual politics found in the literary texts. A prime example of the life of a real queen containing the plot twists of classic tragedy is Olympias, who ruled while Alexander was away at war. She was blamed for the murder of her husband Philip but that was probably unjust, although she did have to plot for her own survival against assorted concubines/secondary wives and their overeager children. Olympias struggled for power against Antipater, who was viceroy in Alexander's absence. Although he supported Antipater, Alexander never gave up allegiance to his mother.

The Hellenistic novels[27] and romances reflected the syncretistic

[26] It is not possible to document the lives of Athenian women with the same breadth as the lives of the later Hellenistic women. As Pomeroy observes, "the apparent formal expansion of women's competence may be attributable to the fact that for the Hellenistic period there exist data from many different areas inhabited by Greeks, while the view of women's position in classical Greece is monopolized by the situation at Athens and the implication that, on the whole, Sparta was exceptional because of a unique social system" (Pomeroy 1975: 125).

[27] Two Latin novels are particularly representative of the genre of ancient novel: Apuleius's *Metamorphoses* (*The Golden Ass*) and Petronius' *Satyricon*. One sees similarities between the raffish dissolute antiheroes portrayed in the Satyricon and the Greek comic tradition, represented by the recently deciphered *Ioolaus*, see Reardon (1989). In the mind of the reader, the motif of conversion of the idealized female in the *Metamorphoses* connects the heroine Isis with her namesake Aseneth.

world in which cultural solidarity was eroding and the closed society was opening up. Where stable traditions were the norm in the classical Greek epics, there were now conflicting desires and centrifugal tendencies, appealing to a heterogenous audience. In a world of large empires, there could not be the same intense interest in local political matters as had characterized the classical city-state. New Comedy was the primary Hellenistic vehicle for romance and entertainment. It reflected the new phenomenon of the individual's self-absorption. Instead of the world of warring deities and cosmic conflicts there was now the individual's war of the soul.[28] The happily-ever-after story appealed to the audience occupied with romantic sentiment and domestic conflicts, in the way that the older forms of tragedy and Old Comedy had interested a populace engaged in public action and civic experience (Reardon 1989: 7). The works of Menander, and even Euripides, continued to be performed in the theaters, but the coarser popular dramas, were more commonly staged. Nonliterate audiences outside the large metropolitan centers, especially women, were attracted to the emotionally dense tales of romanticism and idealism (Hägg 1983: 90).[29]

While the notion that women were attracted to the plays of New Comedy is interesting, I am not satisfied with the standard conclusion which results in the gender stereotyping of women delighted by romantic literary works and men drawn to real hard facts. A prime reason for the interest in comedy, in my view, is its concern with the unequal position of women, visible already in Aristophanes' fifth-century work *Lysistrata*. A second and related reason that women may have enjoyed these performances may be that many of the female characters of New Comedy are either slaves or women whose status and lineage is undistinguished or obscure. These women are more independent than the upper-class women of classical times, and may have come to Athens from

---

[28] André Gide (*Oedipe*: Act II) suggested this psychic shift in his version of the Oedipus myth: "Dans l'état de civilisation avancé où nous sommes, et depuis que le dernier sphinx a été tué par notre père, les monsters ni les dieux ne sont plus parmi les airs or les campagnes; mais en nous."

[29] Hägg (1983) suggests that the people who were attracted to the plays of New Comedy were also those who were attracted to the Mystery religions and Christianity, expecially in the vicinity of Alexandria, and the eastern Mediterranean, the locale in which *Joseph and Aseneth* was probably written.

elsewhere in the Greek world. In the comedies their precarious legal and social positions are reflected.[30] A third reason that women might have been attracted to these performances may be that they were permitted to attend,[31] that the performance was a social occasion, an opportunity to leave the confines of the house.

The fairy-tale plots of the ancient Greek novels[32] are remarkably similar: boy meets girl, boy and girl overcome terrible obstacles to their union,[33] boy and girl marry and live happily ever after. Bakhtin claims that the plots of these novels are composed of identical elements, one work differing from another "only in the number of such elements, their proportionate weight within the whole plot and the way they are combined" (Bakhtin 1981: 87). Part of their appeal, therefore, was in the familiarity of their construction.

According to Hägg the ancient novel was the first literary form to have its main support among women (1983: 95). Again one is faced with interpretive gender stereotyping of a literary audience. While this suggestion of a predominantly female audience is intriguing, one must not be tempted to make the leap into positing female authorship behind the pseudonyms (see Lefkowitz 1991). Chaste, loyal, faithful-to-death, the idealized woman of the ancient novel seems more a male fantasy than a female literary creation. One finds superloyal pious women in the Jewish literary figures of Judith, Esther, Susanna, and Aseneth, all Second Temple period creations. The stories present a range of emotions

---

[30] One such example is the central female character in Menander's *Samia*. Chrysis, a woman from the island of Samos came to Athens and worked as an *etaira* or free companion to men. She becomes a *pallake*, concubine or second-ranking wife, not a citizen wife, but in a rage her husband consigns her to *kamaitupe*, prostitute. He warns her saying, "When you're on the streets, you'll realize what you're really worth. They're not like you, Chrysis, those other women, who for ten drachmas run to dinner-parties and drink themselves to death on unmixed wine, or starve if they're not prepared to do this at the drop of a hat." *Samia* 390–96.

[31] Greek tragedies of the classical era were performed at religious festivals before the entire citizenry, or at least for an audience of male citizens. See Charles Segal (1986: 3).

[32] The five Greek novels which have survived in their entirety are the *Ephesiaca* by Xenophon of Ephesus, *Chaereas and Callirhoe* by Chariton, *Daphne and Chloe* by Longus, *Leucippe and Clitophon* by Achilles Tatius, and the *Aethiopica* by Heliodorus.

[33] The obstacles are often cataclysmic cliff-hangers: shipwrecks, slavery, human sacrifices, near suicides or murders, kidnappings, pirate raids are common plot elements. See Huysmans (1969: 56).

for the female characters and thus give a fuller portrait than the remote stories of the biblical matriarchs. The erotic motifs of Hellenistic romances are found in the extraordinary sex and death scene in which Judith tempts and destroys Holofernes. As I shall show in chapter 6, the banquet scene in the book of Esther as well as the intricate plot details of the book parallel the food–sex–death motifs of the book of Judith, as well as the stories of Jael, Delilah, and Salomé. Both Judith and Esther are temporary heroes, appearing only to save Israel, but then relinquishing their hard-won power to men, Judith to the elders and Esther to Mordecai.

The authors of *Jubilees* and the *Testaments of the Twelve Patriarchs* represent the Jewish community's fears of the influence of the free-wheeling Hellenistic society, with its hedonistic dilution of moral values. Their stern texts tried to point the way back to the values of the biblical patriarchs. While the secular Hellenistic audiences were enjoying a modest display of female power, Jewish writers were attempting to protect the fixed values of their religious communities, or in the reading of Bickerman "to palm off on the reader presumptuous revelations" (Bickerman 1988: 190). Within these Jewish works, the portraits of female figures were the opposite of those in the secular realm. Instead of being free to enjoy the bawdy entertainments of the Hellenistic romances, and enjoying the specter of the female queens accreting power, good Jewish wives were given stories, *haggadot*, whose horizons were still bound by the Euphrates and the Nile, and whose goal was to impress upon the Jewish settlers in Persian Elephantine and in Palestine the lesson of obedience to God. The role of the evil wife with her disruptive sexual passions, as figured in Mut-em-enet, was expanded to emphasize what the Jewish hero was up against. Not only does Mut-em-enet offer herself to the incorruptible Joseph, but she also offers him all her husband's property. The stakes are much higher in Hellenistic times, but the ethically stalwart Joseph is up to the challenge.

The emotional atmosphere thickened in the Hellenistic retellings. In *Joseph and Aseneth*, beset by all the women in Alexandria, Joseph is in a state of anxiety. Following the form of the Greek romance, the beautiful virgin Aseneth converts to the Jewish faith and becomes the ideal woman.[34] At the opposite end of the scale of female figures is the Hellenistic version of Mut-em-enet, whose role has been expanded in both *Jubilees* and the *Testaments of the Twelve Patriarchs*, in which she spends the better part of a year luring Joseph into her bed. Her Egyptian ethnicity was a sharp warning to the Jewish man of the Diaspora who would wander into the house of *ishah zarah*. There was probably a distinction, however, between the wicked *ishah zarah* and a more positive model, that of the loyal foreign wife, such as Ruth or Tamar, and their postbiblical counterpart Aseneth. Aptowitzer argues spiritedly that the foreign wives of biblical heroes were not regarded "as of any hindrance or of any consequence at all, just as in the case of the wife of Moses, inasmuch as their conversion to the religion of their husbands could be assumed as self-evident" (Aptowitzer 1924: 241).[35] This assumption of Aptowitzer in 1924 shows how persistent is the model of the compliant conversion of the foreign wife. In contrast one thinks of Jezebel, who is vilified by the storyteller for remaining foreign and despoiling her husband's piety.

JOSEPH AND ASENETH[36]

The literary genre of *Joseph and Aseneth* is agreed to be a romance, or a roman d'amour (Philonenko 1968: 43). There is narrative unity,

---

[34] Bickerman argues "neither this Joseph [T12P] nor any other hero produced by the Jewish imagination of the pre-Maccabean age made a single convert." This statement of course depends on when one dates *Joseph and Aseneth*, with its extensive report of female conversion. Although he does not refer to the romance, Bickerman does continue his argument by stating that an Egyptian woman would no more become a Jew by worshipping God than she would have become an Athenian by worshipping Athena. Of course citizenship is not the issue in *Joseph and Aseneth*, since it is Joseph who becomes an Egyptian ruler and Aseneth his queen, rather than either of them claiming Jewish citizenship. See Bickerman (1988: 246–48).

[35] Aptowitzer cites post-Tannaitic sources which support intermarriage, so long as the non-Jewish party became a convert. Cf. *Mishnah Yad* iv.4; *Tos. Kid.* v.4; *Ber.* 28a; *Yeb.* 76a; *Mishnah Torah, Issure Biah* xii 17 and 25.

[36] The romance of *Joseph and Aseneth* was composed in Greek between the second century BCE and the first century CE, probably in Egypt. Its textual history is still disputed, but it has been transmitted to us in four Greek recensions and in Slavic, Syriac, Armenian, and Latin versions. For scholarly arguments see Burchard (1967: 18–49; 1978: 68–84). The Greek text used in this study is the emended (and shorter) one in the critical edition of Philonenko (1968). For textual history see Philonenko (1968: 3–26). Philonenko's text does not differ markedly from the earlier edition of P. Battiffol (1889–90) for purposes of comparisons with the other portraits of Joseph in T12P, Josephus, or Philo. English translation by C. Burchard appears in Charlesworth (1985: vol. 2).

the story shows the desire to create heroes for those living under Hellenistic domination, and the "love-sickness" is central. The stock plot elements of the ancient novel are immediately apparent. It bears striking similarities to the tale of Cupid and Psyche and to Apuleius, *Metamorphoses*, especially chapter 11. The ritual of conversion in both the Greek and Roman novels involves the laying on of hands and the conveying of mysteries (16:4), the sacred meal,[37] a holy kiss, almost certainly showing the influence of non-Jewish initiatory rites. Similarities between Aseneth and the goddesses Isis and Neith have also been noted.[38] The ease of conversion for the princess Aseneth also serves to encourage female conversion and to present a model for the steps of renouncing idols and turning toward God.

Let us examine briefly some of the elements of Greek romance and how they appear in the Jewish romance of *Joseph and Aseneth*.

1 Physical beauty of heroes

Aseneth is "tall and handsome and more beautiful than all virgins" (1.4).[39] Joseph is the focalized object of Aseneth, who describes him as "the sun from Heaven, a son of God. For who among men on earth will generate such beauty and what womb of a woman will give birth to such light" (6.2).[40]

---

[37] Eating the honey is equated with the Eucharistic bread, drinking the cup of immortality, and being anointed with the ointment of incorruptibility (16:16; 19:5; see also 8:5,9; 15:5; 21:21). As Chestnutt suggests about this formulaic language, "to live faithfully as a Jew and avoid the contamination of gentile food, drink, and oil – the staples the most susceptible to gentile defilement – is to share the divine food and hence the immortality of angels in paradise (1991: 114). On the topic of bread–cup–ointment, see C. Burchard (1967: 121–33); idem. (1978: 109–17); Chestnutt (1989: 1–16).

[38] Burchard (1978: 84–96) has written about both the comparison with Apuleius and the goddesses. See also Philonenko (1968: 61–79).

[39] Although Aseneth is not called a virgin in the biblical text (Gen. 41:45), Josephus refers to her as *eti parthenon*, "still a virgin" (*JA* 11.92). As Burchard notes, her age of 18 implies that she had been fending off suitors for several years (Burchard 1978: 203, note j).

[40] In Chariton's *Chaereas and Callirhoe*, Dionysius instructs Leonas and the reader about the beauty of women: "A person not freeborn cannot be beautiful. Don't you know that the poets say beautiful people are the children of gods? All the more reason for their human parents to be nobly born" (Reardon 1989: 38). Thus, Aseneth bears the aristocratic pedigree necessary to be a beautiful romantic heroine. After her *metanoia*, conversion, she will have matching Jewish credentials. The idea that Joseph is a son of God fits perfectly with the Greek understanding of romantic hero.

2 Chaste state of the heroes

Joseph prays for Aseneth that the Lord might "bless this virgin and renew her" (8:10) because he knows that as a man of God he may not kiss a woman "who will bless with her mouth dead and dumb idols and eat from their table bread of strangulation and drink from their libation a cup of insidiousness" (8.5).[41] It is interesting to note that in spite of Joseph's refusal to kiss the pagan princess, he does place his hand on her breast, foreshadowing sexual interplay. Both characters are cut to the heart by the other; they appear doomed by the difference in their ethnic and religious station. In a mourning ritual, Aseneth laments her life in the realm of death (10:8–17) and destroys the sacrificial food and drink of her former gods (10:12ff.).

3 The romantic kiss

After her *metanoia*, conversion, to the Jewish faith, Aseneth with seven virgins for company, is ready to meet Joseph, although they have seen each other earlier in the romance, as he is the main hero in biblical accounts.[42] The human heroes are allowed to triumph by the will of the Lord God. Indeed, their triumph proves God's power to the reader. Aseneth is besieged from her tower window; this is the first meeting of the heroes. Joseph does not recognize her, so transfigured is she by her conversion. He is amazed by her beauty and asks who she is.[43]

---

[41] While much scholarly ink has been spilled on the supposition that this is a "meal formula" with ritual implications (see Burchard 1978: 211–12, note i review of the literature) for this study the question of sacramental interpretation is not relevant. The motif underscores the impossibility of an alliance with a pagan woman, and foreshadows the proper, Jewish, use of the bread and cup of wine that will transform Aseneth into an acceptable heroine. Nicklesburg (1984: 2:68, n. 187) suggests that the "imagery of food and drink has probably been developed in polarity to the food and drink of the idolatrous cult."

[42] Nicklesburg (1984: 2:69) notes that *Joseph and Aseneth* differs from other conversion stories in that it makes explicit reference to the author's own time in respect to issues of idolatry and conversion.

[43] In spite of the chastity of the two figures, it should be noted that there are several references to Aseneth's mouth (8:5; 11:2, 9, 15; 12:4f.; 13:13), again focusing upon the sexual relationship to come.

4 The wicked rivals

The son of Pharaoh, dazzled by Aseneth's beauty and jealous of Joseph's connection to her and to his father, becomes Joseph's rival. Trying to turn Joseph's brothers against him and solicit their help in his nefarious scheme, the Pharaoh's son tells them his death-dealing plan, one that will give them all power in the kingdom. He will kill his own father, and they will kill Joseph (24:13–15). "And I will take Aseneth for a wife for myself and you will be brothers to me and fellow heirs to all my wealth." The plot crumbles, and the scene becomes filled with dueling and dying men. The son fails to kill the father and is knocked unconscious by the teenaged Benjamin, riding beside Aseneth in her carriage. The sons of Leah destroy the pharaoh's men in a mighty bloodbath, "six men killed two thousand" (27:6).

5 The difficult separation and the divine rescue

Joseph and Aseneth separate, but he assures her that she will be safe because God will protect her. Indeed, one must note that unlike in the Greek novels, in the Jewish, the Lord God is made the primary male hero by the wicked brothers of Joseph, who surround Aseneth and Benjamin (27:8–9), and she prays to God who has "made me alive again[44] and rescued me from the idols and the corruption of death" (27:10). God of course does rescue the heroine in distress. The attackers' "swords fell from their hands on the ground and were reduced to ashes" (27:11).

[44] The phrase *zoopoiesas me ek tou thanatou*, also found in *JosAsen* 8:10, has particular application to the doctrine of immortality of the soul, according to Philonenko (1968: 215). Burchard (1978: 245) points out (*contra* Philonenko) that the mention of an afterlife of the soul does not by itself prove that the author of JosAsen believes in the immortality of the soul. Burchard suggests instead that it refers to an individual's afterlife in Heaven (8:9; 15:7f.; 22:13), but not to an end of the world or a last judgment (Burchard 1978: 194). Probably Christian scribes preserved the text because of Christianizing echoes in the text, such as the verb *zoopoiesas* interpreting it "to give life," as it does in NT writings, Joseph as the son of God, and Aseneth's rejection of this son of God and then her final acceptance and marriage to the son of God. See Nickelberg (1984: 2:17).

6 *The joyous resolution*

There is a hasty mopping of the plot, in which the action is so speeded up, it reminds one of a Mack Sennett comedy. In a few lines, Benjamin tries to kill the Pharaoh's son, who is dying of a thousand flesh wounds. Levi, making certain that Benjamin does not finish off the Pharaoh's son and bring bloodguilt upon himself, attempts to heal the wicked Egyptian so that "he will be our friend after this, and his father Pharaoh will be like our father" (29:4). Levi does manage to raise Pharaoh's son from the ground long enough for the errant Egyptian to set the record straight with his imperial father. On the third day, the Egyptian dies, leaving the way clear for Joseph to become the heir to the Egyptian throne.

Finally the reversals are complete. The pagan princess has become a pious Jewish bride; the wicked sons of Jacob have reconciled with Joseph and also found a new father in the Egyptian pharaoh. Thus, the ethnic schism between the Egyptians and Jews is healed, as easily as the Pharaoh's son rises from the ground and washes the blood from his face. Finally all the otherness has been removed from the story of *Joseph and Aseneth*, and the heroes are free to rule Egypt and live happily ever after.

A final indication that the story is his story is its final line: "And Joseph was like a father to Pharaoh's younger son in the land of Egypt all the days of his life." Thus, Joseph holds the power and indeed becomes the father figure to a new generation of Egyptian royals. In the last untangling of the plot and in the coda, Aseneth does not appear. Her final act in the story is to beg for mercy for the brother of Joseph and be the peacemaker.

Reducing the role of Aseneth is not surprising since in this only surviving Jewish Hellenistic novel the concern of the community is two fold: how can Joseph marry a Gentile, the Egyptian Aseneth, and what is the relation between Israel and its neighbors? These concerns lead to the major difference between this Hellenistic novel and its Greek parallels: the Jewish novel lacks the overtly erotic elements of the "dark" Greek romance, although as I have mentioned above, there are subtle hints of sexuality and certainly a mutual awareness of the extraordinary physical beauty of each of the main figures. Also missing in the Jewish romance are the dramatic adventurous plot episodes of the pirates, human sacrifices, massacres present in the work of such authors as Tatius, where the heroes are lost in storms and shipwrecks and sold into slavery (Philonenko 1968: 44). In spite of the popularity of such disasters in the Greek novels, as I have shown above, the Jewish text concentrates upon making the pagan heroine suitable for the Jewish hero. Thus, the conversion of Aseneth permits the element of romance to occur: the intrigue with the son of Pharaoh and the brothers of Joseph supply the cliff-hanger excitement.

The treatment of the "wicked woman" is different in *Joseph and Aseneth* from the other retellings under consideration. Potiphar's wife, possibly the mother of Aseneth, has no role in the novel. Nor do Josephus and Philo connect the priest of Heliodorus (Potiphera) with Potiphar as does Jewish tradition. The author of *Joseph and Aseneth* alludes to the biblical incident between the wife of Potiphar and Joseph when Joseph first sees Aseneth standing at her window. He turns from her because of the history of trouble he has had with seductive women (the function of the wicked foreign woman has been broadened [sic] to encompass all wicked foreign women after our hero).

As I mentioned above, there are many parallels between Apuleius' *Metamorphoses*, a Hellenistic romance in which the honorable young hero is frequently "suffering" temptation by wicked women. The conversion of Aseneth can also be compared with the conversion of Lucius (to the cult of Isis) in chapter 11 of *Metamorphoses*. Conversion represents the end of the other, of strangeness; Aseneth becomes self/Jewish/acceptable. In the second part of the nouvella, Aseneth's Jewishness is demonstrated through her relationship with her brother-in-law Levi.

Aseneth loved Levi exceedingly beyond all of Joseph's brothers because he was one who attached himself to the Lord, and he was a prudent man and a prophet of the Most High and sharp-sighted with his eyes, and he used to see letters written in heaven by the finger of God and he knew the unspeakable [mysteries] of the Most High God and revealed them to Aseneth in secret, because he himself, Levi, would love Aseneth very much and see her place of rest in the highest and her walls like adamantine eternal walls, and her foundations founded upon a rock of the seventh heaven. (22:13)

What better proof to a skeptical reader that Aseneth's conversion has not only been complete, but also fully justified than her alliance with the pious Levi. Seen as a City of Refuge in the sharp-sighted eyes of Levi, who can even see the letters written by the finger of God, Aseneth has passed the highest test. The struggle against the other complete, she and Joseph can be joined, self to self. Aseneth's prayer, so similar to that of Joseph in *Testament of Joseph*, underscores the transformation of the other into self. Aseneth's pattern of prayer and fasting is a repetition of Joseph's in *Testament of Joseph* (although it is not clear that the author of *Joseph and Aseneth* knew *Testament of Joseph*). He certainly had the model of Joseph whose *sophrosyne* protected him from the evil other. So with Aseneth prayer and fasting provide the character of protection against the evil pagan suitors who try to enter her castle. Once she has proved worthy of Joseph, however, the focus of the novel shifts from Aseneth to a story of rivalry and jealousy among males.

The second part of the romance focuses on Joseph's seemingly impossible task: achieving imperial power in a foreign, Egyptian, realm. Unlike the readers of the Greek romances, the readers of *Joseph and Aseneth* are deprived of a scene of romance and resolution between the male and female figures. Instead, the audience, living under the domination of foreign rulers, is given another kind of delight: that of a Jewish underdog ruling over an Egyptian kingdom. But something is lost, the voice of Aseneth becomes pious, then silent. Neither she nor the reader is overcome with *jouissance*. Even in a romance bearing the name of the female literary figure, her story is fragmented, and subordinated to the story of the male.

JOSEPH'S VERSION: [EM]BEDDING THE WOMAN

In analyzing the narratological aspects of *TJos*, the effect of voice becomes primary. The device of first-person narration permits the character of Joseph to filter the events of the story through his own point of view. Presented with apparent objectivity, the story bristles with slanted conclusions. Viewed from a structuralist approach, one can see the male story as the opposite of the embedded female story. Since the *TJos* account presents Joseph as the subject and

Mut-em-enet the object, the intention of the story as told by Joseph is to resist the object. For if the righteous man is continuously able to reject the wicked woman, the center will hold. Paternal authority will continue to triumph over unrepressed female sexuality. If the story's subject and object were reversed, the intention would also be upended. The intention of the proposed female story would be the eradication of the resistance. The story, admittedly a different one, would allow the subject and object to fall in love, the obstacles to that love to be removed, and a happily ever after ending. That is the structure of the biblical story of Abigail and David told in 1 Samuel 25, where the husband conveniently dies, leaving Abigail a widow.[45] It is the romance of *Joseph and Aseneth,* where the improper love object becomes a Jewish paragon.[46]

A glance at a few of Joseph's statements in *TJos* will illustrate how they prejudice the reader.

(1) she pretended to regard me as a son (3:7)
(2) she drew me into impurity (3:8)
(3) she came to me under the pretense of instruction (4:4)
(4) she sent me food mingled with witchcraft (6:1)[47]
(5) her officiousness was to lead astray the soul (6:2)
(6) in her madness she was holding fast to my clothes (8:3)

When each of her actions is focalized through Joseph's fear, it becomes an action cloaked in menace. Joseph says she "came to me under the pretense of instruction," but what evidence is there to support such a charge? When Aseneth, another Egyptian woman in a similar situation, decides to convert in order to be a suitable wife for Joseph, no hint of duplicity accompanies the lengthy

---

[45] David is a biblical hero much attracted to women, unlike Joseph. The only woman who does not excite David is Michal, the one given by her father in the traditional manner. Unlike Joseph, David prefers women who belong to other men. Indeed, the future king is anxious to be linked with his paramours. Thus, the husband of Bathsheba is also dispatched so that the subject can have a clear field to pursue his love object. One wonders how David's story would sound in the mouth of *ho sophron.*

[46] For a comparison of Mut-em-enet with these two heroines of Jewish tradition, see below.

[47] The idea of love-philtres and other dangerous magic through which women try to seduce helpless men reflects male fear of female feeding turned into death-dealing. The parade example of this proof of female treachery in the Bible is Jael's offering of milk to Sisera before nailing him. For a description of the thematic elements that structure this scene, see Bal (1987b: 62–64). For an analysis of *pharmakon* within the discourse of love magic in Euripides' *Hippolytus,* see Goff (1990: 48–54).

on of her prayer, fasting, and conversion. In my view
's conversion is valid and Mut-em-enet's a ruse because
h is a suitable desexualized bride and Mut-em-enet is an
per woman, ignoring societal strictures, reaching for erotic
freeoom.

There are twelve brief episodes in Joseph's testamentary
account that play "time after time" on the motif of Joseph as the
victim of passion.[48]

(1) she punishes and threatens Joseph many times (3:1–6)
(2) she pretends to regard Joseph as a son (3:7)
(3) she draws him "openly into impurity" (3:8)
(4) she flatters Joseph (4:1–3)
(5) she pretends to want to convert to his religion (4:4–5)
(6) she offers to kill her husband to marry Joseph (5:1–4)
(7) she sends Joseph magical food (6:1)
(8) she falls ill and threatens suicide (7:1–5)
(9) she tries to force Joseph into a sexual act (8:2–5)
(10) she accuses him and he is sent to prison
(11) she offers to get him released if he will satisfy her (9:1–4)
(12) she falls ill but continues to visit Joseph in prison

Each episode begins with an action of the woman followed by a
reaction from Joseph. Clearly she is the initiator each time. The
final two verses of the story (9:4–5) remind the reader of Joseph's
remarkable achievement, resisting a woman who has tried every
conceivable avenue of seduction.

How often, though she was ill,
did she come down to me by midnight
and listened to my voice as I prayed.
And understanding her groanings[49] I held my peace.

[48] I follow, with a few minor changes, the structure suggested by Hollander and De Jonge (1985). It is interesting to note that the structure as given by these interpreters emphasizes a reading from Joseph's point of view. They divide the story into ten episodes, whereas my structure has twelve episodes.

[49] Groanings or sighings is used three times in Joseph's story: T Jos 7:2, 8:5, 9:4. The Greek word *stenagmos* does not necessarily imply sexual sounds, e.g., in the LXX of Ps. 38(37):9, a similar spiritual pain is indicated: *apo stenagmou tes kardias mou*, "the sighing of my heart." While the context of T Jos 7:2, 8:5, 9:4 might indicate sexual groanings, since emotions connected to sexuality are the only ones attributed to the Egyptian woman, the term could indicate a woman profoundly sick at heart.

> For when I was in her house,
> she used to bare her arms and breasts and legs,
> that I would meet her;
> for she was very beautiful
> splendidly adorned in order to beguile me.
> And the Lord guarded me from her attempts.

The portrait of the woman is consistent. The "time after time" motif of her villainy continues and parallels the "time after time" of his righteousness. Ill and out of control with her obsessive love, Mut-em-enet continues to visit Joseph in his prison. The "groanings" reflect the depth of her pain, sounds that might emanate from a woman lamenting the impossibility of her desire. The narrator hears a malevolent sound, urgent, sexual, which he connects with her nakedness.

Even though Joseph has previously described the groanings as sounds of lost purity, threatening to pollute him, he surrenders for an instant to sexual fantasy. Finally, late into the story, there is confirmation of the woman's beauty. The beauty of the hero has been mentioned at the outset. It is of course his beauty that has first aroused Mut-em-enet. Nowhere in the biblical account or in the expanded accounts is the reader provided with a physical description of the woman. For just a flicker of an instant in Joseph's narration, the curtain of purity is parted and the focalization shifts. The reader sees what Joseph saw: bare arms and breasts and legs, very beautiful, splendidly adorned (9:4). Immediately after presenting this erotic picture, Joseph interprets the woman's body as alien "splendidly adorned, in order to beguile me." Joseph returns to his "understanding" her groanings as sexual, and therefore of evil design. Finally, he cools the heated sensual description of her with a pious reference to God, who "guarded me from her attempts."

In a twist of ironic sexual politics, her sexual/spiritual malaise is bared to an indifferent Joseph; the sympathy she offered the naked man is withheld from her. He undermines the power of her text by not taking it seriously, by displaying indifference to what she has said. When Mut-em-enet saw Joseph naked and powerless, being beaten by a eunuch of the court, instead of turning away from him, she tried to rescue him from his pursuers. Our story exhibits a motif similar to that of 1 Sam. 25, where the woman rescues the younger man beloved of the God of Israel. Mut-em-enet exhibits a devotion to Joseph as strong as that which Abigail had shown to the young David. Each woman attempts to place herself into the public confrontation between the powerful husband and the desperate young hero. Yet the narratorial voice renders opposite judgments on the two women: Abigail is the good wife from Proverbs and the wife of Potiphar is the strange woman. The plot reflects this judgment in the behavior of the two female figures after their encounter with the hero: Abigail returns home and waits for David to act (proper behavior); Mut-em-enet pursues the hero with clear sexual intention (improper behavior). After the iconoclastic moment in the biblical story sexual hierarchy has been reinstated; in *TJos* the female figure perseveres in her attempt to challenge that hierarchy.

A pattern emerges through *TJos* 3–9, in which each mention of the woman's disruptive sexual action is balanced and defused by an admirable reaction from *ho sophron*. The talisman quality of *sophrosyne* that cools the passion of the Egyptian woman is mentioned in 6:7 and 9:2. The reader is not permitted to lose sight of the parenetic/salvific frame: "The wickedness of the ungodly has no power over those who worship God in righteousness (*sophrosyne*)" (6:7). The character of Joseph projects the attitude of a man in distress, who prays, fasts, and weeps, in his extensive request to God for deliverance. Thus, the framed prayer of thanksgiving in *TJos* 1 prefigures Joseph's "time after time" prayers throughout his story.

His most frequent action is to pray for deliverance:

(1) going into my room, I prayed to the Lord (3:3)
(2) I lay upon the ground in sackcloth and prayed and begged God that the Lord would deliver me from the Egyptian woman (4:3)
(3) I gave myself more to fasting and prayer, that God might deliver me from her (4:8)
(4) I prayed to the Lord (7:4)
(5) I knelt before the Lord all day together with all the night; and about dawn I rose up, weeping the while and prayed for a release from the Egyptian woman (8:1)
(6) [she listened to] my voice as I prayed (9:4)

Joseph reminds the reader three times that he fasted, "for God loves him who fasts with chastity (*sophrosyne*) in a den of darkness more than him who lives luxuriously in licentiousness (*akolasias*) in chambers of a palace."

(1) And I fasted (*enesteuon*) in those seven years (3:4)
(2) I drank no wine, nor for three days did I take my food (3:5)
(3) And I gave myself even more to fasting (*nesteian*) (4:8)

He tells us four times that he wept.

(1) I wept (*eklaion*) for the Egyptian woman of Memphis (3:6)
(2) I sorrowed (*elupethen*) unto death.
    and I lamented (*epenthesa*) for her (3:9)
(3) when he had gone out, I wept (*eklaion*) (6:3)
(4) about dawn, I got up, weeping (*dakruon*) all the time (8:1)

The biblical Joseph, who bragged of his superiority in Genesis 37, has undergone no change in personality. In this later version, speaking as an old man, the character is still bragging, this time of his spiritual superiority. The parenesis is clear: every heated female evil intention is met with cool male virtue.

In my view, the structure which appears to support the story of Joseph's beleaguered years in the house of Potiphar also presents a portrait of a woman in love. It is the narratorial frame that polarizes the action, setting up an evil/good dichotomy and prescribing the reader's conclusions of the dangers of uncontrolled female sexuality. This frame functions similarly to the frame in Genesis 39, discussed in chapter 3, as a hermeneutic device to guide the reader's understanding of the text.

MUT-EM-ENET'S VERSION

The distance between the respective psychological landscapes of the chaste male and the lusty female is reflected in the structure of *TJos*. The fear of the male, threatened by the manipulative female, drives his story. In spite of the strategy of first-person narration in which the character Joseph prescribes the reading of his story, seeking out the embedded story allows glimmers of the woman's story to come through the fabula. The male/female dichotomy and its resultant tensions structure the work. Joseph's fear and shame stand as the obstacle between her desire and satisfaction.

The gaps in the biblical version are filled from the outset of the version in *TJos*. As I noted earlier, it is Mut-em-enet who rescues Joseph from the Ishmaelite merchant. In Joseph's account, she continues to be his protector.

> And he [the eunuch] commanded me to be beaten naked.
> But the Memphian woman was looking through the window
> while I was being beaten,
> and she sent to her husband, saying
> Your judgment is unjust, for you punish a free man
> who has been stolen as if he were a transgressor. (*TJos* 14:1)

While Joseph reports her initial kindness to him to contrast it with her eventual perfidy, we can extract pieces of her story even from Joseph's biased account. As Joseph recalls the events from the time of his arrival in Egypt as a slave to his entrance into Pentephres' house, the reader is told of Mut-em-enet's gradual invasion of Joseph's world: first the male enclave of the marketplace, then, the intimate world of his body.

Her persistence structures the second half of *TJos*, much as it did the first. Her attraction to Joseph is no momentary whim. Mut-em-enet's sexual desire is the engine that turns the action. She urges her husband to buy the slave and free him. All the while the merchant is being tried by Pentephres for stealing the slave, and Joseph is being beaten, the woman continues to press for Joseph's release. After the trial, she continues to try to possess Joseph. When she is told by a double-dealing eunuch that the merchants are demanding too large a price for the boy (16:3), she sends a second eunuch to bargain for the young man:

> Even if they demand two *minae*[50] of gold
> take care not to spare gold,
> only buy the boy and bring him.
>
> (*TJos* 16:4)

The pattern has been set: the woman's tenacity is emphasized even before she has spoken a word to Joseph. According to *TJos*, her obsession began when she saw him in the market and

---

[50] A monetary unit, equivalent to 100 drachmas, from the Hebrew *maneh*.

intensified when she saw him naked.[51] The biblical text says only that the woman saw Joseph (39:7), but does not provide such rich detail. Neither the narrator Joseph nor subsequent exegetes comment on the woman's having seen Joseph naked. There are rabbinic and modern speculations about Joseph having fled naked from the bedchamber of the wife of Potiphar in the biblical account since the woman is left holding his garment (*bigdo*) (Gen. 39:12). In *TJos*, however, Joseph defends himself and assures the reader, "not even in my mind did I yield to her" (9:2). Kugel rightly observes that narrative depiction of Joseph as wavering at sexual temptation presents "a Joseph of flesh and blood with whom others can identify and whose example of sudden repentance others might seek to emulate" (Kugel 1990: 98). No commentator, including Kugel, suggests that the sexual attraction may be mutual and indeed the woman may have been given to believe that her feelings for the Hebrew servant were returned. The assurance in *TJos* that "not even in my mind did I yield to her," may have been added by an author anxious to avoid his own fantasies about what happened between Joseph and Mut-em-enet.

In the order of the text, the woman's attention had been drawn to Joseph when she saw him in the marketplace, and her passion was intensified when she saw him naked. The sexual connection had been made before the mistress/servant connection. Not only had she heard about the young man from the eunuchs (12:1), but she has defended him to her husband, identifying the Hebrew as one who possesses grace from Heaven (12:3). Whether the eunuchs have told her that he is a blessed Hebrew or whether she simply

---

[51] Rabbinic tradition is filled with speculation about whether Joseph participated in sexual activity with his master's wife. The speculation comes from the expression *la'soth mela'ctho* (Gen. 39:11), which the rabbis interpret "to satisfy sexual desire." *Bereshit Rabbah* 87.6 insists that Joseph declined her invitation, since he knew that to lie with the woman in this world would assure him of lying next to her in the Gehenna of the world to come. R. Samuel b. Nahman argued that Joseph intended to "do his work," have sex with the woman, but became impotent. Rabbi Isaac pushed the image of Joseph "doing his work" even further, claiming that "his seed was scattered and spilled out onto the ground through his fingernails" (87.7). This onanistic metaphor is an interesting echo of the sexual difficulties of Tamar, another foreign woman who seduces one of Jacob's sons. In both instances, spilling the seed is the man's reaction to undesirable sexual intercourse initiated by the woman. *Sotah* 36b of the Babylonian Talmud argues both sides: (1) Joseph was blameless (2) the two of them [Joseph and the wife of Potiphar] had planned to sin together.

intuits his special relation to the deity must be determined by the reader. But this familiar literary motif of the woman seeing a young man and recognizing him as special to the deity is found in *Joseph and Aseneth* and 1 Sam. 25.[52]

Upon first seeing Joseph from her window, Aseneth realizes that he is the sun from heaven.

Aseneth saw Joseph on his chariot and was strongly cut [to the heart] and her soul was crushed and her knees were paralyzed, and her entire body trembled, and it was if she has been struck with lightning. She feared a great fear. She sighed and said in her heart:

> What shall I now do, wretched that I am
> Did I not speak saying that Joseph is coming,
> the shepherd's son from the land of Canaan?
> And now behold the sun from Heaven has come to us
> on his chariot and entered our house today
> and shines in it like a light upon the earth.

(JosAsen 6:1–2)

As with Mut-em-enet seeing Joseph, the sight of the beloved produces a powerful reaction in Aseneth. Of course, being a marriageable virgin, Aseneth can say, "Let my father give me to Joseph for a maidservant and slave and I will serve him for ever" (6:8). Mut-em-enet can cajole her husband into purchasing Joseph, but she can not overcome the obstacle of her husband. Abigail, upon first meeting the young outlaw David on a mountain pass, recognizes that he is "fighting the battles of the Lord" (I Sam. 25:28)

When Abigail saw David, she hurried and got down from the donkey, and fell before David on her face and bowed to the ground. She fell at his feet and said, "Upon me alone, my lord, be the guilt; pray let your handmaid speak in your ears and hear the words of your handmaid."
(1 Sam. 25:23–24)

Abigail shares with Mut-em-enet the impediment of a husband blocking the fulfillment of her desire for the beloved.[53] After her meeting with David, she leaves him with a petition, "And when the

---

[52] The motif of the unexpected confrontation between the lover (female) and the beloved (male) is frequently found in ancient romances, e.g., Apuleius 5.22–6.5, Chariton 4.1.9. For other examples, see Burchard, *Joseph and Aseneth* in Charlesworth (1985: 25, n. 6c).

[53] My literary analysis of the story of Abigail appears in "The Pleasure of Her Text," in Bach (1990: 25–44).

Lord has dealt well with my lord, then remember your servant" (verse 31). But unlike Mut-em-enet, Abigail is aided by circumstance or (by those reading through the theological code), by unseen but anticipated divine stage-managing. Her husband dies almost immediately after she has seen her beloved.

As I have noted earlier, one of the literary strategies of suppressing the woman's story is to isolate her within the text. In the biblical version and Second Temple expansions of the story of Mut-em-enet, there are no other women to reflect or respond to her experience. There is no confidant or "helper" figure, similar to the stock character of the Nurse found in the Greek version *Hippolytus*. Beginning with *Midrash Tanhuma*, a medieval midrashic collection, a new tradition is added to the narrative spun from Genesis 39. In this tradition, the story encompasses new characters: the women of the Court. At first these Egyptian women were scandalized by the besotted wife of Potiphar. But during a party she arranges to show off her Hebrew servant:

> she took citrons and gave them to each of the women and gave each a knife and then called to Joseph and stood him before them. When they beheld how handsome Joseph was, they cut their hands. She said to them: "If you do this after one moment, I who see him at every moment, am I not all the more so [justified] in being smitten?" (*Midrash Tanhuma Gen 39:7*)[54]

The tradition continues in *Midrash ha-Gadol* and in Surah XII of the Qu'ran. The same basic theme, that other women have the same reaction as the wife of Potiphar to the beauty of Joseph, is found in the work of later Muslim poets and exegetes as well as the medieval Jewish collections of midrash, Chronicles of Yerahme'el, assembled in the late thirteenth or early fourteenth century, and *Sefer ha-Yashar*, an Italian work no earlier than the thirteenth century.[55] When the narrative is focalized through the collective view of the women, a new dimension is added to the story.

> When they saw him, they praised him, and they cut their hands. They said, "God protect us. This no mortal, this is none other than a noble angel." (Surah XII.31)

---

[54] As translated in Kugel (1990: 29). I was unable to find this episode in Buber (1989).
[55] For an extensive, detailed discussion of the medieval development of the theme he refers to as "The Assembly of Ladies," see Kugel (1990: chap. 2).

The blame that had been heaped upon the wife of Potiphar for her foolish behavior is forgotten, and the women's emotions become a mirror of Mut-em-enet's reactions. The Egyptian women of the Court are as captivated by Joseph's beauty as was Mut-em-enet. She is no longer isolated, the woman who behaves improperly. The astonishment of the other women at the sight of Joseph assures the reader that Mut-em-enet has behaved just like a woman.

The episode in these later versions remains under narratorial control, and thus imparts the traditional view that all women are equally treacherous when led by their passions. But the isolation surrounding the female figure in the earlier versions, the isolation that makes her response to Joseph appear unique and her love obsessive and strange, is altered by the scene in which other women confirm her response as universal. Comparing this *mise en abyme*[56] text embedded within the larger narrative with the biblical version in which there are no women to reflect Mut-em-enet's action and feelings will allow us to fill some of the silence surrounding the solitary female figure in the biblical version.

The prefiguring effect of the *mise en abyme* text is maintained in *Midrash Tanhuma* because the reader is already familiar with the primary conflict between the lovestruck Mut-em-enet and the beautiful young Joseph. The reaction of the women, who inflict pain upon themselves with the blades of their fruit knives after beholding Joseph, foreshadows the bloody outcome of Mut-em-enet's having first seen Joseph. In narratological terms, the subtext, or embedded fabula, found in *Tanhuma*, is a sign of the primary fabula, our root story of Mut-em-enet and Joseph.[57] When the character of Mut-em-enet says in the *Tanhuma* to her friends, "If you do this after one moment, I who see him at every moment, am I not all the more so [justified] in being smitten?" she is attempting to align herself with her friends, to normalize her obsession. As Bal

---

[56] A *mise en abyme* text is an embedded text that presents a story which resembles the primary fabula and may be taken to be a sign of the primary fabula. For a description of this mirror-text and the ways in which it may be related to, or reflected back on, the primary fabula, see Bal (1985: 144–50).

[57] Bal has analyzed Mann's use of this tradition in which she observes, "Mut-em-enet planned this event with the explicit purpose of making herself understood. She wants her friends to understand her love at the very same moment they know it; the difference is identification" (Bal 1987: 70).

has observed about this incident as it appears in Mann's novel *Joseph in Egypt*, "she [Mut-em-enet] planned this event with the explicit purpose of making herself understood" (Bal 1987b: 70). I would add to that observation that Mut-em-enet hoped through the power of a community of women to deflect disapproval and judgment from herself.

Another aspect of the woman's story that is suppressed in the biblical version is what happens to her after Joseph is sent to prison. The reader is told nothing of the wife of Potiphar after the episode in which her husband, responding to her accusation, puts Joseph into prison. Eliminating an account of her reaction indicates that the woman's emotions are not central to the story. The narrative in *TJos*, then, is important to the task of recovering the woman's story as it indicates Mut-em-enet's love was not extinguished by the satisfaction of revenge. Indeed, her desire to free Joseph from prison is so intense, one might conclude that some other person had been responsible for his incarceration.

This gap of information, this lack of what happened after the momentous scene of accusation, must have been an irritant to the early readers. For what happened is clearly delineated in the narrative of *TJos*. In this version the narration continues beyond the ending of the biblical version. Instead of leaving the story with Joseph in prison, with the character of the woman erased from the subsequent narrative, the story has been extended in time. Indeed the "time after time" motif of the woman's sexual obsession with the young hero follows him into the recesses of the prison. As we observed earlier, the *sophrosyne* of the character of Joseph was based upon his ability to deflect the sexual advances of the Egyptian woman. That he is locked inside the prison is the external factor blocking her satisfaction. But the permanent block to her satisfaction is his loyalty to the deity and the patriarchal order. It is a version of "Freud's Masterplot," to use Peter's Brooks' term (280–300): an urgent sexual desire faces the factors that block satisfaction until finally love and death join together in the climactic thrust of a symbolic *Liebestod*. The death in our story is the literary death of the female figure, whose subject position is precarious. Her story will be formulated only by a sympathetic reader.

SPEAKING FOR THE WOMEN

As I have argued, the Hellenistic society that would have been reading both the *Testaments* and *Joseph and Aseneth* considered itself most seriously threatened by Eros. That fear of female sexuality had its roots in ancient Near Eastern law codes, which reflect the male suspicion of the dangerous power that a woman might exert inside her house. "If a man seizes a woman in the woman's house, it is the woman's crime and the woman shall be killed" (*ANET* 196). A similar distinction is made in Deuteronomy 22, in which a woman seized inside the city must scream in order to be exonerated. These texts reflect an ancient connection between the woman's ability to control any situation occurring within "her" boundaries and the male fearing himself powerless within her mysterious domain. Male fear is displaced onto Mut-em-enet and resolved in a reassuring manner in the character of the Egyptian princess who converts to Judaism in order to please her beloved. After Aseneth becomes the wife of Joseph, she is rewarded for her piety by the metonymic appellation "City of Refuge, because in you many nations will take refuge with the Lord God, and under your wings many people trusting in God will be sheltered." (*JosAsen* 15:7). After assuring the male that she is a refuge not a deluge, the virginal princess gets the Jewish prince. Pious and devout, having experienced an angelic visitation assuring her of divine approval for her agenda, to be the perfect wife to the patriarchal hero, Aseneth's story need not be suppressed. For her piety, her prayer and fasting, are signs that she is as committed to protecting Jewish tradition as is her hero husband.

The feminist reader, refusing to align herself with the narratorial "we," risks being consigned to ranks of the disloyal and the unfaithful. The story of Mut-em-enet reflects the fate of such a woman: the narrator underscores the uncertainty of her position through the tepid response of her husband. In my view both the universal story and its expansions reflect a desire to enclose women's uncertainty in an image of woman as only the specular reflection of man, thus serving to perpetuate the system in which all that is visible is masculine (Irigaray 1977: 203–17). By giving voice to the suppressed or imagined story of the woman, silenced in both his biblical and postbiblical stories, the reader is protected from being seduced into the writer's world, where women are defined solely in relation to men, that is, by their sexual identity. The embedded woman appears when the reader resists the writer's view that Mut-em-enet behaves "just like a woman."

CHAPTER 5

Signs of her flesh

Or is it that having started with the idea of difference, feminism will be able to break free of its belief in Woman, her power, her writing, so as to channel this demand for difference into each and every element of the female whole and finally, to bring out the singularity of each woman, and beyond this, her multiplicities, her plural languages, beyond the horizon, beyond sight, beyond faith itself.

Julia Kristeva, "Women's Time"

It is worth remembering that biblical narratives are written by men with an ideal audience of men. How does this observation color interpretations? First, there is the idealization of the female object within the social category variously described as wicked woman, sexual object, babe. Even though these are not "real women," the imaginary literary figures possess interpellated bodies, that is, not only does the author imply that these are beautiful women, but the reader accepts such a representation. The widespread assumption is that each of these watched women is worth watching.[1] Second, the narratives are structured in frames: on the level of story the gaze of the male characters directs the narrative, making women objects

---

[1] The term *interpellate* as Althusser has described such a process, involves a social representation which is accepted and absorbed by an individual as her/his own representation, and therefore becomes real, even though it is actually imaginary. A lucid critique of this phenomenon, too often at the root of a reader's interpreting the *legitimate* meanings of a text is made by Modleski, who argues that rather than hypothesizing women readers, one should appeal directly to the experience of real women readers. Feminist readers will keep in mind what they know: that essentializing all female literary figures who are the object of the male gaze as beautiful babes is the major route through which the traumas of gender get inscribed not just in literature, but also in reality. See articles by Modleski, O'Neale, and Russo in de Lauretis 1986. Also on the relation between rhetoric and violence, whether they assume the social "fact" of gender (Foucault) or deny it (Derrida), see the important work of de Lauretis (1987), esp. 33–50.

of their gaze, and on the level of the fabula the powerful male gaze is represented in the look of the author, ideal audience, and traditional interpreter: men looking, telling, explaining. Men call the shots. One must also acknowledge that women today have possibilities for sexual subjectivity and self-creation that did not exist in the past. Except for brief moments of female focalization in biblical narratives, however, the gaze is owned by male characters, authors, and spectators.[2] Indeed this perspective seems natural and unchangeable. The male gaze is assumed.

It is usual for a biblical narrative text to provide the reader with a partial picture of each character, male or female. Following the powerful interpretive gaze of the biblical narrator, traditional interpreters have accepted the biblical narrative conventions that view character as a device to present idealized models of good or bad behavior. For example, in Sternberg's schema the entire personality of marginal characters such as Nabal and Abigail gets telescoped into a single tag line: churl and paragon.[3] Resorting to a description of stock characters robs the story of chiaroscuro and the characters of nuanced interlaced readings. In analyzing the Davidic narrative, critics have inflated this fragmentation of character by defining women as foils for David's development.[4]

[2] I use the term focalization as Bal has defined it, that is, a fine-tuning of the narratologic term point of view. The focalizer is the one who sees within a fabula, and may or may not be the same as the narratorial view. Bal further demonstrates that a focalizer may *see* or understand something unseen by other characters, for example Uriah not seeing what David has in mind in their dialogue. For further discussion, see Bal (1985); Bal (1988a) pp. 122,125, 153,249 et passim; Bal (1991), chap. 4. Also chapter 2, this study. The reader needs to be conscious of reading "with" the focalizer, through his/her eyes, or reading outside the fabula, from an external position.

[3] Sternberg (1985: 325–28). Sternberg sees a primary function of the narrator in using the device of stock characters to *encourage* a reading through the dichotomous moral code, to reach the only "moral" conclusion. Sternberg argues that the reason for such verbal shorthand is to discourage further inquiry into makeup and motivation. He understands omitted features in the narrative to function as "blanks" to remain empty rather than as gaps to be filled by the reader. I read as a gap-filler, accepting that Nabal is by his very name to be thought of as a churl, but taking the narrative power from the narrator to fill in the gaps within the text by comparing Nabal's behavior with that of his wife, or his servants, or with the outlaw David.

[4] It has been quite de rigueur to consider Michal the wife who brings the political connections, Abigail the wife who brings the land and wealth from Judah, and Bathsheba the wife of pleasure and sin. I am not refuting this interpretation, but arguing that basing one's interpretation upon such a unifying analysis deprives the female characters of individual portraits. See Berlin (1983) particularly pp. 23–43; Levenson (1978); McCarter (1984), as well as Alter (1981) and Sternberg (1985).

Saturated with patriarchal needs and desires, interpreters have failed to construct a subject position for Abigail, Michal, and Bathsheba. Satisfied with viewing them as wives, such readers have bound female figures by their gender to the overpowering portrait of their husband David. Such a monolithic system of interpretation has presented feminist readers with a challenge to explore the cracks and fissures of the analytic apparatus in an attempt to rescue female characters from the silence and rigidity of stock roles. As I hope this study demonstrates, a reading that lingers over the collisions and conflicts between characters enhances the reader's pleasure in the text and allows female characters to become subjects, rather than objects, of the reader's gaze.

Reading from the deep-rootedness of the patriarchal unconscious, one presents a literary picture of the objectification of a woman's body as total; she is seen from a masculine subject position as an object to be desired, pursued, controlled. These stereotypes of the feminine, from virgin to whore, are defined in terms of the woman's sexuality. But in each of the stories in this study, the female literary figure experiences a moment of focalization, a moment in which she refuses to blink. After being established as objects of the male narrator's gaze, Mut-em-enet, Bathsheba, Esther, Judith, and Salomé enter into the game. The apparatus of looks converging on the female figure integrates the gaze (male voyeurism) into the conventions of storytelling. On a narratologic level, the female figure's focalizing moment functions as a moment in which power is seized (as well as seen). Mut-em-enet "sees" as she seizes Joseph's warm garment in her hand (see chapter 3); Bathsheba perhaps when she sends a message to David "I am pregnant." Esther and Salomé both respond to the same offer "up to half my kingdom." Confirming their suspicion of sexual power, Delilah gazes upon Samson sleeping on her lap, his hair spread out around him. In the language of film theory, the woman is framed by the "look" of the camera as an icon, an image, that is, "made to be looked at by the spectators as well as the male characters" (de Lauretis 1987: 99).

On a theoretical level, the woman is usually framed: by the male gaze, the scopic drive and desire. In spite of the fact that the characters have been produced by and for the male gaze, there is a reading which permits the female figure to become a mediator between the traditional gaze and the restive spectator. If one makes this strategic move, the courage of the female figures comes not so much from killing the enemy as from returning the gaze, or from acknowledging themselves as sexual objects. Clearly Esther, Judith, Salomé, and Delilah desire to be desired. It is this refusal to drop their eyes that engenders fear in the hearts of men, who are accustomed to owning and directing the gaze. Two further elements enter in: to begin with, men do not simply look; their gaze carries with it the power of action and of possession that is lacking in the female gaze. Women receive and return a gaze, but cannot act on it. Vashti is a prime example of a woman trying to deflect a male gaze. According to the doxic account, when she tries to act, and refuses to display herself for Ahasuerus, her husband, and the men of the Court at a wild bacchanalian affair, they respond out of fear: she is banished from the Court. Since she refused to be the object of the male gaze, the men refused to gaze at her again. After a moment of sublime literary anarchy, Vashti disappears from the narrative. Since no one is looking at her, she cannot return the gaze. She is out of the game (see chapter 6).[5]

Another object of the gaze is Susanna, who is caught in the voyeuristic gaze of the Elders. She cannot escape their gaze, nor can she return it. Unlike Vashti, Susanna does not attempt to deflect the gaze. Naked and powerless in front of her enemies, she needs to be rescued, re-covered, by the young Daniel (see chapter 3). As Bal has shown, the visual interpretation of Susanna's story allows the spectator to understand the display of the female body as commodity, chiefly because the story thematizes the position of the viewer. The female body is the object of what Bal terms indiscreet looking, not so much because it is what the viewer *wants* to look at as

---

[5] While a number of interpreters have observed that Vashti acts as a foil for Esther, one area of their dichotomized behavior has not been sufficiently examined. Vashti is banished from Court because she refuses to display herself for the King. Esther, more adroit than her predecessor at returning the gaze, appears not to have refused the king. At the end of the narrative, she is still performing as Queen. In fact it is her ability to perform and entrance that eventually ends in the death of her enemy Haman and the victory of the Jewish people. For a full discussion of the Esther story, see chapter 6.

because the female body presents the most convincing case for peeping (1991: 161–63). Bal's lucid, extended analysis in *Reading "Rembrandt"* presented a workable paradigm for a kind of seeing that interrupts the overwhelmingly masculine discourse that had driven the majority of biblical-literary readings. Of foremost importance is the lucid manner in which Bal demonstrates the profound consequence of male visual mastery of women, which points to a culture long accustomed to male consumption of women's images, implying a fundamental difference between the ways men and women are interpellated to view one another. Art theorist John Berger captures this gendering of the gaze in his observation, "Men look at women. Women watch themselves being looked at" (46).[6] By casting a cold eye at traditional interpretation, through a combination of feminist literary and visual reading strategies, a reader can freeze-frame the gaze and the object of the gaze. Such a move emphasizes the difference between David's most looked-at wife Bathsheba and the women who desire to be desired. By focusing upon David as the one who controls the gaze, then, Bathsheba can be rehabilitated from the end-of-the-road category of seductress.

SITING BATHSHEBA

Why did it take me so long to shake off the weight of nongendered biblical literary interpretations? First was the necessity of developing new sight lines, borrowing from feminist theory, film theory, and narratology. But equally important has been the insights of cultural studies that have made biblical interpretation and its attendant ideologies a central and essential topic of study. In my search for a narrative space where the female gaze is neither patriarchally feminized nor masculined, I went back to the beginning of recent biblical literary endeavors. Adele Berlin separates the figure of Bathsheba, as an object of adultery in 2

---

[6] The feminized gaze of women functions as the unprivileged term in the masculine–feminine scopic binary because its very existence depends upon the prior discourse of the masculine gaze. See film and literary theorists de Lauretis, Mulvey, Kaplan, Rose, and others who have contested the overwhelming cultural representation of the gaze as an exclusively masculine subject position.

Samuel 11–12, from the active mother Bathsheba attempting to secure the throne for Solomon, her son, in 1 Kings 1–2. While Berlin uses the flattening structuralist term "actant" for the earlier portrait, she uses vivifying categories more akin to the paradigm of traits model suggested by Chatman for Bathsheba the Queen Mother, "with feelings and reactions developed beyond the needs of the plot" (Chatman 1978: 30).[7] Upon first analyzing the Bathsheba and David episodes, I followed Berlin, acknowledging that Bathsheba was a multivalent character in I Kings 2. After comparing the more powerful Bathsheba with other biblical female literary figures, it became clear to me that the second Bathsheba switches roles, is given the power of speech, but possesses no more authority than she did as object of David's desire. She must depend on the prophet Nathan to authorize her son as successor to David. In both episodes Bathsheba remains an unwitting figure in the patriarchal scopic economy in which she is exchanged from one male to another. In such an economic structure, desire and beauty are the keys to inflation; the woman as object of desire is the coin of the realm.

Joel Rosenberg's analysis of the Succession Narrative in *The Literary Guide to the Bible* is an example of careful biblical interpretative scholarship as a male enterprise. Rosenberg attends to the interlacing of the power politics and dynastic building encoded within the narrative. He includes the ironies of David's "encounter and dalliance with Bathsheba," which he terms a moral offense resulting in the "various ensuing immoralities among David's children" (Alter 1987: 134). My intention in highlighting Rosenberg's work is not to denigrate it, but rather to show the silence of the female characters within his interpretive narrative. In spite of its inclusion in a *literary* guide, Rosenberg's contribution, as well as most of the others in the Alter-Kermode work, clearly reflects the historiographic slant of the project. While Rosenberg looks at specific strategies of political machinations within the Davidic narrative, his reading concentrates upon the centrality of male property ownership and male social hegemony. Arguing as if these

---

[7] Berlin (1983). In her recent work Berlin has tried to extricate herself from the category trap and has produced more nuanced readings. However, these earlier readings are heavily anthologized and continue to be cited and incorporated into other scholar's readings.

events are real or historical, Rosenberg does not move beyond a cultural and ideological boundary that is resistant to a female spectator. By reading with the text, and not examining its narrative gaps and silences, he tends to trust the text, to take the biblical narrator at his word. It is the strategies of representation of the characters that are lacking in his and other nongendered readings. And thus the female characters are seen as objects, who provide David with land, dynastic connections, or even a narrative blot on his character. But Michal, Abigail, Bathsheba, Tamar are granted no narrative life in this sort of reading.[8]

As I offered readings in chapters 3 and 4 that questioned the characterization of another biblical virago, the wife of Potiphar, I shall now look at various strategies for developing polyvalent characterizations of Bathsheba. Of primary importance in altering the traditional readings of Bathsheba is to interrupt the masculine gaze, to preclude the singular view of Bathsheba as object of male desire. To collect the shards of Bathsheba's story from the narrator's ongoing tale of David, with the intention of giving Bathsheba a subjectivity beyond her role in the story of David, I shall first look at the doxa, territory that has been well-trod by other literary critics (Bal 1990; Exum 1992, Hackett 1985, Polzin 1993), then compare the biblical portrait of Bathsheba with those of David's other primary wives, Abigail and Michal. An analysis of the Tamar and Amnon episode will demonstrate how echoes of one story can illuminate another. Finally I shall look at a modern retelling of these so-called Davidic narratives by Yiddish writer David Pinski, from his play *David and his Wives* (1930).

SIGHTING BATHSHEBA

In the biblical account the reader first sees Bathsheba when the narrator and David see her – from the monarch's rooftop, bathing. The scene invites the reader to assume the voyeuristic perspective of a spectator squinting at a keyhole. While the doxic account records the gaze but does not blink, Bal has shown that later visual

---

[8] See also Levenson (1978), Levenson and Halpern (1980) and McCarter (1984) for male centered, albeit nongendered, readings of the political codes in David's marriages and sexual conquests.

readings of this scene indicate a possible critique of voyeurism (1990: 225), a blink at the gaze of desire. Let us assume for the moment that Bathsheba is unaware of our gaze. Within a few verses we are introduced to this female character through a list of intimate statements about her body. The reader is privileged to observe signs of her flesh through the narrator's gaze: (1) the woman is bathing (verse 2); (2) the woman is beautiful; (3) the woman is having sex with the king. She is identified in a traditional way: she is the daughter of Eliam and the wife of Uriah the Hittite. Then we are sent more sexual signals: (4) she has just been purified from the unclean state of her menstrual period and is presumably at the fertile time in her cycle; (5) she has conceived and is pregnant.

Bathsheba's only direct speech describes her function in the story, "I am with child." The narration does not provide any details of her state of mind. Not even "I am pregnant with *your* child." We are not told if this turn of events has thrown her into a panic. She is not given the pious extended speech patterns of Abigail, another of David's wives (Bach 1989). Nor does she possess the acid tongue of Michal, who has chastised David a few chapters earlier for getting physical in the sight of Israel. By withholding from the reader Bathsheba's reactions to the sexual demands of the king or to her own act of adultery, the narrator has eliminated a direct route of sympathy between the reader and the female character.

When one approaches the story of Bathsheba and David, a question that echoes and often directs the reading is the much-repeated question posed by Perry and Sternberg: "What did Uriah know and when did he know it?" (Sternberg 1985: 186–229). At least one female reader has been drawn to reverse the Sternberg–Perry question: What did Bathsheba know and when did she know it? Undoubtedly she was the first to know that the evening with the king had resulted in her becoming pregnant. But after she informs David of this messy development, she disappears inside her house. Not until the narrator has reported the incidents surrounding Uriah's death does he bring her out again to be glimpsed by the reader. The spectator will be disappointed if he expects another erotic fantasy. The scene has darkened. The woman is mourning for her husband Uriah. Paralleling the first scene, the monarch sends for her, brings the woman to his house, only this time it is a one-way trip. The narrator chooses two verbal phrases that remind us of her sexual function: she becomes his wife, and she bears him a son (1 Sam. 11:27). This time there is no ogling of her naked beauty; no more is she the delicious fantasy *femme fatale*, appearing wordlessly in another man's bed while her husband is out of town. We can not look at her any more, for she is the king's wife. In her proper role as royal mother, the reader will meet her again.

The question for me, if not for Sternberg, is how did Bathsheba feel about being brought to live permanently with the man who had seized her without a word? Chatman suggests that an audience reconstructs characters from evidence "either implicit or announced in an original construction." Following Chatman's suggestion we may figure Bathsheba as an openly constructed character, allowing the reader the freedom to move beyond the printed page, to view Bathsheba as an independently memorable character (Chatman 1978: 118). I want to imagine Bathsheba as an open-ended character by treating her "as an autonomous being, not merely as a plot function" (119). Wondering about her story prompts questions. Perhaps in lamenting for her husband, she is lamenting her own helplessness. She had no power to resist the king's sexual demands. Has she connected her carrying David's child with Uriah's death? Is what the narrator calls mourning for her husband, perhaps lamenting for her own female destiny?

Since the book of Samuel provides narrative descriptions of David's involvements with two of his wives, Abigail and Michal, before his sighting of Bathsheba, the reader is encouraged to compare these intervals of sexual politics. From the chronological order of wives in David's life, one can posit a setting of priorities of male ambition. First, the connection with the royal house, then the acquisition of personal wealth and the assurance of kingship, and finally a pleasurable sexual liaison. Alter interprets within each of the three "discriminated premarital episodes" a succession of violence. This reading is normative for Alter because he reads each text with David at its center, the object of his interpretive gaze. By not offering an interpretation in which Abigail (or Michal or Bathsheba) is placed at the center of her narrative episode, Alter misses the opportunity of performing a reading in which Abigail's action stops violence. Further, the other female literary figures are not active participants in the premarital episodes that lead to their alliances with David; they are the prizes, the objects of male desire. In the case of Michal, it seems to be the powerful connection with King Saul that sparks desire in David, rather than the eroticism of the woman herself. Put another way, women are objects in the empire of the gaze, especially in a narrative world in which there is such distinct control of the gaze that the object of the gaze becomes a spectacle, one under surveillance. The loss of power of a male figure can be seen as a feminization of the character, as in the story of Samson, who is shown as weak and powerless through his blindness. That undisciplined creature who sold out his faith to the spectacle of women, Samson is not truly powerless until he can no longer see. Deprived of the gaze, he returns to God.

While David sees Bathsheba first,[9] Michal is the one who gazes at David. The power of the male gaze shows us what is lacking in Michal's gaze. Men's desire naturally carries power with it. David's gaze carries the force of action and of possession, both lacking in the female gaze. The first item of information the narrator tells us about Michal is that she loved David (1 Sam. 18:20). The only report in the Bible of a woman loving a man romantically highlights the importance of this situation and explains Michal's intensity toward David, her disloyalty to her father, and her later

---

[9] Jack Sasson suggested to me that Bathsheba may have engineered the initial meeting with David, since she was bathing in the evening, a time marked by a distinct chill in the Jerusalem air. Clearly this is a hyper-realistic interpretation, termed by Roland Barthes "reality effect," in which one thinks that one is embracing the real in its concrete materiality, when in fact one is in the grip of a reality effect. See Barthes, "The Reality Effect" in Todorov, Tzvetan, ed. *French Literary Theory Today: A Reader.*

Thus Sasson uses verisimilitude to achieve veracity in his own interpretation. He imagines for a fictive narrative real weather conditions at a particular time of day, possibly even the light of the moon. Trying to apply this kind of reality effect to the story, I ended up with a bizarre reality indeed. Bathsheba had noticed the monarch pacing his rooftop in the early evening and decided to make herself the object of his gaze, in spite of the chilly bath she would have to endure. Neither surprised nor rendered helpless by David's rapacious actions, in this reading Bathsheba is actually the puppeteer pulling David's strings. Such a reading would support the idea that the pregnancy was a plot twist intended by Bathsheba, who schemed to become the mother of the future king. My continued resistance to such a reading has further underscored to me the strength of the argument that the reader formulates hypotheses about characters based upon the reader's own gaze. Thus, Sasson's speculations and my own reflect the suggestion that there is a literary process in which character is constructed, a process that combines the investment of emotion and interest with the poetics of character.

fury with her unresponsive husband.[10] Her strong love causes her
to rescue her outlaw husband from the deadly intentions of her
father the king. But her gaze is not powerful enough to possess
David sexually. The only time the reader catches David in bed with
Michal, the figure is a stone image, made up of household idols
(*teraphim*)[11] (1 Sam. 19:16), not David in the flesh. The real David has
escaped Michal and her bed. Michal does not possess the object of
her gaze; David does. Before they have exchanged a word, David
has pulled Bathsheba into his bed. Their exchange is sexual, not
verbal.

In contrast there are *no* signs of flesh in the connection between
David and Michal when she helps him elude Saul. No terms of
endearment are exchanged; Michal could have been a loyal ally or
soldier in her only direct speech to David, "If you do not save your
life tonight, tomorrow you will be killed" (19:11). Even in this
critical moment in which she chooses her husband over her father,
there is no sign of intimacy between Michal and David. Even
though she has owned the gaze of the beloved, she could not
dominate him. Michal's acceptance of her powerlessness in the
situation is reflected in her understanding that she needs to cede
the power of the situation to David. Rather than admit to her own
initiation of the escape, she presents a restatement of her words to
David, putting them in his mouth, as she justifies her disloyalty to
Saul by claiming that David had threatened her life; "Help me get
away or I shall kill you" (19:17).

Michal reappears in David's story after David has become king.
The narrator reports that the king has taken "more concubines and
wives; more sons and daughters have been born to David" (2 Sam.

[10] Alter reads the narratorial silence regarding David's feelings for Michal as a device that
reflects the narrator's desire to block access to the private David, "representing him only
as a man in mortal danger" (Alter 1981: 120). Reading with the female character, I suggest
that David's silence emphasizes the one-sidedness of Michal's love and highlights her
predicament and powerlessness. My intention is not to supplant Alter's reading, but
rather to demonstrate the nuance and complexity one can add to characterization by
moving the interpretive gaze onto the female character.

[11] The use in this narrative unit of *teraphim* as objects that a female character uses to effect an
escape from her father clearly recalls the biblical story of Rachel escaping Laban by
stealing his *teraphim* and hiding them under the camel pillow. The allusion reminds the
reader that Rachel and Michal share a decisive choice: they trick their fathers to protect
their husbands. This allusion may foreshadow a fatality shared by the two characters
since Jacob unwittingly curses Rachel because of the theft (Gen. 31:32) (Alter 1981: 119).

5:13–16). The narrator gives a sharp signal of David's sexuality through his report of the names of eleven children who were born to the king in Jerusalem. None of them are children of Michal; her bed and her womb have remained empty. She is absent from the story until she catches sight of her husband "leaping and dancing before the Ark" (2 Sam. 6:16). She is at the window, separated from the sexual heat of her husband. She can merely observe her husband leaping and dancing, verb forms that evoke David's sexuality. The reader observes Michal framed, enclosed, at the window observing David in a moment of physical abandon (see Exum 1990: 45–68). Once again she is distanced from the flesh. From the window, Michal cannot touch him or participate in the joyous frenzy. She is above it all. As her speech reminds us, David is a king without clothes, "*uncovering* himself today before the eyes of his servants' women, just as one of the vulgar fellows shamelessly *uncovers* himself" (2 Sam. 6:20). Michal is a trenchant observer, but no longer one with a gaze of desire. Her no longer beloved David has been uncovering himself before the gaze of women for quite some time, as the report of the eleven named and other unnamed offspring confirms. She has observed the signs of his flesh, but she has not been a player.[12]

In his rejoinder to the wife in the window, David makes clear that God has chosen him above the house of Saul, something Michal knows all too well. And he assures her that he will be even more contemptible in future days, which foreshadows his rapacious activity with Bathsheba a few chapters later. But just as David can risk leaping before the sacred ark of God, so he can leap with another man's wife and survive God's displeasure. Indeed he will even survive my readerly displeasure.

Sternberg refers several times to "Bathsheba's infidelity," ironically permitting her a moment of subjectivity that is also a characterization of blame. Sternberg reads the bedding of Bathsheba in another place as "the love affair between David and

---

[12] Michal is a biblical female figure who has recently been given her due. In a superb collection of articles, Clines and Eskenazi have included not only recent scholarly articles, but also midrashic and "character" studies, Christian sermons, encyclopedia entries, all of which serve the reader well, by presenting cultural contexts for the study of this female literary figure, whose narrative life has survived beyond the Bible. See also Exum 1993a: 46–51, particularly discussion of house as metonymic symbol of woman.

Bathsheba" (202).[13] Whether this phrase is a courtly euphemism or
blind sentimentality, the suggestion of rape of another man's wife
as the sin David has committed would unquestionably make an
ideal reader uncomfortable. It certainly made the Talmudic rabbis
uncomfortable. They presented the situation of David and Bathsheba quite differently, determining that before Uriah had gone off
to battle, he had given Bathsheba a conditional divorce to protect
her in the event he did not return.[14]

The narrator remarks tersely at the close of the narration called by
biblicist Kyle McCarter "The Bathsheba Affair": "The thing that
David had done displeased the Lord" (2 Sam. 11:27). Once again by
reporting divine displeasure, the narrator reminds the reader of his
privileged position, adding a frame of verisimilitude to his story. A
narrator who knows the mind of God certainly must have got his
story straight. The tantalizing ambiguity of the thing that David did,
the sin he committed, remains to tease the reader. Is it his murder of
Uriah? His taking of another man's dearest possession? Is there a
chance that the sin (for both narrator and God) is that of seizing
Bathsheba, first temporarily, then permanently? The answer to this
question gives a clue about the loyalties of the reader.

[13] Other biblical scholars have recently contended with Sternberg. I list them to
acknowledge that my reading of his work should not be considered the only perspective
on this central biblical literary critic's interpretations. Major reviews of *The Poetics of
Biblical Narrative* have been written by Adele Berlin, *Prooftexts* 6 (1986) 273–84; Naomi
Segal, *Vetus Testamentum* 38 (1988) 243–49; Edward L. Greenstein, *Conservative Judaism* 42
(4) Summer 1990. Critical essays by David Gunn. "Reading Right: Reliable and
Omniscient Narrator, Omniscient God and Foolproof Composition in the Hebrew Bible,"
in *The Bible in Three Dimensions* (JSOT Supp. Series), ed. D. J. A. Clines et al. (Sheffield:
Sheffield Academic Press, 1990) 53–64 and Burke Long, "The 'New' Biblical Poetics of
Alter and Sternberg," *Journal for the Study of the Old Testament* 51 (1991) 71–84. The hint of a
dialogue began with Danna Nolan Fewell and David Gunn, "Tipping the Balance:
Sternberg's Reader and the Rape of Dinah," *Journal of Biblical Literature* 110 (1991) 193–211
and Sternberg's reply to this article in *Journal of Biblical Literature* 111 (1992) 463–88.
[14] The rabbinic concern is to avoid placing a woman in the position of an *'agunah* (a woman
whose husband may still be alive, since there's no legal evidence of his death unless
someone either witnessed the act or has found the body). A woman whose husband is
"missing" can never remarry, for fear that the husband might still be alive – unless he had
given her a conditional divorce before going into battle. Thus, as an *'agunah* [lit. chained
or anchored woman], she cannot collect her marriage portion and may become destitute.
Today the practice is still encouraged in Israel for IDF members.
    As Romney-Wegner points out (1988: 123ff.), the problem of the *'agunah* is not merely
that the woman cannot remarry; any children of a later union she forms with a Jewish
male (even if they married only according to the civil law), are in the disastrous status of
mamzerut. See Romney-Wegner 1988: 224, note 60 on the problems of a *mamzer*.

BATHSHEBA HEARD

During one possible unfolding of the so-called Court History Bathsheba is not a player. The political machinations of David and his sons can be interpreted as a male story of power and political gain or loss (Gunn 1978, McCarter 1984, Miscall 1986, Polzin 1989 and 1993). Ignoring the strong sexual connection of David to Bathsheba and Amnon to Tamar, the reader of political codes is left with David losing power by losing sons, first the son of another man's wife, then the son who has raped his daughter, and finally the son of his heart, the son who ends up sleeping with his father's wives. Thus, male sexuality and desire knows no control in the house of David. Neither David nor his sons Amnon and Absalom can turn from their own desire.

A feminist reading must contend with the position of the female literary figure in each of the doxic accounts: the seductive Bathsheba, the victim Tamar. Of course one might read Bathsheba as a victim of David's desire (see Bal 1990; Exum 1993b). As I have shown earlier in this chapter, the more questions the reader poses to the text, the less likely one is to reach a dichotomous, and reductive, conclusion of good or bad, agent or victim. Arguably many modes of reading, including my own, involve comparisons of one text with another, but keeping an eye on each of two texts, a scopic mode of reading, is not the same as searching for the balanced binarisms in a text. In the Davidic narratives, another strategic move for a resistant reader is to acknowledge the persistent connection in David's house between sexual power and political triumph. With one eye on David, a reader can keep the other eye on the female objects of David's desire. The Davidic sexual rampage initiated with his seizing of Bathsheba, is ignited with an imitative scene, Amnon's rape of Tamar. David's sexual power which has built the dynastic house of David is deflated in the derogatory scene in which Absalom rapes his father's concubines. After this scene, the story of David becomes the coda of an old man watching his last vestiges of political power being seized by Bathsheba and the prophet Nathan. Improper sexual advances made David a powerful monarch while they also led to his defeat. He does not seem to declare Solomon king voluntarily. Bathsheba must remind him that he has promised to do so.

At the moment in narrative time that her son Solomon has become an adult contender for the throne, Bathsheba is being transformed by the narrator from sexual object to matriarch. No longer the nubile bather, seen but not heard, she returns to the story, empowered by what? Years of life at Court? A slightly curdled mother's milk? Regardless of the reason for the change in position, Bathsheba can no longer be designated as playing a monoactive role in the narrative. It is this tension between positions and roles that enhances the dissymetry of power within the work (Bal 1988: 36). By following Bathsheba's range of actions, her varying access to speech and power in her first narrative unit (as object of desire) and her second narrative (as matriarch), one can overcome the dichotomous feminist readings that have simplified or flattened the characters under study.

What of the other narratively important wives of David: Michal is barren and Abigail has a "minor" son, Chileab (2 Sam. 3:3) or Daniel (I Chron. 3:1) who is never mentioned as a player in the realm of political power.[15] Thus, Bathsheba returns to the story as she left it, identified as the wife connected with sexuality, with children, with succession. As David's story draws to its conclusion, Bathsheba is the wife chosen to fulfill the stock role of matriarch. Like Rebekah she angles for the prize for her son, unlike Rebekah she does not have to scheme alone. Nathan, the prophet who guided David throughout his reign, helps Bathsheba achieve the monarchy for Solomon. A clue to a reading that promotes the subjectivity of the female figures is Hannah's prayer for a son at the beginning of the Samuel narratives. Following this connection of mother to son, instead of the more usual David and his sons, one finds that Michal has no son, Abigail's son does not

---

[15] There is a rabbinic tradition that claims Chileab was so named because he resembled physically and in his mental powers his father David (*kil'ab*, like [his] father). The name, according to Ginzburg (1911: 275), silenced any misunderstanding about David's hasty marriage to Abigail. The son is clearly the son of David because he resembles him physically. For similar explanation see *Targ. Chron. 3.1.* David's marriage to Abigail seems implicitly to be connected with the marriage of Bathsheba. Although both marriages were impulsive, one was born of improper sexual desire; one was proper. Abigail's good name is protected and echoed by the name of her son.

enter into the political machinations at Court, Bathsheba's infant son dies before she becomes the mother of Solomon, Ahinoam is the mother of Amnon who is killed by Absalom, son of Maacah. Absalom is killed by Joab and his men. Thus of all these mother's sons, only Solomon and Chileab remain alive, and only Solomon has narrative life.

Focusing upon the varied and extended roles of women in the books of Samuel, Hackett notes that they appear in the domestic sphere, the public sphere, and in "the gray area that is the domestic sphere of a ruling family, where private decisions have public consequences" (WBC 1992: 94–95). The narrator resolves the Davidic narrative with some information that seems to parody the earlier story of David and Bathsheba and of course keeps the narratorial focus on David entangled with women, the gray sphere that Hackett describes. David is cold and needs someone to warm his (c)old body. This time the narrator does not invite the reader to peep at the young woman. Abishag the Shunammite is brought to the king. He himself does not choose her or send for her. Like Bathsheba she is described as very beautiful. Abishag, however, is not the object of David's gaze or ours. She will attend David's body as nurse, not as lover. Abishag performs a traditional, and safe, feminine role, while the young Bathsheba, the object of male desire, had been a potential threat. In the narrator's tale of Abishag being brought to David, there is no hint of the eager sexual energy ignited when David saw Bathsheba.[16] David's erotic energy typified by his seizure of Bathsheba in the early years of his reign has vanished. The king now requires a woman in his bed, explicitly not as a sexual companion. Might the omnipotent narrator be sneering a second time at the king's lost potency?

Bathsheba goes to David, who is seen being tended by Abishag, an asexual object. "What do you desire?" asks the king, an ironic twist evoking and recalling his sexual desire that is now dead. Bathsheba is all business, reminding the king that he had promised to make Solomon his heir. Like Abigail before her,

---

[16] I am grateful to Ed Greenstein for reminding me that in *God Knows* Joseph Heller imagines David lying in his sickbed wishing for a final glimpse of (even old) Bathsheba's cheesecake.

Bathsheba uses a verbal strategy of flattery and humility to get David to change his mind at a crucial moment in Israel's history. Like Abigail, Bathsheba is the subject of this scene, reminding the failing king that it is within his power to alter the events of state and halt the power grab of Adonijah. "Now, my lord, the eyes of Israel are upon you to tell them who shall sit upon the throne of my lord the king after him" (1 Kgs. 1:20). Another ironic signal in this scene of reversals. If in the earlier scene, all spectator's eyes had been upon Bathsheba exposed in her bath, now the gaze is fixed upon David faltering on the throne.

To give the necessary authority to the woman's request, Nathan backs up Bathsheba's story, another reversal from an earlier scene: the angry Nathan who had prophesied the death of the nameless infant son, the sexual connection between David and Bathsheba (2 Sam. 12: 1–15), now speaks out in favor of Solomon, the second son of the pair. David then recalls a vow made in an earlier scene:

As the Lord lives, who has redeemed my soul out of every adversity, as I swore to you by the Lord, the God of Israel, saying Solomon, your son shall reign after me, and he shall sit upon my throne in my place, even so will I do this day. (1 Kgs. 1:29–30)

But had he made such a vow to Bathsheba? Nathan's mention of such a vow to Bathsheba (verse 13) is ambiguous. Is this a strategy to convince the muddled monarch that such a vow had been made? This is no textual mention of such a vow. One would also assume that if Bathsheba had been given assurance of her son's ascendancy to the throne, she would not have needed Nathan to encourage her to remind the king of his promise. While the origin of the promise from David to Bathsheba concerning Solomon is draped in obscurity, what is clear is that Bathsheba has been vindicated in the best tradition of patriarchal culture. She has become the triumphant mother, whose son triumphs over the sons of David's other wives. Finally Bathsheba is seen as the mother working to achieve for her son what God intends for him to have. Thus, she has been transformed from sexual object to Queen Mother (see note 25 on *gevirah*). Finally Bathsheba has been cast in the familiar role of good mother, working to protect and extend the tradition. In this final scene she is heard and not seen.

IMAGINING BATHSHEBA

The biblical storyteller is clearly not interested in Bathsheba's feelings about David. The biblical text supplies no direct details about Bathsheba's reactions to her suddenly altered status as wife to the King of Israel and Judah. By comparing her story with that of the other narratively important wives of David, Michal and Abigail, another storyteller might excavate embedded signals that add to the laconically narrated portrait of Bathsheba. There is no story that does not have embedded within it the question of how it continued, what happened next. Yiddish playwright David Pinski asks such questions of the biblical narrative in *David and his Wives*, while seeking to find answers within the scope of traditional Jewish loyalty to King David.

First, let us note that the Talmudic sages have set their rabbinic minds to cleansing David of any immoral mud that may have stuck to him by the narratives as related by the biblical narrators. There are of course problems that the narration of David's sexual life presents. First, there is the problem that David may have actually married sisters – Michal and Merab (I Sam. 18:17–28), although the biblical text is ambiguous. The sticking point is whether Adriel (Merab's husband) had taken David's place in Merab's life before her marriage to David or after it (similar to the Palti issue in Michal's narrative). R. Yossi maintains that Merab was married to David. But his students are surprised. Could David be married simultaneously to two sisters (forbidden by both Lev. 18:18 and rabbinic law)? R. Yossi assures them David married Michal after the death of her sister Merab. R. Yehoshua Ben Karha's explanation is that the marriage to Merab was not a valid one because it would have been impossible for Saul to have given his daughter to David in lieu of the promise of riches (the reward for killing Goliath). (*Sanh.* 19B). This same *gemara* contains a lengthy discussion whose intention is to prove that Palti was not Michal's husband, but rather her guardian. I cite these talmudic interpretations not so much to reach a halakic conclusion, but rather to show the reader the strategies the rabbis employ to clean up David's image considerably. Of equal interest for this study is the way the literary figures of David and his wives are discussed by the rabbis as though they are real people, thus illustrating how deeply characters take root in the readerly mind.

David Pinski deals with the problem ceded to him by the biblical narratives about King David. Unlike the rabbis, who persevered in finding law to exonerate the crimes of the hero David, Pinski uses humor and irony to eradicate any nagging readerly doubts about the King as Israel's hero. The Pinski play is divided into five scenes: Michal, Abigail, Bathsheba, In the Harem, a collective scene in which all the wives and concubines converge and show their true colors: as mothers deftly trying to achieve a better royal position for their sons. In the final scene, Abishag, David assures the young woman that she is indeed his wife, his "virginal, immaculate, eternal flame that must never cease to burn" (185). The play ends with Abishag's dance, which "grows wilder and more voluptuous." Thus, she has become David's erotic self, doing the dance that he can no longer perform.

Pinski's work is filled with explicit and often exaggerated stage directions that function as narratorial commentary. With its rather flat dialogue, the play reads more as a narrative using the genre of drama than as a play that would benefit from dramatic production. In each of the first three scenes, Michal, Abigail, and Bathsheba, Pinski uses the female characters to reflect the honor and purity of David. However, the interesting aspect of the play for this study is that Pinski returns to David all the honor and respect an ideal audience could award him through exploring gaps in the male–female interplay in the biblical narrative.

The most confounding gap in the story of Bathsheba occurs because Bathsheba will never get to tell her story, to identify her sexual encounter with David. Was it traumatic? Was it kismet? Pinski's version "solves" one question: David definitely is the sexual aggressor. At the very moment that Nathan is prophesying David's royal future as the beloved of God, in Pinski's version, David's attention is caught by a movement outside his window. "(Stage Direction) Leans over the balustrade and looks with utmost interest upon something down among the trees . . . Slowly raises his left hand in a defensive gesture, but remains as if transfixed" (1923: 100). After Nathan identifies the woman and warns the king against the sin of looking at her, David avows: " I take the sin upon myself most willingly." Acknowledging that Bathsheba is a beautiful work of the Lord God, and ignoring Nathan's lengthy and impassioned pleas to let the woman alone, David orders the woman brought to him.

The young Bathsheba's entrance is described in Pinski's dramatic style: "She is dragged in by the soldiers. She tears herself free and runs to the middle of the roof. The Guards disappear at a signal from David. He looks at Bathsheba sharply" (1923: 107). Where she has no dialogue at this point in the biblical narrative, Pinski gives her voice so that she becomes an active participant in the events that unfold. First she explains her situation with an economy of phrase reminiscent of her "I am pregnant" in the Bible. To David she says, "I am married. And I love my husband." In spite of David's desire for her, she remains steadfast in her resolve. "Were you even an hundredfold more [than a king], I would love only Uriah." Undeterred by her words, David tries to get her drunk, then tries sweet words, but to no avail. Finally, afraid of his ardor, Bathsheba calls out to Uriah, who "enters immediately comprehending the situation, he trembles as if struck by a thunderbolt. Meeting the king's glance, however, he falls on his knees before David" (113–14).

The stage is set, the characters have been introduced. The audience sees Bathsheba approaching her husband, who is kneeling, not at her feet, but at the feet of the king, a clue to where his loyalty lies. Now the comedic interplay begins. While Bathsheba is relieved and comforted by the sight of her husband, Uriah has eyes only for his liege David. Disgusted that Uriah's arrival has destroyed his sexual opportunity, David leaves the stage. Bathsheba thinks Uriah is ignoring her because he has misread her part in the situation.

You are angry with me. Your heart is turned to stone against me. You do not want to look upon me. But I have not sinned – neither against God nor against you, Uriah. I did not come hither willingly. Uriah, do you hear me? The king's will brought me here. He beheld me while I was bathing, and his soldiers drove me, dragged me here. Yet I resisted him, and the king has not yet touched me . . . Look at me! Uriah! Save me and yourself. (1923: 116)

Upon hearing that the king fancies Bathsheba, Uriah's response is immediate. "The king wants you! The king's wish be fulfilled." Following is an unsurprising husband and wife argument that is funny because of its role reversals: the woman is trying not to commit adultery and the husband is offering her, like an open box of chocolates, to the king. When it becomes clear that Uriah will not come to her defense, Bathsheba becomes a diva.

Are you perhaps afraid of death? Uriah, I will die together with you. Rather will I die than survive my shame. Take your sword and stab me. How sweet to me will death be from your hand! Will you die together with me? Then death will be a dance to me! (1923: 121)

A servant enters with the news that Uriah must return to the front. Uriah refuses Bathsheba's demands that he kill the king for trying to seduce her. "Never shall my hand be raised against my king," Uriah assures her. After more melodrama, in which Bathsheba's hysterical reactions can be seen only as farce, Bathsheba has a moment of recognition.

Am I nothing to you? Is the king so much dearer to you than I? Do you know where the king is sending you to? (1923: 123)

She has been given the power to inscribe her own truth. Predictably Uriah remains obdurate; Bathsheba caves in to the inevitable. Her final speech restores her own honor by a complete about face: she is eager for her alliance with David.

I laugh at myself. I mock myself. I loved a slave, hahahaha! Now I must go to the king! He must cleanse me of my impurity. He must sanctify me! Ah-h-h! I have loved a slave. Now I shall love a king. (1923: 126)

Pinski's play can be viewed as subversive of the biblical narrative. He certainly fills the biblical gaps in women's stories within the Davidic material. But this is not a truly Bakhtinian carnival, created to subvert the patriarchal codes structuring the biblical narratives. More likely *David and his Wives* functions as a carnival conceived by the institutional authority to explain the possible indeterminacy caused by the gaps in the biblical text. Thus, Pinski's effort to fix meaning, to procure eternal honor for David, results in an idealization of the biblical figures, especially David. Pinski's gap-filling is an attempt to restore authority to the hero rather than to resist authority through the participation in a carnival of laughter. Bakhtin explains in *Rabelais and his World* that the carnival of laughter that celebrates a temporary liberation from the prevailing truth and from the established order is marked "by the suspension of all hierarchical rank, privileges, norms and prohibitions . . . the feast of becoming, change" (10). This sort of carnival laughter has a different valence from usual laughter because it is opposed to the official, the authoritative. Thus, the comic carnival may be seen as an event staged by Pinski so that female spectators drown out their own voices through the laughter of recognition but not the laughter that opposes authority. The discourse never tempts the spectator to suspend its acceptance of authority. Rather the festive laughter is temporary and returns the woman to silence and compliance.

In spite of the rabbinic effort to rehabilitate David through a creative reading of the law, considering Bathsheba a divorced woman does not alleviate the problem of David demanding sex from her. It does remove the legal problems of damaging another man's property. And it does erase the accusation of adultery – since she would be unmarried. But it takes Pinski's characterization of Bathsheba as desiring David to tidy up the damage caused by David's wandering eye. Pinski's wry viewpoint renders everyone happy: in the Pinski play Bathsheba is the familiar loyal wife who when scorned and shamed by her husband's overpowering loyalty to his king is pleased to exchange her devotion and loyalty to one man for loyalty and devotion to another. Thus, he renders both Bathsheba and David innocent of crimes. And Bathsheba comes out a winner; she trades a servile subject for a king. In neither the rabbinic nor the Pinski versions does the male interpreter lose control of the narrative, of the power to define the heroic models in the narrative.

Neither is my disappointment in not finding a single interpretation that matches or supports my own desires to excoriate David and recover or recreate the voices of the women who surround him alleviated through the recent feminist reading in which David is judged to be a rapist and Bathsheba his victim. Upon first reading the suggestion of pushing the text to characterize King David as a rapist made me uncomfortable. God's beloved, a rapist? Suggesting such a violent filling of the gaps has been instructive. That reading is merely a focus upon the opposite end of the dichotomy of David as the beloved of God. Neither polar opposition provides me a readerly respite. Even the analysis of a male fantasy of sexual primacy does not result in a reinvented text of female potency. No wonder Bathsheba grieves. But is the idea of rape so distant from the story of David's Bathsheba? In 2 Samuel it is a scant chapter away, in the narrative of David's son Amnon raping David's daughter Tamar. Does the activity of the father foreshadow the activity of the son?

TAMAR: STORY OF A DOUBLE TAKE

There are many paradoxes in the story of Tamar, but the most intriguing is that the rape of Tamar actually supports the ideology of the text. The episode of Tamar and Amnon illustrates the Bakhtinian notion that the author of ancient epic desires to impose a single world view upon the text.[17] Amnon wants Tamar and acts upon his desire in spite of the recognition that incest is against the law.[18] As David knew that Bathsheba was the wife of Uriah before

---

[17] I refer the reader to Bakhtin's distinction between the classic genres of epic, lyric, and tragedy, which he terms monologic, and the modern novel, which he terms dialogic. In their effort to forge a unified world view, classical authors suppress the inherently dialogic quality of language. The novel allows the dialogic nature of language and culture to pierce the monologic voice through direct, indirect, and doubly indirect (parodic) speech. The novel's carnivalesque irreverence toward all types of repressive monologic forms prevents a novelist from imposing the monologic form even if he or she wanted to. It is important to remember that Bakhtin is not suggesting a dichotomy between classical and modern forms of storytelling, since he acknowledges that the roots of the novel are found in Socratic dialogues, Menippean satire, and the satyr play, as well as the carnival folk culture which kept alive this resistant voice during the Middle Ages until the Renaissance. The clearest statement of Bakhtin's theories can be found in Bakhtin (1973, 1981). An interesting application of these theories by a novelist and literary critic is David Lodge's *After Bakhtin: Essays on Fiction and Criticism* (London and New York, Routledge: 1990), particularly 75–153.

[18] The Bible explicitly forbids incest in both cultic law (Lev. 18:9, 11; 20:7) and Deuteronomic law (Deut. 27:22). See also the prophetic example of social and political dissolution: "One commits abomination with his neighbor's wife; another lewdly defiles his daughter-in-law; another in you defiles his sister, his father's daughter" (Ezek. 22:11).

What is confounding in the Tamar/Amnon text is Tamar's statement "He won't keep me from you!" (verse 13). Perhaps the prohibition of marriage between siblings was a late development (Daube 1974: 77–79) or consanguinity was thought only to exist through the blood of the mother (de Vaux 1961: 19–20). McCarter suggests that marriage between half-brother and sister would have been permitted (325). Whatever the prevailing law or custom at the time of the redacting of the book of Samuel, the phrase that Tamar utters

his sexual encounter with her, so Amnon knew that it was forbidden for him to rape Tamar. While the story of David's son violating a woman explicitly, as opposed to the more guarded story of his father's semiotic rape of Bathsheba (Exum 1993a: 184–90), can be read as a continuation of the father's behavior by the son, and thus, control a unified viewpoint of character within the larger Davidic story, an interpreter can resist such a monologic interpretation by supplying the dialogic voice herself. This narrative strategy, to refuse interpretive closure by adding another voice to the author's attempt at monologic imperialism, is essential to a feminist reading, one that intends to disrupt the order determined unilaterally by the author/narrator.

In the previous chapter, 2 Samuel 12, the one that acts as a moral bridge between the David and Bathsheba episode and the Amnon and Tamar story and secures the unified narratorial vision, the divine position is revealed through Nathan.

Now therefore the sword shall never depart from your *house*, for you have despised me, and have taken the *wife* of Uriah the Hittite to be your *wife*. Thus says the Lord: I will raise up trouble against you from within your own *house*; and I will take your *wives* before your eyes, and give them to your neighbor, and he shall lie with your *wives* in the sight of this very sun. (2 Sam. 12:10–11)

Note the repetition of the words *house* and *wife* in this verse, which reflect the use of *Leitwörter* throughout the chapter.[19] Polzin notes that the following chapter in which the divine punishment begins to be played out simultaneously examines the family of David through a narrative microscope (1993: 133). The emphasis on the punishment coming to David through his wives has received little gendered commentary. In the text of Chapter 13 the word

---

"He won't keep me from you," reminds the reader of the star-crossed lover theme recurrent in Western literature. Such a suggestion also crenelates the fabric of character provided for Tamar. Did she have feelings for Amnon that were destroyed by his rough treatment of her? Were her shame and grief doubled by the realization that he would not marry her?

19 Gunn shows clearly the play of the *Leitwörter bayit* and the verbal and allusive connections between the house of David and the house of Israel in his article "In Security: The David of Biblical Narrative" (1989). Rosenberg in *King and Kin in Israel* (1986) and Polzin in *David and the Deuteronomist* (1993) also work with this central intertwined theme. Polzin particularly emphasizes the multiplicity of voices that permit familial expressions and plots to carry with them national and tribal implications.

"son" occurs 9 times, the word "brother" 13, the word "sister" 9 times. This repetition of such words emphasizes familial relationships, but the use of "sister" (*'ahot)* also underscores the connection of Tamar as sister, dependent by social and filial connections to her father's sons, her brothers. It becomes clear through the patterning of language that the family microscope is focused upon the actions of men while the punishment is to be lived out through the pain of women, particularly Tamar.

If the reader believes that God intends to make good on his punishment to David, thus recognizing the unified theological code, Amnon's rape of Tamar is not a surprise. Rather it amplifies and refers the reader back to David's taking of Bathsheba. I make this assertion in spite of the fact that some interpreters, like McCarter, characterize David as a "gentle king and doting father" (327). This saccharine figuration does not seem to come from a careful reading of the textual evidence. After watching David toy with Michal, snatch Bathsheba, and appear diffident over the rape of his daughter, I prefer to characterize David's behavior with women as the dark backing behind the bright mirror. Reflected in the paradoxical mirror, the rape of Tamar supports the patriarchal order twice: by showing how Absalom fulfills his social obligation through avenging his sister and by David fulfilling his proper social obligation by going to war with his murderous son. What remains secondary in the narrator's story is the sexual politics played out by Amnon and Tamar. According to the divine reasoning the taking of another man's wife (Bathsheba) is equivalent to the incestuous contact that Amnon effects.

Now therefore the sword shall never depart from your house, for you have despised me, and have taken the wife of Uriah the Hittite to be your wife. Thus says the Lord: I will raise up trouble against you from within your own house; and I will take your wives before your eyes, and give them to your neighbor, and [Absalom] shall lie with your wives in the sight of this very sun. (2 Sam. 12:10–11)

The narrator seems to have trouble keeping his agenda straight: as Rosenberg and others have argued, there is a distinct parallel between the political/military narratives of men and war and the personal/sexual destruction of David's house. Fokkelman's division of the MT attempts to solve this problem. Is the narrator/theologian creating a symmetry between the sexual and the political? The way in which these codes are so carefully intertwined indicates that in the narrator's mind they reflect each other (Schwartz 1991: 45–51). A feminist reader invariably does a double take when analyzing the figure of the raped woman in the Bible. For the rape of Tamar, like the rape of Dinah and the Levite's wife, functions to explain violence between groups of men. The stories are painfully similar: male politics are inscribed upon women's bodies. When Amnon dismisses Tamar as "this (woman)"(*zo't*), he attempts to consign her to that nameless invisible category of other biblical victim women, notably the Levite's wife[20] who is twice raped, once by her "brother" and, as Exum puts it, once by the pen (1993, chap. 6, esp. 176–88).

There are echoes of other biblical male/female encounters in this brother/sister event that illustrate biblical signs of the flesh. A primary parallel is found in the account of David's encounter with Abigail on the hillside at the time of the sheep-shearing (*gozezim*) (I Samuel 25) and in the sheep-shearing festival held by Absalom in which Amnon is killed. In both these parallel encounters, a fundamental law that knits together the social fabric is ripped apart. Abigail's life-altering meeting with David occurred at the time of sheep-shearing (conveniently the foul Nabal died a few verses later, freeing her to go to David legitimately). Absalom avenges his sister at the time of a similar feast. There is additional irony in that David gained Abigail as a wife after one sheep-shearing holiday, and lost his firstborn son Amnon after another.

An intriguing linguistic association is made between the name *nabal* (Abigail's husband) and the word *nebalah*, meaning sacri-

---

[20] Polzin (1993) draws stunning and convincing comparisons between the narrative of Tamar and Amnon and the narrative of the Levite's concubine. Through both linguistic details and similarities in plot structure, Polzin demonstrates that what happens to brothers in the house of David becomes "another, more concrete way of telling the reader what is happening to brothers within the house of Israel" (1993: 138). In spite of his concentration on the male-centered civil wars in both stories, Polzin does point out the all-important lack of protection of the ravaged women by their male protectors, whether the men be brothers in the familial sense or brothers in the sense of tribal relationship. He notes that the word brother (*'ah*) denotes familial connection in about two-thirds of the cases in 2 Samuel, whereas in Judges 19–21, the word is used to indicate the sons of Israel as national or tribal brothers five out of six times (136).

lege.[21] The insertion of the idea of sacrilege into the story of Tamar and Amnon makes the narrator's view of the rape clear, but what is more subtle is the hint of sacrilege in Nabal's behavior toward David. Nabal's failure to pay off David and his outlaws in return for their sparing his sheep and herders is a violation of the social contract between these two parties: landholders and brigands. David outlines the understanding succinctly:

now your shepherds have been with us, and *we did them no harm*, and they missed nothing, all the time they were in Carmel. Ask your young men, and they will tell you. Therefore let my young men find favor in your sight; for we have come on a feast day. Please *give whatever you have at hand to your servants and to your son David*. (I Sam. 25:7–8, italics mine)

Nabal's rude refusal to honor the unspoken agreement with David threatens the safety of Nabal's entire household. Understanding that the balance has been upset, Abigail rushes to David to offer him armloads of bread and meat and cakes and skins of wine to appease him and to restore the social balance. Amnon also demands food, but he does not accept it as the medium of exchange with Tamar. Tamar's offering of cakes is not successful in restoring the balance in her family. When it becomes clear that Amnon wishes not to eat her cakes, but to devour her, Tamar suggests explicitly the appropriate substitute, that Amnon marry her, but he refuses. She had played her role, as nurturing sister-cook; he had renounced his role as protective brother. Thus, part of her grief at having him abuse her body is her shame at having failed to protect the familial social order.

There is a strong echo of another sexual encounter in the story of

---

[21] I follow McCarter, who reinterprets the term *nebalah* as a "general expression for serious disorderly and unruly action resulting in the breakup of an existing relationship whether between tribes, within the family, in a business arrangement, in marriage or with God. It indicates the end of an existing order . . ." McCarter (1984: 322–23). Polzin adheres in his commentary to the earlier meaning, that of foolishness or vile thing, but points out that the word, except for the instance of Achan's stealing of the Lord's things in Josh. 7:15, is confined to acts of sexual misconduct (1993: 137).

Schwartz provides an elegant literary association between the explicit *nabal* and David, who after his initial sexual encounter with Bathsheba becomes an implicit *nabal*. "The roles of Nabal and David have reversed: now, David is the Fool. The king is greedy, as Nabal had been, and he denies his neighbor what is rightfully his, as Nabal had denied David provisions from his livestock and hospitality . . . When women are stolen, rather than peaceably exchanged, the relational directions reverse, from friendship toward fear, from alliance toward hostility" (47).

Mut-em-enet and Joseph. The foreign woman, the seducer, is paralleled by David's firstborn son. The reversal of gender in the two stories tempts one to add to Amnon's characterization the negatives associated with the foreign woman (*ishah zarah*). Both refuse to accept their place within the familial social order, Mut-em-enet as the wife of a highly placed Egyptian courtier, and Amnon as the son who is to become the future king of Israel. It is interesting to note that the idea of seducing Joseph comes directly from Mut-em-enet, through a narratorial report, while the author of Samuel distances himself as well as the character of Amnon from the rape. He frames the Tamar/Amnon episode with the stage-managing of Jonadab, known to be a very crafty man (2 Sam. 13:3). In direct speech Jonadab presents to Amnon the idea of seducing Tamar, and the exact details of the plan (verse 13:5). Later on this same Jonadab reports to David that Absalom has killed Amnon. While the details of Absalom's plans are related indirectly through the narrator, Jonadab connects the murder with the rape: "Let not my lord suppose that they have killed all the young men the king's sons; Amnon alone is dead. This has been determined by Absalom from the day Amnon raped his sister Tamar" (verse 32). Through the use of direct speech, the biblical narrator is cleared of having thought up the sacrileges that led to the fall of David's house or of having pronounced sentence on either of David's sons.

As Mut-em-enet longed for Joseph "day after day" (*yom yom*) (Gen. 39:10) so Amnon longed for his sister "morning after morning" (*babboker baboker*) (2 Sam. 13:4). The most direct linguistic connection is the repetition of the unusual "long garment with sleeves" (*ketonet passim*), worn by Joseph and Tamar exclusively in the Bible. The clothing serves as a marker of the wronged character in the narrative – in the book of Samuel it reminds the reader of the Genesis text, in which Joseph was a member of a familial social network that is about to unravel. In their similar garments Joseph and Tamar represent a powerless figure, yet one who paradoxically is at the center of the rupture of the family. The blood on Joseph's *ketonet* "coat" is goat's blood and ultimately does not signal Joseph's death. The blood on Tamar's garment is her own blood, a sign of her stolen virginity, death for a woman in the ancient world.

Part of the paradox in the Tamar/Amnon episode is that the

rape is of little consequence to the narrator and to David. As the ensuing two years in which neither David nor the Court acts to avenge Tamar indicates, it is Absalom's anger, and his desire to defend the honor of the house of David, not the rape itself, that destroys Amnon. Similarly, Mut-em-enet's rapacious desire for Joseph results in her misrepresenting Joseph as the sexual predator. As I discussed earlier in this study, such a determination would result in certain death if God's protection of Joseph had not been more powerful than Mut's slanderous accusations. In traditional interpretation Amnon's rape also has a plot-kindling function, that is, it "provides the knowledge of private matters necessary, in our narrator's opinion, for a correct understanding of the public events recounted in chaps. 15–20" (McCarter 1984: 327).

Just as Mut-em-enet planned her encounter with Joseph when no one was in the house (Gen. 39:12), so Amnon, following the advice of Jonadab, pretends to be ill so that he may see Tamar alone. The major difference in the plots of the two accounts is that Amnon is successful in possessing the object of his desire, and Mut-em-enet is not. Not completely powerless because he is under the protection of yhwh, Joseph is able to flee. Apparently under no one's protection, Tamar is raped.

Amnon refers to Tamar as my sister directly twice: once when he is repeating Jonadab's suggestion, he says to his father, "Let my sister Tamar (*'ahoti*) come and give me something to eat" (verse 6); the second time also occurs in direct speech. Amnon says what he truly wants. "Come lie with me, my sister (*shikvi 'immi 'ahoti*)" (verse 11), is an echo of the shortest seductive phrase in the Bible, the identical request that Joseph heard from Mut-em-enet. In order to make the sexual request vile, sacrilegious, Amnon must add the phrase, "my sister" *'ahoti*. From the married Mut-em-enet to Joseph, the servant, *shikvah 'immi* is in itself an adulterous suggestion. From Amnon, the relational connection *'ahoti* must be made explicit to the reader. Again the narrator uses the convention of direct discourse to distance himself from the deed. At the beginning of the story he had identified Tamar as the sister of David's son Absalom, and then related that David's son Amnon had fallen in love with her. In that simple well-balanced phrase the narrator has concealed his own perspective by putting the greatest distance between Amnon and Tamar, as the object of his desire. After the rape, when Amnon's desire has become revulsion, he orders her out of his house *qumi lekhi* without the vital filial connection. She is no longer his sister.

For a feminist reader an interesting element of narrative investigation is whether a female character gets to tell her story or is allowed to show even a fragment of her feelings to the audience or to the other characters. Bathsheba sends a message to David, saying succinctly "I am pregnant," which certainly serves to announce the beginning of their combined story. But she is not given emotions until the death of her infant child. And then the emotions are described indirectly. The narrator reports that "David consoled his wife Bathsheba, and went to her, and lay with her; and she bore a son, and he named him Solomon." The progression of events in this verse are reflected in the succession of male-subject verbs: he consoled, he went in to her, he lay with her, [she bore him a son], and he named him. The activity after the death of the child is summed up through David's actions. The entire report of the illness and subsequent death of the child is focalized through the servants of David. Bathsheba is invisible until the mention of her in relation to David's mourning. Her appearance functions to assure the audience that David is returning to life as usual. Part of David's consolation is to reassert his sexual primacy. The male ideology of the story is apparent through this series of events that ensures the legitimate male role is to dominate the woman. The consolation of Bathsheba is merely a preamble to reasserting her role as producer of children. As such she renders possible the redemption of David through the birth of his son who will become king.

Tamar is disconsolate after being raped by Amnon. Whereas the reader is provided with no dialogue between David and Bathsheba before either of their sexual encounters, there is direct discourse surrounding the rape episode in 2 Samuel 13. Tamar's dialogue reinforces the ideology of the text. She only wants to be taken properly so that she will be able to perform her social obligation.

She answered him, "No, my brother, do not force me; for such a thing is not done in Israel; do not do anything so vile!
As for me, where could I carry my shame? And as for you, you would be as one of the scoundrels in Israel. Now therefore, I beg you, speak to the king; for he will not withhold me from you." (2 Sam. 13:13)

After the rape, Tamar retains the power of speech. She does not give up trying to re-establish the social contract. She tries to protect her status within the family and the royal community; through her pleading, she demonstrates her resolve not to be shamed and her understanding that her ability to reassert "respectability" depends in part upon Amnon not being relegated to the category of scoundrel. Once again she begins her speech with the phrase "No, my brother." Then she inserts the double take into the story. As though she has already contended with the rape, she tries to reason with Amnon. "For this wrong in sending me away is greater than the other that you did to me." But his disenchantment with her is total. Her moment of recognition does not become his. He has her thrown outside the boundary of his house. Like the Levite's wife she is thrown outside the arena of familial/tribal "brotherly" protection.[22] Like Bathsheba she survives her shame, but unlike David's queen, Tamar has no powerful man to find her another role in the narrative.

Dressed in mourning clothes, Tamar put ashes on her head, and "tears the long robe that she was wearing; she put her hand on her head, and went away, crying aloud as she went" (13:19). Mourning for her lost virginity, mourning for the irrevocable split in the family, Tamar's life is ruined not by the rape, but by Amnon's subsequent rejection. Hidden inside Absalom's house, Tamar is no longer a sign of the flesh.

SHOOTING BATHSHEBA

Bathsheba has captured the imagination of visual artists since the Middle Ages. In several medieval Books of Hours, she is pictured as a thin grayish figure shivering in her bath. David, fully clothed in

---

[22] In declining to refer to the Levite's wife as "concubine," as the tradition has, I follow Bal (1988a: 83–86) and Exum (1993: 177–81). Bal argues that the father's warm reception of the Levite indicates that of a relation, *hoten*, "father-in-law" (Judg. 19: 4). To emphasize the importance of the term *house* in the story, Bal refers to the Levite's wife as *Beth*. For a complete analysis of the roles of daughters in the book of Judges, see Bal's *Death and Dissymmetry*. Exum calls the Levite's wife *Bath-sheber*, "daughter of breaking," "on the analogy of Bath-sheba (daughter of an oath or daughter of seven)" (Exum 1993: 176). Rather than use either name, I refer to the character as the Levite's wife, knowing that I am leaving her to the anonymity to which patriarchy had consigned her.

royal red and gold, is gazing at her. Bathsheba's eyes are unfocused. Her frail arms are ineffective at covering her body. In *Reading "Rembrandt"* Bal has dealt at length with visual figuring of the biblical Bathsheba. Rather than rework the ground she has covered so completely and so brilliantly, I'd like to rerun the tale of David and Bathsheba one final time, casting the narrator as filmmaker.

There is a Hollywood version of *David and Bathsheba* (1951), about a moody David, many sheep (a few shepherds), and a love-struck Bathsheba.[23] In this version the story has been altered to suit an ideal American Fifties viewing audience and the Hollywood star system. Lest the audience think it is the most honorable Gregory Peck who has seduced Bathsheba, the tempestuous Susan Hayward confesses to the monarch, whom she has met a few frames earlier, that her marriage to Uriah was of six-day duration, arranged by her father, and lacking in love or vitality. She has known that David paces his rooftop each night, and thus she has arranged her bath as a performance to dazzle him. She has heard that no woman has ever made him happy, and she is prepared to make him *completely* happy, to serve his every wish. But only if it is forever.

Perhaps the scene most disconsonant with the biblical world is that of the wedding of David and Bathsheba toward the end of the film, a wedding that takes place in a lavish setting that mimics a Renaissance cathedral. The bride wears a splendid white wedding gown, trimmed in gold rope, a garish tiara and gauzy wedding veil. Composer Alfred Newman has scored for the event a sentimental chorale rendition of the twenty-third psalm. While the organ gushes, the players are held in a tight shot, their eyes focused on high. The audience is led to believe that David has composed this musical extravaganza for the occasion since he has picked out the tune on his lyre earlier in the film. The anachronistic perspective is most apparent in the final half-hour of the film, which is mostly a

---

23 The film *David and Bathsheba* was written for the screen by Philip Dunne; produced by Darryl F. Zanuck; directed by Henry King; released in 1951 by Twentieth Century Fox Film Corporation. Cast: Gregory Peck, Susan Hayward, Raymond Massey, Kieron Moore, Jayne Meadows. Credits: director of photography, Leon Shamroy; special photographic effects, Fred Sersen; film editor, Barbara McLean; music, Alfred Newman.

debate about whether David should give up Bathsheba to a mob eager to stone her. The stoning is right and proper, as David and Nathan both reiterate: "it is the law" and "we are a nation of laws." Stoning of an adulterous woman must be reminiscent to a Christian audience of the difference between David and the soon to come upon the scene Jesus, who would stop such mistreatment of women. Finally while the nation is suffering a Hollywood spectacle drought, with black funnel clouds, writhing sheep, and camel drivers blown about by hissing winds, David realizes that God will not be mocked. Thus, he prays at the Ark that God remember him as the young David, full of love for the Lord, who subdued Goliath and was anointed by the aged Samuel. God consents, the rains fall, and David and Bathsheba walk into the damp night together.

As one can see from the tone of my analysis, the way a viewer accepts the story is all-important to its interpretation. In analyzing biblical films, I became increasingly aware of the function of the audience as author. The multiple identities of each audience member determines the film's various interpretations. Scholars of religion have the foundational text inscribed upon their hearts and will hear biblical echoes whispering underneath the modern voices. Cultural theorists will see how thoroughly and profoundly the appropriations of the biblical material have been achieved and encoded within popular media. It will be clear from the mainstream interpretations of film theorists that women were represented as either idealized objects of desire or as threatening forces to be tamed. Clearly these are not attempts to establish female subjectivity but rather reflect the search for male self-definition. Thus, popular films are said to belong to the patriarchy, leaving the female audience to identify with the male-as-subject and the female-as-object.

While it is instructive for biblical scholars to analyze popular cooptions of biblical texts as one level of interpretation (see chapter 7), I want to propose in this chapter an examination of an imagined female gaze, first as spectator of the Hollywood film, and second, as director of an imagined feminist film version of Bathsheba's story. The reader will note in this imagined shooting script that the subject and object positions do not remain constant. The identification of Bathsheba as the object of the gaze – masculine or feminine, compliant or seductive, victim or virago – depends on both the directorial/camera eye and the spectatorial eye.

In the Hollywood version, the most direct signal that the male narrator/director is engaged in the eroticization of woman can be seen by the way he controls and limits what we see. The narrator performs the function of camera, slowly panning over the female body. The first frame reveals the length of her entire naked body at her bath, and then a tight shot directs our gaze to a more intimate record, as the narrator discusses the woman's fertility cycle. She is prime to become pregnant. The narrator's report that David lies with her seems redundant. The taking of the woman is his erotic fantasy.

The woman's identity is not important. Learning that she is the wife of Uriah or the daughter of Eliam does not alter David's desire.[24] The narrator shows his hand in these first few frames by emphasizing male ownership of the woman's body's fertility and its interiority; at the same time he shows her vulnerability since her body is not inviolable. The scene has been constructed for a male spectator. The woman has been completely objectified. The male figure commands the scene; he articulates the look and creates the action.

Signs of male domination remind us that our cinematic narrative has been constructed by men for male spectators. While female spectators may be part of the audience, as Kaplan argues in *Women in Film*, they must either identify with the woman as object or they must appropriate the male gaze. When Bathsheba announces that she has conceived, David does not respond to her, but sends for Joab, his trusted intermediary, and Uriah, the man he has wronged. In a narration that reveals nothing of the woman's response to the king, her silence reinforces the power relationship between the king and a woman brought to his bed. A male viewer might well share the narrator's voyeuristic pleasure in this scene,

---

[24] If one understands *halo'-z't* as "isn't that" as a rhetorical question from David, "Isn't that Bathsheba daughter of Eliam, the wife of Uriah the Hittite" (2 Sam. 11:3), and thus that David knows well the identity of Bathsheba, then perhaps a different reading will result, that is, that part of the desire for her comes from the fact that she is another man's wife.

picturing the woman as enigma, as other, viewed as outside of male language, in which deals are cut.

Once the tension of wanting has been broken by fulfillment, the narrative searches for direction. Does the king become mildly disenchanted with Bathsheba to foreshadow his son Amnon's total disenchantment with Tamar after he has raped her? If the film remains within the male scopic gaze, and that gaze is allied with David, then Bathsheba must be the one who seduces the king (as in the Hollywood film) or she must struggle against his wishes, as she does comically in Pinski's story. But what of our imagined female version in which Bathsheba refuses David – the story stops. Remaining inside the biblical metanarrative, the ideal female audience is shut out of the picture. One way to find a site for a female spectator might be to reinscribe the scene of Tamar and Absalom into the story of David and Bathsheba. Absalom recognizes his sister's trauma, and tries to temper the traumatic by engaging his father, which fails, and finally through killing Amnon, the offensive male. But what Fifties audience wants to see a Gregory Peck David as the offending party, not only with the seductive Bathsheba (forgivable), but also with his daughter Tamar (unforgivable).

To cut the deal for Solomon to become David's successor, Bathsheba needs words. No longer the eroticized object of male sexual desire, she now plays the game like the loquacious Abigail, who convinced David to change his plans with honeyed words. Bathsheba in her plea to the king sounds much like Abigail, docile, compliant. The sexual Bathsheba has been replaced by a safer queen. Speaking in the familiar cadences of a deferential wife, she is no longer dangerous. Like Michal who saved David from Saul, Abigail who saved him from bloodguilt, Bathsheba now plays an acceptable social role. She saves David from appointing the wrong son king.[25]

---

[25] Bathsheba is the first *gebirah* or Queen Mother in the Bible. Whether she enjoyed particular status, either cultic or political, as *gebirah* has been the matter of much scholarly debate. The high status is thought to be demonstrated in the episode in I Kgs 2:13–25, in which Bathsheba petitions her son Solomon on behalf of Adonijah. On the intriguing question of the high status of the Queen Mother (*gebirah*), see J. Pedersen (1953); T. Ishida (1977: 155–60); R. N. Whybray (1968: 40); J. W. Flanagan (1983: 48–49); Z. Ben-Barak (1994: 170–85).

But let us consider this final scene as a cinematic midrash employing elements of the earlier films and literary versions. Remember Bathsheba, the nubile young woman, rosy in her bath? Now she is seen as clothed, driving, ambitious, just like the men surrounding her. Through the Hollywood lens, she would be played closer to Jayne Meadow's Michal, the sarcastic and savvy queen who appears to see through her husband David as though he were the color of water. But this version of Bathsheba would deliver the Fifties audience, both male and female, into David's hands. As the unsympathetic portrait of Michal reflects, no one wanted to cheer for a woman who put down her man.

How would one film the older Bathsheba, the one who is no longer the object of the camera's gaze? In order to make sure that Bathsheba is not seen by the audience as turning into an out-of-control stage mother, pushing her son Solomon forward to solidify her position as Queen Mother, the Hollywood camera eye would need to record a benign Nathan writing Bathsheba's dialogue with the king, signaling that her ambition is not to be feared. She is no longer luscious, the object of the desirous gaze. As she delivers Nathan's words to an indifferent David, the audience is assured that Bathsheba is supported by the divine prophet. She is repeating male mandates, not creating female ones. So the male desires, ownership of beautiful women and the political triumph of the "right" son becoming king, are fulfilled, happily ever after. But the camera's eye is restless. Searching for another object on which to fix its gaze, it roams over the eager Abishag, desperately trying to become the new Spectacle queen in the empire of the gaze. Ironically it is too late. Nearing death, David no longer reigns as the owner of the gaze. The camera moves on. There is almost a mutuality of gaze at this point – but it is Bathsheba, through speech and alliance with two powerful males, Nathan and Solomon, who has the power of the gaze – or at least of returning the patriarchal gaze. One must stay with the story of the gaze until it is has played itself out in order to subvert its power, to assure that all power relations in the text are not subsumed under one monolithic ocular apparatus (eye, camera, telescope, etc.).

The patriarchal perspective of the Hollywood version can be

seen through the film's assumption that fulfillment is a proper marriage that protects Bathsheba from stoning and David from gossip. Imagine instead a film that ended with the coronation of Bathsheba – perhaps in the same rosy-hued Renaissance cathedral as the wedding scene. In such a scene Bathsheba would dominate the screen. All eyes including the camera would be on her. David would have been buried in the preceding scene, assuring the audience that the time of succession was at hand. Stripped of their expected poses of shrewdness and complicity, the sons would be powerless and silent, no longer the subject of the story. As Queen regnant, our Bathsheba has retained her hegemonic position as the subject of the cinematic gaze. Through her eyes, we can look at the sons, corralled into a corner, dressed identically, not distinguishable, played by unknown actors, unimportant. Our gaze remains with Bathsheba. Stripped of the double-fringed eyelashes of Susan Hayward, this older, wiser, "womanly" Bathsheba might have remained in the spectator's mind as one who would have been disinterested in the king's erotic gaze so long ago on a spring evening in Jerusalem.

Authors usually try to create the illusion that the gap between the narrator and the reader is narrow; the ideal narrative audience is firmly planted within the elements of this fiction. We have followed the biblical narrator's gaze, blinked when he blinked, turned a blind eye when he wanted acts concealed. The Talmudic rabbis, reading with the biblical texts, have exerted halakic force to exonerate David from various legal and moral difficulties his behavior has caused. Pinski offers another, intimate view of the Davidic court. But none of these interpretations speaks for the women in the text. I hope I have suggested possibilities for eye-opening readings in which an irritable or suspicious narratee can question the story told through a narrator's fixed gaze and can surreptitiously glance around the fictive landscape to pick up clues about the story that didn't tempt the narrator. One can bring the women of the Court together in the mind of the reader, comically as Pinski has done. Or in a darker reading, tinged with the rape of Tamar, one can cite the torn clothes and spirit of Tamar, the narrative disappearance of Abigail. In the instance of Bathsheba one can refuse to stand watch with the narrator and David on the rooftop. As feminist readers we can employ insight, avert our gaze, and go somewhere else. When faced with an authoritative over-viewing narrator, we can cast a cold eye.

CHAPTER 6

Wine, women, and death[1]

> The Dark Continent is neither dark nor unexplorable. It is
> still unexplored only because we have been made to believe
> that it was too dark to be explored. Because they want to
> make us believe that what interests us is the white continent,
> with its monuments to Lack.
>
> Helene Cixous

BEYOND SEEING

In the previous chapters I have focused primarily on the way
women are visualized or perceived by a male audience – the
sighting of women. Through the narratologic analyses of these
texts, I have suggested some connections between vision, language,
authorship, reading, and conceptions of the self. By this point, I
hope the reader is convinced that biblical narratives operate in the
same way as modern narratives in which male characters attempt
to hold steadily to the subject position through controlling the gaze.
Judah looks over his daughter-in-law Tamar, although he does not
understand whom he is seeing; the Elders arrange forbidden views
of Susanna; as king, David gazes at Bathsheba bathing, and, as
outlaw, he watches Abigail riding down the mountainside to
placate him. There is also a gender reversal in which the female
character adopts the pivotal role of focalizer. Women are caught
gazing at beautiful men: Mut-em-enet gazes at Joseph almost

---

[1] Much of the discussion of the power of the details of fragrance and food found in the
narratives that are the subject of this chapter has grown out of fulfilling talks with
Geraldine Heng during a shared year at the Stanford Humanities Center. Over lunch,
over coffee, we have performed feminist readings. Her wisdom and humor have inspired
and enlivened this chapter.

fanatically in the *Testament of Joseph*, and Aseneth watches him from her high-tower window; Michal watches David from a similar privileged vantage point. Both Jezebel and the mother of Sisera await their fate, at the hands of their enemies, from a tower window. All these female characters who dare to look at men, however, are covered with narrative and doxic scorn. Looking is an aggressive maneuver, seeking to hold the object in its view. Looking must be controlled by the male. Driving the aggressive ownership of the gaze is the fear of becoming an object, that is, a fear of being looked at. I need to look so as not to be looked at. I must control the gaze, lest the gaze control me and engulf me.

The holder of the gaze has, not surprisingly, privileged it among the senses. Sight has always held a central place in Western culture, although it has been argued about the ancient Mediterranean world that the Greeks were a visual and the Hebrews an auditory culture.[2] "If the Jews could begin their most heartfelt prayer, 'Hear, O Israel,' the Greek philosophers were in effect urging, 'See Oh Hellas.' "[3] This distinction seems far too superficial; the biblical culture was not as hostile to the eye as scholars have argued.[4] The Hebrew marker *hinneh lo* "behold" is one such sign of visual epistemology. In Hebrew syntax *hinneh lo* transforms seeing into believing, and it simultaneously encourages the believing reader to fabricate reality from representation through the force of the narrative voice heralding divine intervention.

[2] Classic studies by Auerbach (1953) and Boman (1960) and more recently Handelman (1982). Boman's argument suffers from the polarized and positivistic values of his time, e.g., Greeks concentrated upon the nude body in their statuary and Hebrews "spoke" of clothed figures. The Hebrew prohibition against visual images of the deity strengthens his case for orality over ocularity, but does not take into account the mental spectacle created by narrative discourse nor that the deity was seen by the biblical ancestors, much as the Greek gods were manifest to humankind. Handelman's argument is more nuanced, but neither acknowledges the importance of the reader expanding the visual clues offered within Hebrew narrative writing. I am not disputing that the Greeks privileged sight over the other senses, nor that Western discourse has not been primarily ocularcentric, but rather that Hebrew narrative also had vital scopic elements.

[3] This citation does not reflect the depth of Jay's elegant argument, which traces the movement of specular thought from its central position (seeing is believing) to its postmodern diffusion (Jay 1993).

[4] One of the plainest indications of the importance of ocularity in the Bible would be the deity's choice to create light first. Each time God finishes the work of a day, he sees or looks at (*r'h*) what he has done and says that it is good. One could argue, therefore, that sight/light is almost equivalent to hearing/speaking in Genesis 1.

I am not disputing the view that Western thought has privileged sight above the other senses, but rather that biblical literature, even within the conventions of Hebrew narrative, is often ocularcentric *for the reader,* or as Jay suggests, one reads with a "plurality of scopic regimes." While it is not the purpose of this study to debate the hierarchizing of the senses within ancient literatures, it is important for the reader to consider the evocation of the senses as potential strategies for the biblical authors in their attempts to characterize female figures. Thus, the reading strategy I employ in this chapter will privilege the senses of smell (aroma, fragrance) and taste (food, banquets, wine), senses that recall early or infantile sexuality.[5] This period is synonymous with the rule of the mother, before entrance into the Symbolic, patriarchal Law. A patriarchal regime might fear the return to a pansexual eroticism, with its nongenital economy that does not focus upon the phallic, but takes pleasure on generalized touching, smell, texture, taste.

In premodern Western cultures, smell was associated with essence and spiritual truth, while sight was often deemed a superficial sense, revealing only exteriors.[6] It was not until the Enlightenment focus upon science and its allegiance to seeing/knowing that the importance of the sense of smell declined and Western culture became firmly ocularcentric.

The sixteenth century did not see first; it heard and smelled, it sniffed the air and caught sounds. It was only later, as the seventeenth century was approaching, that it seriously and actively became engaged in geometry, focusing attention on the world of forms with Kepler . . . vision was unleashed in the world of science as it was in the world of physical sensations and the world of beauty as well.[7]

---

[5] For a superb analysis of the ways in which language gives rise to desire while it simultaneously sets limits to the representability of desire, see Butler (1995). Feminist paradigms for thinking about desire and gender in classical texts are analyzed by Halperin (1990b); Keuls (1985); Winkler (1990a). The subtle analyses found within this new-directed classical scholarship has showed me the problems with setting up too strict a correspondence between masculinity, rationality, and active desire on the one hand and feminity, matter, passive desire on the other.

[6] In his social history of smell in France, Corbin argues that "the sense of smell has suffered from an unremitting process of discrediting since the eighteenth century" (Corbin 1986: 5).

[7] It is pointless to try to determine the hierarchy of the senses in Western thought. While some argue for smell, and some for touch, there is agreement that ocularcentrism is connected to the developing scientific discourse (Febvre 1982).

Smell and taste are strongly engaged by authors to add to the sensual depiction of their characters. Magic, sexual power, and healing were connected with olfactory signs in ancient texts. Biblical texts may not be as explicit about these odors as other literatures, due to the classical Hebrew authors' spare style and disinterest in languorous descriptions, but the suggestions of aromas would be enough to elicit associations in the reader familiar with ancient Mediterranean cultures. I have provided a number of textual examples of olfactory and alimentary codes employed in classical literary texts to offer the reader insight into the pervasiveness of fragrance and food in ancient daily life. Smell and taste, fragrance and food, were proof of a material existence that brought verisimilitude to ancient narratives. The locus of such dailiness was the inside of the house, the domain of the maternal woman, metonymic for the protected pleasurable pansexuality of the pre-phallic life. By privileging the codes of nongenital pleasure, one can reach back to the forms of pleasure that predate seeing, gazing, knowing. Food is a displaced trope for sexual pleasure: the erotic written as noneroticized (and therefore a safe, recreational, even ceremonial form of) pleasure. The pleasures of eating return us to the infantile sexuality of "polymorphous perversity," a stage in Freud's cosmos where the erotic encompassed more than genital sexuality, with its fixation on *telos* – tumescence, genital orgasm, climax – where eroticism was distributed to all points of the body envelope (hearing, taste, touch, smell) and any and all stimuli might be erotic(ized).

To return to the Bible, one has only to think of the odors of Noah's sacrifices being pleasing to the deity in Gen. 8:21 "and YHWH smelled (*ryḥ*) a pleasing [lit. soothing] smell" to recall the centrality of smell in early Israelite rituals.[8] This reference to a Yahwistic ritual is followed by many references to the incense altars

[8] The etymology of the word perfume (L. *fumare*, to smoke) literally "to smoke through" indicates its association with aromatic smoke and incense. The *terminus technicus* in the Hebrew Bible for aromatic sacrifices that propitiate the deity is also found in reference to other ethnic peoples' sacrifices "wherever they offered pleasing odor to all their idols" (Ezek. 6:13), and to YHWH's acceptance of Israel, "there they offered their sacrifices and presented the provocation of their offering" (Exod. 20:28 and also verse 41); the term refers to aromatic sacrifices, both cereal and animal offerings, pleasing to YHWH seventeen times in the book of Leviticus; eighteen times in the book of Numbers.

(*hammanim*) associated with the high places (*bamoth*), sometimes associated with YHWH, frequently with other gods.[9] These altars have been described as "small cuboid incense altars made of limestone, known from the sixth through the fourth century throughout the west Semitic world" (Ackerman 1992: 184). Ezekiel describes the nefarious ritual practices in which these altars were used as common:

> For when I had brought them into the land that I swore to give them, then *wherever* they saw any high hill or any leafy tree, there they offered their sacrifices and presented the provocation of their offering; *there they sent up their pleasing odors*, and there they poured out their drink offerings. (Ezek. 20:28, emphasis mine)

Ackerman has determined that there may well have been a cult centered in Lachish which "perceived the burning of incense to YHWH on small altars as legitimate regardless of whatever practices the priests and prophets in the sixth century and Ezra in the fifth century had defined as normative" (1992: 181).[10]

Is there a connection between aromas as mediating signs in the sacrificial offerings humans offer to the deity in the Semitic and the classical world and the odors that form sensual connections between women and men? Any recall of an all-powerful mother, the source of nourishment and pleasure – female power in its earliest form, and as the infant understands it – surely threatens masculine regimes of power, which are posited on (1) specularity or the politics of the gaze, in which the masculinized gaze dominates a feminine object; (2) teleological sexuality, the dominance of the phallus as the operator of pleasure and focus of the sexual act, and

---

[9] Incense offerings are associated with, although no altar is specifically mentioned in, I Kgs 3:3; 13:2; 22:44; 2 Kgs 12:4; 15:4, 35; 16:4; 17:11; 23:5,8.

[10] See also on the shrine at Lachish and the small limestone incense altars (*hammanim*) found there, Y. Aharoni, "Trial Excavation in the Solar Shrine at Lachish. Preliminary Report," *IEJ* 18 (1968) 163–64; idem. "Excavations in the Solar Temple at Lachish," *Qadmoniot* 2 (1969) 131–34 (Hebrew). See also W. F. Albright, "The Lachish Cosmetic Burner and Esther 2:12," *A Light Unto My Path: Old Testament Studies in Honor of Jacob M. Myers* (ed. H. N. Bream, R. D. Heim, and C. A. Moore), Philadelphia: Temple University Press, (1974) 25–32 for an explanation of the cosmetic burner in the book of Esther as referring not to a religious or cultic object, but rather to an object from "the secular world of cosmetics and beautification of women" (25). Albright connects these incense burners with the ones stipulated in the marriage contracts from Elephantine by the father of the woman to his daughter.

the organization of these regimes into a communal dynamic.

Detienne has shown that sacrifice and marriage are the two major human institutions in which aromatic spices play a role in classical Greek culture. According to his theory, the union of the two [spices/marriage, spices/sacrifice] have opposite valences; in sacrifices spices are positive and in marriage the role of myrrh and perfume becomes dangerous and negative. "If they are allowed to predominate in the conjugal union, instead of their effects being first restricted and later totally eradicated (a matron is supposed to eliminate all perfumes both on her own person and on her husband's) the marriage is destroyed, not by overreaching itself but by being perverted."[11] The more limited the role of fragrances, and thus the more finite the role of the woman, the more successful the marriage will be in Detienne's scheme.[12] The pivotal figure for Detienne in the alliance between seduction and spices is Pandora. Unleashed during the summer-dry Dog days, she is fire, heat, enchantment, created to make men pay for Prometheus' theft of fire from the gods.[13]

What other associations might an author make between gender and aromas and tastes to add details of characterization?[14] For our purposes the most important function of the culinary sign, or other portion of the alimentary code, is to represent the erotic transformation of an object into a body, in this case the eroticization of the female character *through* her connection to the food she prepares or offers to the male. The odors ascribed to women reflect a hushed

[11] From the supremely lucid introduction by J.-P. Vernant (Detienne, 1994: xxvi).

[12] Winkler has pointed out that Detienne has imposed a masculinist view upon the interpretation of the events of the Adonai and the identity of the women as courtesans (1990a: 200–02). My purpose is not to validate Detienne's reading over Winkler's, but rather to show the parallels between Detienne's diagnosis of "ideology in hermeneutic disguise," connecting codes of fragrance with the construction of women with a possible similiarity in biblical texts.

[13] It is during the time of the dry Dog days that frankincense and myrrh are produced and collected. For the Pandora myth, see Hesiod, *Works and Days*, lines 60–104.

[14] The scope of this study does not permit a review of the anthropologic and cultural contexts of food in antiquity. Nor is this book a place to open a discussion of culinary discourse in ancient literature. But the reader is referred to the classic trajectories outlined by Levi-Strauss from the raw to the cooked (and from honey to ashes), as well as Bourdieu's study of the formation of taste and distinction as models and values functioning powerfully on social classes. Mary Douglas has deciphered a meal by involving religion, sociology, and culture. Bourdieu (1985), Douglas (1966, 1975, and 1987), Levi-Strauss (1966).

dialogue between the male author/narrator and his reader, codifying women as safe or dangerous through the aromas with which she is associated. For the purposes of this analysis, I have adapted anthropologist Constance Classen's classification of three types of women and the generalized odors with which they are connected. (1) Wives and mothers, the good women, are connected to the odors of food and flowers. These are figured also as matriarchs, who use the spices for ritual and religious purposes, e.g., Sarah baking bread for the angels of the Lord. These are positive uses of the spices, which have the recognized virtue of summoning the gods to the sacrifice being offered to them. The aromatic spices have become integrated, as it were, into cultivated life (Detienne 1994: 127). (2) Garlanded with floral crowns, young virgins, such as the Graces, are identified with pleasant odors, and are described as wearing garments scented with crocus, hyacinth, and blooming violets. Sour old maids, a threat to the reproductive power of society, are accorded a stale odor. A most excessive example is described by Horace, who abhors an older woman smitten with him. "What sweatiness and how rank an odor everywhere rises from her withered limbs."[15] (3) Sexual women are associated with "heavily sweet and spicy odors, the sweetness of the scent signifying their beauty and attraction, and the spiciness and heaviness their exotic status and overwhelming powers of fascination" (Classen 1993: 88).

There is a temptation to include in this third group a goddess associated with the pungent incense offered at the *bamoth* sanctuaries, to a deity other than YHWH. That deity is Asherah. A symmetry exists between the feminine heat of Detienne's courtesans, whose rituals occur in the scented garden of Adonis, and the implied sexuality of the Canaanite/Israelite ritual activities described in Hos. 4:12–13.

My people consult a piece of wood, and their divining rod gives them oracles. For a spirit of whoredom has led them astray, and they have played the whore, forsaking their God. They sacrifice on the tops of the mountains, and make offerings upon the hills, under oak, poplar, and terebinth (*'elim*), because their shade is good. Therefore your daughters

[15] Horace, *The Odes and Episodes*, with an English translation by C. E. Bennett. Loeb Classical Library 33. Cambridge, MA: Harvard University Press, 1927. Ode 12.

play the whore, and your daughters-in-law commit adultery. (See also
Jer. 2:20; 3:6, 13)[16]

The seeded garden of Adonis is here feminized by the verdant
places of sacrifice: upon the hills, under oak, poplar, and terebinth.
Central to the evocation of female sexuality is the mention of
terebinth. The linguistic connection between biblical Hebrew
[*'elath* > 'elat] terebinth and the goddess Asherah (whose presence
in biblical religion is now being examined through the work of
Ackerman, Dever, Olyan, and others) is found in the biblical
Hebrew place name Elat.[17] In Greek writings, eating terebinth is
stereotypical of the "East," particularly Persia. Associated with the
initiation of Persian kings (Artaxerxes 3.2), terebinth were intended
to keep alive the memories of the halcyon old days of Cyrus. A
similar connotation is found in Strabo's description of Persian
educational practices (15.3.18). The cultural connection with
terebinth (at least in the Greek evidence) is with life in the wild,
bravery, and authority. One can certainly assign each of these
attributes to the dangerous goddess Asherah as well.[18] Further, one
can understand why the patriarchal narrators are concerned to
close down such potentially dangerous intimations of female
sexuality.

William Albright notes the great variety of spices associated with

[16] A further connection is made between the sacred groves of Adonis and those *'elim*
(terebinths) of the Bible. Zohary describes such forests in the Lower Galilee, and the
valleys of Huldah and Dan. "In these forests, according to Zohary, evergreen oaks, styrax
trees, and terebinths predominate . . . These trees are deciduous, thus the season Hosea
describes here is the summer, when the trees are leafed out. The summer is of course the
dry season in Israel, and it is easy to understand why fertility rituals involving sexual
intercourse would be practiced during that season when the forces of drought and sterility
threatened the fruitfulness of the land" (Ackerman 1992: 188, n. 92).

[17] This etymology is found in Albright (1968: 189). See Ackerman (1992: 185–202) for full
discussion of the figuration of Asherah as sexual/fertility deity and her connections both
to aromatic vegetation and trees and her suppressed cultic presence within the biblical
texts – and within Israelite popular religion.

[18] For a thorough discussion of Persian royal meals, meats, and spices, see Sancisi-
Weerdenburg (1995). The author reviews Greek sources for food items typical of the
peoples comprising the Persian Empire and states in relation to terebinths: "in view of its
common occurrence in the ancient Near East, its use by the Persians is not at all unlikely.
Its relative rarity (textually) compared with references to dates, apples, and other
cultivated fruits may point to its being gathered in the wild" (289). The terebinth was
ubiquitous in the ancient Near East, its fruits are reddish and purplish, about the size of
blackcurrants and turn coppery green upon drying. The tree is still commonly found on
the mountain slopes of Kurdistan.

the South Arabian spice burners, most of them being sweet smelling, and hence referring to some kind of perfume. Emphasizing that these spices are in no cases recipes for religious incense, he cites Baker's vivid description of the different perfumed spices most in demand by women from the traveling native merchants.

The women have a peculiar method of scenting their bodies and clothes, by an operation that is considered to be one of the necessaries of life and which is repeated at regular intervals. In the floor of the tent or hut . . . a small hole is excavated sufficiently large as to hold . . . a fire of charcoal . . . into which the woman about-to-be-scented throws a handful of various drugs. She then takes off the cloth or tope which forms her dress, and crouches naked over the fumes while she arranges her robe to fall as a mantle from her neck to the ground like a tent. (Albright 1968: 28–30)

The erotic mix of fragrant perfume and woman's body is remarkable in this text. Not commenting directly upon the powerful erotic description that he himself has provided us, Albright suggests that the variety of spices mentioned directly or implied in the text of Esth. 2:12 were a specific combination of spices (*besamim*) and the period of six months in which they were applied indicated that this period was one of "fumigation, which would have had both hygienic and therapeutic value" (32). I include his conclusion merely to show how this provocative text tempts many interpretations associated with and tangential to female sexuality.

Albright's interpretation of the association of spices with the women of Ahasuerus' harem illustrates well how in the Bible, as in other ancient literatures, the signs connected to food and fragrance may be read as direct or reversed. They may be used to convey pansexual pleasure or irony, to foreshadow abundance or dearth, to structure narrative, or to highlight or counterpoint other action in a text.[19] Of course one need not have alliance to a psychoanalytic mode of reading. The ritual nature of celebrations, marked by food and celebration, also figure in the biblical and ancient Near Eastern cultures and form the basis for much biblical interpretation. Important stages in the life cycle are marked by celebrations, orchestrated with food and drink, from the wedding feast to the

---

[19] See Sharon (note 20) for illustrations of these categories within biblical narrative texts.

honoring of the dead at the *marzeah*. The matrix of food/life cycle that connects the figures who are the primary subjects of this chapter marks a greater event than an initiation or passage into a life stage, however. The banquets and feasts have a transformative function, a reworking of the traditional female role, as the female figure turns from maternal nurturer to murderous mother, using food as bait to trap her enemy.

First, I would like to examine a biblical story in which food is encoded within the confines of the patriarchal narrative. While I am not ready to argue that the encoding language for food and cooking in such texts is an example of woman's culture breaking through the dominant male narrative, I do believe that the entry of food into the story does allow for a transformation of the identity of the female figure. Let us consider a subtle aromatic sign linked to the ritual meal prepared in I Samuel 28 as a conveyer of characterization of a female biblical figure, although in this text the main literary sign would be the meal itself.[20] In this story the Medium of Endor, a literary figure whose small narrative unit is usually not accorded interest by scholars except as it reflects ancient notions of ghosts, superstition, and possible remnants of oracular rituals, calls forth the shade of Samuel to warn Saul of his impending defeat and death.

One way to read the signs of the meal would be as ritual fragrances pleasing to the shade being called forth. But one can also approach the codes from an opposing point, a narrative journey from the spirit world to the mortal realm. A level of realism is added to this fantasmic story in the final scene in which the woman cooks a meal for the emotionally exhausted dispirited Saul. While the author does not explicitly describe the aroma of the cooking meat or bread, the

---

[20] Bakhtin's extensive study of all the semiotic elements in banqueting and Barthes' essays on the semiology of the meal have influenced my decision to add a culinary reading of the biblical texts: Bakhtin (1965) Barthes (1975). Fictional meals and their semiotic importance in biblical narratives needs further study. In her dissertation *The Literary Functions of Eating and Drinking in Hebrew Bible Narrative with Reference to the Literatures of the Ancient Near East* (Ph.D., Jewish Theological Seminary of America 1995), Diane Sharon has examined the ways in which meal narratives operate to introduce an oracle, either positive or negative. This pattern appears to underlie and reinforce accounts of the establishment of an entity when the oracle is positive, or the condemnation of an entity when the oracle is negative. Generally she has argued that meals serve as versatile literary devices that reinforce or undermine narrative messages, suggesting intertextual readings.

reader having experienced such familiar cooking smells can easily fill such a sensual gap. The association between the comforting smells of cooking food and ordinary life serves to mitigate the threat of the woman as seer. The cooking of food transforms her momentarily into a wifely character. Using the standard convention of a good woman soothing or nurturing a man with food, the author defuses the alarm of Samuel's appearance and warning. Thus, the author gives us details of dailiness, of a very real world, to contrast with the eerieness of the spirit world.[21] The concrete nature of the hearth serves as a sign to remind the reader that the Medium is not a total outcast, but possesses the alimentary elements, bread and meat, of any civilized woman in the community. This small narrative unit illustrates one way in which the alimentary code may operate as a literary device to provide textual subtlety and nuance the female figure. In the case of I Samuel 28, the role of the woman is transformed from the seer to the wife, a reversal of the expected transformation from traditional role to exceptional act, as food marks the narratives of Judith, Esther, and Jael.

Clearly sensual evocations can sharpen desire in the reader, as intended by descriptions of a somewhat benign subset of the category of seduction, personal attraction. Both men and women wore similar fragrances on their hair, breast, legs, and feet. Demetrius Poliorcetes (third century BCE king of Macedonia) exhausted his stock of perfumes trying to find the perfect scent to render him irresistible to a certain female flute player (Classen 1994: 28). What was surprising about the woman anointing Jesus' feet in the Gospel of John was not the powerful fragrance of the perfume, but the lavishness of her act in using such an expensive ointment. Similar fragrances emanating from the two lovers in the Song of Songs emphasize their mutuality and the way their narrative roles blend and intertwine.[22]

Greek and Roman texts reflect a cultural concern with the

[21] The reader might connect Saul being served by the female seer with the occasion on which he was chosen to become king-elect (*nagid*) of Israel by Samuel, an occasion of a celebratory or ritual meal, as described in I Sam. 9:23–24.

[22] I use the term mutuality in relation to the Song with a light touch, acknowledging the critical nuance provided by Pardes' reading. Following her, I think the female lover's desire for a free sexual experience must be framed by "the patriarchal character of the society within which the amorous dialogue takes place" (Pardes 1992: 132). For an elegant analysis of the Song, see Landy, whose prose captures the lyrical beauty of the Song.

breath, both fragrant and foul. Needless to say, the fragrance of a lover's kiss would be associated with the freshest most delightful signs, as in Martial's catalogue of kisses:

perfume such as when the blossoming vine blooms with early clusters; the scent of grass which a sheep has just cropped; the odor of myrtle, of the Arab spice-gatherer, of rubbed amber; of a fire made pallid with Eastern frankincense; of the earth when lightly sprinkled with summer rain. (Classen 1994: 27)[23]

In a love song composed for the marriage of the king whom God has anointed with the oil of gladness, the psalmist adds aromatic notes to his picture: "Your robes are all fragrant with myrrh and aloes and cassia" *mor va'ahalot qetsi'ot* (Ps. 45:8). Spices accelerate pleasure and sensuality in the Song of Songs, frequently also in relation to the male character: "nard and saffron, calamus and cinnamon, with all trees of frankincense, myrrh and aloes, with all chief spices" (Song 4:14). The Song is filled with sensual descriptions of aromas meant to entice both the male lover and the reader. "His cheeks are like beds of spices, yielding fragrance. His lips are lilies, distilling liquid myrrh" *(mor 'over)* (Song 5:13). "Your anointing oils are fragrant, your name is perfume poured out; therefore the maidens love you" (Song 1:3). Spiced fragrance is not solely connected to the male lover; the Song also figures the woman as a scented garden. "My beloved has gone down *to his garden,* to the beds of spices, to pasture his flock *in the gardens*" (Song 6:2). The multiple fragrances of the woman create a vital sensual connection to the man.

How sweet is your love, my sister, my bride! How much better is your love than wine, and the fragrance of your oils than any spice! Your lips distill nectar, my bride; honey and milk are under your tongue; the scent of your garments is like the scent of Lebanon! (Song 4:10,11)

One notes in the translation of these verses from the Song of Songs the paucity of language that specifically defines or describes

---

[23] Modern fragrances also make use of natural scents to create sensual images. Popular colognes currently on the market are called Earth, Ocean Breeze, Grass, Clouds, and Summer Rain.

smell. The reader would need to have an association with the sensual words honey, nectar, and milk, as well as a familiarity with the scent of Lebanon, to fully appreciate the mingled fragrances of the woman.

Landy has noted that both flowers and spices are markers of time in the Song, that is, flowers blossom and fade, fragrance is intense and wafting. The temporal nature of the Garden in the Song is what distinguishes it from the static perfection of the Garden in Eden (1983: 192–93). Since the narrative of the lovers is engaged in their celebration of each other, there is an ephemeral quality to the story narrated in the Song. The precision that would be gained in identifying specific plot points is lacking in this narrative; instead this narrative is truly a biblical case of writing the body. Functioning as both setting and plot, the Garden in the Song is a cultivated garden that signifies activity of human pleasures and human cultivation. The conversion of leaves, blossoms, and bark into aromatic oils and spices requires human diligence and desire to become part of the natural world.[24] Thus, the movement of the story embraces the lovers and human connections to sensuality. A connection between sensuality, fragrance, and pleasure seems inevitable: in the biblical texts containing the most positive and overt sexual codes, the vocabulary of fragrance and spice is most frequently used.

Other than the poetry redolent of images of flowers, perfumes, and oils found in the Song, probably the most extensive biblical sensual evocations occur in the Book of Esther. The alimentary code and the sensations associated with ancient banquets will be considered later in this chapter in the discussion of biblical narrations of banquet preparations. First, I want to consider the references to personal fragrances as triggers to desire. These occur immediately following the rejection of Queen Vashti, who has not behaved like a proper woman, with the information that the young girls of the harem are preparing for their special night with King Ahasuerus. The narrator delights the reader with the mental image

---

[24] Landy observes that "spices are a supreme cultural achievement, whose function is to make nature acceptable by disguising it and thereby enhancing it, to make food palatable and women attractive" (1983: 192). I would amend his observation to indicate that spices intensify a mutual sexual experience since both male and female lovers in the garden are equally adorned with fragrance.

of young nubile women spending twelve months under special beautifying regulations, "since this was the regular period of their cosmetic treatment, six months with oil of myrrh (*beshemen hammor*) and six months with perfumes (*babbesamim*) and cosmetics for women (*betamruqe hannashim*)" (Esth. 2:12). The female in this text is figured as the object of male desire. One can easily imagine a male fantasy in which a harem of beautiful girls is thinking of nothing but ways to please a man. What do these projections tell us about the people and the culture which nourish such fantasies?

While Esther is seen as a positive literary character for the traditional Jewish reader,[25] an individual less inclined to read with the official line of thought might look at the descriptions of beauty and banquet preparations as metonymic for a seductive woman, using her beauty as power to achieve her ends. Reading these codes of sensations, one could compare the description of the preparation of the young girls for their tryout night with Ahasuerus with the description of Pandora, as she has been prepared by Aphrodite and Athena as a temptation for men. Anointed with perfumes, crowned with myrrh, clothed in a wedding tunic and veil, the enchantress heads for Epimetheus. When she lifts the lid of the spice jar, hard work, illness, deteriorating old age, and death are released into the world.[26] The "magic" contained in Esther's spice jar results in the death of Haman, as well as the reversal of the political enmity toward the Jewish people. In both instances the beauty of one woman effects an entire populace, not just the man who is the object of the seduction. Read this way, Esther becomes another of those female characters who exert power over men through their seductive wiles.

The pleasures of the body, as offered by the temptress, are frequently used as negative signs, particularly as elements of female

---

[25] Some of the major contemporary readings of the character of Esther as Jewish and/or feminist heroine are found in Berg 1979; Bickerman 1967; Moore 1971 and 1977; J. F. Craghan, "Esther: A Fully Liberated Woman," *Bible Today* 24 (1986) 7–10; S. A. White, "Esther: A Feminine Model for Jewish Diaspora," in Peggy Day (ed.), *Gender and Difference in Ancient Israel* (Minneapolis: Fortress Press 1989) 161–77.

[26] The biblical parallel to evil being introduced into the world involves a woman offering a fragrant fruit to her male companion. One can argue with traditionalists that Pandora is intentionally set into the world as the bearer of evil, and that the woman in the second Genesis creation story chooses to disobey the deity. Or one can see the stories as parallel tales of misogyny.

characterizations. Often women smell *too* good, and such hyper-fragrance is understood to be for the express purpose of seduction. In these instances the authors employ sensual signs to subvert the intentionality of the subject who desires. The author of Proverbs connects the perfumed woman with sexual temptations and promises. "I have perfumed my bed (*mishkavi*) with myrrh, aloes, and cinnamon," the *ishah zarah* sings, beckoning to the hapless youth (Prov. 7:17). She taunts the young man with other phrases associated with fragrance. "I had to offer sacrifices, and today I have paid my vows" (Prov. 7:14). Are these sacrifices at the Temple or cultic sacrifices to Asherah or another pagan god? Wisdom, representing the good woman, resides in a world free of spices and aromatic allusions (see especially the narratives in which Wisdom speaks: Prov. 1:20–33; 8:22–31).

The mention of quantities of spices can serve also as a sensual allusion, leaving an aromatic gap for the reader to fill. "Never again did spices come in such quantity as that which the Queen of Sheba gave to King Solomon" (1 Kgs. 10:10.) The mysterious unnamed ruler supposedly came from the southern Arabian peninsula, the primary locus of ancient spices, the source of exotic powers. While the Bible is taciturn about the relationship between the Jewish king and the mysterious Queen, later literatures award them a fecund love life.[27] Thus, the references to the spices, offered by her and accepted by him, point to a drama of sexual difference in which the discourse of desire plays itself out. The Queen, who controls the trade in spices, seduces the king and eventually is held responsible for his downfall. King Solomon gave to the Queen of Sheba every desire that she expressed (1 Kgs. 10:13).[28] Rashi insists that *he satisfied all her desires* refers to

[27] Pseudo Ben Sira identifies the Queen of Sheba as the mother of Nebuchadnezzar (through her liaison with Solomon). Her son will usurp the power of Solomon and defeat Israel, send the people into exile, and destroy the Temple that his father Solomon has built. Thus the Queen of Sheba is a nefarious mother, whose offspring strips Israel of its house of David, its house of God, and its homeland. (Lassner 1993: 21–25). Since the Queen brings great quantities of spices from her homeland, the source of the spices, one can connect this surfeit of fragrance with the third category of women, whose use of spices has a negative effect.

[28] The report, expanded in 2 Chr. 9:12, hints at the later midrashic conclusions. "King Solomon granted the Queen of Sheba every desire that she expressed, well beyond what she had brought to the king."

wisdom and wisdom alone. However, an interpolation printed in Rashi's commentary adds a sexual gloss. "He had intercourse with her and she gave birth to Nebuchadnezzar, who destroyed Israel." Holding the supreme power of the spices, the Queen overwhelms even King Solomon.

A negative encoding of fragrance, where seduction becomes prostitution, can also be found in the figuration of Israel as destructive woman, such as the text in which Trito-Isaiah connects aroma and female carnality. "You journeyed to Molech with oil, and multiplied your perfumes; you sent your envoys far away, and sent down even to Sheol" (Isa. 57:9). It is presumably up to the reader to determine whether the woman making love in her scented bed in the Song of Songs is of a different sexual class than the strange woman in Proverbs who has decked her couch with coverings, and perfumed her bed with myrrh, aloes, and cinnamon (7:16–17). According to Classen's classification, both are *femmes fatales*, associated with heavily sweet and spicy odors. Their modern-day parallels are found among perfume ad models and sex-goddess moviestars (see chapter 7). But if one chooses to privilege the codes of fragrance (myrrh, aloes, and cinnamon) and touch (colored spreads of Egyptian linen), one can avoid the negative encoding so important to the patriarchal narrator, who fears such powerfully threatening, potentially excessive hints of sexuality. In spite of these narratorial attempts at suppression, reading as a woman, one is returned to the pleasurable pansexual pre-phallic world of the mother.

Greek writers of the classical and Hellenistic periods often figured both goddesses and mortal women as a perfume too strong, *overpowering*. Sparkling with desire, laden with aromas, women use the senses as tools of sorcery. Often writers use the senses lightly, allowing small gestures to betray female characters. Pseudo-Lucian describes a man slipping out of his paramour's bed, "saturated with femininity."[29] Lucretius observes that all women, even the beautiful ones, "reek of noisome smells in private."[30] In comparing the "sensations named for Aphrodite," with the equivalent delights performed by boys, Achilles Tatius

---

[29] Quoted in Calasso's mellifluous novel, *The Marriage of Cadmus and Harmony* (1993).
[30] Cited in Classen (1994) from Lucretius, *On the Nature of Things*.

in the novel *Leucippe and Clitophon*[31] tips his hand in the direction of male–male sensuality.

> Women are false in every particular, from coquettish remarks to coy posturing. Their lovely looks are the busy contrivance of various ointments: they wear the borrowed beauty of myrrh, of hair dye, even chemical preparations. If you strip them of their many false attractions, they would be like the fabled jackdaw who lost his feathers. A boy's beauty is not carefully nurtured by the odor of myrrh nor enhanced by other scents of insidious intent. Sweeter than all a woman's exotic oils is the honest day's sweat of an active lad. (Reardon 1989: 207)

Tatius claims that the young boy kisses from instinct, the woman by technique. In his mind, and that of other Greek Hellenistic authors, a boy's sweat has a finer smell than anything in a woman's mysterious makeup box. Of course the reader must determine what the smell of a boy's sweat and of a woman's makeup box are. These determinations will vary with cultural associations.

When Christianity rose to power in the fourth century, the importance of fragrance declined. With the fall of the Roman Empire, the role of fragrance as marker of the high life ended. Communal use of incense was condemned as an indication of idolatry. Origen called it a "food for demons." Personal use of perfumes was considered frivolous; "Attention to sweet scents is a bait," warned Clement of Alexandria. "It draws us into sensual lusts." If the ancient deities made their presence known by spicy fragrances, it was not until the Middle Ages that incense was widely used as a symbol of prayer in Christian ritual.

In the ancient Mediterranean world, then, both food and fragrance served as markers or codes to indicate texts in which women's roles were heightened, altered, or transformed. For the contemporary reader, food and fragrance are problematic but

---

[31] *Leucippe and Clitophon* was written in the late second century BCE and was one of the most popular Greek novels in Greco-Roman Egypt. I have used John J. Winkler's superb translation published in Reardon (1989). Winkler categorizes the novel *Leucippe and Clitophon* as "sophisticated criminal fiction. Quite unmatched for sheer staginess . . . the apparatus of melodrama [killed] by analytic asides that dissect the physiology of emotions" (1990: 174). For a classic translation with commentary and introduction, see Plepelits (1980). Bartsch argues that the descriptions found in Tatius' novel, often thought of as needless ornamental devices, are employed to lure the reader into the text and heighten the reader's connection with the text. I would argue similarly for the less extensive but equally powerful sensual descriptions in biblical literature (Bartsch 1989).

central elements of femininity, and as such play a part in the literary interpretation of gender roles. While culinary codes and banquet settings are not found in the majority of biblical narratives, they are important to mark transitions within the life-cycle, alterations in the expected role of a character, or interplays of sexual desire and possible danger.

"FOOD IS NOT FEED"[32]

From the very first biblical narrative set in the Garden of Eden, women have offered men dangerous food. Within male-created narratives, it stands to reason that women's weapons would be chosen from the female arsenal. Since feeding is one of women's primary cultural roles, it becomes the key to their seizing of power. Thus, when God forbids the eating of the fruit of a particular tree, the man trusts that the woman will feed him only the safe food. Instead the woman feeds him the forbidden fruit, thus linking, from the beginning of the biblical narratives, a connection between food and death. A dual connection between food and sex is made simultaneously. As a result of eating the magical fruit, the couple discovers desire and gratification in each other's bodies. As part of the divine punishment, God must emphasize what is sacred (and therefore denied to the human couple) and what is profane (and part of the human world). Of course the greatest difference between God and human beings is death, which both male and female will experience.

Of the gendered experiences, the woman will have pain in childbirth; the man will get bread only through sweated labor. Production is separated from reproduction. Instead of delighting in food, humans shall eat in sorrow. A shadow falls over food; it is no longer the delicious, desirous commodity so plentiful in the Garden, food that did not even need processing or cooking. Only through work will grain become bread. Separation from God occurs at the moment that the woman swallows (and thus represses)

---

[32] This phrase, coined by Mary Douglas, refers to the conjuction of the social and culinary. "Food is a blinding fetish in our culture . . . [of which] our ignorance is explosively dangerous" (1975: 7). She further emphasizes its danger for women, since feeding is a primary part of women's role in our culture.

her new-found knowledge with the last sweet vestiges of the fruit.[33] After a moment of initiation, or disobedience, she is returned to her role as the submissive partner of the couple, who will become food for future storytellers. Within the male fantasies produced by the joined tropes of woman and food is that the food either symbolizes sexual pleasure or accompanies it. A graphic image of the woman's body connected to the supplying of food is found in the *Tosefta Niddah*, where the Talmudic sages report that the girls in the villages who did the grinding of the flour from the time they were very young developed much larger breasts than the girls who grew up in towns and could purchase flour and bread from a baker (6.9). Through those breasts, the woman's body becomes the supplier of food. Thus the circle becomes complete. The one who supplies food can be transformed into the one who offers death through the food she supplies. The nurturing mother becomes a murderer; the food that she serves – poisonous, intoxicating, magical – operates at the center of the trope. An offer of a bowl of curds precedes the killing of Sisera; banquet wine acts as a narcotic upon Holofernes. Food then takes on an aura of warning when women violate the primary connection they have to food and nurturing. This paradox permeates all the biblical stories of women who are murderers. They do not use the weapons of men to kill men; they assume power through the ordinary elements available to all women. Such a connection between food and murder goes far to explain the unease and alarm with which men viewed these female figures. The horror of beheading men immediately after luring them with food and drink is so great that domesticated female readers are protected from identity with such creatures.

At the beginning of the story of Amnon and Tamar, love is visualized as an irresistible food. When Amnon admits his love for Tamar to the clever Jonadab, the latter suggests that he request that Tamar prepare him something to eat – in the intimacy of his rooms. Amnon wants the food prepared in his sight. No one else is to be present. He want to eat from her hand (2 Sam. 13:4–7). He appears to be obsessed with his sister. To be obsessed is to be enslaved, to lose the power of choice.

---

[33] The importance of grain as food was so great that the ancient rabbis compared it with the Tree of Knowledge. Genesis Rabbah 15.7.

Tamar makes the requested food (verse 8), special dumplings (*lebibot*) that are hearty (McCarter 1984: 314–15) or heart-shaped (Newsom 1992: 93). Whether the noun is used as an intentional play on *lebab*, "heart," as I think is the case, or is simply a term for the dumplings, the noun makes a clear connection between food and body. The image of Tamar kneading the dough and shaping the dumplings "in his sight" reminds the reader that Tamar herself is within his sight, the object of his gaze. When she offers him the cooked dumplings, he refuses to take them from her. His obsession has been broken. Instead of loving her, he seizes her. As quickly as she had turned the dough into dumplings, Amnon's love is transformed into violence.

What is of particular interest is that Tamar does not seem to be the seducer, the one offering the intoxicating food to her lover. She is not the *femme fatale*, luring men with food or wine. She has not initiated the idea of the dumplings to soothe her supposedly ill half-brother; she has not played the role of Tricky Female and got him alone in the house, as the wife of Potiphar did to Joseph. The shocking gender reversal, the man using food to trap the woman, functions to reinforce the evil nature of Amnon. He is not worthy to receive his inheritance as king of Israel. He is no better than a scheming woman.

More often it is the trope of the consuming female, the one who entraps and then kills the male, who represents the rebellion within patriarchal culture that threatens to bring down the whole society. Once again Eve is accused of causing the death of Adam with forbidden fruit. Male warnings about women's potions and potables have been expressed in each of the classical literatures. Circe uses creams, ointments, and fragrant potions in her seductions of sailors who arrive at the rocky island of Aiaia. To lure the men to her, she offers them a brewed drink concocted of barley meal, wine, honey – as well as a pinch of a mysterious drug (*pharmacon kakon*) that robs them of human form. She is then often pictured as raising a stick or wand (*rhabdos*) to drive the trapped swine into her inner house. While the drugged drink is usually considered the agent that allows her to turn men into swine, Yarnall has argued that this moment of female dominance over the male seems to flow from the stick (*rhabdos*) which in her hands gains potency, a symbol of phallic powers improperly assumed (12). Thus, Homer provides us with an equation of terror: a winey brew (offered by a woman) plus a common object (harmless when properly used by a man) equals the destruction of the male.[34] Circe's wand is Jael's hammer, Judith's sword.

What narrative elements do these stories of wine, women, and death share? Jael, Judith, and Esther have been traditionally celebrated as salvific heroes for killing or causing to be killed an enemy of Israel. Always hungry for positive stories about women, feminist Bible scholars have feasted upon these female figures (Berg, Craven, Day, White). Esther is termed a role model for Diaspora Jews suffering a minority status (Newsom 1992: 129).[35] Judith, a model of Jewish piety and feminine demeanor, like Esther, uses her beauty to dispatch an enemy. Jael exhibits the same courage and efficiency in nailing Sisera.[36] How do these warrior women differ from Delilah and Salomé, two other inhabitants of the dark continent? The latter kill the wrong men. Samson and John the Baptist are on our side, that is, the side of the traditional readers of the biblical texts. But the tropes of beautiful women seducing men with food or wine and killing them instead of soothing them are basically the same, and in my view represent the generalized male fear of the courtesan as killer.

Most feminist readers have avoided dealing directly with the murderous aspects of the characters of Esther and Judith by transforming them into brave acts committed on behalf of the Jewish people. The problem with such a limited reading is that it ignores the constructedness of the characters in each of these narratives. The woman who risks her life to protect her community is as much a construction as the woman who uses cosmetics and

[34] Of course Homer protects his hero Odysseus from falling victim to Circe. Hermes gives the hero a herb charm to defend against the drug, his sword will overcome her wand. When Odysseus agrees to Circe's request to "mingle in lovemaking and trust each other in friendship" (*Odyssey* 10.334–5), she becomes a beneficent being. Thus, Odysseus becomes one of the few heroes who mingles sexually with a goddess and does not later suffer for his presumption.

[35] Also Craven for a spirited connection between Judith (the Jewess) and the Jewish nation.

[36] Sidonie White argues for the author of Judith's dependency upon the Jael/Deborah material. While I find that claim unconvincing, I do think the tropic parallels cited in White's article, especially within Judith's prayer and the song of Deborah, point toward symmetries in the narratives (White 1992).

finery to seduce a man into fulfilling her political desires. Just as the loyal matriarch praying for sons is a construction, a stock characterization, as recognizable to the audience as the foolish foreign ruler, such as Pharaoh and Ahasuerus who make idiotic edicts that eventually become the very lever that incites popular rebellion. If the reader remains satisfied with the stock reading, remaining within the doxa, the valorous reading will remain primary. Only by cracking open the facets of characterization will a female literary figure reflect individual colors of light.

A reading dependent on genre categories will similarly result in an analysis pleasing to the dominant interpreters. Alter acknowledges the fictive nature of the book of Esther, by referring to it as "a comic fantasy utilizing pseudo-historical materials" (34). I would extend Alter's observation to suggest that most of the stories in which women play a key role in the biblical narratives, especially Exodus 1–2 (Exum 1983), *Joseph and Aseneth* (see chapter 4), and the story of Judith (Levine 1992), share exaggerated comic details. All of these stories of wine, women, and death are indeed comic fantasies produced by male authors. The comedic element contains a central clue to my readings in this chapter, that is, assurance to the ideal reader that this story is, on the surface, entertainment. Women are returned to their safe asexual place at the margins of the text. Resting below, at the level of male fantasy and anxiety, is the warning about women who overflow their boundaries.

As I have argued throughout this study, one strategy for breaking the dichotomous good woman/bad woman analysis is to avoid building one's reading around the stock nature of female literary figures, and to eliminate the temptation to assign a category of victim or agent to the female character or to the story in which she appears. Each of the stories of a phallic woman by its very existence challenges the smooth running of the system and the masculine monologic discourse of oppositions. For within each story it is the female body that suggests the failure which its society wants to keep hidden. Clearly Delilah and Salomé appear to fit this structure, since their actions are blamed for showing up a Jewish male figure. But both of these female figures share with Judith, Esther, and Jael silence in the face of institutional power. The latter group is not a conscious affront (they are after all on "our" side, and thus are role models rather than villains). Nevertheless, all five female characters exhibit transgressive behavior and demonstrate the limits and contradictions in gender roles. Each reflects the failure of *individual* male power. None questions the normalcy of that power.

The earlier works that have reviewed the historical elements, linguistic properties, and literary structure of the books of Esther (see Berg, Moore, White) and Judith (see Craven, Moore) are widely available and remain within the traditional genre of commentary in which the text is studied in the linear fashion in which it was written. In an effort to avoid adding another voice to this well-scripted discourse, I shall focus upon the tropes of feeding or feasting to illustrate how they form a brisk warning of being eaten up by fear of the other, the dark unexplored territory of woman. Concomitantly I shall tease out the elements of the alimentary subtext, the places at which the presentation and serving of food or drink leads to erotic conquest. The erotic elements of the banquet fuse to become the acrid scent of female power, if only fleetingly. Through their physical "charms," perfumed and bejeweled bodies, the female figure in each of these stories exposes male desire by revealing the voyeuristic man as subject to her powers. Thus, for even a moment one can experience the narrative pleasure of the power of woman's subversion. However, the moment is short-lived since none of these stories indicate that women can maintain their position of power by forming a community of strong women. The example of Vashti and her ill-fated banquet reminds the reader of who holds the ultimate narrative power in these stories.

One possible strategy that enables a reader to break the hegemony of the gaze is to allow the codes of food and fragrance to inundate the text, to return the reader to an earlier pansexuality. Such a reading is not satisfied by a purely phallic model, as I have argued, but shows that the text contains hints of other eroticization of body envelope – food, spices, aromas, silks, and sweet wine.

A BANQUET OF POLYPHONIC CODES

The name Esther can be connected to the word *hester* (*'astir*), meaning concealment.[37] For concealment is a major theme that runs throughout the story. The power Esther gains in her role as Queen is possible only because Vashti has concealed her body; Esther conceals her Jewishness; Esther conceals her plans for Haman amid the food and drink of a banquet; Esther conceals her desire to use the king's power with her glamorously arrayed costumes and seductive speech. Esther conceals her connection to Mordecai – indeed even Haman does not connect the alluring Queen with the irritating Jew sitting in sackcloth at the gate. There is of course the well-argued concealment of God in the story, although I find this less convincing than interpreters insist. For a faithful reader, each of the "coincidental" plot points is the intrusion of the deity into the story. In my view the greatest concealment, the most tempting *hester*, is that of the silence about sexual play within the story. The author toys with the audience much as Esther toys with Ahasuerus who comes upon her and Haman struggling on the couch. There is a tableau, a feast for the eyes, which each individual spectator/reader tastes, as well as all the sensual codes that lead the reader to a heated reading of the story.

The figure of Ahasuerus (Heb. *Ahashwerosh*) is clearly based upon a typical Oriental potentate, connected with the king of the same name in Ezra 4:6 and Dan. 9:1. As Radday observes, Jews have had "much experience of such unpredictable rulers from antiquity until modern times" (1990: 296). Part of the ludic fun in the tale is that the banquet that lasted half a year left no one in charge of the realm. Of course constructing a narrative atmosphere of historicity is far different from actual historical writing. Reading with Greenstein, I prefer to concentrate upon the strong "influence of

---

[37] As Brenner and Radday have shown, comic codes are often bound to naming in the Bible. The book of Esther is no exception. Word play between *'astir* and *masteret* was pointed out in Tractate Hullin. The verse "and I will surely hide (*'astir*) my face (Deut. 31.18) is connected to Esther, implying that Esther would rescue her people at a time when the face of the deity was concealed (B. Hul. 139B). While Esther is the non-Hebrew name of the figure, often connected to the Semitic goddess Ishtar, the more interesting connection is Radday's observation of the word play between the non-Hebrew name Esther and the word *hester*, meaning concealment (1990: 300).

the surrounding carnival-like Purim scene" (1981: 225) than to subject the book of Esther to historical analysis. A kind of twisting of historical names and events is another clue to comedic narrative found in both the books of Esther and Judith. Then there is the situation of women who are thought to move outside their appropriate roles for moments of sexual play and narrative glory. Since each of these female figures is put in her place by disappearing from the biblical metanarrative, the stories can be viewed as comedic entertainments for the male reader.

Detienne poses the central question about the seeming paradox of texts which glorify sexual attraction found within a religious tradition that clearly understands sexuality to be solely for procreation. In other words, what are the connections between the pleasures of eroticism and a pragmatic sexuality that proscribes intercourse except to establish a legitimate line of descent? In his description of the Adonai, the courtesans whose celebration of Adonis includes a "ritual whose every characteristic constitutes a negative imprint of the model forms of conjugal union" (1994: xxiv), Detienne argues that rather than a simple inversion of the positive codes of fragrance and spices, the Adonai represent a necessary condition to gaining access to spices. Our spicy biblical heroines function similarly to the Adonai in that they use fragrances and other codes of female sexuality in their campaigns to destroy enemies of Israel. Other female characters who threaten biblical heroes (Delilah, Salomé, and Jezebel) are more marginal, but still perform within the same system. To transform the negative to a positive sign, one need only reverse the reader's identity. Delilah would be a hero in the mind of her own people, that is, like Esther and Judith, she kills an enemy threatening the state. Salomé represents a more subtle distortion, for she eliminates a personal enemy of her mother. But the common thread connecting these characters and providing a key to a feminist mode of reading remains the detailing of rituals of beauty and banquets each uses to achieve her ends.

Esther has understood that her power comes from being the object of the gaze and has exploited that power. But the site that Esther chooses for her seduction is not the bedroom but the banquet hall. It is food, wine, and spectacle that Esther uses rather than her body to get the king to order Haman's death. A reader expecting to find descriptions of succulent meals, dainty dishes, or elaborate delicacies in the book of Esther will be disappointed. Metonymic of the courtly way of life, the meals are not even meagerly described. The pleasure of the palate is not an issue in the biblical narrative, but rather the banquets are used as loci of female power. Esther's power is as fleeting as the banquet itself, but as memorable. The author points toward the importance of spectacle and feasting in his tale by inventing a setting of splendor in the opening scene:

There were white cotton curtains and blue hangings tied with cords of fine linen and purple to silver rings and marble pillars. There were couches of gold and silver on a mosaic pavement of porphyry, marble, mother-of-pearl, and colored stones. Drinks were served in golden goblets, goblets of different kinds, and the royal wine was lavished according to the bounty of the king. Drinking was by flagons, without restraint . . . (Esth. 1:6–8)

The reader is surrounded by the splendor and opulence of the Persian king, first by the descriptions of the palace, then by the excessive feasting, and finally by the exaggerated elements of the search for the perfect woman to replace Vashti.[38] The Orientalized imaginings of the cultural other emanating from the biblical author's text is a stock characteristic of the Hellenistic romance and

---

[38] Greenstein refers to these narrative elements as the "comedic hyperbole that permeates the text" (1989b: 226). Modern Jewish readers, such as Greenstein and Sasson, acknowledge that the book of Esther is a Jewish triumph, Jews celebrating their own survival. Both these interpreters, however, move past the reading of a theological code to analyze the narrative through its narratologic elements. For a review of medieval Jewish commentators' exegetical interpretation and midrash on the book of Esther, see Walfish.

It is instructive to review the ways in which medieval readers fill the gaps of description of the Persian palace with *medieval* details, e.g., Joseph Kara, who refers to the colored hangings in 1.6 as suspended from the capitals and pillars. As Walfish notes, the practice of hanging tapestries on the walls for special occasions was widespread during the Middle Ages. Other medieval scholars dream up increasingly exotic decorations: elegant billowing canopies, crenelated curtains covering the ceiling, curtains suspended by purple silken ropes tied to marble pillars set into silver wheels (1993: 102–26). Walfish's carefully researched work reflects the power of the reader to create any interpretation, as the medieval exegetical work signals to the modern reader not only the individual exegete's dreams of ancient exotic Persia but also the way "it must have been" based on each one's own cultural context, e.g., Moorish kings of Seville and Granada. Thus, even at a time in which making the story "true" was a fundamental objective of the interpretation, the exegetes were attempting to add historicity by incorporating elements familiar to their readers.

is used in other Pseudepigraphic romances, such as Judith, Tobit, and Susanna, as well as *Joseph and Aseneth* (see chap. 4). As I have noted earlier, the women are objects of desire in each of these stories.

The Jewish protagonist as other is also a well-used plot type within the Bible. Joseph and Daniel, like Esther, are trapped, alone, isolated from family and Jewish community, in the world of the other. Through their wit and skill, and primarily because they are the elect of God, whether acknowledged in the text or woven into the plot structure of the story, each one gains the eye of a benefactor in the foreign court. Joseph has the Egyptian Potiphar, Esther the harem chief Hegai, Daniel the wise men in the Babylonian court. Through the aid of their benefactors, each of the displaced characters is elevated to the highest position in the foreign court. Joseph becomes viceroy of Egypt and marries Aseneth (Gen. 41:40–44), Esther marries Ahasuerus, and Daniel is appointed by Nebuchadnezzar as ruler over the province of Babylon (Dan. 2:48) and eventually becomes third ruler in the kingdom (Dan. 5:29). However, the similarities do not make these stories congruent. The most important difference points to the analogy between race and gender and the politics of the deployment of both forms of otherness. When a man is the object of desire, as Joseph is, and is also the cultural other, by virtue of his membership in a dominant gender community he is still less vulnerable and less under threat than when a woman is simultaneously the object of desire and the cultural other. Esther as doubly other must siphon power from Ahasuerus and gradually replace herself with Mordecai, who then more closely parallels Daniel and Joseph as a male Jew maintaining power within a foreign nation.

From the moment she enters into the Court of Ahasuerus, Esther is trained to be an object of desire.[39] For a year in the citadel of Susa under custody of Hegai she is perfumed, oiled, primed for her one-night stand with the king (2:3). Her teachers are Hegai and the other eunuchs of the Court, sexually ambiguous creatures. With them Esther is masquerading, learning to put on the feminine guise. Thus, when Esther finally has her night with the

---

[39] The text reads "the girl who looked good *in the eyes (be'ene)* of the king", emphasizing the power of the gaze.

king, she is performing for the first time. Her skill or her strategy of engaging the male gaze continues until she achieves her goal.[40] Her reliance on Hegai to help make her the primary object of the male gaze is hinted at in the biblical text, which reports that she asked for nothing except what Hegai advised (2:15). Her reliance upon Mordecai is woven throughout the text, and her reliance upon the king to grant her requests fulfills her story.

From her first mention in the story, the character of Esther undergoes several category changes: when she first is being prepared as a candidate for the king's pleasure, Esther is referred to by the narrator as a young girl (*na'arah* 2:7,9,13), concurrently as a virgin (*betulah* 2:2,3,17). These terms merit close attention. In her analysis of the narrative of Judges 12, the sacrifice of the daughter of Jephthah, Bal distinguishes between the term *betulah*, a life stage, which one confronts, and betulah, virgin. In the Judges narrative, Bath, so named by Bal, turns away from the house and the father, and heads instead in the direction of the mountains, the wilderness. Her expression, *betulah*, "then, is more independent from the narrator's than we are accustomed to assume possible, used as we are to a realistic, psychological narrative discourse" (Bal 1990:22). If one uses the sense of life-stage, of ripeness, for the term *betulah* in the book of Esther, the same sense of female self-definition slips into the narrative of male pleasure. Unlike the other candidates whose category becomes concubine (*pilegesh* 2:14),[41] Esther changes in

---

[40] Note the textual emphasis upon Esther's instant progression through the Court hierarchy. As the king's favorite she would have special beauty preparations and special delicacies to eat. "The girl pleased him and won his favor, and he quickly provided her with *her cosmetic treatments* and *her portion of food*, and with *seven chosen maids* from the king's palace, and *advanced her and her maids to the best place in the harem*" (Esth. 2:9).

The question of Esther's eating of the king's "unclean" food figures prominently in most interpretations of the book of Esther and makes Esther a less pure and pious heroine than Judith, who, tradition assures us, brings her own kosher food with her when she seeks out Holofernes. For the discussion of Esther's eating habits, see Berg and Moore, and note The Prayer of Esther (Additions c 28): "Your servant has not dined at Haman's table; nor have I extolled the royal parties or drunk the wine of libations."

[41] The translation of the term *pilegesh* "concubine" is problematic as I mentioned in chapter 5 (see pg. 153, note 20). While concubine is a traditional translation, Bal has argued in *Death and Dissymmetry* that *pilegesh* most probably refers to a wife who lives in the house of her father, while the husband has no stable dwelling, but follows the flocks, as a transhumant nomad. As Bal notes, this situation is termed by Morgenstern a *beena* marriage, a less usual type of marriage arrangement, but one found in Gen. 22:24; 25:6). See Bal 1988: 80–93.

status from the category of girl (*na'arah*) to the designation of
Queen. In fact the indication of her victory, that she has won the
contest, is that the king awards her the honorific title of Queen and
calls her by name.

Radday argues that eroticism is kept to a minimum in the text
because the author does not fill in the gaps between Esther's
advancement from one category to the next: he does not disclose
how long Esther had to wait for her turn with the king, whether she
was recalled for a second or third night, if she had to spend time in
the concubine quarters. While I agree with Radday that the
narrative gaps are wide in relation to the other young women, the
text becomes very specific – the gaps narrow dramatically – when
Esther takes her turn.

When Esther was taken to King Ahasuerus in his royal palace in the *tenth
month*, which is *the month of Tebeth, in the seventh year of his reign*, the king loved
Esther more than all the other women; of all the virgins (*betulot*) she won
his favor and devotion, so that he set the royal crown on her head and
made her queen instead of Vashti. (Esth. 2:16–17)

The immediacy of her coronation contrasts with the year in
which the king was indecisive and sorting through young women,
night after night. Once he has met Esther, this amorphous time
period ends. Thus, I would argue that if this passage, with its
detailing of treatments of six months duration with oil of myrrh and
another six months of fragrances and cosmetics, is not titillating to
the reader, it is because the reader has moved on to contemplate
Esther, the new Queen. The erotic nature of the story depends on
the audience's participation or willingness to hear an erotic story
when only suggestions or details are offered. Lingering upon the
codes of fragrance and oils might widen the gaps the text offers,
permitting a more erotic reading.

The myriad of details of each of the banquets accounts for much
readerly pleasure in the text. Indeed the word *mishteh*, which occurs
forty-six times in the entire Hebrew Bible, occurs twenty times in
the book of Esther, emphasizing the importance of eating and
drinking to the story. I prefer not to look at these festive occasions
symmetrically, in chiastic groups (*contra* Berg), but rather to analyze
each banquet and the ways in which it differs from the one that
precedes it. The first *mishteh* held by Ahasuerus is an excessively

lavish half-year celebration at which practically the entire population participates. The author uses this first gala as an occasion for
setting the scene of royal wealth and pointing toward a story of
exaggeration and excess. The second banquet that the ruler holds
is only seven days in length and for a much smaller guest list. This
B-list banquet that takes place in the courtyard of the garden of the
king's palace marks the downfall of Vashti. The occasion is
described in great detail. The drinking of wine in vast amounts is
emphasized, although the food is not mentioned.

> When these days were completed [180 days], the king gave for all the
> people present in the citadel of Susa, both great and small, a banquet
> lasting for seven days, in the court of the garden of the king's palace.
> There were *white cotton curtains* and *blue hangings tied with cords of fine linen and*
> *purple to silver rings and marble pillars.* There were *couches of gold and silver on a*
> *mosaic pavement of porphyry, marble, mother-of-pearl, and colored stones.*
> *Drinks were served in golden goblets,* goblets of different kinds, and the *royal wine*
> *was lavished* according to the bounty of the king.
> *Drinking was by flagons,* without restraint; (Esther 1:5–8)

By contrast the author does not provide any details of Queen
Vashti's parallel drinking party (*mishteh nashim*), the third banquet.
It is given minimal narratorial importance. The reader must
choose to interpret the textual silence as providing a subtext of
male power – the king's banquet is of interest; the Queen's is not –
or that the furnishings would be similar at both parties. A third
mode of reading would reflect the male author's ignorance about
what might take place at a female *mishteh.* This ill-fated banquet
held solely for women can be contrasted with the successful
banquet held by Esther solely for two men, King Ahasuerus and his
vizier Haman, the fourth in the series. The banquet at which
Vashti is vanquished lasts for seven nights. Esther's banquets by
contrast are only one evening each.

The fourth banquet is called by Ahasuerus to celebrate the
coronation of his new Queen. In fact he calls it "Esther's banquet"
(although the LXX reads more accurately "a banquet in honor of
Esther"), shifting the focus of the text onto his new Queen. After
the embarrassment with Vashti, who has concealed herself, he gets
to show off his Queen to the male courtiers at a banquet, albeit a
different Queen and one swathed in coronation robes. This fourth

banquet marks the end of Ahasuerus' flashy entertaining in the narrative. Esther's banquet can be seen as a rewriting of the second one, one in which the male ruler uses the female presence to reflect his own triumph and importance. The coronation banquet eradicates the shame of Vashti's absence at the king's second banquet by the substitution of Esther's coronation. Female arrogance has been transformed into female compliance, restoring the king's honor. The king has regained control of women in his kingdom, at the same time reassuring the restive men of the court that women have been put in their place. Ahasuerus' position as flamboyant ruler is certainly to be envied by his male audience since he has engaged in a well publicized year of "auditioning" girls, a veritable sexual banquet, before he found the tastiest morsel.

The following two banquets are Esther's creations, rather than Ahasuerus'. The author indicates what care Esther took in preparation of the banquets, equal with that of her own toilette. At the same time as she is preparing delicacies for the Babylonian king and his vizier, Esther denies food and drink to the Jews. The banquet is replaced by its opposite, the fast. While preparing the banquet for her two guests, Esther is neither eating nor drinking. For this time, at least, she is not part of the food and drink that distinguishes Ahasuerus' reign. She may use the feast as a tool, but she herself is one who fasts. Thus, regardless of her food habits for the year, she is in the harem; while she is at prayer and asking God for the success of her act, she is not eating the Persian food of the court.

Since it is unusual for the Queen to initiate a banquet, Esther must prepare the king to accede to her invitation. Esther informs the reader that her second move is unusual and possibly life-threatening: she is risking an uninvited appearance before the king.[42] The author frames and dramatizes this information by

---

[42] I agree with Moore's observation that the author of Esther is using the "non-fact" that no one is permitted uninvited into the king's presence as a strategy to heighten the story's suspense and the heroine's daring (52). If the reader wishes to focus upon the character of Esther, a slightly different perception can be teased out of the text. The reader familiar with ancient Babylonian courtly customs would appreciate this further example of Esther's great skill at assessing the men with whom she is dealing. Esther would have every reason to be leery of approaching the mercurial king with a large request. In spite of her great beauty, the king might very well react suddenly as he had with the banishment of Vashti. Thus, the suspense in the encounter is generated through this second interaction between the king and his beautiful queen.

setting it in dialogue. Esther tells Mordecai in direct discourse the substance of her heroism:

Go, gather all the Jews to be found in Susa, and hold a fast on my behalf, and neither eat nor drink for three days, night or day. I and my maids will also fast as you do. After that I will go to the king, though it is against the law; and if I perish, I perish. (Esth. 4:16)

She requests through Mordecai that the Jews fast for three days, the time period of her preparations for the private banquets. Since the Babylonian Jews are not mentioned in relation to the earlier banquets, one may assume that they participated in the national festivals. Jews eating the same food as the Babylonians does not seem to be an issue for the author of Esther, although it becomes an irksome detail for later readers. What is significant in the report of Esther calling for a fast is that she and her maids are said to fast too. This communal fast connects the Jewish population of Susa, and it ties Esther directly to them. For the first time the Jews are delineated as different from the Babylonians through the marker of food.

After demanding that all the Jews observe a three-day fast, Esther prepares herself carefully, wrapping the splendid royal robes around her. Coming to the king unbidden, hidden in a robe, she has told us, is a mark of her power.[43] Whereas Vashti was asked to display her naked beauty to the Court,[44] Esther is the covert object of his gaze and indeed the narrator assures us that she has played the situation exactly right. "When the King saw Queen Esther standing in the Court, she found favor in his sight" (5:2). He holds out the golden scepter to her, and in accepting it, she understands that she possesses a piece of his power. One element of that power is that her beauty is for his eyes only. She has the power of intimacy with him that Vashti did not have.

[43] The Additions add vivid details of Esther's preparations and costume for her appointment with the king. I cite them here because they will aid the reader in seeing how carefully Esther displayed herself as object of the king's gaze, how the Greek author's gaze was fixed upon the beautiful Oriental woman, how the gaps were filled by these ancient readers. Note also that Esther calls upon the "all-seeing" God to see her through this delicate mission. "After she had called upon the all-seeing God and savior, she looking absolutely radiant, took with her two maids, leaning daintily on the one, while the other followed, carrying her train" (D2, Moore's translation). Once again through her actions, Esther proves that she is the mistress of the tableau.

[44] This reading illustrates the difference between a doxic interpretation with its force of cultural assumptions and a close reading of the text.

In the following two evenings of wine and feasting, Esther reiterates the formula of her deal with the king: *if I have found favor in your sight*. The audience knows that Esther will be victorious, that she has indeed found favor in the king's sight. There is also a sly play here. Esther is not seen by Haman, that is, Haman does not "see" who Esther really is. Flattered by her attention, he has no idea that she is his Pandora, blinding him with her beauty to the reality that she is bringing him death. Toying verbally with the enemy, a pleasure that both Esther and Judith enjoy, indicates that their speech is pleasing to the ideal reader as much as to their immediate addressee of their speech, whose ear is cathected as a zone of pleasure.

Haman's braggadocio to his wife in the scene intercalated between the banquets heightens the reader's pleasure at his imminent fall. At his wife's suggestion, he constructs the gallows that will become the instrument of his death. Amid the spectacle of food and splendor, Haman becomes the spectacle. Caught up in his own fright, he has no idea of the sexual tableau he is presenting to the king.

When the king returned from the palace garden to the banquet hall, Haman had thrown himself on the couch where Esther was reclining; and the king said, "Will he even assault the queen in my presence, in my own house?" (Esth. 7:8)

If one were reading "with Haman," Esther might appear to be the initiator of sexual play. Like the *ishah zarah* in Proverbs 7, whose perfumed couch is covered with colored spreads of Egyptian linen, in this reading, Esther would be figured as spicy, sexy, offering goblets of wines that confuse Haman and make him forget his proper station. Either Esther is spunky and uses her beauty to save her people, or she is spicy and uses her sexuality to trip up a besotted man. Or perhaps she is both.

As kings besotted by female beauty are wont to do, Ahasuerus offers Esther half his kingdom. Like Salomé, who receives the same offer, there is a literary gasp at this point, in which the reader understands at the same time as the female character that she has won, she will get her wish. The rest of the story is concerned with watching the female character navigate the male shoals of the story, fulfilling her own deadly desires.

Once her objectives are achieved, and Haman has been executed, the characterization of Esther changes along with the tension in the story. She is no longer described as a continuing object of the male gaze. Her detailed beauty preparations are not mentioned in the final third of the book. She properly falls at the king's feet and turns on the tears, reassuring the ideal reader of her predictable womanly (weak) behavior. She knows in whose hand the scepter still resides. After the king signals that he is willing to share the power – Esther may make a request – we are reminded of her former triumphs in engaging the male gaze: she prefaces her request for the death of Haman with the magic words *if I have found favor in your sight*. As Mordecai's power increases and the political status of the Jews is assured at Court, reflected in the Babylonians converting just to be on the safe side (8:17), Esther's beauty is no longer mentioned in the text. The narrator does not return to the king's desire for her. Rather Esther becomes the helper to Mordecai, the position the reader has known her to occupy throughout the story.

Like Bathsheba, who had been initially the object of David's scopic gaze, seen and not heard, Esther the beauty queen finally gets to be heard and not seen. The male gaze locks upon Bathsheba in her bath, upon Esther in her year-long beauty regimen. As a mature woman, Bathsheba was counseled by Nathan in cutting the deal with an impotent David to gain the kingdom for her son Solomon. As a mature queen, Esther depended on Mordecai when gaining power in the kingdom for her people. At the moment when Bathsheba and Esther are transformed from sexual to political Queen, men have been delivered from the unstable terrain of the dark continent. When she is signing edicts and improving the lot of the Jews, there are no details about what Esther wears, how she smells, or who is looking at her. The emphasis on her beauty until Haman's death edict is signed, and her hand has enclosed the king's golden scepter, not once but twice, marks the moment at which she becomes the one who gazes.

Queen Esther daughter of Abihail, along with the Jew Mordecai, gave *full written authority*, confirming this second letter about Purim. (Esth. 9:29; emphasis mine)

After being a fetishized or voyeuristic object of the gaze, Esther reverses the relationship and appropriates the gaze for her own power. Finally, she is described as having "full written authority," power equivalent with that of a male. The powerful woman using her beauty to triumph over the king adds to the pleasure of the female spectator who identifies with her. This active role of female returning the gaze is more appealing than women's passive acceptance of her narrative portrayal as object of desire.

The sense of performance is most clearly marked out by Esther's appearance before the king at the beginning of the banquet and the tableau of her and Haman on the couch. Both are tableaux arranged to increase male desire for Esther, just as the dance of Salomé functions to ignite King Herod. Both invite the male spectator to share the pleasure of the gaze. To a reading which privileges the gaze, reading through the codes of food and fragrance highlights the subtle movements of the female figure in the text. Multiple coded readings show the connections between women and food, danger and desire, even more sharply than a reading in which the woman is seen solely as the object of the gaze.

KILLING US SOFTLY

The book of Judith shares so many structural parallels with the book of Esther that one cannot help raise the question of the power of genre. By the very nature of these narratives, clearly marked as stories, they do not strike directly at the institutions of power in the way an actual occurrence might. Intentionally playing with time and place, conflating both events and historical personages, both works assure the reader that these female figures are presented as models of courage for moral entertainment. Greenstein connects Esther with the folktale of Cinderella, a happily-after story that permits its female readers to dream but does not challenge the construction of girl as beauty queen, where being the object of male desire is her only means to success. She is also Snow White waiting for her prince in a harem of young men instead of a cottage of minuscule men. Older and wiser, Judith resists the fairy-tale image – for she requires rescuing by no prince. Instead she is the crone shining her power on a confused community.

The parallel structures of the books of Esther and Judith share more than the genre of historical romance. (1) In each narrative, Israel is threatened by a foreign nation, more powerful than Israel. Thus, Israel itself is figured as feminine, and as such must depend on *her* wits, as well as *her* male God, to rescue *her* from the male invader. Levine's analysis of the metaphoric connection between the heroine and the community is important.[45] As Levine has demonstrated, sexuality as well as gender is a crucial shared characteristic. "Faithful Israel is sexually controlled; her faithless antitype is sexually loose. Consequently the chaste widow Judith, like the virgin Dinah (Jdt 9:9–10), represents the holy community" (Levine 1992: 211). I would expand her connection to include the virgin Esther.[46] In my view the figure of Esther also functions as a metaphor for the holy community of Israel, that is, she is sexually controlled, first in the harem supervised by Hegai, and then as the Queen. The metaphor of the pliant woman can easily be figured as Israel when she is good, obedient to the male god, responsive to his desires, loyal to his name.

(2) Both narratives play on the concept of virginity or sexual abstinence. The central female figure is not introduced in relation to a husband, father, or son. In the book of Judith, the locale is Bethulia, which has been noted by a number of interpreters to share a resonance with *betulah*. The community of Bethulia in which the widow Judith lives is as asexual as the community of women, the harem of virgins, in which Esther lives until she departs for the king's palace. While Judith and Esther first enter the narrative "unmanned" in a positive way, another deadly figure, Delilah, is unmanned in a dangerous roving way. Unattached means unprotected and unsupervised by a male family member. Jael and Deborah are both unmanned throughout their stories. Jael is referred to as wife of Heber the Kenite and Deborah as wife

---

[45] See Levine (1992). For my analysis of the character of Judith I have been influenced to a great degree by this article as well as private discussions with A. J. Levine about the phallic woman, for which I am grateful.

[46] For a Christian community the virginity of Salomé is connected to her appeal to King Herod as well as her naiveté in fulfilling her mother's death-dealing desire. Salomé's purity, however, is quickly contrasted with the violence of her request. Later interpreters also have connected her dance and her love for the Baptist as being endemic of the sexual disorder of the community. For a full analysis of Salomé, see chapter 7.

of Lappidoth, but neither husband has narrative presence. Each unmanned woman uses her freedom to help her own community fell an enemy. After her act of courage, Judith is rendered safe, returned to an asexual position in the book of Judith, as well as a place of narrative silence. Levine has observed that Judith is not a threat to her admiring audience because the text never indicates that she has erotic desire (1992: 13–15). This observation can be extended to each of the female characters under consideration. Further, the reader's eroticism can be controlled by the limited sparks of sexual politics in the text. Each female flicker of erotic display is short-lived, just enough to underscore the construction of woman as sexual temptress, and nothing over.

(3) Both narratives share a theological pattern in which the ritual of prayer and fasting acts as fulcrum in the story and precedes the decisive action of the female figure. After the act of the woman, God allows Israel to get revenge on its enemy. The theological influence is clearly stated in the book of Judith (Esth 10–13), in the story of Deborah and Jael (Judges Jdt. 4–5), and in the LXX version of Esther (Esth. 5.1/e/D8)[47]

(4) Fasting and banquet motifs abound. In Judith the people of Bethulia are engaged in an enforced fast. They are deprived of both food and water. Esther calls for the Jews to fast from food and drink for three days before her banquets for the king and Haman. Both stories end in feasts of celebration for the Jews, where their victory over their foreign enemy frees the people to indulge in food and drink.

(5) Each woman adorns herself before confronting her male enemy. Similar codes of fragrance and spices prefigure the woman's sexual weaponry. The preparations of Esther have

---

[47] The Hebrew version of Esther implies the presence or approval of God, I would argue, in chapter 6, and especially in chapter 8. I am thinking particularly of the "coincidences" in chapter 6, such as the insomniac king, who gave orders to bring the book of records, the annals, to be read to him. Here he is reminded of Mordecai's valor on his behalf. In chapter 8, the king gives Mordecai his golden signet ring and Esther his golden scepter. From powerless nameless subjugated people in Ahasuerus' kingdom, the Jews' prayers are answered royally, symbolically. All the plot reversals take place here too: the fall of Haman becomes the rise of Mordecai, the life threats to the Jews become threats to the Babylonians. The pagan feast of Ahasuerus from the beginning of the story becomes the Jewish festival at the end. All this symmetry represents the hand of God to the faithful reader.

already been discussed in this chapter. The reader will want to compare Judith's toilette:

she laid aside the sackcloth which she had put on and divested herself of her widow's garb, and washed her body all over with water, and anointed herself with costly (thick and heavy) ointment, and combed and perfumed the hair of her head, and put upon it a tiara, and clad herself in her gayest attire . . . she took sandals for her feet and put on anklets and bracelets[48] and rings and her earrings and all her finery, and adorned herself so as to beguile the eyes of as many as should behold her. (Jdt. 10:4–5)[49]

The text of Judith is much fuller than the MT of Esther in its descriptions of food, perfumes, clothing. The Greek Additions to Esther does fill out these gaps, although not as lavishly as the details found in the book of Judith, such as the alimentary preparations that Judith carried with her to the camp of Holofernes: a leather bottle of wine and a cruse of oil, and a pouch of barley-groats and a cake of figs and loaves of fine bread (10:5). This collection of food is so close to the provisions that Abigail packs when she hurries to appease the outlaw David (I Sam. 25:18) that one wonders if there is a subtextual scrap of woman's culture here involving food that is pleasing to men. Ruth 2:14 mentions bread, wine, and parched grain as the foods that Ruth and Boaz share. The narratologic difference in the book of Ruth is that Boaz offers the food to Ruth, keeping control of the narrative and of the gaze with the male, where it belongs. At this point in the narrative at least, Boaz continues to control the gaze; he is not afraid that it will control him.

(6) Esther and Judith both toy verbally with the enemy, possibly suggesting that their speech is pleasing and that the pleasures of listening are directed at the ideal reader as much as the immediate address of their speech, whose ear is cathected as a zone of pleasure. Neither Haman nor Holofernes "sees" beyond the dazzling raiments to the real meaning of the woman's words. The *doubles entendres* in which the reader is protected from the verbal

[48] I am grateful to Geraldine Heng, who suggested that Judith's anklets and bracelets in this speech reflect sound as well as sight. The details of the tinkling, jangling sounds would also draw the male's attention (both the apparent and the intended addressee of the speech) to the body of the female character, adding another degree of pleasure.

[49] For translations in the book of Judith, I have relied upon Enslin, *The Book of Judith*, Greek Text with an English translation commentary and critical notes. Leiden, E. J. Brill, 1972.

trickery of the female character by being in on the joke also serves to separate the male reader from the buffooned male figure in the text. The ideal male reader knows what the dim "enemy" male can not hear and thus his pleasure in the word play is not diminished.

These biblical narratives of Judith and Esther emphasize how visible gender differences are when connected to the tropes of food and desire. Perhaps the details of fragrance of the food and fragrance of the woman heighten the reader's pleasure and anticipation of a narrative of sex and pleasure. Since women's roles are usually figured in connection with food, often displaced as Mother, the ambiguous nature of the women in these texts may be understood through the use of food as weapon rather than celebration. The expected connection between women and feeding, so-called women's work, defined woman as maternal; these texts can be considered as maternal only if one reads maternal as protecting the children of God from the enemy. But the reader, male or female, for whom the killing of Haman or Holofernes is more horrific than salvific will find the maternal woman transformed into virago.

"SO THE WITCH WON'T EAT ME . . ."

Having considered the way sensual details can increase the reader's connections to a biblical text and to a narrative of desire, I want to acknowledge briefly the assumptions modern readers make within the metanarrative of sexuality, Freudian style. It was not Freud who invented the inferiority of women, but he mustered everything in his analytic arsenal to explain women's inferior position, make it logical, and therefore inevitable. The culturally loaded paradigms of biblical narratives, where women come second, informed the work of Freud, as they did most other cultural attitudes that formed the Western metanarrative.

The real trouble arises in uprooting the assumptions of one's reading position. Does one come to the biblical text immersed in popularized Freudian analysis and thus expect to find sexual women who strike terror into the hearts of fallible men? How much does that readerly position affect one's determination to read the biblical story as true, as reflections of the ways in which women behave toward men in real life? Once the barest outlines of Freudian views have taken up a permanent place in the reader's mind, the inferiority of a female literary figure which could be observed socially and theologically takes on a scientific appearance; in the mind of the modern reader Freud's feminine equations are transformed into universally familiar adages. As many feminist theorists have observed, "Freud is certainly not the first who built up *his* truth into an objective seeming science; he is the first to parley *his* sexuality into a universal sexuality."[50]

How is this observation about the Freudian attempt to adapt women to men important for readers of biblical texts? Let's begin at the beginning. The latent theme is creation itself. The Western metanarrative in which God's creation of the universe – of the man, of the woman, of the laws of the Garden – has in our culture taken on the force of natural law. The creation of the woman as a companion for the man is a theme that continues to run through much of our own popular culture. And finally the male dream of controlling creation, especially the creation or construction of the woman. In traditional interpretations God made Eve from the flesh of Adam, as Freud made feminine sexuality from male libido. They are one and the same myth, that is, fantasies produced by a patriarchal unconscious in which, throughout history, men have been considered superior, and women kept down. In both the biblical genesis and psychogenesis, woman is born from and for man. In other words the linear narrative which has the transition to patriarchy as its crowning *telos* is simply the counterpart of a theory which, arguing from the creation of Eve after Adam in Genesis 2, would posit the male as the definitive *arche* or beginning.

If Eve has attempted to pluck power away from the deity, by offering her companion the forbidden fruit, then she must be *over*-powered in order for the fear of her to be quelled. Recent feminist critics have used psychoanalysis to theorize the necessity of displacement concurrent with both the construction of Woman

---

[50] This vital understanding of the shaping of literary interpretations through Freudian prisms of gender has formed a matrix of feminist psychoanalytic interpretation. The scholarly literature is much more varied than this basic selection indicates. The reader is referred to Brennan (1992), Canto (1986), Case (1990), Creed (1993), de Lauretis (1987), Doane (1987), Felman (1977 and 1981), Irigaray (1977), Kofman (1985), Konstan (1994).

and also the masculine gendering of the gaze. The ideal spectator is generally assumed to be male and the image of woman is designed to flatter him. In Mulvey's description, the active male protagonist is the scopophilic gazer, wary of the woman, whose heat might sear him. He must neutralize the woman's poisonous brew of desire and death by a re-enactment that repeats both the original trauma of the castrating female and the process of the male gazer overcoming her.

In the biblical narratives under consideration, women offer all sorts of deceitful delicacies to men, who greedily reach out for them no matter what the dangers. The most obvious corollary to the bowl of curds Jael offers Sisera, the banquets staged by Esther, Judith, and Herodias/Salomé, the grapes Delilah probably dangled before Samson, is the decadent and aromatic gingerbread house that tempted Hansel and Gretel into the dark world of the witch. As Bettelheim has shown in his Freudian analysis of the tale, the gingerbread house is a symbolic representation of the mother and stands for oral greediness and what fun it is to give in to it. The warning embedded in the tale is that men who have become subservient to the id reach out for tempting women and receive death instead of gratification (1976: 161–62).

Offering themselves as tasty gingerbread, objects of the male's greedy gaze, Esther, Judith, Jael, Salomé, and Delilah turn the tables and punish men for looking. The woman/witch, it turns out, time after time, is as bent on eating up Hansel as he is on feasting off her house. The image of Woman as difference, lack, loss, clearly troubles and endangers the owner of the gaze, be he author, ideal audience, unlucky biblical figure, or young Hansel within the forest.

The male owner of the gaze overcomes the offer of the food of deceit through narratives that reveal woman as spectacle, whose visual presence tends to freeze the flow of action in moments of erotic contemplation. The storyteller reduces the impact of the feminine locus of details of food and pansexuality by returning to the safe world of spectacle – seen and controlled by the male gaze. In other words an Esther or Judith, who tricked an appropriate man with her beauty and fed his desires, oscillated between desire and death in the male fantasy. The biblical authors throw cold water on feminine flames. Judith is returned to her proper place to live a solitary asexual life as demure widow. Descriptions of Esther's beauty and body are replaced by accounts of her cleverly worded edicts, her acting as helpmate to Mordecai and dignified consort to Ahasuerus. Each woman is transformed into a cooler more reassuring portrait than one whose sexuality is still rampant, such as Salomé or Delilah, who may be continuing the dance of desire. As Freud, the interpreter with the unblinking male gaze, would see it, Delilah's next victim could well be another one of us.

Signing edicts with the approval of the king and Mordecai, Esther is complementary to the male, both Babylonian and Jewish, fulfilling his desires. The moments when desire blinded male judgment have passed. The male audience, as well as the surviving male characters, have escaped the dark continent. But the anxiety and fear of castration remain in the unconscious. At least as strong, I would argue, is the accompanying male desire to conceal their dread of these women. For Freud, the basis of the dread is the fear of castration, cutting off of male power. Jael *thrusts* her tent peg deep into the skull of Sisera. Esther arranges for Haman to be hanged, his head cut off from his body; Judith herself lops off the head of Holofernes with his own sword, which she borrows from the victim for the job. The patriarchy attempts to glorify Esther and Judith, by naming books of the Bible after them, since these women have been simultaneously the source of their cravings and their dread. But this attempt seems half-hearted. Underneath the heroine status of Esther and Judith lie female characters who perform the same threatening death-dealing acts as Delilah, Salomé, and Jael.

Let us look more closely at this characterization of a woman who tricks a man into reaching out for her goodies and then cuts off his gaze, in cutting off his head. What of the woman who is *not* returned to a safe female space, but survives narratively to do the deed again? This is not anybody's nurturing mother, patriarchy warns us, but a greatly feared witch, who rules the dark continent, a spicy woman whose power comes from her misuse of food and sexuality. In psychoanalytic terms, she is the phallic mother, a fantasmatic caricature. Defining these biblical characters as phallic mothers will not teach us about women or mothers in the biblical world, although it will shed light on the historical construction of them as categories, and, to a certain extent, on how these categories have been invoked to oppress women and other "others." In the cases of Salomé and Delilah, who are not put back into their proper places, male relief is sought and found in the disparagement of these women, witches who might eat you up. Like Hansel pushing the witch into the oven, patriarchy pushes these women into an interpretive oven, where they are suffocated with contempt.

But what about the good women: Judith and Esther, who even have books named for them. Aren't they also phallic mothers? Surely as literary figures who cut off men's heads, they are dangerous. But as role models they also are representative of good women. To make sense of this seeming contradiction, the phallic mother who is to be emulated, I think psychoanalytic metaphors are helpful. Possibly the most central gift that psychoanalysis has offered to literary readings is "Freud's definition of the psyche as the realm where the law of noncontradiction does not apply" (Ian 1993: 9). In other words the seeming contradiction of fear and desire can coexist in the unconscious, as I think they do in the cases of these biblical literary figures who are murderous heroines. Desire requires an obstacle to exist, and fear is surely a central one. For underneath the laudatory aspect of Esther and Judith causing enemies of the Jewish people to disappear, acting at times when Jewish males are powerless to protect the community, lies the incontrovertible "fact" that they are females who have stolen male power. They function like their phallic sisters, Delilah and Salomé, who simultaneously are the object of greatest male desire and his greatest fear. The difference emerges when one follows the cultural attempt to repress the failed moment of containment of the virago in patriarchal culture. Thus, the reader does not merge the qualities of female figure as killer and as heroine, but rather allows them to coexist. A sign of this ambivalence is found in the books of Judith and Esther, in which the heroines are communally useful; only the mechanisms through which they accomplish their usefulness are potentially as dangerous to the individual masculine subject (if not to the community) as their usefulness. In other words, in spite of the manipulation of a threatening, powerful, and potentially excessive female sexuality glimpsed in their narratives, neither Esther nor Judith is ethnically other, figured as uncontrollable sexuality, as in the narratives of Delilah and Salomé.[51]

In this chapter, I have analyzed biblical stories of women who use food and sexuality to seduce men. While the tropes of food, wine, and murder are common to these stories, there are critical differences that illustrate how cautious the male must be in the presence of female sexuality, even within narratives. Esther and Judith are the women who are communally useful (indeed essential) and therefore heroines. But the mechanisms through which they accomplish their heroism are potentially as dangerous and murderous (to the individual masculine subject, if not the community) as their usefulness whenever the manipulation of a threatening, powerful, and potentially excessive, uncontrollable female sexuality is glimpsed in their narratives. That the biblical narratives do not exploit that potential – indeed are concerned to close it down – testifies to the necessary operations of patriarchal culture. But the very act of closing down on the potential acknowledges that the potential *is* there (seen in the characters of Delilah, Salomé, and Jael), and must be disengaged. Wicked women, therefore, signify failed moments of containment by patriarchal culture.

---

[51] I use the term ambivalence here in its psychoanalytic definition. In a footnote to "Instincts and their Vicissitudes" (1915), Freud credits Bleuler with the invention of the term *Ambivalenz*, which Freud applies to the psychophysics of instinct, whose behavior is compared to that of waves in order to show that numerous instincts can be in flux at the same time and still not use their separate identities (*SE* 14:131). Thus, they are ambivalent, not equivalent.

CHAPTER 7

Calling the shots: directing Salomé's dance of death

> Actually there is no story for which the question as to how it continued would not be legitimate. The novelist, on the other hand, cannot hope to take the smallest step beyond that limit at which he invites the reader to a divinatory realization of the meaning of life by writing "Finis."
>
> Walter Benjamin

Long before Oedipus encountered the Sphinx at Thebes, people were trying to solve the riddle of the woman-headed monster whose deep brooding wings and lion-muscled torso threatened to slash and devour any man who did not please her. Every passerby was set a riddle and if he could not answer it, she sprang at him.[1] Is the sphinx a threatening figure? A female demon?[2] When I saw a reproduction of a classical sphinx for the first time, I thought it was the best combination possible: a large brave lion's body guided by

---

[1] For complete references to the classical and modern sources of these mythic figures, see Reid (1993).

[2] There are two "sphinx" mythic traditions, one classical, referred to in this chapter, and one Egyptian, in which the sphinx is a royal protector, often figured as male. The great sphinx at Giza in indeed male, and so are most other Egyptian sphinxes. They are depictions of the king, expressing in animal form (similar to the gods who are figured with their animal heads) some of the king's attributes. The lion's body has overtones of majesty and power, and the wings that are seen (usually folded over the back) in detailed examples refer to his identity with the falcon-god Horus. The Amarna period female sphinxes are not protectors of the queens, they are representations of the queens themselves, paralleling the depictions of the king in this mode. They are of course female, with the heads of the queens themselves. (Nefertiti is figured with her famous blue crown.) They are figured with the same power as the male sphinx: trampling foreign enemies. In the case of the kings, these enemies are male; but in the case of the queens they are female. Queen Hatshepsut, the queen regnant several generations earlier, is also shown as a sphinx in her mortuary temple, trampling male foreigners; but then she was also depicted with a beard, which raises other questions about the stability of the gender of the sphinx.

the intelligence and vision of a woman. No one had explained to me what the sphinx was supposed to be. I had not yet heard her narrative. I knew nothing of the use *fin de siècle* artists made of the Sphinx as a symbol of female evil. Reading the image without its accompanying strands of cultural narrative lead to a confused interpretation.

As a child lacking cultural associations to the figure of the sphinx, I interpreted her as brave and intelligent. I was not yet conscious of the archetypal image of the female as dangerous, predatory. Nor had I examined the cultural expressions of the fear of woman, what Burton in *The Anatomy of Melancholy* classifies as "[of] woman's unnatural, insatiable lust, what country, what village doth not complain?" Historically the image of the devouring woman tends to wax and wane, much as various cultures attributed different powers and characteristics to the sphinx. In periods of great social upheaval, such as the fifteenth and sixteenth centuries, woman's carnality has been perceived as overwhelming.[3] "All witchcraft comes from carnal lust, which is in women insatiable," say Kramer and Springer, authors of the official witch-hunters' guide, *Malleus Maleficarum.* "For the sake of fulfilling the mouth of the womb, [women] consort even with the devil." One medieval version of the Salomé/Herodias legend portrays a monstrous Herodias who cuts one of the dead John's eyes with a knife. In other folkloric versions from this period, the villainous woman was transformed into a witch, conflated with other demons, and blamed for various natural disasters.[4]

Further social causes of the anxiety over women's uncontrollable hungers appear to peak during periods when women are becoming independent and are asserting themselves politically and socially. During and after the first waves of feminist theories, in the second half of the nineteenth century, a flood of visual and verbal images were produced that focused upon the dark, dangerous, voluptuous, and viraginous woman: "sharp-teethed, devouring

---

[3] Bordo describes this fearful flooded feeling as a cultural expression of the fear of woman as "too much; extravagantly and excessively needful" (Bordo 1993).

[4] Kuryluk 1987: 190–91. Both Kuryluk, and Meltzer provide excellent historical recapitulations of the Salomé legend before the nineteenth century.

Sphinxes, Salomés, and Delilahs, biting, tearing, murderous women." According to intellectual historian Peter Gay, "no century, depicted woman as vampire, as castrator, as killer, so consistently, so programmatically, and so nakedly as the nineteenth."[5] Gay constructs the era as a dialectic of action and reaction in which women's demands shape male anxieties and conversely, these male anxieties encouraged further social and political activity by women (Gay 1984: 207). One of the female figures who most completely engaged the *fin de siècle* male imagination was Salomé, whose image, like that of the Sphinx, has become embedded in our imaginations so effectively that we can recall representations in the verbal, visual, and musical arts. In spite of her shadowy appearance in the Gospels of Mark and Matthew, one can create a full-bodied dangerous Salomé through the examination of these *fin de siècle* and popular cinematic representations of the mysterious dancing girl who became an icon of seduction. I have chosen Salomé because the mythification of her body in art and literature as excess so perfectly typifies the moment in the late nineteenth century when "the male loses access to the body, which the woman then comes to *overrepresent*" (Doane 1991: 2). An analysis of the emergence of Salomé as a *femme fatale* becomes a narrative about the representation of a woman caught in the act.

The story of Salomé in the New Testament is not even a story of Salomé. Matthew calls the dancer *he thaugater tes hrodiados* "the daughter *of* Herodias," (14:6); Mark *tes thugatros autou* "*his* daughter Herodias" (6:22). The details of the story are spare: the setting is the ruler Herod's birthday banquet; after his young stepdaughter has danced for the guests, Herod offered her anything up to half his kingdom, presumably as a reward for her crowd-pleasing performance. In the Markan account she leaves the banquet hall to consult with her mother Herodias, who advises her to ask for John's head. The girl herself adds the detail of "serving the head upon a charger." In keeping with biblical narrative's predilection for not

---

[5] Gay (1984: 201–07). Further, Bordo points out that this period emphasizes an obsession with the medical control of female sexuality. Treatment for excessive sexuality and sexual excitement included placing leeches on the womb, clitoridectomy, and removal of the ovaries (also recommended for "troublesomeness, eating like a ploughman, erotic tendencies, persecution mania, and simple cussedness") (Bordo 1993: 161).

expanding plot points, neither the dance nor the costumes or food at the banquet are described. Most important, there is no hint of eroticism or sexuality either in the report of the dance or in Herod's reaction to the young girl. The text details none of the emotional connections among the characters in the story, although the narrator does indicate Herod's disinclination to kill the Baptist, whom the Tetrarch fears.

The connection of the tropes of devouring women and their male victims was common in the ancient Mediterranean world. As I discussed in chapter 6, there are a series of stories in the Bible in which a woman is responsible for the death and decollation of a narratively significant male figure. Haman is hanged at Esther's request, Judith severs Holofernes' head with his own sword, Jael smashes in the head of Sisera, Delilah is responsible for the haircutting and subsequent blinding of Samson. Food and drink are two of the temptations that lead to sexual desire and death in each of these stories. Scenting these tropes are the senses of smell and taste which add to the reader's formulation of character, especially marked in the descriptions of female characters, where sexuality and fragrance are related. Spicy ointments and other beauty preparations that women employ in their seductions mark the woman as sexual predator.

Early Mediterranean traditions other than the one preserved in the Bible contain accounts of decollation as a symbol of power over an enemy. The legends are built around the figure of the consul Flaminius who was expelled from the Roman Senate (184 BCE). One of the earliest accounts appeared in Caesar's *De Senectute*, in which Caesar writes in the persona of Cato, "It was a disagreeable duty that I performed in expelling Lucius Flaminius from the senate . . . but I thought that lust merited the brand of infamy. For, when in Gaul during his consulship, at the solicitation of a courtesan at a banquet, he beheaded a prisoner then under condemnation" (Loeb xii, 42). Plutarch further publicized this incident, writing a compilation of historical accounts in the "Life of Flaminius" a more detailed version of the account recorded by Caesar. I shall quote his text at length so that the nuances of character of Flaminius and the details of plot may be available to the reader. Plutarch's summary story may be of particular interest to readers tracing the Salomé legend because of the appearance of similar tropes in both versions.

> Titus named Scipio first member of the senate; and involved himself in a quarrel with Cato, on the following unhappy occasion. Titus had a brother, Lucius Flaminius, very unlike him in all points of character, and in particular, *low and dissolute in his pleasures*, and *flagrantly regardless of all decency*. He kept as a companion a boy whom he used to carry about with him, not only when he had troops under his charge, but even when the care of a province was committed to him.
>
> One day *at a drinking bout* when the youngster was wantoning with Lucius, "I love you sir so dearly," said he, "that preferring your satisfaction to my own, I came away without seeing the gladiators, though I have never seen a man killed in my life." Lucius delighted with what the boy said, answered: "let not that trouble you; *I can satisfy that longing*," and with that ordered a condemned man to be fetched out of the prison and the executioner to be sent for, and commands him to strike off the man's head before they rose from table.[6] (italics mine)

While the classical versions of the story all involve Lucius Flaminius and his infatuation with a young boy, there is one version in which the young lover is a girl. Plutarch insists on the correctness of his version with a male–male topos.

> Valerius Antius only so far varies the story as to make it a woman for whom he did it. But Livy says that in Cato's own speech the statement is that a Gaulish deserter coming with his wife and children to the door, Lucius [Flaminius] took him *into the banqueting room*, and *killed him with his own hand to gratify his paramour*.

The additional detail of the banquet, as well as the coldness of Flaminius in taking the man from his wife and children and then killing him within a celebratory setting purely to satisfy the whim of his young male lover, add a subtext of horror to the scene. While the Gaulist was a military deserter and John the Baptist was a religious zealot speaking against the ruler and his wife, the two versions reflect similar tropes: both men were killed to satisfy a need of the ruler to please a young figure of desire. The order of death is not related to any actual crime committed by the victim.

---

[6] The translation of Plutarch's *Lives* is by John Dryden, although the italics are mine and have been added to show the similarities of trope with the Salomé legend. Plutarch (1932).

While the biblical text does not indicate that Salomé and Herod had any sort of sexual involvement, he accedes to her wish because she has pleased him and he wishes to please her. In the classical story the consul Flaminius wants to please his lover. Pleasure in both cases overrules justice. Similarly each sexual story overwrites the political one.

The dance motif was not a strong element in early versions of the Salomé story. Concentration upon the dance became prominent during the eleventh century. One startling example of the dancing Salomé is found on the bronze doors of San Zeno's Church in Verona, where "the sinuous line of the dancing princess's body likens her to a snake"(Kuryluk 1987: 196). In an English Psalter from the beginning of the thirteenth century, Salomé is pictured in a contorted backbend, with her long hair brushing the ground. Her own neck is exposed, vulnerable, while the folds of her gown fall into a V outlining her legs and directing the spectator's gaze to the area of her body just above her thighs. In the miniature following this one, the decollated head of the Baptist drips into a cup, while his headless body forms the reverse of Salomé's arched back above. His mutilated body arches forward, as it might have in a sexual encounter with the princess lying "on her back" in the previous picture. Another picture from the end of the twelfth century, on the tympanum of the Cathedral of Saint John the Baptist and John the Apostle in Rouen, is notable for a similar acrobatic fantasy, in which the artist imagines Salomé dancing on her hands. Kuryluk interprets this metaphor as "a monstrous world standing on its head."[7] A figure dancing on her hands, turning her body upside down, would invite the spectator to gaze at her sexually. In most of the medieval illustrated Bibles that depict Salomé, the manuscript is concerned with the life of John the Baptist, not with the figures of Herodias or her daughter. Salomé, as the voluptuous virago wordlessly demanding his death, is used solely as a sharp contrast to the character of the "good women" of medieval Christianity, John's virtuous mother Elizabeth, who rejoiced so in the miracle of

---

[7] Kuryluk 1987: 196. According to Kuryluk this odd way of dancing was invented by Herrade of Landsberg, the famous prioress of the Sainte-Odile nunnery, who towards the end of the twelfth century illustrated the *Hortus deliciarum* (the manuscript was kept in Strausberg and destroyed there in 1870, but it is known through copies).

John's birth, and of course with the increasingly important Virgin Mary.

During a period of fifty years in the nineteenth century, the Salomé story danced its way throughout the artistic imagination of Europe. Critics, poets, dramatists, and visual artists were concerned with embellishing and transforming cultural motifs and legends rather than creating entirely original stories. Several elements served to bind together and unify the creative visions of artists of this period: their iconoclastic irreverence and mordant wit, their desire to transcend stale conventionality, their delight in the pure gesture of revolt, perhaps, as Huysmans writes, as a response to a century concerned with

virtues and vices of a quite healthy and robust order, with the peaceable activity of brains of a perfectly ordinary confirmation, with the practical reality of current ideas, with never a thought of morbid depravations, with no outlook beyond the pale of everyday; in a word the speculations of these analysts of human nature stopped short at the ordinary classification of human acts by the Church into good and evil; it was all the simple investigation, the mere examination into normal conditions of a botanist who watches minutely the foreseen development of the everyday flora growing in common earth. (1961: 133)

Heine retold the Herodias/Salomé legend in his satiric *Atta Troll* (1840),[8] Mallarmé wrote a poem entitled "Heródiade," Oscar Wilde wrote a play in French about a tortured Salomé (1893), Strauss composed an opera based on Wilde's work,[9] and Flaubert

---

[8] Heine's satiric poem *Atta Troll* (1840) was primarily concerned with the political and social situation in Germany, and the era's insistence "upon reducing art to the role of handmaiden to the state." In the poem Heine deprecates the design to utilize literature as a cultural and moral leveller. Heine himself translated the work into French (1847) and included a long episode about the Herodias figure, whom he construed as a heroine. For an analysis of *Atta Troll*'s possible influence on the post-romantic treatments of the Salomé legend in France, and Mallarmé's interpretation, see Zagona (1960) and Pressly (1983).

[9] Max Reinhard's immensely successful 1902/3 production of Wilde's play at the Kleines Theater in Berlin probably provided the connection between Wilde and Strauss. Richard Strauss' opera *Salomé* premiered at the Königliches Operhaus in Dresden on 9 December 1905. In a letter meant to discourage Strauss from going forward with a version of the Wildean play, Romain Rolland wrote, "Oscar Wilde's *Salomé* is not worthy of you . . . Wilde's Salomé and those who surround her, save only that brute of a Iohanaan, are unhealthy, unclean, hysterical, or alcoholic, oozing with a perfumed and mundane corruption . . . You surpass your subject, but you cannot make one forget it." Quoted in Jane Marcus, "Salomé: The Jewish Princess was a New Woman," *Bulletin of the New York Public Library* (1974) p. 100, n. 28.

wrote a novella, *Heródiade*, possibly inspired by Moreau's paint-ings.[10] The cultural elision of the relationship between Salomé and Herodias that is found in some of the nineteenth-century represen-tations of "Salomé" is significant. In the original story, one can not distinguish the daughter's desire from the mother's. The reader can not tell whose desire animates and initiates the action, which returns, therefore, the suspicion of the mother's presence, power, desire. It is in the interest of a patriarchal cultural system to evacuate the mother, by concentrating upon the daughter – Salomé's inexplicable request for the head to be presented on a platter – to elide over the reality, trace, or force of the relationship of the mother/daughter pair, whose existence recalls the insepara-bility of that early dyad prior to the entrance of the third term – or paternal signifier – of mother and infant.

Among the other *fin de siècle* artists who expressed the narcissistic sensuality of the Judean princess were Lovis Corinth, the Marquis von Bayros, Lucien Lévy-Dhurmer, George Privat Livemont, Franz von Stuck. Bram Dijkstra writes spiritedly about the artists who cranked out their obligatory Salomés for the salons. "In the minds of many the separate entities of the mother and daughter had blended into a single image of ferocious vampire bloodlust with a touch of Ophelia thrown in for good measure" (1986: 387).

How did the *fin de siècle* Salomania begin?

The first writer to emphasize the connection between the literary veils of Salomé and their visual mystery was J. K. Huysmans. Through acquaintance with the character of Des Esseintes, an alterego of the author himself, and the several chapters of *A Rebours* (*Against the Grain* 1884) that describe in great bibliographic detail his library and his literary affinities, the reader is by turns assaulted and amused by the vitriolic effusions of Huysmans about the canon of the educated European man. One

---

[10] Massenet's opera *Heródiade* was based on Flaubert's story. The Massenet libretto, written by Paul Millet and Henri Gremont, departs from Flaubert's tale, rendering it far more sentimental and conventional. Salomé falls in love with John the Baptist in the first act, a love eagerly returned by John by the final act. Salomé pleads unsuccessfully with Herodias for her beloved's life. Broken hearted, Salomé rather expectedly kills herself.

   Showalter reflects upon the operatic tradition of Salomé productions that the diva usually overpowers the role of the young princess, perhaps because "it demands a powerful singer often physically at odds with the image" (159).

can imagine Huysmans expostulating to his friends in literary
Paris, insisting on the value of some artists and the failure of others,
firmly encouraging his admirers to read against the grain. In the
imaginary café of the book, the narrator enumerates for the reader
the different tastes of the *fin de siècle* artists – on whom he was such a
major influence. Thus, Huysmans succeeds in becoming the
arbiter of taste for *fin de siècle* Paris, much as he has given this role to
his character Des Esseintes. Within the minds of both Des Esseintes
and his creator, the sublime majesty of medieval church music and
illuminated prayer books clash violently with his consistent vision
of the Church as morally corrupt. Through his focus on two of
Gustave Moreau's paintings of Salomé, Huysmans is able to tie his
Decadent revision of Salomé with a challenge to both the genre of
theological storytelling and traditional Church piety.

The interplay of visual and verbal heightens the sensual effect
that Huysmans uses to lure his audience to the figure of Salomé,
brought to life for destroying the traditionally drawn power of the
male ruler. In his novel *A rebours*,[11] his protagonist and alterego Des
Esseintes is haunted by his fantasy of a monastery for free-thinkers,
those who appreciate his sense that the Church has become a
worn-out legend. If the story of Salomé represents the Church at its
recalcitrant worst, the character of Salomé allows Huysmans to
challenge the conventional confines of morality through the artifice
of her creation by Moreau, with exotic jewels, iridescent silks, and
the physical appearance of the magical head itself. The head
"glows eerily in an embracing sinister gaze," having left the
charger and "risen into the air, the eyes staring out from the livid
face, the colorless lips parted, the crimson neck dripping tears of
blood" (1969: 68). The visual portrait created in words by
Huysmans is as vivid as the colors of the original Moreau painting.
Words evoke images as powerfully as the betrayer of John the
Baptist evokes simultaneous fascination and fear of the female.

In spite of his detailed knowledge of medieval Bibles and
theological treatises, Huysmans neither describes these early
renditions of the Salomé tradition nor does he connect any of these
early visual portraits of Salomé with the central focus of his work –

---

[11] References to *A Rebours* will be to the English translation *Against the Grain* found in
Huysmans (1969). All other references to this work will be found in the text.

Moreau's two paintings of the voluptuous princess mesmerized by her desire for the head of the Baptist, the result of her heart-stopping request to Herod. Moreau's watercolor *L'Apparition* tempts the reader to see through Huysmans' eyes. As the dazzling heavily jeweled woman has made appear the other-worldly specter of the head of the Baptist, an impossible sight, so Huysmans' work has challenged the possible and broken taboos, with its eroticizing of the Christian story.

But Huysmans is not concerned with either any historical or cultural route that Salomé might have taken into the imagination of his own des Esseintes, of Moreau[12] or of the other Decadent artists. If his characterization of Salomé has any connection to the biblical character, she functions as she will very soon afterwards for Oscar Wilde, as a biblical figure magnified, eroticized, and intensified. If the biblical figure of the unnamed dancing daughter of Herodias plays a very minor role in the biblical text, presenting her as the protagonist of a visually horrific and exotic tale challenges the drear biblical telling and the conventional tensions between good and evil, much as Huysmans challenges the moralistic tracts of the later Church throughout *A Rebours*.

While the plot of *A Rebours* lags and falters and is clearly of minor interest to Huysmans, he succeeds in his goal of transforming the novel from a plot-driven genre to a work engaging philosophic ideas as well as visual images. If one survives the polemic thrust of the prose, the reader does become intimate with the ideas and passions of protagonist Des Esseintes, the only viable character in the novel. Huysmans is so agonizingly precise in elaborating upon his literary *bêtes noires* that the reader comes close to adopting his

---

[12] "In his various renderings of woman as the embodiment of earthly temptation (*The Sphinx, Salomé, Delilah*) Moreau expressed one of the preoccupations of the period: "an obsession with woman as the agent of the Devil, but also as the symbol of beauty and purity." Goldwater (1979: 153–55).

Moreau's two paintings *Salomé Dancing Before Herod* and *L'Apparition* received much attention when they were first shown. Moreau made eighty studies of the oil painting and about fourteen of the watercolor. The long period of gestation is documented by a pair of studies dating from 1872 and 1874. According to Kaplan, Moreau's *Salomé* was probably influenced by the dancing figure of Delacroix's *Jewish Wedding* (Louvre 1839), Regnault's *Salomé*, which had won a prize in the Salon of 1869 (Paris), as well as Rembrandt's *Christ Driving the Moneychangers from the Temple*, "in which small figures are placed in a huge architectural setting" Kaplan (1982: 62–63). For critical analysis of Moreau's work, see Mathieu (1991); Pressly (1983); Treuherz (1993); also Moreau (1974a).

opinions as one's own. Full of contempt for the Latin Augustan age, Huysmans through Des Esseintes terms Horace a detestable clown; he is repelled equally by Caesar's dry constipation and Cicero's fat redundancy; Juvenal, Livy, Tacitus, and Plautus could delight only those of faux-literary tastes. For Huysmans Petronius was the only gold among the dross because the Roman's ironic wit anticipated the contemporary French novelists he so admired. Since Apuleius was another of his Latin favorites, it is odd that Huysmans did not connect Apuleius' lavish corrupted banquet scenes with the Herodian court in which the *fin de siècle* Salomé danced. While the lavish, erotic worlds of Verlaine and Mallarmé, like Huysmans himself, shaped the anti-classical age in France, following the lead of Baudelaire, the viraginous Salomé drew her inspiration from an allergy to traditional religious morality.

Termed Decadent by the more traditional critics, such art was described disparagingly by those who viewed suspiciously the Decadents' and Symbolists' revolt against the previous generation's positivistic scientific attitudes that affected both literature and painting.

A style of decadence is one in which the unity of the book is decomposed to give place to the independence of the page, in which the page is decomposed to give place to the independence of the phrase, and the phrase to give place to the independence of the word.[13]

But for those artists who were committed to seeking the new, the rare, the strange, Walter Pater described their credo:

Our one chance lies in . . . getting as many pulsations as possible into the given time. Great passions give us this quickened sense of life. The love of art for arts' sake has most, for art comes to you proposing frankly to give nothing but for the highest quality to your moments as they pass, and simply for those moments' sake.[14]

Having schooled the reader in the virtues of some and the vilification of other literary artists, but having no literary use for the biblical or medieval connections with Salomé, Huysmans turns his eye unblinkingly toward contemporary visual images of Salomé. In fact his use of the paintings is to reveal further the sensibilities of

---

[13] Quoted in Huysmans (1969: xvi).
[14] Walter Pater, *The Renaissance*, 1873, cited in Showalter (1990: 170).

Des Esseintes, who owns Moreau's two greatest paintings of Salomé and hangs them in his study, the most private room of his house. The aesthete meditates on the images deep into the night, his obsessive fascination providing him a kind of thick-tongued pleasure. What Des Esseintes sees as he stares at Moreau's *Salomé Dancing Before Herod* is the soaring architectonics of myth and structure.

In the work of Moreau. . .Des Esseintes realized at last the Salomé, weird and superhuman, he had dreamed of. No longer was she merely the dancing-girl who exhorts a cry of lust and concupiscence from an old man by the lascivious contortions of her body. . . She was now revealed in a sense as symbolic incarnation of world-old Vice, the goddess of immortal Hysteria, the accursed Beauty exalted above all other beauties by the cataleptic spasm that stirs her flesh, and steels her muscles – a monstrous Beast of the Apocalypse, indifferent, irresponsible, insensible, poisoning, like the Helen of Troy of the old classic fables, all who come near her, all who see her, all who touch her. (53)

In the second picture, *L'Apparition*, a watercolor, Huysmans understands Moreau to have painted Salomé's terror at the sight of the bodiless head. "With a gesture of horror, Salomé repulses the appalling vision that holds her nailed to the floor, balanced on her toe tips; her eyes are dilated, her hand grips her throat convulsively" (1969: 54–55). While some interpreters interpret the painting as Huysmans does, insisting that Moreau painted the arm repelling the head, that the facial expression shows Salomé's horror at what she has wrought, I struggle to break the intellectual hold Huysmans has upon my critical faculties. I see another narrative revealed in the painting.[15] The figure of Salomé is covered only by a diaphanous veil and ornate jewelry, her body is open, not protected or coiled in fear, but rather proudly gesturing toward the result of her power play. Her bejeweled nakedness is the weapon she uses to transfix the members of the Court as precisely as the executioner uses the ax to sever the head of the Baptist.

The narrative gap in the painting, inherent in visual stillness, allows the viewer to decide whether the extended arm of the bejeweled Salomé is beckoning or repelling the specter of John's

---

[15] Another counter-interpretation can be found in Dijkstra, who considers Salomé reaching out to the head in ecstatic hunger.

floating head. One interpreter suggests that the severed head serves as a metaphor for the plight of the frigid woman, as understood in the male unconscious. The satisfaction [Salomé] so "ardently desires hovers just out of reach, while at the same time she both covets and threatens the instrument through which it must be achieved."[16] Another viewer claims that the figure of Salomé in the watercolor is "less imposing, but more ensnaring to the senses than the Salomé of the oil painting." *A Rebours* illustrates precisely Bal's theory that images trigger readings. Huysmans' gaze fills gaps in the story:

the dreadful head flashes and flames, bleeding always, ripping gouts of dark purple that point the beard and hair. Visible to Salomé, alone, it embraces in the stare of its dead eyes neither Herodias, who sits dreaming of her hate satiated at last, nor the Tetrarch, who, leaning rather forward with hands on knees, still pants, maddened by the sight of the woman's nakedness, reeking with heady fumes, dripping with balms and essences, alluring with scents of incense and myrrh. (55)

Thus, it becomes clear that the interpretations of visual texts are no more fixed than interpretations of literary ones. Contained within the spectatorial gaze is the resolution of the question of whether Salomé was attracted or repelled by the head – of whom? – the imprisoned prophet who spurned her advances, as Wilde would envision it, or the desert leader who threatened her mother's life, as the biblical narrative suggests. The answers to the question of John's identity reveal the cultural pressures exerted upon the biblical author, Wilde, and the reader.

In *L'Apparition*, in my view, the full figure of Salomé is equal in importance with the truncated radiant head of the Baptist. They make equivalent claims upon the spectator's attention. Salomé as subject points toward her work with pride. The Baptist is enclosed within the fire of the cosmos. He is as complete as Salomé, an unearthly specter to balance the very earthy woman. She is the figure with a body who has subsumed his. Like Des Esseintes, the figure of Salomé is mesmerized by her passion, fixated on the head as trophy or possession, as Des Esseintes is fixed upon the icon of the painting which he possesses.

---

[16] Lucie-Smith (1991 (rev. edn): 233).

Moreau's oil painting *Salomé Dancing Before Herod* exemplifies an Orientalized dream of the Judean princess who personified female eroticism out of control. Precisely detailed, crowded with allegory, painted in a palette of yellows, coppers, and golds, Moreau's vision contains a natural association of poetry and painting. The executioner stands to the right of the seated Tetrarch and a black panther is seated in the right foreground of the picture. In the midground an elegantly draped and jeweled Salomé dances before a still-as-a-statue Herod. Among the central details filling the painting are the statues that are placed above the head of Herod. Above him, in the vaulting Moorish arches are statues of Diana of Ephesus, a goddess of fertility, flanked by two smaller and identical images of Mithras, an exclusively male deity. Partially hidden Herodias is seated to the left behind a seated musician, clearly separated and less important than her daughter. The central image is that of Salomé, although her iridescent body is static, unyielding. Since all the figures in the painting are frozen, the scene appears transfixed in time, holding the viewer's attention to the moment before Salomé's request is granted. Although the Baptist is not figured in this picture, for those viewers who know the story of Salomé, the picture stops time: at the moment in the painting the decadence of the Herodian court has not yet been turned into an immortal evil.

Mesmerized by the visual elements of her story – a half-naked woman, a sensual esoteric dance before an Oriental court, and the severed head of a Christian martyr, Moreau was stimulated by a century of archeological discoveries and publications, and shared an interest in oriental and near-Eastern themes with Flaubert, Mallarmé,[17] Gautier, and other contemporary artists. The idea of the woman as sexually dominant, as the castrating female over whom men lost their heads, became prominent in the second half of the

---

[17] In his *Heródiade* Mallarmé characterizes the narcissism of Salomé as she gazes at her reflection in the mirror. Note the recurring antinomies of cold/heat; and snow, white/night connected to Salomé that are found also in Flaubert and Wilde.

> The horror of my virginity
> Delights me, and I would envelope me
> In the terror of my tresses, that, by night,
> Inviolate reptile, I might feel the white
> And glimmering radiance of thy frozen fire,
> Thou that art chaste and diest of desire
> White night of ice and of the cruel snow.

nineteenth century. For these artists, then, the character of Salomé represented both flesh and idea. In this period, the figure of Salomé is shown partially nude, either before the gaze of the court of Herod or alone with one of the icons of her story: the charger or the decapitated head. Corinth's *Salomé* (1899) leans barebreasted over the charger or platter as she caresses the decollated head with bloodied hands; von Stuck's three versions of Salomé (1906) emphasize the sensuality of the dance as well as the erotic currents in the encounter of Salomé with Herod, John, and the male members of the Court. In the Corinth painting, the violent deed has already been performed. Thus, the spectator can gaze at the dangerous woman whose breasts are tumbling toward him from the safe distance of the frame. Reminiscent of Japanese woodblocks, and as different from the style of Moreau's lush paintings, are Aubrey Beardsley's flat black and white drawings. The sinuous lines define an overbearing domineering Salomé who scandalized even a society titillated by decadence and familiar with the mythic figure of Salomé. Both artists orientalize the figure and story of Salomé, emphasizing her foreignness to the *fin de siècle* European sensibility.

THE PRE-TEXT OF SALOMÉ

While the biblicist may well have read the Gospel versions of the so-called Salomé narrative before considering other cultural appropriations of the story, a reader not as conversant with the Bible may well have read the Gospel accounts after seeing a Hollywood version of the story, after reading Wilde's *Salomé*, or Flaubert's *Heródiade*, after attending a performance of the Strauss opera. Regardless of the order of one's reading, what is immediately apparent is the difference between the story as reported by the biblical writers and the later literary, musical, and visual interpretations of the figure of Salomé.

Salomé in the Gospel accounts is an unnamed young woman, daughter of Herodias and Philip, step-daughter of Philip's brother Herod.[18] The character of the young girl, later called Salomé, exists

---

[18] The complicated Herodian genealogy is not important to this chapter. Briefly Herod Antipas was married to the daughter of Aretas IV, king of Nabatea, until Herod fell in love with Herodias, who was married to his half-brother Philip. Herodias agreed to marry

narratively for only a few verses in the Gospels of Mark and
Matthew. The name Salomé appears only twice within the New
Testament, in Mark 15:40 and 16:1. In both verses the name refers
to one of the three women disciples of Jesus. This Salomé figure
appears again in extracanonical traditions and in subsequent
Christian midrashic literature. Josephus gives the name Salomé to
the daughter of Herodias although he does not credit her with a
dance that results in either Herod or JBap losing their heads (*Ant.*
XVIII 5, 1–4). He understands the death of the Baptist to be
politically motivated and credits the inplaying of the decadent
Herodian clan with the crime. In their theological readings, both
the biblical authors and Josephus connect Herod's beheading of
the Baptist with the Tetrarch's subsequent loss of power.

> But to some of the Jews it seemed that Herod's army had been destroyed
> by God, who was exacting vengeance (most certainly justly) as satisfaction
> for John, who was called Baptist. For Herod indeed put him to death,
> who was a good man and one who commanded the Jews to practice
> virtue and act with justice toward one another and with piety toward God
> and [so] to gather together by baptism. (*Ant.* xviii, 116–17)

Josephus considers John to be a good man (*agathou andra*), who
has God on his side. The historian clearly is on the side of the Jews
who consider John to have been unjustly killed by Herod. It is
tempting to connect Josephus' judgment of Herod with that of
Caesar against Flaminius, since both rulers have ignored the
ethical demands of their communities.

The biblical versions of both Mark and Matthew are structured
as flashbacks, indicating that the surprise effect of the demand for
the severed head is not of interest to the biblical storytellers. The
audience knows that John has been beheaded before the story of
his imprisonment is related. The reader of Mark and Matthew is

Herod Antipas after he divorced his first wife. She returned to her father Aretas, who
subsequently went to war against Antipas, soundly defeating him in battle. A thorough
investigation of the figure of John the Baptist and his relation to the reign of Herod
Antipas is found in Webb. See note 23.

For most of the significant early Christian references to Salomé, see Smith (1973). For a
discussion on the identity of this Salomé – is she both disciple and sister of Jesus, or are
there two figures sharing the name – see Smith (1982); Bauckham (1991). Bauckham
provides detailed Patristic references in his effort to correct Smith's mistaken conflation of
the sister of Jesus and the second Salomé, whom Bauckham identifies as the namesake of
the disciple of Jesus (246).

first offered the link between Tetrarch and prophet: Herod's understanding that Jesus is John "raised from the dead" (Mark 6:14,16; Matt. 14:2). The story of the Baptist's silencing and death also points to the political unrest in the Jewish community, provides a reason for the military defeat of Herod Antipas by Aretas, and functions narratively to foreshadow unjust actions taken by a Judean ruler on behalf of Rome. But these two elements of the story are not the primary explanation offered for the death of the Baptist. As I read the text, the political struggle between Herod Antipas and his enemies is not the precipitating event for the Gospel writers that it is for Josephus.

In the final version of the Markan account the effect of intercalating the story between two stories of Jesus' expanding ministry underscores the deep connection between the baptizer John and the one who shall baptize by fire and the Holy Spirit. As John's ministry is coming to its close underground, his enemies struggling to still his prophetic voice, Jesus is beginning to instruct his apostles (*apostoloi*) on their ministry (6:7–13). As Jesus is becoming more visible, John is fading from sight. One can hear the Baptist, through his berating of Herodias, but it is Jesus who has become visible and central to the narrative. Regardless of the biblical text's lack of concern with formulating a character for Salomé, the killing of the prophet is clearly assigned to the female Herodias. First, her act of adultery has ignited John's wrath, and then her machinations result in his death.

The Matthean account parallels the Markan narrative quite closely. After explaining parables, Jesus, surrounded by his family, begins to make himself known to the people, not without irony and foreboding. "Jesus said to them, 'Prophets are not without honor except in their own country and in their own house.'" (Matt. 13:57; Mark 6:4 par.). Immediately following in both biblical accounts is the narrative of the death of the Baptist, a startling reminder of a prophet without honor, or life, in his own country. In the Matthean account it is Herod who connects Jesus with the troublesome Baptist, prophesying from the dank prison below ground, although not in the specific direct discourse of Mark, "But when Herod heard of it, he said, 'John, whom I beheaded, has been raised.'" (Mark 6:16). In the Matthean version the scene between Herod and the daughter of Herodias is not as dramatic, for the ruler's foolish vow is not presented in direct speech, as it is in Mark: "Whatever you ask me, I will give you, even half of my kingdom." (Mark 6:23). The interchange between Herodias and the daughter is also indirect in Matthew, flattening the account. Because of the lack of direct speech in the Matthean account, the audience does not realize that the daughter has amended her mother's account.

> She went out and said to her mother, "What should I ask for?" She replied, "The head of John the baptizer."
> Immediately she rushed back to the king and requested, "I want you to give me at once the head of John the Baptist *on a platter.*" (Mark 6:24–25)

Thus, although the information gleaned from the accounts is equivalent, the Markan account allows more of a spectacle to emanate from the account. The reader of the Markan account is faced with the carnality of the execution, emphasized in the repetition of the phrase, "head of John the Baptist." The gore of the scene is grayed by the indirectness of the Matthean style.

The biblical accounts provide no narrative hint that the daughter of Herodias possessed the glitter that transforms her into the *belle dame sans merci* of *fin de siècle* Europe. First it is highly unlikely that a young girl would have appeared at all at a *symposium* or banquet. As I discussed in chapter 6, in the first century, proper women of the Court would have been excluded from male entertainment (the *symposium* following the banquet). Even Queen Herodias' presence would have been doubtful. Men and respectable women celebrated such occasions separately, both in Greco-Roman and in Hellenistic–Jewish practices.[19] The only women to be found at such gatherings were "evil" women, ones who danced or entertained the men after the meal. Thus, Herod's request for a dance shows the ambiguous nature of his desire for Salomé, who performs as a *hetaira* (courtesan or party girl). Here one can compare the success of Herod in turning his stepdaughter into a courtesan and the failure of Ahasuerus' attempt to force Vashti to perform such a dance, which would change her role from that of

---

[19] For detailed descriptions of Greco-Roman, Jewish, and early Jewish-Christian meal practices, both ritual and banquet settings, see Corley (1992) esp. chapter 2; Murray (1990). See chapter 6 of this study for detailed discussion of the nexus of women, food, and sexuality in the biblical texts.

Queen/wife to the role of *hetaira*. In *The Sacrifice of Cain and Abel* Philo warns that the only type of woman who accompanies men to a banquet occasion is a "party girl." Although Philo does not use the term *hetaira* in this passage, it seems clear that the woman whose role is designated as pleasure giver is what he is describing:

So pleasure comes languishing in the guise of a harlot (*porne*) or courtesan (*chamaitune*). Her gait has the looseness which her extravagant wantonness and luxury has bred . . . her costly raiment is embroidered lavishly with flowers . . . a strumpet of the streets, she makes the marketplace her home.

In a passage that extends the sensual caricature of the strange woman "*ishah zarah*" presented in Proverbs 5 and 7, Philo sounds much more like Huysmans than the Gospel writers who would have been his contemporaries.

Sweet modulations of melodious sounds, costly kinds of food and drink, abundant varieties of delicious perfumes, amours without ceasing, frolics unregulated, chamberings unrestricted, language unrepressed, deeds uncensored, life without care, sleep soft and sweet, satiety ever filled. I will join you in considering what food and drink would charm your palate, what sight would please your eyes, what sounds your ears, what perfume your nostrils.

In describing the daughter of Herodias, the Markan author uses the word *korasion*, a diminutive of *kore*, the Greek word for girl or maiden. Young, uncultured, she would be connected metaphorically to the wildness of Artemis, her elements being "thorny plants and acorns." Before becoming marryable, she would have to rid herself of the wildness, become a creature of wheat and bread (Detienne 1994: xv). That progression of the female figure from girl to wife is precisely what is missing in the Salomé version of the *kore* story. Herodias has not rid herself of wildness; on the contrary, as the Baptist relentlessly reminds the reader, her wildness is an offense against the Jewish community, her refusal to become a creature of wheat and bread is an offense against God.

A secondary meaning of the word *kore* is pupil of the eye. I like to think that there is a connection between the two meanings because of the tiny reflected image found there. Thus, a young girl like Salomé could see herself reflected in the male gaze; she would know that she was the apple of Herod's eye.[20] And just as the mythic Kore is abducted and shut away in the underworld by Hades, so Salomé has been living in the underworld of Herod's mind. Given the widely varied cultural appropriations of the figure of Salomé, the reader may well have gazed at the girl, and taken her captive in the underworld of the mind, long before reading the Gospel account. Simultaneously wild and held captive by her mother's power, the young Salomé is led toward her violent request by her mother, making clear that she is not mothered by the female guardian of grain and nourishment. In the ordinary development of the myth, the *kore* (virgin) is contrasted with the *gune* (wife), a woman of different age and status. *Kore*, not its later diminutive form *korasion*, was used in classical Greek to refer to maiden goddesses, such as Kore and Artemis. The word indicated virginity, the period up to that of bride. Thus, the *kore* was a term familiar to ancient readers for a young girl, not one schooled in seductive practices. But Herodias remains in part a *kore*, the apple of Herod's eye, a *kore* who has never lost her wildness, never acceded to the cultivated state of grower of grain, producer of the family bread. What makes Herodias doubly dangerous is that she has shed the innocence of the virgin, but has ripened into a viraginous woman, not a mother figure. Perhaps Salomé's embellishment of the request, to present the head of the Baptist *on a platter* is an unconscious reflection of the murderous mother, who offers the food of death instead of the bread of life. This elision of the mother–daughter that is sometimes found in versions of the story can be explained as an erasure of the necessary distinction between *kore* and *gune*, virgin and wife. Both female figures occupy the same liminal space, each casting a shadow into the category forbidden to her. The *kore* acts in a sexual manner, tempting the male to do her bidding; the *gune* puts her own daughter and husband in danger, and thus does not act with the expected selflessness of the mother.

Central to my reading, then, is the oscillation between the two women, found in the crucial detail that the girl is obeying her

---

[20] *korasion* is also the word used in Mark 5:41, 42 to describe Jairus' twelve-year-old daughter who is cured by Jesus (see note 22). The LXX reading of the book of Esther uses *korasion* to describe Esther and the other young virgins in the harem trying to gain the favor of King Ahasuerus (Artaxerxes in the Greek version).

mother in making her ghoulish request. In both Gospel accounts, it is Herodias, the wife of two men, who is constructed as the phallic mother, the woman who ignites male sexual desire and fear. The young girl is fulfilling her mother's wish to have the troublesome Baptist silenced, not her own. The Baptist has threatened Herodias because she has not lived as a good wife and mother; by "marrying" Herod Antipas she has scoffed at the laws that protect a woman's womb for her legal husband, Philip. An indication that leads the reader to a "cool" reading of the girl's dance is the Greek word *aresen* that defines the kind of pleasure that the daughter's dance evokes (Mark 6:22), a word that refers not to erotic pleasure but rather to "accommodating someone, or doing something that someone will approve, or find pleasant" (Anderson 1992: 122).[21] One can connect this sort of innocuous pleasure with the girlishness of the *korasion*. Matthew uses the same verb and refers to the girl as *korasion* (14:11) and also calls the daughter of Jairus *korasion* (Matt. 9:24, 25).[22] Flaubert also has understood the character of the biblical Salomé as the virginal tool of her overbearing mother, the genuine figure of power in the text. The daughter is not the subject of power, but rather its carrier. Flaubert fills the gaps in the story with a similar innocent carnality. He imagines a girl who is not personally eager for the head of the Baptist, but rather a girl who is not yet the central character in the story.

The girl depicted the frenzy of a love which demands satisfaction. She danced like the priestess of the Indies, like the Nubian girls of the cataracts, like the bacchantes of Lydia. She twisted from side to side like a flower shaken by the wind. The jewels in her ears swung in the air, the silk on her back shimmered in the light, and from her arms, her feet, and her clothes there shot out invisible sparks, which set the men on fire. A harp sang, and the crowd answered it with cheers.

I read with Flaubert in preserving the biblical account of the dance as innocent, a child charming an adult audience. In both my reading and in Flaubert's *Hérodiade* the female power belongs to

---

[21] Other New Testament uses of *aresen* as accommodation appear in Acts 6:5; Rom. 8:8; 15:1–3; Gal. 1:10; I Cor. 7:33, 34, 10:33; I Thess. 2:4, 15, 4:1; 2 Tim. 2:4.

[22] Mark refers to the daughter of Jairus as both *korasion* (5: 41, 42) and *paidion* "Why do you make a commotion and weep? The child (*to paidion*) is not dead but sleeping." (5:39; also 5:40 (twice)). Mark "translates" Jesus' Aramaic *talitha cum* as *korasion* (5:41); while Matthew does not use the Aramaic, but simply refers to the young girl as *korasion* (9:24; 25).

Herodias, who controls the movements of her daughter. Because Herod liked to listen to the Baptist (Mark 6:20), the Queen's options in annihilating her enemy were limited. It is the cleverness of Herodias in manipulating her daughter and the foolishness of King Herod's open-ended promise that combine to cause the death of John the Baptist. She is the *femme fatale*, who choreographs the performance that mesmerizes the male ruler. Herodias seems, therefore, to confound the power of patriarchy, gaining agency through the body of her own daughter. However, it would be a feminist misreading to understand Herodias as a heroine in the narrative; she is not the subject of feminism but a symptom of male fears about feminism. Doane has recognized the seductive trap for the feminist who accepts the *femme fatale* as a sign of strength and warns such a reader to recognize that the construction of the *femme fatale* involves "an unwritten history [that] must also and simultaneously involve an understanding and assessment of all the epistemological baggage she carries along with her" (1991: 3). Acknowledging the connection of the *femme fatale* or viraginous woman with deception or secretiveness within these narratives encourages a feminist reader to exploit the figure's more disruptive connotations, to unveil male fears about her.

A ruler's similarly foolish promise is found in the book of Esther, where besotted King Ahasuerus, at a banquet, promises the young Queen Esther, also termed *korasion* in the LXX, the apple of his eye, that she may have anything she desires up to half his kingdom. Both stories involve women manipulating men through wining, dining, and gazing at delicious feminine beauty. Each of the all-powerful kings ends up ordering a man killed although he may not truly want to execute the man. Each ruler violates legal authority with impunity because each has had his mind "poisoned" by desiring a very tasty female dish. What is ambiguous in the Salomé story is who that dish is – Herodias or her daughter. As I read the story, the child-daughter in the text that will inform the doxa is as compliant as a daughter should be. The central importance of the wickedness of Herod and his "illegal" wife Herodias is shown through John's repetitive warnings that they are breaking the law. Herodias is desperate to silence the righteous and holy voice of the prophet. The seriousness of the crime of adultery to the Jewish audience, underscored by the prophet's citing of the Levitical law, is played against the frivolity of the dance of the unnamed daughter. While the girl's dance is the overt act that leads to the death of the Baptist in both New Testament accounts, the dance is of minor narrative importance. There is no suggestion of the perfumed heat of the *ishah zarah*, who would have transformed the princess from a young obedient girl (*korasion*) to a steamy courtesan (*porne*). The audience might have thought simply by the presence of Herodias and her daughter that "extravagant wantonness" was occurring at Herod's banquet. After all, he and Herodias were already being berated by John for living as adulterers. Whether the young daughter would be swept along by the tide of their guilt is not clear, especially since the Markan author emphasizes twice that the girl asks the mother what to request, and then presents the trophy head to her. Salomé seems to be a mere conduit, or condiment, to the main course of female evil.

The Markan text connects the two banquets of betrayal, the birthday celebration of King Herod and the seder which became the Last Supper of Jesus and his disciples, through the use of the word *eukairon*, "opportunity," a term referring to a history-changing rent in the fabric of plain time. "But an *opportunity* (*eukairou*) came when Herod on his birthday gave a banquet for his courtiers and officers and for the leaders of Galilee" (6:21). The Gospel writer uses the term at a second crucial moment in the narrative, Mark 14:11, "So he began to look for an *opportunity* (*eukairos*) to betray him," where the noun designates Judas' determination to find the opportune moment to betray Jesus. Thus, the betrayal of John foreshadows the betrayal of Jesus. Herodias/Salomé becomes an eroticized iconic Judas, who presents the storyteller with the added dimension of sexual betrayal to the legend.

An intertextual reading of Salomé with the book of Esther (see chapter 6) prompts the reader to interpret the diffident description of the daughter's dance in the Gospel accounts as an allusion to the lavish entertainment at Ahasuerus' birthday entertainment in the book of Esther. When one reads the two texts together, the comparison of the refusal of Vashti, the first queen of Ahasuerus, to dance for the king and his male Court, and the compliance of the young daughter of Herodias in performing her dance, leads one to speculate about an undercurrent of parody in the Gospel account of Herod's banquet. A parodic reading would connect the two kings, one a pagan Babylonian and one a Jewish puppet of the Roman regime, through their lavish celebrations. Vashti, a pagan queen, refuses to perform in spite of her husband's command; the daughter of Herodias, an adulterous improper Jewish queen, dances even before being offered the prize. In such a reading it is probably Herodias who is the match of Queen Esther, for it is Herod's love and fear of his Queen that makes him fulfill her request in spite of his own misgivings. Salomé in the biblical text has no knowledge of John, and does not desire his death, except as it will please her mother. Herodias, like Esther, knows that the way to manipulate the king is through the female body – Herodias uses her daughter's body, Esther her own. But both figures are probably more the symptom of male fears than they are proper subjects of a feminist "heroic" discourse.

Since the accounts of the banquet and the after-dinner entertainment seem to be of little interest to the biblical storytellers, one is impelled to unearth possible reasons for these male authors not lingering upon such a tempting narrative dish. Unlike classical narrations of banquets and erotic entertainments, these texts are striking for their omission of the details of steaming platters of food, flagons of drink, women clothed in softly woven fabrics, jewels glinting in the firelight, the *plink* of a lute or lyre accompanying the dance. The Markan and Matthean writers dutifully report that the daughter of Herodias[23] danced, but they do not imagine her dance.[24] She is not of central interest to writers concerned with a

[23] The familial connection between Herod and Herodias is immediately apparent in the closeness of the two names. Josephus records that Herodias had two husbands Herod Antipas, the son of Herod the Great, the figure mentioned in the Gospel accounts, and earlier, a second Herod, possibly Herod Philip, another son of Herod the Great, *Antiquities* 18:5–14. Marriage to a brother's wife (while the husband is still alive) is forbidden to Jews in Lev. 18:16, 20–21. This explains the fierce antipathy between John the Baptist, who was continually speaking out against the breaking of Jewish law by the Hellenized Tetrarch and his wife Herodias. Not incidentally the punishment of the woman for adultery (the situation of Herodias since Herod Philip was very much alive) was death by stoning.

[24] What Salomé danced is one of the narrative gaps that has been filled spectacularly by choreographers and visual artists from Victorian times to the present. Michael Fokine choreographed the Dance of the Seven Veils to the music of Strauss for a staging of Wilde's play in St. Petersburg in 1908 starring the Russian dancer and actress Ida

paternalistic theological agenda. What is at stake is the connection between the Baptist and Jesus, not the sexual politics of an imagined banquet evening. The hegemony of the theological code explains the insertion of the story into the Gospel accounts as parallel narratives of the public betrayal of John the Baptist and Jesus. The erotic elements of the narrative can be restored through a gendered reading, or through the desire to imagine the erotic, as in Wilde's *Salomé*.

If one were to read through the historical–political code in each text, and disregard the gendered aspects of the story, the character of Herodias would have no parallel in the Esther story. If she were to have a parallel, ironically, it would be to one of the political male characters in the text, Mordecai or Haman. Mordecai is a pious man, obeying Jewish law, making a comparison with the Jewish adulteress unlikely. And Haman, while a confidant of the king, as is Herodias, and surely as narcissistic as she, loses his power and his head to his enemy, while Herodias uses her daughter to destroy her enemy and gain his head. "Half a kingdom," is offered to both Salomé and Esther, by their male admirer–rulers, forging an echo in the mind of the Gospel reader familiar with the Esther story. The Babylonian ruler must be guided by Esther and her adviser Mordecai in order to do the "right" thing, to halt his kingdom's legal persecution of the Jews. There is no ethical or "right" voice to guide Herod, since Herodias is as corrupt as her husband and the courtiers do not figure in the story. The only pious Jewish voice, that of John, is ignored, then silenced, whereas the voice of

Rubinstein. Leon Bakst designed the sets and costumes for this staging and for a later production in Paris in 1912. Tamara Karasavina danced in Diaghilev's 1914 Paris production of Robert d'Humières' poem *Le tragédie de Salomé* set to music by Florent Schmitt. Karasavina made her entrance on stage in a peacock cape inspired by Beardsley's designs. The Schmitt piece was performed in 1907 by Loie Fuller, "who reportedly finished in the nude" (Pressly 1983: 16). The popular dancers of the early decades of this century capitalized on the new-found interest in the exotic Dance of the Seven Veils, making it as erotic as the theater owners would permit. The most popular interpretation was Maud Allen's *Vision of Salomé*, first performed in Munich in 1907, and in London the following year where it played for 200 performances. Mlle Dazié starred in the first of the Ziegfield Follies in New York in 1907 as a lushly choreographed Salomé. For further descriptions of performances of Salomé, see Pressly, and for a short history of Rubinstein's life in the theater, as well as other descriptions of the figure of Salomé interpreted in dance, see Koegler (1977). For a colorful and engaging history of the *fin de siècle* decadent dance as it relates specifically to the figure of Salomé, see Ellis (1995) and Showalter (1990).

Mordecai is heard through Esther. If the Gospel story were a parallel instead of a reversal of the Esther story, then Salomé would be guided by the Baptist to reform her mother and stepfather. Ironically the closest "match" to this version of the story is the interpretation found in the Fifties Hollywood version of the Salomé story that I shall discuss below.

SALOMÉ GONE WILDE

Oscar Wilde's retelling of the Salomé story illustrates the theoretical notion that reading is changing. After reading many of Wilde's works, it becomes clear that his art is one of inversion, or discrediting the ideals of unity of thought and predictability of action. One sees in *The Importance of Being Earnest* that each person becomes his secret or hidden opposite: Algy becomes Bunbury, Jack Ernest. Gender inversions are marked symbols of the essential changing that occurs through reading. The women in the play read heavy German philosophical works and attend university courses, while the men lounge about on couches, daintily nibbling at cucumber sandwiches. The last words on these inversions of gender are given to Gwendolyn, when she praises her own father for conceding that a man's place is in the home and that a woman can safely be entrusted to deal with public affairs. When Wilde wrote *Salomé*, he was disaffected with the English literary world and drawn to what he perceived as the freedom of French intellectual life and dreamed of having his play produced in Paris with Bernhardt as Salomé. The influence of Huysmans and Mallarmé on Wilde's version of the story is apparent

Through his characterization of Salomé as a moon princess, whose being is a reflection of light rather than the light itself, Wilde seems to be arguing that seeing is reflecting as well. All his characters in *Salomé* are described through their attempts to see, a combination of vision and insight, except the prophet, who defines himself by language; his sense is hearing and listening. The structure of the opening scenes of the play, in which the minor characters observe the main characters and comment upon their actions, places the spectator in the position of being a double observer: (1) of the interplay among Salomé, Herod, and the

Baptist, and (2) of the framing commentary of the secondary characters. This hearing about seeing, verbal descriptions of the visual, presents a gelid tableau that adds to the mysterious mythic quality of the play. The spectator is not seeing the action performed so much as the action reflected – thus the act of seeing becomes a parallel to the iconic figure of Salomé – a reflection (the moon) rather than a source of energy (the sun).

Wilde's eye-trapping art, as well as his public persona, was founded on a critique of the Victorian urge to construct and adjudicate between polar opposites, between English and Irish culture, between male and female, master and servant, good and evil. He does not seem interested, however, in the contrast between Roman and Jewish cultures that interested Flaubert. "He [Wilde] inveighed against the specialization deemed essential in men fit to run an empire, and showed that no matter how manfully they tried to project qualities of softness, poetry and femininity on to their subject peoples, these repressed instincts would return to take a merry revenge."[25]

One illustration of Wilde's desire to transform a cultural polarity can be found in his descriptions of Salomé. A number of scholars have noted the linguistic parallels between the figure of Salomé and the female lover in the English version of Song of Songs. Note, however, that Wilde expresses his fondness for character inversion by reassigning the male lover's description of the female lover in the Song to Salomé's musings about the beauty of Iohanaan. Nowhere does Wilde's character Iohanaan speak the language of love to Salomé that the male lover speaks to the female lover in the Song. One can see immediately that the mutual honeyed discourse of fragrance with which the language of the Song is laden is one-sided in *Salomé*. Frequently the words used in the biblical Song (in the voice of the male lover) to describe the woman are used in *Salomé* to describe the prophet. Salomé dreams of kissing the prophet rather than being kissed by a male lover. Thus, she sees herself as both the lover and the beloved; the irony comes in the total absence of mutuality. See Table 1.

---

[25] Kiberd (1994). In this critical essay Kiberd suggests that Wilde is the perfect illustration to the question "Was there ever an Irish man of genius who did not get himself turned into an Englishman as fast as he could?"

Table 1. *Echoes of Song of Songs in* Salomé

Song 1:2 ¶ Let him kiss me with the kisses of his mouth! For your love is better than wine.	*Salomé*: Suffer me to kiss thy mouth. *Salomé*: Ah, thou wouldst not suffer me to kiss thy mouth, Johanaan. I will kiss it now. (34)
Song 2:1-2 ¶ I am a rose of Sharon, a lily of the valleys. As a lily among brambles, so is my love among maidens.	*Young Syrian*: She is like a narcissus trembling into the wind . . . she is like a silver flower.[i]
	Salomé: I am amorous of thy body, Johanaan. Thy body is white like the lilies of the field that the mower hath never mowed . . . The roses in the garden of the Queen of Arabia [are not] so white as thy body.
Song 4:1 ¶ How beautiful you are, my love, how very beautiful! Your eyes are doves behind your veil. Your hair is like a flock of goats, moving down the slopes of Gilead.	*Young Syrian*: She is like a dove that has strayed. (5) Her little white hands are fluttering like doves that fly to the dovecote. (4)
Song 4:3 Your lips are like a crimson thread, and your mouth is lovely. Your cheeks are like halves of a pomegranate behind your veil.	*Salomé*: Thy mouth is like a pomegranate cut in twain with a knife of ivory. (12) I will look at thee through the muslin veils. (8)
Song 4:4 Your neck is like the tower of David, built in courses; on it hang a thousand bucklers, all of them shields of warriors.	*Salomé*: Thy mouth is like a thread of scarlet on a tower of ivory. (12)
Song 4:16 ¶ Awake, O north wind, and come, O south wind![ii] Blow upon my garden that its fragrance may be wafted abroad. Let my beloved come to his garden, and eat its choicest fruits.	*Salomé*: I am athirst for thy beauty; I am hungry for thy body; and neither wine nor apples can appease my desire. (35) *Salomé*: Thy body was a garden of doves and lilies of silver.
Song 5:1 ¶ I come to my garden, my sister, my bride; I gather my myrrh with my spice, I eat my honeycomb with my honey, I drink my wine with my milk. Eat, friends, drink, and be drunk with love.	*Salomé*: Neither the floods nor the great waters can quench my passion . . . I was a virgin and thou didst take my virginity from me. I was chaste and thou didst fill my veins with fire. Wherefore didst thou not look at me? If thou had looked at me, thou hadst

Table 1. (cont.)

Song 5:7 Making their rounds in the city the sentinels found me; they beat me, they wounded me, they took away my mantle, those sentinels of the walls.	loved me. Well I know that thou wouldst have loved me, and the mystery of love is greater than the mystery of death.
Song 5:8 I adjure you, O daughters of Jerusalem, if you find my beloved, tell him this: I am faint with love.	
Song 8:6 ¶ Set me as a seal upon your heart, as a seal upon your arm; for love is strong as death, passion fierce as the grave. Its flashes are flashes of fire, a raging flame.	
Song 8:7 Many waters cannot quench love, neither can floods drown it. If one offered for love all the wealth of his house, it would be utterly scorned.	

[i] While the three varieties of lily mentioned in the Song of Songs are white, and thus contrast sharply with the skin of the female lover, I think the "silver" in *Salomé* would have the same visual effect, especially by moon-light, so central to Wilde's staging.

[ii] "The shepherdess begs the breezes to blow strongly upon the trees in the garden, severing their delicate springs and starting the trickle of their "wholesome sap" (Feliks 1983: 82). The intensity of the natural imagery here, as the author, a "biblical botanist" interprets it, underscores the reader's crucial role in extending interpretation.

Although Wilde's language closely parallels the descriptions in the Song, the character references to Salomé are much closer to the character of the Whore of Babylon in the book of Revelation, "he has judged the great whore who corrupted the earth with her fornication," (Rev. 17:5).[26] "The woman was clothed in purple and scarlet and adorned with gold and jewels and pearls" (17:4) recalls

---

[26] Other verses in the Book of Revelation also point to the scorn in which a traditional narrator/reader constructs Salomé in Wilde's play: "But I have this against you: you tolerate that woman Jezebel, who calls herself a prophet and is teaching and beguiling my servants to practice fornication and to eat food sacrificed to idols" (Rev. 2:20). Salomé beguiles the Syrian to release the prophet to her.

"And the ten horns that you saw, they and the beast will hate the whore; they will make her desolate and naked; they will devour her flesh and burn her up with fire." (Rev. 17:16) As his last act in the play Herod orders. Salomé killed. This verse in Revelation parallels the *cul de lampe* illustration of Beardsley, see page 247.

the pearls and jewels offered to Salomé by Herod as well as the pearls that connect her with the moon. "And I saw that the woman was drunk with the blood of the saints and the blood of the witnesses to Jesus" (17:6) could be a reference to Salomé with the head of the Baptist. Finally, "for his judgments are true and just; and he has avenged on her the blood of his servants" (19:2) could serve as a coda for *Salomé*.

Wilde seemed irritated by the "docility" that drives the biblical character of Salomé, who demands the head in obedience to her mother. The inadequacy of the biblical characterization, its lack of imagination and passion, according to Wilde, makes it necessary "for the centuries to heap up dreams and visions at her feet so as to convert her into the cardinal flower of the perverse garden" (Ellmann 1988: 344). Struggling against the positivism of his time, Wilde understood well his own passion for creating an excessive heroine, one who is by turns passionate, agitated, disturbed, "too much." Moving from the biblical text and the traditions of the Salomé figure that constitute the doxa, Wilde connected his fascination with the figure to that of Huysmans. "I flee from what is moral as from what is impoverished . . . I have the same sickness as Des Esseintes," he wrote to his friend Gomez Carrillo.[27]

Wilde never varied in his understanding of the princess demanding Iohanaan's death, after the prophet refuses to respond to her. While the biblical account does not indicate that the young girl has ever had contact with the Baptist, that contact is essential to Wilde's understanding of the story. She must be initiator of the crime in order to render her power central to the story. Because Salomé demands the prophet's death not out of any connection or loyalty to her mother, but rather out of unrequited love, she becomes a goddess-like symbol of violent love for Wilde (Ellmann 1988: 334). He describes her as the moon herself, "like a mad woman who is seeking everywhere for her lovers." Jane Marcus, while not connecting Salomé directly with the moon, thinks that playing the character would be a tempting vehicle for a woman, since Wilde's play is "a parable of the woman artist's struggle to

---

[27] Quoted in Ellmann (1988: 344).

break free of being the stereotype of sex object" (Marcus 1974: 96).[28] If one connects the figure of Salomé with Wilde himself, then the desire to break free of the stereotype of sex object provides a glimmer of his own difficulties with Bosey and other young men, who became traps for him, both stimulating and defining his artistic subjects.

From the opening lines of the play the dialogue of the Young Syrian and the Page direct the spectator's gaze toward a blending of the moon and the gelid princess – through a verbal interplay intentionally intertwining each for the other.

SYRIAN How beautiful is the Princess Salomé tonight.
PAGE Look at the moon. The moon has a strange air. One would say it was a woman rising from the grave. She appears like a dead woman. She seems to search for the dead.
SYRIAN She has a very strange air. She resembles a little princess who wears a yellow veil, and with silver feet. She appears as a princess with feet like little white doves. One would say that she dances. (29)

The pronoun "she" is used like a mirror that reflects simultaneously the moon and Salomé. The Syrian is gazing at Salomé, the Page at the Moon. Each is wrapped in his own visions; neither responds directly to the words of the other. Rather their different visions blend for the spectator through the verbal play of symbolic twinning of the moon and the princess. The Syrian continues in the following scene, "She seems like the reflection of a white rose in a silver'd glass." The Page warns, "Do not look at her. You look at her too much" (33). While one assumes that the Page is referring to the princess, the ambiguity of the pronoun tempts the spectator to imagine that the young men recognize a mystic connection between Salomé and the moon.

Wilde was certainly not the first to connect woman with lunar mythology. Among the *fin de siècle* writers, Jung thought of the moon as a representative of the unconscious and wrote of men who were trapped in the "dark imperium of the mother in a sublunar

---

[28] I agree with Gagnier that Marcus overreads the New Woman, who was not a *sexual* creature, as was Salomé. Gagnier's reading places *Salomé* within a more politicized social context than the majority of literary and psychoanalytic readings that have characterized Wildean scholarship over the years. For a review of the literature see Gagnier (1986), esp. chap. 4 and 228–31.

world." This verbal description could be the inspiration for the Beardsley illustration in which the overbearing heavily drawn female [called Herodias] is drawn much larger than the men in the picture. The inflated size of the woman with swollen almost bursting breasts is shown from the perspective of a spectator at level of the ground. This odd perspective, looking up at the woman, suggests a child lying in bed awaiting the mother or a man imagining the erotic visit of the moon goddess. In the frontispiece of the series, Beardsley playfully acknowledged Wilde's visions of the moon woven throughout Salomé by using Wilde's caricatured features as the face of the moon entitled "The Woman in the Moon." Wilde's play, however, is illuminated by images of the moon, not in a systematic manner, but rather in a pattern like splattered moonlight.

Salomé's connection with the moon cannot save her from being destroyed by her own excess. Similar to the character of Des Esseintes, Salomé wills her passion "beyond human limits, beyond the grave even" (Ellmann 1988: 345). This squeezing of character from the frozen perfection of the moon to the heat of maddened monstrosity illustrates the way convention is challenged and reversed by *fin de siècle* writers. Wilde's Salomé, in observing the moon, is describing herself and suggesting what makes her so attractive to the men who are gazing at her, as she is gazing at the moon.

How good it is to see the moon! She looks like a little piece of money. One might call her a tiny silver flower. She is cold and chaste is the moon. . . I am sure she is a virgin. She has never been soiled. She has never given herself to men, like the other goddesses. (1894: 39)

Salomé's curiosity with the prophet stashed in the cistern below the palace leads her to tease Narraboth, the Young Syrian, into letting the prophet come upstairs, into the light, so that the Princess may gaze at him. Immediately the Page to Herodias remarks, "Oh how strange the moon looks. She seems the hand of the dead which tries to cover herself with a shroud. Indeed she has a strange look. She might be a little princess with amber eyes" (43–44). Clearly Wilde has the audience as an ally in laughing at the seemingly innocent remarks of the players, while each of their speeches is

1 Beardsley's enormous overbearing Herodias/Salomé figure is transfixed by the dripping bodiless head. Note the eyes of the Baptist, closed perhaps in ecstasy, rather than death?

2 In this Beardsley interpretation, the Herodias/Salomé figure is almost the
opposite of the one in Illustration 1. She is not rooted to the ground. She
seems to be performing an ethereal dance with the object of her affection,
the head of the Baptist. Note the lightness of the drawing in comparison with
the heavy, cloaked female figure in Illustration 1.

redolent with the *doubles entendres* that Wilde uses to invert the meanings of language at the very time the actors are speaking the words.

Iohanaan is the only character whose speech is plain and cannot be misread. In decrying Herodias, his intention cannot be misunderstood or inverted:

Where is she who having seen men painted on the walls, the figures of the Chaldeans painted in colours, has let herself be carried away by the lust of the eye and has sent ambassadors into Chaldea. (1894: 44)

Unafraid of the consequence of his plain speech, Iohanaan in the hearing of Salomé, continues to malign her mother, using motifs of the strange or evil woman found in the book of Proverbs.

Tell her to rise from her bed of shamelessness, from her bed of incest that she may hear the words of one who prepares the way of the Lord; so that she may repent of her sins. Although she will never repent, but will remain among her abominations, tell her to come, for the Lord has his scourge in his hand. (1894: 47)

If Iohanaan will not sell out God, at least Herod will sell out Iohanaan. Not that Wilde portrays Herod as wanting to order the death of the prophet. Quite the contrary. In confessing to his weakness for Salomé, to having looked too much, Herod tries to dissuade her from her request.

Perhaps I have loved you too well. So do not ask this of me. It is horrible it is appalling to ask this. In truth I do not believe that you are serious. A bodiless head is an ugly thing, surely? It is not a thing that a virgin ought to look at. What pleasure could it give you? None. No, no you do not wish for that . . .
. . . You are saying that only to make me unhappy, because I have looked at you too much all through the evening. Well, yes, I have looked at you through out the evening. Your beauty has troubled me. Your beauty has troubled me terribly and I have looked at you too much. (1894: 95)

The tetrarch tries first to tempt the princess with jewels to enhance her moon self. "I have a collar of pearls in four rows. They seem like moons caught in a silver beam. They seem like fifty moons caught in a haze of gold" (1894: 99). His offer is met with silence. Then he tries to distract her with jewels that acknowledge and reflect her animal heat. "I have topazes which are as yellow as the eyes of tigers, and red topazes which are red like the eyes of pigeons and green topazes like the eyes of cats." And lest the metaphoric associations with her dual nature of heat and cold be lost upon any listener,

> I have opals which are always burning with a flame which is very cold, and opals which sadden the spirit and have fear of darkness. I have onyxes which are like the pupils of dead women. I have signets which changes with the moon and become pale when they see the sun. (99–100)

When none of these possibilities engages the greed of the princess, the Tetrarch offers her "the veil of the sanctuary," the ultimate sellout that he as a Jew can make, to offer her a veil far more precious than any she might now possess – the veil that has protected the Holy of Holies, the most sacred arena of his religion. This offer to desecrate the Temple probably does not contain so much an anti-Semitic flavor, as it illustrates Wilde's idea that all art must contain the essential criticism of its prevailing codes, in this case religious or pious ones. Another reading might suggest that this veil of veils is a reference to the Dance of the Seven Veils. Herod's veil which is unaccountably more meaningful than Salomé's seductive dancing veils actually instead of screening or covering up the individual possesses the power and inner eye of God, and therefore would pierce the mystery of the veiled princess.

But Salomé's triumph as she embraces the head is short lived. As Herod has noted, the moon has turned red.[29] Salomé caresses the horrific head as though it were one of the jewels offered to her by Herod. She understands that he has deflowered her by refusing to look at her. But she seems indifferent to the reality of his eyes now unable to gaze at her. "The mystery of love is greater than the mystery of death," she croons to the head in a long soliloquy. Her last act is one of ecstasy: she kisses his lifeless mouth, confusing the bitter taste of death with the taste of love (see Illustration 2).

Wilde demands of his henchman Herod that the coquette be immediately killed. The male ruler is outraged that he has been tricked into destroying truth because of a momentary infatuation

---

[29] Note the similarity in Acts 2:20. "The sun shall be turned to darkness and the moon to blood, before the coming of the Lord's great and glorious day."

with an impure half-truth, female sexual desire, tricked but not surprised. Herod has been tricked by the Jezebel, the great whore, of Revelation. The tragedy for Wilde is that one is incapable of saving or preserving truth: Wilde kills the silvery moon goddess, as each man kills the thing he loves: as Herod has killed Salomé, as Wilde's own intense infatuation with Bosey separated them, first by Wilde's years in Reading Gaol, and then by the estrangement that came from Bosey's coldness and Wilde's exhaustion. Viewed from the perspective of Wilde's life, the figure of the doomed Salomé kissing the lifeless lips of Iohanaan illustrates the apothegm from Dorian Gray, "all excess, as well as all renunciation, brings its own punishment."

Beardsley's black and white illustrations for the 1894 English edition of Wilde's play telegraph fixation and alarm: both male fear and fascination with the sexually dominant woman who reduces the male to a dripping impotent head.[30] At the time of their publication, these drawings achieved an even greater notoriety than the play itself and helped to popularize the image of Salomé as a perverse young temptress who lusted for the saintly Iokanaan. Wilde appreciated their power, inscribing a copy of the original printing to Beardsley as follows: "For Aubrey, the only artist who besides myself, knows what the dance of the seven veils is, and can see that invisible dance. Oscar" (Hart-Davis 1962: 334).

Beardsley, perfectly in tune with Wilde, Huysmans, and Mallarmé, reifies a minor biblical girl into the divine Salomé, a figure containing the ultimate corruption and ecstasy. His drawings for *Salomé* reflect a desire similar to Wilde's to challenge and transform the conventional symbols and styles of the period. One need only compare the highly detailed and repetitive decorative art of William Morris with the asymmetrical, stark black and white illustrations of Beardsley to see that the artist is playing not only

---

[30] Beardsley worked rapidly, executing all the drawings between May and November of 1893. As he began this work, he wrote excitedly to a friend, "Behold, me, then, the coming man, the rage of artistic London, the admired of all schools, the besought of publishers, the subject of articles . . . I have fortune at my feet . . . and I really have more work on my hands than I can possibly get through and have to refuse all sorts of nice things" (cited in Slessor 1989: 42). Four years later, at the age of 28, he was dead from tuberculosis. For further analysis of the Beardsley paintings, see Dijkstra (1986); Langenfeld (1989); Zatlin (1990).

CURTAIN.

3 Found at the end of Wilde's Salomé, this drawing echoes a pièta, with the
sacrificed figure a female. The figure on the left is probably a caricature of
Wilde himself, leading the viewer to share in Beardsley's sardonic comment
on the play's ending. The pièta imagery is clearly tongue in cheek since the
sarcophagus is a powder box, adorned with the fluff of a powder puff.

with the images of the biblical bad girl but also with the popular Art
Nouveau style of his time. Beardsley's surprising use of flat planes
of pure black and white, linked by lines which vary in strength,
suggests something of the frozen, transfixed quality characteristic
of a bas-relief, such as the paintings on classical Greek vase
paintings. In the final illustration (*cul de lampe*) of his series (see
above), Beardsley draws Salomé's lifeless nude figure as a pièta,
borne away by the conventional horned devil. Observing the scene
with a somewhat benevolent smile is a caricatured Oscar Wilde.

Finally the tempting erotic figure of Salomé has been unveiled. To the male gaze she is naked, unresponding, safe. The devil who holds her legs (together or apart?) can be seen as the one who succeeds in deflowering the virginal princess, with the moon-faced Wilde presiding over the act. Beardsley with a few strokes of his pen connects Wilde and his muse Salomé forever in a seamless bond of sex and death.

SALOMÉ GONE HOLLYWOOD

As my gaze shifts from literary to cinematic appropriations of the character of Salomé, a word needs to be said about representation itself. Every representation exacts some cost, in the loss of immediacy, in the gap between intention and realization, between original and copy. Too often one must agree with Browning's painter that

> Paint
> must never hope to reproduce the faint
> Half-flush that dies along her throat

In film, as in painting when gazing at "her" face, the spectator shares with Browning the knowledge that the picture represents "my last Duchess painted on the wall," but it is removed from the woman herself, "*Looking as if she were alive.*" Film has presented us with a similar representational gap to fill, that between life and death. As postmodern scholars have argued widely in works of film and cultural theories, there are only copies now. What is an original, if not a copy of something earlier?

It is not within my purview to provide a detailed analysis of the cinematic Salomés. However, I think a brief survey of the way filmmakers have appropriated the character of Salomé will illustrate how characterization is altered and augmented through its cinematic presentation. Further, the tension between original and copy is central to this study because it extends the scope of biblical narrative, which usually focuses solely upon texts produced in the ancient Mediterranean world. As I have argued throughout this study, one's mental representations of characters, whether they be from films, novels, paintings, or children's responses to the doxa, reflect backward onto the biblical text and serve to fill the reader's gaps. Thus, acknowledging and analyzing these later literary and visual representations help to trace the process of characterization as it functions in the interpreter's mind. Such an analysis prevents the reader from harmonizing or universalizing characterization – Salomé as loyal daughter and dishonorable Jew, Salomé as virgin or virago – and creates a healthy web of antagonisms among all these cultural representations.

"Representation, even purely aesthetic representation of fictional persons and events," writes Mitchell, "can never be completely divorced from political and ideological questions." Representations of Salomé as subject, as in Moreau's painting, or as object, as portrait of the artist's gaze as in Regnault's gypsy portrait of Salomé, tempted me to see how viewing a collection of visual Salomés would affect my reading of the biblical narrative itself. Analyzing the ways in which artists have used the biblical characters, and how they have reinvented them in the context of their own cultural, political, and historical perspectives, provides the biblical scholar with another series of interpretations against which to examine characterizations offered in the usually terse biblical narratives.

Film theory, like the narrative theory from which it draws its primary strength, presents the opportunity to examine the fluid relations between narrative versions of Salomé and iconographic interpretations.[31] The analysis of the process of reading acknowledges that a visual image (or images) is in itself a reading, or retelling, not merely an illustration of a reading, but a new text in itself. Like verbal analysis, cinematic analysis assumes that both readers and viewers bring to texts and images their own cultural

---

[31] Feminist film theory is particularly helpful to this study because a major aspect of its developing concern focuses on the spectator and the effect of the film's subject (usually male) and object (usually female) on the spectator, who was first assumed to be male. See esp. Laura Mulvey, "Visual Pleasures and Narrative Cinema," and Mulvey's response to her own assumption that the spectator is male, "Afterthoughts on 'Visual Pleasures and Narrative Cinema'" inspired by *Duel in the Sun*, *Framework*, no. 15, 16, 17 (1981) 12–15; E. Anne Kaplan, "Is the Gaze Male?" Mary Ann Doane, "Film and the Masquerade: Theorizing the Female Spectator," *Screen* vol. 23, nos. 3 and 4 (1982) 74–88; also Teresa de Lauretis, *Alice Doesn't*, esp. chap. 1, "Desire in Narrative." Special issues of *Screen*, *Wide Angle*, and *Film Reader* also deal at length with this subject.

assumptions. The medium of film underscores that there is not one chair from which to view the narrative in this virtual space beyond the word-image opposition. Meanings collide and swirl much like the various Salomés in their dancing. When viewed together, the images provide testament to the lack of coherence in this sweep of cultural images of Salomé. Reading through the director's lens gives a Technicolor testament to the absence of a universal story of Salomé. More than stamping out similar interpretations, a montage combining visual, cinematic, and verbal images shows how each cultural production makes of the biblical icon a reflection of its own values, not of the ancient culture in which the story was rooted. Each of the Hollywood Bible films proclaims itself as a recitation of shared cultural history, but also accedes to the strong current of belief in its intended Christian audience. A topic that merits further exploration is the anti-Semitic current that overwrites the portrayals of Jews within these modern adaptations of Hebrew Bible narratives.

My montage of these images, "Calling the Shots" provides just such a visual and verbal experience of images of Salomé as they have been changed by the cultures that have created them. Due to complexities of copyright law, I can not provide the film to readers; I thus refer to the visual montage as a verbal metaphor, which is not my first choice. It is possible, however, for any reader, to set in motion a montage of the literary characters they hold in their minds.

My initial reasons for creating a film seemed quite clear. (1) I wanted to explore the challenge of juxtaposing iconographic and narratologic elements to create a new work. Instead of imitating the linear versions presented by the Jesus spectaculars, I have created a circuitous strategy, so that the spectator feels as though s/he is continuously moving, watching the film from many angles. (2) Technology to create a montage of still pictures, film clips, audio tracks, is readily available, so that the print or oral presentation of interpretive work can no longer claim priority. (3) Probably the most compelling reason was to make a visual text that would illustrate some of Mieke Bal's theories in *Reading "Rembrandt,"* in which she creates links between visual and textual appropriations of biblical icons. Her book showed me that images meant to illustrate well-known biblical stories may function as a replacement for texts but they do so "on the basis, not of total redundancy or replication, but, on the contrary, of overwriting the previous text" (Bal 1991b). While these reasons are easy to articulate verbally, the film, a predominantly visual medium, showed the power of images over theories. The artistic process exerted itself, claiming a discontinuity of images at the same time as a basic narrative thread reasserted itself. The process of interpretation continues; the film offers an alternate interpretive view that takes the reader/viewer further from the doxa while simultaneously returning narrative attention to the pre-text found in the Gospels.

In order to explore the connections between visual and verbal readings, I shall use the device of an imagined film montage that will focus upon the visual culture that has grown up around the biblical figure of Salomé. My imagined film encompasses Victorian images, *fin de siècle* drama, and various films ranging from a 1920s two-reel adaptation of Oscar Wilde's *Salomé* to Rita Hayworth's Technicolor dance in the Hollywood of the Fifties. I also include Salomé's moments in the Jesus biopics of Nicholas Ray (*King of Kings*, 1961), George Stevens (*The Greatest Story Ever Told*, 1965), Franco Zeffirelli (*Jesus of Nazareth*, 1977), and Martin Scorsese (*The Last Temptation of Christ*, 1988). One advantage of envisioning a cinematic metaversion of Salomé is that I can create a twirling circular narrative that is not situated in a single spectatorial view, recounting the story of Salomé in linear motion. Following the metaphor of the dancing Salomé, the film follows many rhythms that have changed the nameless girl who danced at her uncle's birthday banquet in the New Testament into the *femme fatale* whose erotic dance dominated artists' and writers' visions almost two millennia later.

I have attempted to chart Salomé's cultural trip from bit player in a religious drama to female sphinx, whom no man can resist. The first hint of the *fin de siècle* Salomania to come is Henri Regnault's painting exhibited in 1870 that presents a petulant self-indulgent Salomé, flowing hair, dressed in exotic Orientalized attire. One can almost hear her sigh with impatience, imagine her swinging her bare foot, as she anticipates the head to be placed on the ornate silver charger. Or perhaps the head has already been removed and she carries the charger like armor, as the icon of her triumph. In many of the paintings, the artists' fascination with the exotic ancient Hellenic world is apparent.

Painters' fantasies about Salomé are clearly defined in their portrayal of her facial expression: there are crude sensual Salomés, narcissistic pouty Salomés, vacant expressionless Salomés, gilded golden Salomés. Herod, John the Baptist, Salomé, and Herodias are all figured differently by film makers, visual artists, and choreographers.[32] There is one recurring motif, however: the young woman who could awake the sleeping passions of men, "bewitching, subjugating more surely his will with her unholy charm, as of a great flower of concupiscence born of a sacrilegious birth, reared in a hothouse of iniquity."[33] The painters as well as the male subjects in their paintings, are mesmerized by the pale young girl – she is neither pale nor young, but rather, the sprite that dances in each one's unconscious.

In looking at the "sword and sandal" genre of Hollywood films containing the story of Salomé, my central focus is on the treatment of the character as she is played by a major star, Rita Hayworth. In comparison, other "unknown" cinematic Salomés swirl and slither around her. In comparing Dieterle's *Salomé*, both with the Wildean stage version which preceded it by fifty years and the later Hollywood versions in which Salomé was played by an unbilled actress with a fashion model's disengaged sensuality, one gets the picture of American puritan sexuality and the treatment of women in the Indian summer of Hollywood's heyday. In 1953, the time of the cold war and the organization man, Rita Hayworth's dance of the seven veils was filmed as a Technicolor confection that drove Charles Laughton into an overfed pudgy-fingered frenzy. In contrast to the out-of-control Tetrarch, the ideal film audience doesn't overdose on Rita's goodies. Moviegoers by the mid-Fifties were trained in having

[32] In October, 1994, I saw a performance of Salomé, loosely adapted from the Wilde play in which Salomé was played in classic Japanese style by an aged Kabuki actor. There is just a squint of familiarity in the staging of this two-actor play when one looks at the Beardsley pen-and-ink drawings, almost one hundred years earlier, that evoke a Japanese style.

[33] Huysmans 1969: 56.

their cake and eating it too. They were experienced in responding to these dramas of temptation, and "would never swallow the lures and desires, allowing them to override their fundamental morality" (Sklar 1994: 95).

The body stocking constructed for Rita's dance made headlines in the popular press. No actress had revealed so much skin, albeit stockinged, in a feature film. It was reported that Marlene Dietrich ordered an identical garment for her private use. Rita's dance compared with the other cinematic Salomés, whose task it is to seduce Herod, is as salacious as the heroine of a hygiene film made for bored seventh graders. Her perfect-postured virginal portrayal reveals more about the Hollywood star system and male fears and fantasies of the Fifties than it shows a Lolita-sexy Salomé figure. Indeed the entire montage is most effective at showing how many different interpretations there are of this ancient princess who danced to please her step-father and her overbearing mother.

In the glitzy Fifties version, the most telling plot point is that Rita was a good girl, indeed she was trying to *save* the Baptist. The girl next door, even in a body stocking and seven Technicolor veils, is a proper subject of male fantasy. An out-of-control dominating sex goddess was the subject of horror films; hardly the domain of a box office star like Rita, who was not the sort to be cast against audience sympathy. In her most well-known role, *Gilda*, Hayworth had a carefully choreographed dance, in which she was also a sex symbol, not a sex goddess. Slowly unpeeling her long black satin gloves, she teases the male audience into imagining her revealing much more than her supple beckoning arms. Film theorist Mary Ann Doane reads the striptease in *Gilda* as more of a cleansing than a seductive act. The striptease is metaphoric for the narrative peeling away of the evil, the lip-licking luscious availability that is the surface persona of Gilda/Rita. "Evil on the part of the woman is only a discardable garment – her threatening aspects can be detached, peeled away like layers from a core, which is basically 'good'" (1987: 107–08). It is the good girl, of course, that has hold of the spectator's imagination. As Gilda, the ever-popular Rita wasn't really crooked, just a little out of line. Similarly in *Salomé* as the veils drop, the spectator "sees" a girl so devoted to saving the Baptist that she is willing to dance for her stepfather, who is drawn as solidly evil, with no inner goodness to relieve the audience of its distaste for him. Continuing Doane's argument, I would add that the striptease is reversed by the spectator, who is more invested in the goodness of the heroine than in peering at her body. Doane thinks that in spite of the intended protecting of the "goodness" of Hayworth, the striptease works too well in *Gilda*. For Doane, Rita's dance overpowers the metaphoric intention of the narrative. She exudes too much heat to retreat into holiness. I do not agree. In both roles Hayworth is oddly wooden as a coquette, as though she really has no interest in the men she dazzles.[34] It is quite easy for a spectator to domesticate the Hayworth heroine as the girl who had a bad break, fell in with the wrong crowd, was misunderstood. In Salomé the actress seems to be focusing on a choreographer's instructions. One can imagine her counting her steps rather than the admiring glances from the men of the Court.

In Dieterle's *Salomé* the death-dealing demand for the head of the Baptist as the final delicacy to be served at the banquet is put into the mouth of Judith Anderson. No sexual fantasies gone awry there. The casting of Judith Anderson is inspired: she was well known for her portrayals of monstrous maternal figures on both stage and screen: she played the title role in *Medea* (1947 and 1949) and Mrs. Danvers, the housekeeper in Hitchcock's *Rebecca* (1940). The older woman, no longer an object of the male gaze, can scheme and even kill with a calculated impunity. Her evil is political, thoughtful, not the erotic temptation of the Eve figure who makes men forget their responsibilities and obligations. Like the rest of the characterizations in this version, there is no nuance or subtlety here. Anderson's Herodias is a one-note venomous character, dependent upon her daughter's beauty to save her own life. In Stevens' interpretation Rita Gam is a classically beautifully Herodias, costumed like an Italian statue of Nefertiti. It is easy to see why her Herod would risk breaking the Law to possess such a

[34] According to the magazine that chronicles popular culture, *People*, Hayworth developed in a short time from pinup queen to major star and finally to goddess. "By 1941's *Blood and Sand* (with Tyrone Power), studio execs had changed a dark-haired Rita into a strawberry blonde. Hayworth's place as a goddess was secure after her heated performance in 1946 *Gilda* (with Glenn Ford), in which she provocatively peeled her gloves." "A girl is a girl," noted Hayworth, "It's nice to be told you're successful at it." June 1, 1987.

4   Salomé (Alla Nazimova) and Herod at the banquet (*Salomé* 1922 version).

woman. In Stevens' version Salomé has become petulant, languorous, and diffident to her powers to hold in thrall the entire court of
Judea. Her mother is manipulating the scene, but with a feather-
light touch. Gam's Herodias is much more threatening than the
horrific Anderson because Gam is still an object of male desire, a
much riper fruit than her adolescent daughter.

Herod in the silent film is a grinning fool, wearing a rakish crown
of olive leaves as a reminder of his royal but pagan bearing. He is a
buffoon as are the members of his Court. As he and Herodias slug it
out with exaggerated gestures, it is difficult to connect them with
rulers of any civilized country. Charles Laughton gives his Herod a
pudgy studied lip-licking sexuality in the 1953 *Salomé*. In Nicholas
Ray's *King of Kings*, Herod is played by an unknown actor, Frank
Thring, whose obese sybaritic posturing bears a striking resemblance to the caricature of Oscar Wilde that Beardsley has playfully
included in his drawing of Herod. None of these three Herods

5   Herod (Charles Laughton) regrets his offer to Salomé (*Salomé* 1953 version).

seems intellectually capable of performing the duties of a Tetrarch, much less of surviving the political machinations of the Herod family. But the ruler of a wanton Court, a ruler who would destroy Christian values, provides a formidable connection for a Cold War audience who had less than a decade earlier lived through the madness of Hitler.[35]

José Ferrer, the pale, cerebral Herod in *The Greatest Story Ever Told* is the only Hollywood Herod who gives a nuanced performance. Stevens is also the only director whose Herod projects an image of stony authority. The sexual debauchery that underlines the corruption of the Herodian court is gone from this film, in which Ferrer plays Herod as a troubled politician frightened by the spiritual unrest in his kingdom. The relaxation of sexual mores in the

[35] For an analysis of Fifties Bible films as cultural responses to the Cold War, see Forshey (1992): esp. 27–55. Also Gow (1971); Driver, November 28, 1956.

1960s in the USA may be responsible for the less stereotyped sexual interplay. Like the short-lived Camelot of the Kennedys, Ferrer's Herod contains aspects of both the intellectual governor and erotic dreamer. The dance in this version is performed in half-light for Herod alone. It is an idyllic fantasy in which the female remains veiled and the camera rests on Ferrer's face, eyes closed, expressionless. Stevens tries to soften the pious aspect of his film by emphasizing that he is making a film about ideas, not about religion. This was the time of change in the Roman Catholic Church under the rule of Pope John XXIII and the Second Vatican Council. Protestants were experiencing a burgeoning ecumenical movement; technocratic control increased as the race into space program and military-industrial complex were reshaping American ideas of the sacred and the ethical. At the same time sex and roll and roll, peace, and love were being affirmed in the youth counterculture. As Forshey points out, Stevens wanted to be relevant to his time, but in doing so he ended up making the wrong film at the wrong time (Forshey 1992: 102–04). His audience was the mainstream churches at the very moment at which the social order was being rent by wide divisions of ethical opinions. Two weeks before the film opened, cultural images bombarding the news were those of African-Americans being beaten with cattle prods and sprayed with tear gas as they tried to cross the Edmund Petrus bridge in Selma, Alabama. A month after the film opened, the drive for the Voting Rights Act became a reality and the first teach-in against the war in Vietnam was held at the University of Michigan.[36]

The figure of John the Baptist plays a larger role in my montage than in most of the films themselves. In the Wildean version the Baptist like Salomé herself is transformed from a biblical figure to an icon of a very secular sort. Wilde conceives of the Baptist as a symbol of pure beauty, pure truth. Like Rita Hayworth, Alla Nazimova recognizes that John is the embodiment of Truth. Unlike Rita, the girlish actress, a dead ringer for Mary Pickford, does not ally herself with an armored man to save John. Pouting and pursing her lips, feverishly trying to coerce an unresponsive ethereal prophet into selling out his faith for her, Nazimova plays

---

[36] For a classic analysis of the profound American religious shifts in the Sixties, see Cox (1965).

the role as a little girl, not understanding the consequence of her lascivious poses or indeed of her death-dealing demand. Showalter provides a succinct but vivid sketch of this Russian-born actress who at the age of forty-four played a girl less than half her age.

She became a brilliant success in New York in productions of Ibsen and Chekhov. Her movie career was even more dazzling; her house on Sunset Boulevard had a swimming pool in the shape of the Black Sea and her wild parties were the talk of Hollywood . . . Salomé first appears as a Mack Sennett bathing beauty in a sequined gym suit and a wig of big bubble-shaped pearls on little antennae, copied from one of the Beardsley drawings of Salomé's curls. (Showalter 1990: 162–3)

Of particular note in the 1922 production is the dance of the seven veils, in which Nazimova seems to get caught or trapped inside the fog-colored diaphanous veils with her pingpong-curls bobbing suggestively. For the Decadents of the *fin de siècle*, and the early filmmakers of the 1920s, Salomé is more a figure of ridicule than a fully conceived sex goddess. It is difficult to imagine her as an erotic figure, seducing men other than the equally ridiculously drawn Herod. Perhaps, from the days of the Decadent versions of Salomé, the erotic element came out of her defiance of the Baptist's sacred authority and Herod's secular rule. "Both in dramatizing a rebellious woman and in portraying male–male desire," argues Dellamora, "*Salomé* puts normal masculine representation under pressure (see Illustration 4)."

Salomé can be possessed by men only in death. They are no longer threatened or mesmerized by her limp unresponding figure. Bristow suggests that Wildean eroticism is fated because "there is no escape from the doom-laden consequences of desire."[37] As she claimed the head of John, seemingly unaware that the head once was joined to a living body, so the courtiers of Herod claim her body. But through Wilde's words and Beardsley's sharp pen-and-ink drawings, her position has moved from peripheral to central, from nameless girl to obsession. The costumes and sets for the 1922 film production of Salomé were adapted from Beardsley's drawings and set designs.

A more market-driven Hollywood, not willing to let a box-office

---

[37] Bristow (1995: 49). Note particularly for this study, "Wilde's Fatal Effeminacy," 16–55.

baby be martyred, or indeed be the cause of male viewer discomfort, banishes all thought of Rita/Salomé as genuinely wicked. The scriptwriter handily converts her to Christianity after an intimate meeting with the Baptist in the dungeon. When her dance calculated to buy time for a rescue of the Baptist from the dungeon has the opposite effect, the scriptwriter constructs an even holier happy ending as Rita is reunited with Stewart Granger, a handsome Roman centurion, also a secret convert to this new religion. In the film's final scene they are seen with a cast of thousands crowded onto a Jerusalem hillside, like college students at a rock concert, listening to the Sermon on the Mount broadcast from a divine echo chamber. Through a stiff scream of horror, Salomé has been exonerated from the crime. Eagerly embracing the teachings of the new prophet, listening to the words of Jesus himself, perhaps the martyred John reborn, Rita/Salomé remains a good virginal maid, looking forward to a happily-ever-after life, now and in the world to come.

The final visual image that is central to the Salomé story is the head itself. The head that renders Salomé a demonic castrating figure. The images of the head shown separate from an image of Salomé I find most interesting. An anonymous polychrome-painted carved wooden head appears to be a Christ-like ascetic head resting upon a platter that functions as the Baptist's mark of martyrdom, his halo. On closer comparison a surprising number of these heads show John's lips slightly parted and a sly smile upon his lips. He appears to be a man who has just been sexually satisfied. Even without the seductive dancer or the executioner, the head is easily recognized as the head of John the Baptist. If the severing of the head is not an image meant to brand Salomé and her kind as castrating women, why not demand an ear, his prophetic tongue, perhaps a thumb or hand? Because those demands are merely bizarre. Requesting the head is a double-edged blow to the masculinity and power of the male figure.

WHY SALOMÉ?

The figure of Salomé, then, can be regarded as a place-holder for all the biblical literary figures caught in the tropes of wine, women,

6   Rita Hayworth screaming when she realizes she has been tricked into being the Salomé of the doxa story instead of the Christianized good girl with box-office appeal.

and death. Male narratives, whether visual or verbal, about beautiful women seducing men with food or wine and killing them instead of soothing them possess basic similarities, regardless of later interpretive salves or salvos. As I have argued in chapter 6, the female figures whose beauty draws the male to them represent a generalized male fear of courtesan as killer. In the confrontations of Jael and Sisera, Judith and Holofernes, Salomé and Herod, the man is not the husband or suitor of the woman, but rather a man powerless to resist the sexuality that the woman exudes. Samson is the suitor of Delilah, but it is a wrong match, and ends with the same defeat of the male figure. Esther is the only wife who uses the combined effect of her beauty and a banquet successfully to negotiate for the death of her enemy, but her husband is not the object of her plan. Haman, like Sisera and Holofernes, is a national enemy, whose death is desired by the ideal reader.

7   The cinematic head, replete with all the horror Rita's scream requires,
served up to an eager audience.

Why were some of these female heroes transformed into warrior
women, fetishized with biblical books named for them, when
Delilah and Salomé have been openly demonized? They are by no
stretch of the imagination anybody's nurturing mother, patriarchy
warns us, but examples of the witch who rules the dark continent.
Gustav Klimt's painting *Judith II* was also entitled *Salomé*. It clearly
identifies the heroine's rapturous seizing of the head with the
sexual climax. While some critics argue that the anti-Semitic
feeling in *fin de siècle* Vienna could easily have interpreted Judith as
such a *femme fatale*, the traditional story is that the painting was at
first mislabeled. While there are artistic evidences of Judith and
Esther as seductive muse, what made Salomé the one to be dressed
in diaphanous splendor, sewn into her interpretive fabric a
permanent warning label – a witch who might eat you up? The film
montage suggests various answers to the question about
Salomania.

I have suggested that the characterization of Salomé as *femme fatale* is more of a symptom of male fears of women and feminism than a creation of an erotic muse. There is probably some of each aspect in the erupting versions of Salomania from the nineteenth century until the present time. While the Decadent writers may have wanted to convert Salomé into the cardinal flower of the perverse garden, the reader who has mentally stored away the creation of several Salomés can choreograph a dance that is neither biblical nor Wilde, neither sacrosanct nor sacrilegious, but rather one of the reader's own creation. Thus, a reader dances both forward and backward in time, gazing at the *femme fatale*, and then accepting the *korasion*, and in a circular way creating an ever-changing character in the mind. The process of characterization is continuous, not linear. Thus, Salomé is not punished or killed permanently, but rather she spins and swirls as the mind of the reader vacillates. Sometimes she need not dance at all.

Bibliography

Ackerman, S. (1992). *Under Every Green Tree: Popular Religion in Sixth-Century Judah*. Cambridge, MA: Harvard University Press.

Albright, W. F. (1918). Historical and Mythical Elements in the Story of Joseph. *JBL* 37, 111–43.

(1968). *YHWH and the Gods of Canaan*. Garden City, NY: Doubleday.

Alexandrian, S. (1969). *Surrealist Art*. New York: Praeger Publishers.

Alon, G. (1977). *Jews, Judaism, and the Classical World*. Jerusalem: Magnes Press.

Alonso-Schekel, L. (1975). Narrative Structures in the Book of Judith, *The Center for Hermeneutical Studies in Hellenistic and Modern Culture* (Vol. Colloquy 11, pp. 1–20). Berkeley, CA: Center for Hermeneutical Studies in Hellenistic and Modern Culture.

Alter, R. (1981). *The Art of Biblical Narrative*. New York: Basic Books.

(1989). *The Pleasures of Reading in an Ideological Age*. New York: Simon and Schuster.

(1992). *The World of Biblical Literature*. New York: Basic Books.

Alter, R., and F. Kermade (eds.) (1987). *The Literary Guide to the Bible*. Cambridge, MA: Belknap Press of Harvard University Press.

Amaru, B. H. (1988). Portraits of Biblical Women in Josephus' Antiquities. *JJS* 39, 143–70.

Anderson, J. C. (1992). Feminist Criticism: The Dancing Daughter. In J. C. Anderson and S. D. Moore (eds.), *Mark and Method: New Approaches in Biblical Studies*. Minneapolis, MN: Fortress Press.

Appignanesi, Lisa. (1993). *Freud's women*. New York: Basic Books.

Aptowitzer, V. (1924). Asenath, The Wife of Joseph: An Haggadic Literary Historical Study. *HUCA*, I.

Ardener, S. (1978). *Defining Females: The Nature of Women in Society*. London: Oxford University Press.

(1981). *Women and Space: Ground Rules and Social Maps*. London: Oxford University Press.

Arnheim, R. (1974, c1954). *Art and Visual Perception: A Psychology of the Creative*

Eye. (New version, expanded and revised). Berkeley: University of California Press.

(1982). *The Power of the Center: A Study of Composition in the Visual Arts.* Berkeley: University of California Press.

Arthur, M. B. (1984). Early Greece: Origins of the Western Attitude Toward Women. In J. P. Sullivan (ed.), *Women in the Ancient World: The Arethusa Papers.* Albany: SUNY Press.

Attridge, H. W. Josephus and his Works. *CRINT* II(2), 185–232.

Auerbach, E. (1953). *Mimesis: The Representation of Reality in Western Literature* (Willard Trask, trans.). Garden City, N.Y: Doubleday.

Babington, B., & Evans, P. W. (1993). *Biblical Epics: Sacred Narrative in the Hollywood Cinema.* Manchester: Manchester University Press.

Bach, A. (1991). Mieke Bal and the Method Which is Not One, *Union Seminary Quarterly Review* 44 3/4: 333–41.

(1993a). Breaking Free of the Biblical Frame-Up: Uncovering the Woman in Genesis 39. In *The Feminist Companion to Genesis.* Ed. A. Brenner. Sheffield: Sheffield Academic Press.

(1993b). Signs of the Flesh: Characterization in Biblical Narratives, *Semeia* 63.

(1993c) Good to the Last Drop: Viewing the Sotah (Num. 5:11–31) as the Glass Half Empty and Wondering How to View it Half Full, *The New Literary Criticism and the Hebrew Bible*, eds. J. Cheryl Exum and David J. A. Clines, Sheffield: JSOT Press.

Bach, A. (ed.). (1990). *The Pleasure of her Text: Feminist Readings of Biblical and Historical Texts.* Philadelphia: Trinity Press International.

Bailey, J. L. (1987). Portrayal of the Matriarchs. In L. H. Feldman & G. Hara (eds.), *Josephus, Judaism, and Christianity* (pp. 154–79). Detroit: Wayne State University Press.

Bakhtin, M. (1965). *Rabelais and his World* (Helene Iswolsky, trans.). Boston: MIT Press.

(1973). *Problems of Dostoevsky's Poetics* (R. W. Rosel, trans.). Ann Arbor, MI: ArdisBooks.

(1981). *The Dialogic Imagination* (Caryl Emerson and Michael Holquist, trans.). Austin: University of Texas Press.

Bal, M. (1981). Notes on Narrative Embedding. *Poetics Today* 2(2), 41–59.

(1985). *Narratology: Introduction to the Theory of Narrative.* Toronto: University of Toronto Press.

(1986). *Femmes imaginaires: l'ancien testament au risque d'une narratologie critique.* Utrecht: HES/Montreal, HMH.

(1987a). *Lethal Love: Feminist Literary Readings of Biblical Love Stories.* Bloomington: Indiana.

(1987b). *Murder and Difference: Gender, Genre, and Scholarship on Siesera's*

Death (Matthew Gumpert, trans.). Bloomington: Indiana. University Press.

(1987c). *Mythe à la lettre*. In S. Rimmon-Kennan (ed.), *Discourse in Psychoanalysis and Literature*. New York: Methuen.

(1988). *Death and Dissymmetry: The Politics of Coherence in the Book of Judges*. Chicago: University of Chicago Press.

(1990). Dealing/With/Women: Daughters in the Book of Judges. In R. M. Schwartz (ed.), *The Book and the Text: The Bible and Literary Theory* (pp. 16–39). Cambridge: Basil Blackwell.

(1991a). *Reading "Rembrandt" Beyond the Word-Image Opposition*. Cambridge: Cambridge University Press.

(1991b). His Master's Eye. In *Modernity and the Hegemony of Vision*. D. M. Levin (ed.). Berkeley: University of California Press.

Balsdon, J. P. V. D. (1974). *Roman Women: Their History and Habits*. London: Bodley Head.

Barret-Ducrocq, F. (1989). *Love in the Time of Victoria: Sexuality, Class and Gender in Nineteenth-Century London*. London: Verso.

Barthes, R. (1975). *Mythologies*. New York: Hill and Wang.

Bartsch, S. (1989). *Decoding the Ancient Novel: The Reader and the Role of Description in Heliodorus and Achilles Tatius*. Princeton: Princeton University Press.

Bataille, G. (1962, c1957). *Erotism: Death and Sensuality* (Mary Dalwood, trans.). San Francisco: City Lights Books.

(1988, c1967). *The Accursed Share* (Trans. by Robert Hurley). (Vol. 1). New York: Zone Books.

(1991, c1976). *The Accursed Share*. (Trans. by Robert Hurley). (Vols. 2 and 3). New York: Zone Books.

Battiffol, P. (1889–90). Le livre de le prière d'Aseneth, *Studia Patristica* (Vol. 1.2). Paris: Leroux.

Batto, B. F. (1974). *Studies on Women at Mari*. Baltimore, MD: Johns Hopkins University Press.

Bauckham, R. (1991). Salomé the Sister of Jesus, Salomé the Disciple of Jesus, and the Secret Gospel of Mark. *Novum Testamentum*, XXXIII(3), 245–75.

Becker, J. (1970). *Untersuchen zur Enstehungsgeschichte der Testamente der zwölf Patriarchen*. Leiden: E. J. Brill.

Beer, G. (1970). *The Romance*. London: Methuen.

Ben-Barak, Z. (1980). Inheritance by Daughters in the Ancient Near East. *JSS*, 22–23.

(1994). The Status and Right of the *gebirah* in A. Brenner (ed.), *A Feminist Companion to Samuel and Kings*. (Sheffield: Sheffield Academic Press, 170–85.

Benjamin, W. (1978). *Reflections: Essays, Aphorisms, Autobiographical Writings* (Jephcott, Edmund, trans.). New York: Schocken Books.

Benstock, S., & Ferriss, S. (eds.). (1994). *On Fashion*. New Brunswick, N J: Rutgers University Press.

Berg, S. B. (1979). *The Book of Esther: Motifs, Themes, and Structure / I*. (Vol. 44). Missoula, MT: Scholars Press.

Berger, J. (1972). *Ways of Seeing*. London, BBC: Harmondsworth, Penguin.

Berlin, A. (1983). *Poetics and the Interpretation of Biblical Narrative*. Sheffield: Almond.

Bernal, M. (1991). *Black Athena: The Afroasiatic Roots of Classical Civilization*. (Vol. II: The Archaeological and Documentary Evidence). New Brunswick: Rutgers University Press.

Berube, M. (1994). *Public Access: Literary Theory and American Cultural Politics*. London: Verso.

Bettelheim, B. (1976). *The Uses of Enchantment, the Meaning and Importance of Fairy Tales*. New York: Alfred A. Knopf.

Beye, C. R. (1987). *Ancient Greek Literature and Society*. (2nd revised edn). Ithaca: Cornell University Press.

Bickerman, E. (1962). *From Ezra to the Last of the Maccabees*. New York: Schocken Books.

(1967). *Four Strange Books of the Bible: Jonah, Daniel, Koheleth, Esther*. New York: Schocken Books.

(1979). *The God of the Maccabees: Studies on the Meaning and Origin of the Maccabean Revolt*. Leiden: E. J. Brill.

(1988). *The Jews in the Greek Age*. Cambridge, MA: Harvard University Press.

Bird, P. (1974). Images of Women in the Old Testament. In R. R. Ruether (ed.), *Religion and Sexism*. New York: Simon and Schuster.

(1989a). The Harlot as Heroine: Narrative Art and Social Presupposition in Three Old Testament Texts. *Semeia* 46, 119–39.

(1989b). Women's Religion in Ancient Israel. In B. S. Lesko (ed.), *Women's Earliest Records: From Ancient Egypt and Western Asia* (pp. 283–98). Atlanta GA: Scholars Press.

Bloom, H. (1990). *The Book of J* (translated from the Hebrew by David Rosenberg). New York: Grove and Weidenfeld.

Boman, T. (1960). *Hebrew Thought Compared with Greek*, Eng. trans. of *Das hebraische Denken im Vergleich mit dem Griechischen*. (Jules L. Moreau, trans.). London: SCM Press.

Bordo, S. (1993). *Unbearable Weight: Feminism, Western Culture, and the Body*. Berkeley: University of California Press.

Bottero, J. (1992). *Mesopotamia: Writing, Reasoning, and the Gods* (Zainab Bahrani and Marc Van De Mieroop, trans.). Chicago: University of Chicago Press.

Bourdieu, P. (1985). *Distinction: A Social Critique of the Judgment of Taste* (Richard Nice, trans.). Cambridge MA: Harvard University Press.

Boyarin, D. (1985). Rhetoric and Interpretation: The Case of the Nimshal. *Prooftexts* 5, 269–76.

(1986). Voices in the Text. *Revue Biblique* 93–94, 581–97.

(1990a). *Intertextuality and the Reading of Midrash*. Bloomington: Indiana University Press.

(1990b). The Song of Songs: Lock or Key? Intertextuality, Allegory, and Midrash. In R. M. Schwartz (ed.), *The Book and The Text: The Bible and Literary Theory* (pp. 214–30). Cambridge: Basil Blackwell.

(1993). *Carnal Israel*. Berkeley: University of California Press.

Braun, M. (1938). *History and Romance in Graeco-Oriental Literature*. Oxford: Basil Blackwell.

Bremmer, J., & Roodenburg, H. (eds.). (1991). *A Cultural History of Gesture*. Ithaca: Cornell University Press.

Brennan, T. (1992). *The Interpretation of the Flesh: Freud and Femininity*. London: Routledge.

Brenner, A. (1985). *The Israelite Woman: Social Role and Literary Type in Biblical Narrative*. Sheffield: JSOT Press.

(1990). Come Back, Come Back, The Shulammite. In Y. Rattay and A. Brenner (eds.), *On Humor and the Comic in the Hebrew Bible*. Sheffield: Almond Press.

(1993). *On Gendering Texts*. Leiden: E. J. Brill.

Brisman, L. (1990). *The Voice of Jacob: On the Composition of Genesis*. Bloomington: Indiana University Press.

Bristow, J. (1995). *Effeminate England: Homoerotic Writing After 1885*. New York: Columbia Univeristy Press.

Bronfen, E. (1992). *Over her Dead Body: Death, Feminity, and the Aesthetic*. New York: Routledge.

Brooks, P. (1982). Freud's Masterplot: Questions of Narrative. In S. Felman (ed.), *Literature and Psychoanalysis: The Question of Reading Otherwise* (Vol. 55/56, pp. 280–300). New Haven: Yale French Studies.

(1984). *Reading for the Plot: Design and Intention in Narrative*. New York: Alfred A. Knopf.

(1993). *Body Work: Objects of Desire in Modern Narrative*. Cambridge MA: Harvard University Press.

Broude, N., & Garrard, M. D. (eds.). (1982). *Feminism and Art History: Questioning the Litany*. New York: Harper and Row.

Brown, P. (1971). *The World of Late Antiquity*. London: Harcourt, Brace, Jovanovich.

(1985). The Notion of Virginity in the Early Church. In B. McGinn, J. Meyerforff, & J. Leclerq (eds.), *Christian Spirituality: Origins to the Twelfth Century* (pp. 427–43). New York: Crossroad.

(1988). *The Body and Society: Men, Women, and Sexual Renunciation in Early Christianity*. New York: Columbia University Press.

Brownlee, W. H. (1979). *The Midrash Pesher of Habakkuk*. (Vol. 24). Missoula MT: Scholars Press.

Bruns, G. L. (1982). *Inventions: Writing, Textuality, and Understanding in Literary History*. New Haven: Yale University Press.

(1987). Midrash and Allegory: The Beginning of Scriptual Interpretation. In F. Kermode & R. Alter (eds.), *The Harvard Guide to the Bible* (pp. 625–46). Cambridge, MA: Harvard University Press.

(1990). The Hermeneutics of Midrash. In R. M. Schwartz (ed.), *The Book and The Text: The Bible and Literary Theory* (pp. 189–213). Cambridge: Basil Blackwell.

Brunsdon, C. (ed.). (1986). *Films for Women*. London: British Film Institute.

Bryson, N., Holly, M. A., & Moxey, K. (eds.). (1994). *Visual Culture: Images and Interpretations*. Hanover: Wesleyan University Press.

Buber, M. (1989). *Midrash Tanhuma* (John T. Townsend, trans.). Hoboken: NJ: Ktav.

Bucknell, B. (1993). On "Seeing" Salomé. *English Literary History (ELH)* 60(2), 503–26.

Budde, K. (1899, 1906). *The Religion of Israel to the Exile*. New York, London: G. P. Putmans Sons.

Burchard, C. (1967). *Untersuchungen zu Joseph und Aseneth: Uberlieferung-Ortsbestimmung*, WUNT 8 (Tubingen: Mohr, 1965).

(1978). *Joseph und Aseneth neugriechisch*. *NTS* 24, 68–84.

(1987). The Importance of Joseph and Aseneth for the Study of the New Testament: A General Survey and a Fresh Look at the Lord's Supper, *NTS* 33, 109–17.

Burke, Kenneth (1970). *The Rhetoric of Religion: Studies in Logology*. Berkeley: University of California Press, 1970.

Burkert, W. (1992). *The Orientalizing Revolution: Near Eastern Influence on Early Greek Culture in the Early Archaic Age* (trans. Walter Burkert and Margaret E. Pinder). Cambridge MA: Harvard University Press.

Butler, J. (1995). Desire. In F. L. and T. McLaughlin (eds.). *Critical Terms for Literary Study* (pp. 369–87). Chicago: University of Chicago Press.

Bynum, C. W. (1984). Women's Stories, Women's Symbols: A Critique of Victor Turner's Theory of Liminality. In R. L. Moore & F. E. Reynolds (eds.), *Anthropology and the Study of Religion* (pp. 105–25). Chicago: Center for the Scientific Study of Religion.

(1991). *Fragmentation and Redemption: Essays on Gender and the Human Body in Medieval Religion*. New York: Zone Books.

Bynum, C. W., Harrell, S., & Richman, P. (eds.). (1986). *Gender and Religion: On the Complexity of Symbols*. Boston: Beacon Press.

Calasso, R. (1993). *The Marriage of Cadmus and Harmony*. New York: Alfred A. Knopf, Inc.

Callaway, M. (1986). *Sing, O Barren One: A Study in Comparative Midrash*. (Vol. 91). Atlanta: Scholar's Press.

Camp, C. (1981). The Wise Woman of 2 Samuel: A Role Model for Women in Early Israel. *Catholic Biblical Quarterly* 43, 14–29.

(1985). *Wisdom and the Feminine in the Book of Proverbs*. (Vol. 11). Sheffield: JSOT/Almond Press.

(1988). Wise and Strange: An Interpretation of the Female Imagery in Proverbs in Light of the Trickster Mythology. *Semeia* 42, 14–36.

(1991). What's So Strange About the Strange Women? In Jobling, Day, & Sheppard (eds.), *The Bible and the Politics of Exegesis*. Cleveland: The Pilgrim Press.

Camporesi, P. (1981). *Le pain sauvage: L'imaginaire de la faim de la Renaissance au XVIIIe siècle* (Monique Aymard, trans.). Paris: Le Chemin vert.

Canto, M. (1986). The Politics of Women's Bodies: Reflections of Plato. In S. Suleiman (ed.), *The Female Body in Western Culture* (pp. 339–53). Cambridge MA: Harvard University Press.

Carson, A. (1990). Putting her in her Place: Women, Dirt, and Desire. In D. M. Halperin, J. J. Winkler, & F. I. Zeitlin (eds.), *Before Sexuality: The Construction of the Erotic Experience in the Ancient Greek World* (pp. 339–53). Princeton: Princeton University Press.

Case, S. (1990). *Performing Feminisms: Feminist Critical Theory and Theatre*. Baltimore: Johns Hopkins University Press.

Cassuto, U. (1973). The Story of Tamar and Judah, *Biblical and Oriental Studies* (vol. 1). Jerusalem: Magnes.

Castelli, E. (1986). Virginity and its Meaning for Women's Sexuality in Early Christianity. *Journal of Feminist Studies in Religion*, 2, 61–88.

Charles, R. H. (1908). *The Greek Versions of the Testaments of the Twelve Patriarchs*. Oxford: Clarendon Press.

Charlesworth, J. (1976). *The Pseudepigrapha and Modern Research*. (Rev. edn 1981 edn). Missoula MT: Scholars Press.

Charlesworth, J. (ed.). (1985). *The Old Testament Pseudepigrapha*. (Vol. 2). Garden City, NY: Doubleday.

Chatman, S. (1978). *Story and Discourse: Narrative Structure in Fiction and Film*. Ithaca, NY: Cornell University Press.

Chestnutt, R. D. (1989). Bread of Life in Joseph and Aseneth and in John 6, in J. E. Preiest (ed.). *Johannine Studies in Honor of Frank Pack*. Malibu, CA: Pepperdine University Press. 1–16.

(1991) Revelatory Experiences Attributed to Biblical Women. In *Women Like This: New Perspectives on Jewish Women in the Greco-Roman World*. Ed. A J. Levine. SBL Early Judaism and its Literature. Atlanta: Scholars Press. 107–27.

Cixous, H. (1993). Bathsheba or the Interior Bible. *New Literary History* 24(4), 820–36.

Classen, Constance. (1993). *Worlds of Sense: Exploring the Senses in History and Across Cultures.* London: New York : Routledge Press.

Classen, C., David Howes, and Anthony Synnott. (1994). *Aroma: The Cultural History of Smell.* London: Routledge Books.

Clement, C. (1983). *The Lives and Legends of Jacques Lacan* (Arthur Goldhammer, trans.). New York: Columbia University Press.

Clifford, J. (1988). *The Predicament of Culture: Twentieth-Century Ethnography, Literature, and Art.* Cambridge, MA: Harvard University Press.

Clifford, J., & Marcus, G. E. (eds.). (1986). *Writing Culture: The Poetics and Politics of Ethnography.* Berkeley: University of California Press.

  (1973). The Joseph Story and Ancient Wisdom: A Reappraisal. *CBQ* 35, 285–97.

Coats, George W. (1976). *From Canaan to Egypt: Structural and Theological Context for the Joseph Story.* (Vol. 4). Washington: Catholic Biblical Association of America.

Cohen, J. (1989). *"Be Fertile and Increase, Fill the Earth and Master It:" The Ancient and Medieval Career of a Biblical Text.* Ithaca: Cornell University Press.

Cohen, S. J. D. (1976). *Josephus in Galilee and Rome.* Leiden: E. J. Brill.
  (1984–85). Solomon and the Daughter of Pharoah: Intermarriage, Conversion, and the Impurity of Women. *JANES* 16–17, 23–37.
  (1993). *The Jewish Family In Antiquity.* Atlanta, GA: Scholars Press.

Corbin, A. (1986). *The Foul and the Fragrant: Odor and the French Social Imagination* (M. Kochan, R. Porter, and C. Prendergast, trans.). Cambridge, MA: Harvard University Press.

Corley, K. (1992). *A Place at the Table: Jesus, Women, and Meals in the Synoptic Gospels.* Claremont: University Microfilms.

Cox, H. (1965). *The Secular City.* New York: Macmillan.

Craik, J. (1994). *The Face of Fashion: Cultural Studies in Fashion.* London: Routledge.

Crapanzano, V. (1992). *Hermes' Dilemma and Hamlet's Desire: On the Epistemology of Interpretation.* Cambridge, MA: Harvard University Press.

Craven, T. (1983). *Artistry and Faith in the Book of Judith.* Atlanta GA: Scholar's Press.

Creed, B. (1993). *The Monstrous-Feminine: Film, Feminism, Psychoanalysis.* London: Routledge.

Culler, J. (1982). *On Deconstruction: Theory and Criticism After Structuralism.* London: Routledge & Kegan Paul.

Cunningham, V. (1994). *In the Reading Gaol: Postmodernity, Texts and History.* Oxford: Basil Blackwell.

Daube, D. (1974). *The New Testament and Rabbinic Judaism*. London: University of London, Athlone Press.

(1974). *Daube noster: Essays in Legal History for David Daube*; edited by Alan Watson. Edinburgh, Scottish Academic Press; London, distributed by Chatto and Windus.

Day, P. (1989). (ed.) *Gender and Difference in Ancient Israel*. Minneapolis, MN: Fortress Press.

(1991). Why is Anat a Warrior and Hunter? In Jobling, Day, & Sheppard (eds.), *The Bible and the Politics of Exegesis*. Cleveland: The Pilgrim Press.

de Certeau, M. (1984). *The Practice of Everyday Life* (Stephen Randall, trans.). Berkeley: University of California Press.

de Jonge, M. (1978). *A Critical Edition of the Greek Text*. Leiden: E. J. Brill.

de Lauretis, T. (1987). *Technologies of Gender: Essays on Theory, Film, and Fiction*. Bloomington: University of Indiana Press.

de Lauretis, T. (ed.). (1986). *Feminist Studies/Critical Studies*. Bloomington: Indiana University Press.

(1994). *The Practice of Love: Lesbian Sexuality and Perverse Desire*. Bloomington: Indiana University Press.

de Vaux, R. (1961). *Ancient Israel: its Life and Institutions*. New York: McGraw Hill.

Dellamora, R. (1990). *Masculine Desire: The Sexual Politics of Victorian Aestheticism*. Chapel Hill: University of North Carolina Press.

Derrida, J. (1987, c1978). *The Truth in Painting* (Geoff Bennington and Ian McLeod, trans.). Chicago: University of Chicago Press.

Detienne, M. (1994, c1972). *The Gardens of Adonis: Spices in Greek Mythology* (trans. by Janet Lloyd). Princeton: Princeton University Press.

Detienne, M., & Vernant, J.-P. (1991, c1974). *Cunning Intelligence in Greek Culture and Society* (trans. by Janet Lloyd). Chicago: University of Chicago Press.

Dijkstra, B. (1986). *Idols of Perversity: Fantasies of Feminine Evil in Fin de Siècle Culture*. New York: Oxford University Press.

Dimant, D. (1988). Use and Interpretation of Mikra in the Apocrypha and Pseudepigrapha. In M. J. Mulder (ed.), *Compendium Rerum Iudaicarum ad Novum Testamentum* (Vol. Section 2, *Mikra*). Assen: Can Gorcum & Fortress.

Doane, M. A. (1987). *The Desire to Desire: The Woman's Film of the 1940s*. Bloomington: Indiana University Press.

Doane, M. A. (ed.). (1991). *Femmes fatales: feminism, film theory, psychoanalysis*, New York: Routledge.

Donald, J. (ed.). (1989). *Fantasy and the Cinema*. London: British Film Institute.

Dottin, M. (1989). Laforgue fumiste: Salomé Floupette. *Romantisme Revue du Dix-Neuvieme Siècle,* 19(64), 17–28.

Douglas, M. (1966). *Purity and Danger: An Analysis of the Concepts of Pollution and Taboo.* London: Routledge and Kegan, Paul.

——— (1975). Deciphering a Meal, in *Implicit Meanings: Essays in Anthropology.* London: Routledge and Kegan Paul.

Douglas, M. (ed.). (1987). *Constructive Drinking: Perspectives on Drink from Anthropology.* Cambridge: Cambridge University Press.

Driver, T. (November 28, 1956). Hollywood in the Wilderness. *Christian Century* 73, 1390–1.

Duby, G. (ed.). (1988). *A History of Private Life.* Cambridge: The Belknap Press of Harvard University Press.

DuPlessis, R. (1985). *Writing Beyond the Ending: Narrative Strategies of Twentieth Century Women Writers.* Bloomington: Indiana University Press.

During, S. (ed.). (1993). *The Cultural Studies Reader.* London: Routledge.

Eagleton, T. (1983). *Literary Theory: An Introduction.* Oxford: Basil Blackwell Publishers.

Egger, B. (1993). Women and Marriage in the Greek Novels: The Constraints of Romance, in Tatum (ed.). *The Search for the Ancient Novel.* Baltimore MD: Johns Hopkins University Press.

Eilberg-Schwartz, H. (1990). *The Savage in Judaism: An Anthropology of Israelite Religion and Ancient Judaism.* Bloomington: Indiana University Press.

Ellis, S. C. (1995). *The Plays of W. B. Yeats: Yeats and the Dancer.* New York: St. Martin's Co.

Ellmann, R. (1988). *Oscar Wilde.* New York: Alfred A. Knopf.

Ellmann, R., Johnson, E. D. H., & Bush, A. L. (1966). *Wilde and the Nineties: An Essay and an Exhibition.* Princeton: Princeton University Press.

Emerton, J. A. (1975). Some Problems in Genesis xxxviii. *VT* 25, 338–61.

Enslin, M. (1972). *The Book of Judith.* Greek text with an English translation, commentary and critical notes. Edited with a general introduction and appendices by Solomon Zeitlin. Leiden, Brill.

Eron, L. J. (1987). *Ancient Jewish Attitudes Toward Sexuality.* Unpublished Dissertation, Temple University.

Exum, J. C. (1990). Murder They Wrote: Ideology and the Manipulation of Female Presence in Biblical Narrative. In A. Bach (ed.), *The Pleasure of Her Text.* Philadelphia: Trinity Press International.

——— (1992). *Tragedy in Biblical Narrative: Arrows of the Almighty.* Cambridge: Cambridge University Press.

——— (1993a). *Fragmented Women.* Sheffield: JSOT Press.

Exum, J. C., & Bos, J. (eds.). (1988). *Reasoning With the Foxes: Female Wit in a World of Male Power.* (Vol. 42).

Exum, J. C., & Clines, D. J. A. (eds.). (1993b). *The New Literary Criticism and the Hebrew Bible.* (Vol. 143). Sheffield: JSOT Press.

Febvre, L. P. V. (1982). *Problème de l'incroyance au xvie siècle, la religion de rabelais. The Problem of Unbelief in the Sixteenth Century: The Religion of Rabelais* (Trans. by Beatrice Gottlieb). Cambridge, MA: Harvard University Press.

Feliks, Yehuda (1983). Song of Songs: Nature Epic & Allegory. Jerusalem: Israel Society for Biblical Research.

Felman, S. (1977). Turning the Screw of Interpretation. *Yale French Studies* 55/6.

(1981). Rereading Femininity. *Yale French Studies* 62, 19–44.

(1987). *Jacques Lacan and the Adventure of Insight: Psychoanalysis in Contemporary Culture.* Cambridge, MA: Harvard University Press.

(1993) *What Does a Woman Want?: Reading and Sexual Difference.* Baltimore, MD: Johns Hopkins University Press.

Felman, S. (ed.). (1982). *Literature and Psychoanalysis: The Question of Reading, Otherwise.* Baltimore, MD: Johns Hopkins University Press, c1982.

Fischel, H. (1973). *Rabbinic Literature and Graeco-Roman Philosophy: A Study of Epicurea and Rhetorics in Early Midrashic Writings.* (Vol. 21). Leiden: E. J. Brill.

Fish, S. (1976). Interpreting the *Variorum. Critical Inquiry* 2, 473–85.

(1989). *Doing What Comes Naturally: Change, Rhetoric, and the Practice of Theory in Literary and Legal Studies.* Durham and London: Duke University Press.

(1994). *There's No Such Thing As Free Speech, And It's A Good Thing, Too.* New York: Oxford University Press.

Fishbane, M. (1979). *Text and Texture: Close Readings of Selected Biblical Texts.* New York: Schocken Books.

(1985). *Biblical Interpretation in Ancient Israel.* Oxford: Clarendon Press.

(1989). *The Garments of Torah: Essays in Biblical Hermeneutics.* Bloomington: Indiana University Press.

J. W. Flanagan (1983). Succession and Genealogy in the Davidic Dynasty. In H. B. Huffmon, F. A. Spina and A. R. W. Green (eds.), *The Quest for the Kingdom of God: Studies in Honor of George E. Mendenhall* (Winona Lake: Eisenbrauns, 48–49).

Fokkelman, J. P. (1975). *Narrative Art in Genesis.* Assen: Van Gorcum.

Foley, H. P. (1982). The Concept of Women in Athenian Drama. In H. P. Foley (ed.), *Reflections of Women in Antiquity.* London: Gordon and Beach.

Forshey, G. E. (1992). *American Religious and Biblical Spectaculars.* Westport, CT: Praeger.

Foucault, M. (1970). *The Order of Things: An Archaeology of the Human Sciences.* New York: Vintage Books.

(1980). *The History of Sexuality* (Robert Hurley, trans.). (Vol. 2). New York: Random House.

(1985). *The Use of Pleasure* (Robert Hurley, trans.). (Vol. 2, History of Sexuality). New York: Random House.

(1986). *The Care of the Self* (Robert Hurley, trans.). (Vol. History of Sexuality 3). New York: Random House.

Freedberg, D. (1989). *The Power of Images: Studies in the History and Theory of Response*. Chicago: University of Chicago Press.

Freud, S. (1973). *Introductory Lectures on Psychoanalysis* (Strachey, James, trans.). (Vol. 1). London: Penguin Books.

Freund, E. (1987). *The Return of the Reader*. London: Methuen & Co.

Frye, N. (1976). *The Secular Scripture*. Cambridge, MA: Harvard University Press.

Frymer-Kensky, T. (1981). Patriarchal Family Relationships and Near Eastern Law. *Biblical Archaeologist*, Fall 1981, 209–14.

Fuchs, E. (1987). Structure and Patriarchal Functions in the Biblical Betrothal Type-Scene: Some Preliminary Notes. *Journal of Feminist Studies in Religion* 3, 7–13.

(1988). For I Have the Way of Women: Depiction, Gender and Ideology in Biblical Narrative. *Semeia*, 42, 68–83.

Furman, N. (1989). His Story versus Her Story: Male Genealogy and Female Strategy in the Jacob Cycle. *Semeia*, 46, 141–49.

Fuss, D. (1989). *Essentially Speaking: Feminism, Nature, and Difference*. New York: Routledge.

Gagnier, R. (1986). *Idylls of the Marketplace: Oscar Wilde and the Victorian Public*. Stanford, CA: Stanford University Press.

Gallop, J. (1985). *Reading Lacan*. Ithaca: Cornell University Press.

(1988). *Thinking Through the Body*. New York: Columbia University Press.

(1992). *Around 1981: Academic Feminist Literary Theory*. New York: Routledge.

Gaster, T. H. (1969). *Myth, Legend, and Custom in the Old Testament*. New York: Harper).

Gay, P. (1984). *The Bourgeois Experience: Victoria to Freud*. (Vol. One: Education of the Senses). New York: Oxford University University Press.

Genette, G. (1972a). *Figures II*. Paris: Seuil.

(1972b). *Figures III*. Paris: Seuil.

(1982). *Figures of Literary Discourse* (trans. Alan Sheridan). New York: Columbia University Press.

(1988). *Narrative Discourse Revisited* (trans. by Jane E. Lewin). Ithaca: Cornell University Press.

Gesenius, W. E., Kautzsch, & Cowley, A. (1910). *Hebrew Grammar*. Oxford: Oxford University Press.

Gide, A. (1932). *Oedipe*. 9th edn. Paris, Gallimard, Editions de la Nouvelle Revue Française.

Ginzberg, L. (1911). *Legends of the Jews*. Trans. by Henrietta Szold. Vol. 3. Trans. by Paul Radin. Philadelphia: Jewish Publication Society.

Girard, R. (1977). *Violence and the Sacred* (trans. P. Gordon). Baltimore, MD: Johns Hopkins University Press.

Goff, B. E. (1990). *The Noose of Words: Readings of Desire, Violence and Language in Euripides' Hippolytos*. New York: Cambridge University Press.

Goldin, J. (1977). The Youngest Son or Where Does Genesis 38 Belong? *JBL* 96, 27–44.

Goldman, S. L. (1986). *The Jewish Story in Jewish and Islamic Lore*. Unpublished Dissertation, New York University.

Goldwater, R. (1979). *Symbolism*. New York: Harper and Row.

Goodwin, S. W., & Bronfen, E. (eds.). (1993). *Death and Representation*. Baltimore, MD: The Johns Hopkins University Press.

Goody, J. (1982). *Cooking, Cuisine, and Class: A Study in Comparative Sociology*. Cambridge: Cambridge University Press.

Goux, Jean-Joseph (1994). *Monnayeurs Du Langage. The Coiners Of Language*. Norman: University of Oklahoma Press.

(1990) *Selections. Symbolic Economie*. Ithaca: Cornell University Press.

Gow, G. (1971). *Hollywood in the Fifties*. New York: A. S. Barnes & Co.

Gowers, E. (1993). *The Loaded Table: Representations of Food in Roman Literature*. Oxford: Clarendon Press.

Greenblatt, S. J. (1990). *Learning to Curse: Essays in Early Modern Culture*. New York and London: Routledge.

Greenspahn, F. E. (1994). *When Brothers Dwell Together: The Pre-eminence of Younger Siblings in the Hebrew Bible*. Oxford: Oxford University Press.

Greenstein, E. L. (1981). Biblical Narratology. *Prooftexts* 1, 201–08.

(1982). An Equivocal Reading of the Sale of Joseph. In G. L. et al. (ed.), *Literary Interpretations of Biblical Narrative* (pp. 114–25). Nashville: Abingdon.

(1985). Sources of the Pentateuch. In P. J. Actemeier (ed.), *Harper's Bible Dictionary* (p. 983). San Francisco: Harper.

(1988). On the Genesis of Biblical Prose Narrative. *Prooftexts* 8, 347–55.

(1989a). Deconstruction and Biblical Narrative. *Prooftexts* 9, 43–71.

(1989b). *Essays on Biblical Method and Translation*. Atlanta GA: Scholars Press.

Grosz, K. (1989). Some Aspects of the Position of Women in Nuzi. In B. S. Lesko (ed.), *Women's Earliest Records: From Ancient Egypt and Western Asia*. Atlanta GA: Scholars Press.

Guillory, J. (1993). *Cultural Capital: The Problem of Literary Canon Formation*. Chicago: University of Chicago Press.

Gunkel, H. (1901). *Genesis*. (3rd edn): Vandenhoek & Ruprecht.

(1967). *The Legends of Genesis*. New York: Schocken.

(1987). *The Folktale in the Old Testament* (Michael D. Rutter, trans.). Sheffield: Almond.

Gunn, D. (1978). *The Story of King David: Genre and Interpretation.* (Vol. 6). Sheffield: JSOT Press.

(1989). In Security: The David of Biblical Narrative. In J. C. Exum (ed.), *Signs and Wonders: Biblical Texts in Literary Focus.* Atlanta: Scholars Press.

Gutting, G. (ed.). (1994). *The Cambridge Companion to Foucault.* Cambridge: Cambridge University Press.

Hackett, J. A. (1985). In the Days of Jael: Reclaiming the History of Women in Ancient Israel. In Atkinson, Buchanan, & Miles (eds.) *Immaculate and Powerful: The Female in Sacred Image and Social Reality.* Boston: Beacon Press.

Hägg, T. (1971). *Narrative Technique in Ancient Greek Romances.* Stockholm. (1983). *The Novel in Antiquity.* Berkeley: University of Caifornia Press.

Hagstrum, J. H. (1992). *Esteem Enlivened by Desire: The Couple from Homer to Shakespeare.* Chicago: University of Chicago Press.

Hallett, J. P. (1984). *Fathers and Daughters in Roman Society.* Princeton: Princeton University Press.

Halperin, D., John Winkler, Froma Zeitlin (eds.). (1990a). *Before Sexuality: The Construction of Erotic Experience in the Ancient Greek World.* Princeton, NJ: Princeton University Press.

Halperin, D. M. (1990b). *One Hundred Years of Homosexuality.* New York: Routledge Press.

Halpern, B. (1983). *The Emergence of Israel in Canaan.* Chico: Scholars Press. (1988). *The First Historians: The Hebrew Bible and History.* New York: Harper and Row.

Handelman, S. (1982). *Slayers of Moses: The Emergence of Rabbinic Thought in Modern Literary Theory.* Albany, NY: SUNY Press.

Harrington, D. J. (1975). Joseph in the Testament of Joseph, Pseudo-Philo, and Philo. In G. W. Nickelsburg (ed.), *Studies on the Testament of Joseph.* Missoula: Scholars Press.

Harris, R. (1989). Independent Women in Ancient Mesopotamia. In B. S. Lesko (ed.), *Women's Earliest Records: From Ancient Egypt and Western Asia* (pp. 145–57). Atlanta: Scholars Press.

Hart-Davis, R. (ed.). (1962). *Selected Letters of Oscar Wilde.* Oxford: Oxford University Press.

Hayman, Ronald (1995). *Thomas Mann.* New York: Scribner.

Heinemann, J. (1986). The Nature of the Aggadah. In G. H. Hartman & S. Burdick (eds.), *Midrash and Literature* (pp. 41–56). New Haven: Yale University Press.

Hendricks, M., & Parker, P. (eds.). (1994). *Women, "Race," and Writing in the Early Modern Period.* London: Routledge.

Hengel, M. (1974). *Judaism and Hellenism*. Philadelphia: Fortress Press.

Hochman, B. (1985). *Character in Literature*. Ithaca: Cornell University Press.

Hollander, H. W. (1981). *Joseph as an Ethical Model in the Testament of the Twelve Patriarchs*. Leiden: E. J. Brill.

Hollander, H. W., & de Jonge, M. (1985). *Testaments of the Twelve Patriarchs: A Commentary*. Leiden: E. J. Brill.

Hollis, S. T. (1982). *The New Egyptian Tale of Two Brothers: A Mythological, Religious, Literary, and Historico-Political Study of the Papyrus d'Orbiney*. Unpublished Dissertation, Harvard University.

(1989). The Woman in Ancient Examples of the Potiphar's Wife Motif, K2111. In P. L. Day (ed.), *Gender and Difference in Ancient Israel*. Minneapolis, MN: Fortress Press.

Horney, K. (1967). *Feminine Psychology*. New York: W.W. Norton & Company, Inc.

Hubert, H., & Mauss, M. (1964). *Sacrifice: Its Nature and Functions* (W.D. Halls, trans.). Chicago: University of Chicago Press.

Humphreys, W. L. (1973). A Life-Style for Diaspora: A Study in the Tales of Esther and Daniel. *Journal of Biblical Literature* 92, 211–33.

(1976). Joseph's Story, *Interpreter's Dictionary of the Bible: Supplementary Volume*. Nashville: Abingdon Press.

(1988). *Joseph and his Family*. Columbia: South Carolina University Press.

Huysmans, J. K. (1959). *Against Nature*. London: Penguin Books.

(1961). *A Rebours*. Paris: Bibliothèque Charpentier Gasquesse Editeurs.

(1969). *Against the Grain (A Rebours) with an introduction by Havelock Ellis*. (Reprint of Three Sirens Press edn (1931) edn). New York: Dover Publications.

Ian, M. (1993). *Remembering the Phallic Mother: Psychoanalysis, Modernisms, and the Fetish*. Ithaca NY: Cornell University Press.

Irigaray, L. (1977). Quand nos lèvres se parlent, *Ce sexe qui n'en pas un*. Paris: Editions de Minuit.

(1985a). *The Sex Which is Not One* (trans. C. Porter with C. Burke). Ithaca: Cornell University Press.

(1985b). *Speculum of the Other Woman* (trans. G. C. Gill). Ithaca: Cornell University Press.

Irvin, D. (1978). *Mytharion: The Tales from the Old Testament and the Ancient Near East*. Levelaer: Butzon & Bercker.

Iser, W. (1989). *Prospecting: From Reader Response to Literary Anthropology*. Baltimore, MD: Johns Hopkins University Press.

Ishida, T. (1977) *The Royal Dynasties in Ancient Israel* (BZAW 142; Berlin: de Gruyter, 1977) 155–60.

Jackson, M. (1987). 'Facts of Life' or the Eroticization of Women's

Oppression: Sexology and the Social Construction of Heterosexuality. In P. Caplan (ed.), *The Construction of Sexuality*. London and New York: Tavistock Publications.

James, H. (1934). *The Art of the Novel*. New York: Charles Scribner's Sons.

Jameson, F. (Autumn, 1975). Magical Narratives: romance as genre. *New Literary History*, 7(no. 1), 133–36.

Jardine, A., & Smith, P. (eds.). (1987). *Men in Feminism*. New York: Routledge.

Jay, M. (1993). *Downcast Eyes: The Denigration of Vision in Twentieth-Century French Thought*. Berkeley: University of California Press.

Jenkyns, R. (1980). *The Victorians and Ancient Greece*. Cambridge, MA: Harvard University Press.

Johnson, B. (1980). *A Critical Difference*. Baltimore, MD: Johns Hopkins University Press.

 (1987). *A World of Difference*. Baltimore, MD: Johns Hopkins University Press.

Jones, A. H., & Kingsley, K. (1983). Salome in Late Nineteenth-Century French Art and Literature. *Studies in Iconography*, 107–27.

Josephus, F. (1926). *Antiquities*. Cambridge, MA: Harvard University Press.

Jouon, P. (1947). *Grammaire de l'hebreu biblique*. (2nd edn). Graz, Austria: Akademischen Druck- u. Verlagsanstalt.

Kamuf, P. (1982). *Fictions of Feminine Desire: Disclosures of Héloise*. Lincoln: University of Nebraska Press.

Kaplan, J. (1982). *The Art of Gustave Moreau: Theory, Style, and Content*. (Vol. 33, The Avant-Garde). Ann Arbor: UMI Research Press.

Kaplan, J., & Stowell, S. (1994). *Theatre and Fashion: Oscar Wilde to the Suffragettes*. Cambridge: Cambridge University Press.

Keuls, E. (1985). *The Reign of the Phallus: Sexual Politics in Ancient Athens*. New York: Harper and Row.

Kiberd, D. (1994, December 16). Wilde and the English Question. *Times Literary Supplement*.

King, J. R. (1987). The Joseph Story and Divine Politics. *Journal of Biblical Literature* 106(4), 577–94.

Koegler, H. (1977). *The Concise Oxford Dictionary of Ballet*. London: Oxford University Press.

Kofman, S. (1985). *The Enigma of Woman: Woman in Freud's Writings* (Catherine Porter, trans.). Ithaca: Cornell University Press.

Konstan, D. (1994). *Sexual Symmetry*. Princeton: Princeton University Press.

Kornfeld, W. (1950). L'adultère dans l'Orient antique. *RB* 57, 92–109.

Kraemer, D. (1989). Images of Childhood and Adolescence in Talmudic

Literature. In D. Kraemer (ed.), *The Jewish Family: Metaphor and Memory*. New York: Oxford University Press.

Kraemer, R. (1979). Ecstasy and Possession: The Attraction of Women in Rome and Egypt. *HTR* 72, 59–65.

(1986). Non-Literary Evidence for Jewish Women in Rome and Egypt. *Helios* 13, 85–101.

(1988). *Maenads, Martyrs, Matrons, Monastics: A Sourcebook on Women's Religions in the Greco-Roman World*. Philadelphia: Fortress Press.

(1992). *Her Share of the Blessings: Women's Religions Among Pagans, Jews, and Christians in the Greco-Roman World*. Oxford: Oxford University Press.

Krauss, R. (1993). *The Optical Unconscious*. Cambridge, MA: The MIT Press.

Krecher, J., & Muller, H. P. (1975). Vergangenheitsinterresse in Mesopotamien und Israel. *Saeculum* 26, 30–44.

Kugel, J. L. (1990). *In Potiphar's House: The Interpretive Life of Biblical Texts*. San Francisco: Harper Collins.

Kuhrt, A. (1989). Non-Royal Women in the Late Babylonian Period: A Survey. In B. S. Lesko (ed.), *Women's Earliest Records: From Ancient Egypt and Western Asia*. Atlanta: Scholar's Press.

Kuntzmann, R., & Schlosser, J. (1984). *Les Etudes sur le Judaisme hellenistique*. Paris: Les Editions du Cerf.

Kuryluk, E. (1987). *Salome and Judas in the Cave of Sex: The Grotesque: Origins, Iconography, Techniques*. Evanston: Northwestern University Press.

Lacey, W. K. (1968). *The Family in Classical Greece: Aspects of Greek and Roman Life*. Ithaca: Cornell University Press.

Lambert, G. W. (1960). *Babylonian Wisdom Literature*. Oxford: Clarendon Press.

Landy, F.(1983). *Paradoxes Of Paradise*. Sheffield: Almond Press.

Langenfeld, R. (ed.). (1989). *Reconsidering Aubrey Beardsley*. Ann Arbor: University of Michigan Research Press.

Lanser, S. S. (1992). *Fictions of Authority: Women Writers and Narrative Voice*. Ithaca: Cornell University Press.

Laqueur, T. (1990). *Making Sex: Body and Gender from the Greeks to Freud*. Cambridge: Harvard University Press.

Larson, C. (ed.). (1992). *An Intimation of Things Distant: The Collected Fiction of Nella Larsen*. New York: Anchor Books/Doubleday.

Lassner, J. (1993). *Demonizing the Queen of Sheba: Boundaries of Gender and Culture in Postbiblical Judaism and Medieval Islam*. Chicago: University of Chicago Press.

Lefkowitz, M. R. (1983). Influential Women. In A. Cameron & A. Kuhrt (eds.), *Images of Women in Antiquity* (pp. 49–64). Detroit: Wayne State University Press.

(1991). Did Ancient Women Write Novels? In *Women Like This: New*

Perspectives on Jewish Women in the Greco-Roman World. Ed. A J. Levine. SBL Early Judaism and Its Literature. Atlanta GA: Scholars Press. 107–27.

Lefkowitz, M. R., & Fant, M. B. (1982). *Women's Lives in Greece and Rome*. Baltimore, MD: Johns Hopkins University Press.

Leiris, M. (1992, c1939). *Manhood: A Journey From Childhood into the Fierce Order of Virility* (Richard Howard, trans.). Chicago: University of Chicago Press.

Leitch, V. (1983). *Deconstructive Criticism: An Advanced Introduction*. New York: Columbia University Press.

— (1988). *American Literary Criticism from the 30s to the 80s*. New York: Columbia University Press.

Lemche, N. P. (1991). *The Canaanites and Their Land*. (Vol. 110). Sheffield: JSOT Press.

Lerner, G. (1986). *The Creation of Patriarchy*. London: Oxford University Press.

Levenson, J. (1978). I Samuel 25 as Literature and as History. *CBQ* 40.

Levenson, J. D., and Baruch Halpern. (1980). The Political Import of David's Marriages. *JBL* 99, 507–18.

Levi-Strauss, C. (1966). *From Honey to Ashes: Introduction to a Science of Mythology*. (Vol. 2). New York: Harper and Row.

Levine, A. J. (1992). Sacrifice and Salvation: Otherness and Domestication in the Book of Judith. In J. C. VanderKam (ed.), *No One Spoke Ill of her: Essays on Judith*. Atlanta GA.: Scholars Press.

— (1995). Hemmed in on Every Side: Jews and Women in the Book of Susanna. In A. Brenner (ed.), *A Feminist Companion to Esther, Judith, and Susanna* (pp. 303–23). Sheffield: Sheffield Academic Press.

Levine, A. J. (ed.) (1991). *Women Like This*. Atlanta GA: Scholars Press.

Lieberman, S. R. (1975). *The Eye Motif in Ancient Near Eastern and Classical Greek Sources*. Unpublished Dissertation, Boston University Graduate School.

Logue, C. (1991). *Kings: An Account of Books 1 and 2 of Homer's Illiad*. New York: Farrar, Strauss, and Giroux.

Lombardo, P. (1989). *The Three Paradoxes of Roland Barthes*. Athens: University of Georgia Press.

Lowenthal, E. I. (1973). *The Joseph Narrative in Genesis*. New York: Ktav.

Lucie-Smith, E. (1972, 1991 rev. edn). *Sexuality in Western Art*. New York: Thames and Hudson.

Luck, G. (1985). *Arcana Mundi: Magic and the Occult in the Greek and Roman Worlds, A Collection of Ancient Texts* (Georg Luck, trans.). Baltimore, MD: Johns Hopkins University Press.

Malherbe, A. (1977). *Social Aspects of Early Christianity*. Baton Rouge: Louisiana State University Press.

Malina, B. (1986). *Christian Origins and Cultural Anthropology: Practical Models for Biblical Interpretation.* Atlanta GA: John Knox Press.

Mann, T. (1938). *Joseph and his Brothers.* New York: Alfred A. Knopf.

Marcus, J. (1974). Salome: The Jewish Princess was a New Woman. *Bulletin of the New York Public Library,* p. 100, n. 28.

Marcus, M. (1993). *Filmmaking by the Book: Italian Cinema and Literary Adaptation.* Baltimore, MD: Johns Hopkins University Press.

Mathieu, P.-L. (1976). *Gustave Moreau.* Boston: New York Graphic Society.

 (1986). *Le Musée Gustave Moreau.* Paris: Editions de la Réunion des musées nationaux.

 (1991). *Tout l'oeuvre peint de Gustave Moreau.* Paris: Flammarion.

McCarter, P. K. (1984). *II Samuel, A New Translation with Introduction and Commentary.* (Vol. 9). Garden City, NY: Doubleday, Inc.

Meeks, W. A. (1983). *The First Urban Christian: The Social World of the Apostle Paul.* New Haven: Yale University Press.

Melamed, E. Z. (1988). *Halakhic Midrashim.* Jerusalem: Magness.

Meltzer, F. (1987). *Salomé and the Dance of Writing: Portraits of Mimesis in Literature.* Chicago: University of Chicago Press.

Meyers, C. (1983). Procreation, Production, and Protection: Male–Female Balance in Early Israel. *Journal of the American Academy of Religion* 51, 569–93.

 (1988). *Discovering Eve: Ancient Israelite Women in Context.* New York: Oxford University Press.

 (1989). Women and the Domestic Economy of Early Israel. In B. S. Lesko (ed.), *Women's Earliest Records: From Ancient Egypt and Western Asia* (pp. 265–78). Atlanta GA: Scholars Press.

 (1991). To her Mother's House: Considering a Counterpoint to the Israelite *Bet'ab.* In Jobling, Day, & Sheppard (eds.), *The Bible and the Politics of Exegesis.* Cleveland: The Pilgrim Press.

Milgrom, J. (1981). The Case of the Suspected Adultress, Numbers 5:11–31: Redaction and Meaning. In R. P. Friedman (ed.), *The Creation of Sacred Literature* (pp. 69–75). Berkeley: University of California Press.

 (1990). *Numbers.* Philadelphia: Jewish Publication Society.

Miscall, P. (1978). The Jacob and Joseph Stories as Analogies. *JSOT* 6, 28–40.

 (1986). *1 Samuel: A Literary Reading.* Bloomington: Indiana University Press.

Mitchell, J., & Rose, J. (eds.). (1982). *Feminine Sexuality: Jacques Lacan and the école freudienne.* New York: W.W. Norton and Company.

Mitchell, W. J. T. (1981). *On Narrative.* Chicago: University of Chicago Press.

(1994). *Picture Theory: Essays in Verbal and Visual Representation*. Chicago: University of Chicago Press.

Moi, T. (1985). *Sexual/Tectual Politics: Feminist Literary Theory*. London: Methuen.

Moi, T. (ed.). (1986). *The Kristeva Reader*. Oxford: Basil Blackwell.

Momigliano, A. (1977). *Essays in Ancient and Modern Historiography*. Middletown: Wesleyan University Press.

Monaco, J. (1981, c1977). *How to Read a Film: The Art, Technology, Language, History, and Theory of Film and Media*. (Revised edn). Oxford: Oxford University Press.

Moore, C. A. (1971). *Esther: Introduction, Translation and Notes*. (Vol. 7B). Garden City, NY: Doubleday.

(1977). *The Anchor Bible: Daniel, Esther, and Jeremiah: The Additions*. Garden City, NY: Doubleday.

(1990). Judith the Cast of the Pious Killer. *Bible Review* (Feb.), 26–36.

Moreau, G. (1974a). *Catalogue des peintures, dessins, cartons, aquarelles exposés dans des Galeries du musée Gustave Moreau, Paris*. Paris: Editions des musées nationaux.

(1974b). Gustave Moreau. Los Angeles: Los Angeles County Museum of Art.

Moriarty, M. (1991). *Roland Barthes*. Stanford: Stanford University Press.

Murray, O. (ed.). (1990). *Sympotica: A Symposium on the Symposion*. Oxford: Clarendon Press.

Nead, L. (1992). *The Female Nude: Art, Obscenity and Sexuality*. London and New York: Routledge.

Neider, Charles (1948). *Short novels of the masters*. New York: Rinehart.

Neusner, J. (1971). *The Rabbinic Traditions About the Pharisees Before 70*. Leiden: E. J. Brill.

Newsom, C. A. (1989). Woman and the Discourse of Patriarchal Wisdom: A Study of Proverbs 1–9. In P. L. Day (ed.), *Gender and Difference in Ancient Israel* (pp. 142–60). Minneapolis, MN: Fortress Press.

Newsom, C. A., & Ringe, S. H. (eds.). (1992). *The Women's Bible Commentary*. (WBC) Louisville, KY: Westminster/John Knox Press.

Nicholson, L. J. (1986). *Gender and History: The Limits of Social Theory in the Age of the Family*. New York: Columbia University Press.

Nickelsburg, G. W. E. (1972). *Resurrection, Immortality, and Eternal Life in Intertestamental Judaism*. (Vol. 26). Cambridge, MA: Harvard University Press.

(1981). *Jewish Literature Between the Bible and the Mishnah*. Philadelphia: Fortress Press.

(1984). Stories of Biblical and Early Postbiblical Times, *Jewish Writings of the Second Temple Period, Compendium Rerum Iudaicarum ad Novum Testamentum*. Assen: Van Gorcum & Fortress Press.

Nicol, G. G., Revd., BD, DPhil. (1988). Bathsheba, a Clever Woman? *The Expository Times* 99, 360–63.

Niditch, S. (1979). The Wronged Woman Righted. *Harvard Theological Review* 72, 143–49.

(1987). *Underdogs and Tricksters: A Prelude to Biblical Folklore.* New York and San Francisco: Harper and Row.

(1989). Eroticism and Death in the Tale of Jael. In P. L. Day (ed.), *Gender and Difference in Ancient Israel.* Minneapolis, MN: Fortress Press.

Niditch, S., & Doran, R. (1977). The Success Story of the Wise Courtier. *Journal of Biblical Literature* 96, 179–93.

Niehoff, M. (1992). *The Figure of Joseph in Post-Biblical Jewish Literature.* Leiden: E.J. Brill.

Noerdlinger, H. S. (1956). *Moses and Egypt: The Documentation to the Motion Picture The Ten Commandments.* Los Angeles: University of Southern California Press.

North, H. (1966). *Sophrosyne: Self-Knowledge and Self-Restraint in Greek Literature.* Ithaca: Cornell University Press.

Olivier, C. (1980). *Jocasta's Children: The Imprint of the Mother* (George Craig, trans.). London: Routledge.

Ortner, S. B., & Whitehead, H. (1981a). Introduction: Accounting for Sexual Meanings. In S. Ortner & H. Whitehead (eds.), *Sexual Meanings: The Cultural Construction of Gender and Sexuality.* Cambridge: Cambridge University Press.

(1981b). *Sexual Meanings: The Cultural Construction of Gender and Sexuality.* Cambridge: Cambridge University Press.

Ostriker, A. S. (1993). *Feminist Revision and the Bible.* Oxford: Basil Blackwell.

Pagels, E. (1979). *The Gnostic Gospels.* New York: Random House.

Paradise, J. (1980). A Daughter and her Daughter's Property at Nuzi. *JCS* 32, 189–207.

Pardes, I. (1992). *Countertraditions in the Bible: A Feminist Approach.* Cambridge, MA: Harvard University Press.

Parker, R., and G. Pollock, (eds.). (1987). *Framing Feminism: Art and the Women's Movement,* 1970–85. London: Pandora Press.

Patte, D. (1975). *Early Jewish Hermeneutic in Palestine.* (Vol. 22). Missoula MT: Scholars Press.

Pederson, J. (1953). *Israel: Its Life and Culture.* London: Cumberlege, III, IV.

Pembroke, S. (1965). The Last of the Matriarchs: A Study in the Inscriptions of Lycia. *JESHO* 8, 217–47.

Perry, B. E. (1967). *The Ancient Romances: A Literary-Historical Account of Their Origins.* Berkeley: University of California Press.

Pervo, R. (1975). Testament of Joseph and Greek Romance. In G. W.

Nickelsburg (ed.), *Studies on the Testament of Joseph* (pp. 15–28). Missoula: Scholars Press.

(1976). Joseph and Aseneth and the Greek Novel. In G. MacRae (ed.), *SBLSP 1976* (pp. 171–81). Missoula MT: Scholars Press.

(1987). *Profit With Delight: The Literary Genre of the Acts of the Apostles.* Philadelphia: Fortress Press.

(1991) Aseneth and her Sisters: Women in Jewish Narrative and in Greek Novels. In *Women Like This: New Perspectives on Jewish Women in the Greco-Roman World.* Ed. A. J. Levine. SBL Early Judaism and Its Literature. Atlanta: Scholars Press. 107–27.

Philonenko, M. (1968). *Joseph et Aséneth: Introduction, Texte critique, traduction et notes.* (Vol. 13). Leiden: E. J. Brill.

Pick, Z. M. (1994). *The New Latin American Cinema: A Continental Project.* Austin: University of Texas Press.

Pinski, D. (1923). *King David and his Wives.* Translated from the Yiddish by Isaac Goldberg. New York: B. W. Huebsch.

Plepelits, K. (1980). *Achilleus Tatios: Leukippe und Kleiphon.* Stuttgart.

Plutarch. (1932). *Lives of the Noble Grecians and Romans.* New York.

Polzin, Robert. (1980). *Moses and the Deuteronomist: A Literary Study of the Deuteronomic History.* New York: Seabury Press.

(1989). *Samuel and the Deuteronomist: A Literary Study of the Deuteronomic History.* San Francisco: Harper & Row.

(1993). *David and the Deuteronomist.* San Fransisco: Harper Collins.

Pomeroy, S. B. (1975). *Goddesses, Whores, Wives, and Slaves: Women in Classical Antiquity.* New York: Schocken Books.

(1984). *Women in Hellenistic Egypt: From Alexander to Cleopatra.* New York: Schocken Books.

Pressly, N. (1983). *Salomé: la belle dame sans merci* (Catalog for Exhibition: 1 May–26 June 1983). San Antonio Museum of Art: San Antonio Museum Association.

Prince, G. (1982). Narratology: the form and functioning of narrative. Berlin New York: Mouton. Janua linguarum. Series maior.

Propp, V. (1968). *Morphology of the Folktale.* (2nd rev. edn). Austin: University of Texas Press.

(1984). *Theory and History of Folktale* (A. Martin and R. Martin, trans.). (Vol. 5). Minneapolis: University of Minnesota Press.

Rabinowitz, N. S. (1986). Female Speech and Female Sexuality: Euripides' *Hippolytos* as Model. *Helios* 13, 127–40.

Rabinowitz, N. S., & Richlin, A. (eds.). (1993). *Feminist Theory and the Classics.* New York: Routledge.

Rabinowitz, P. J. (1987). *Before Reading: Narrative Conventions and the Politics of Interpretation.* Ithaca: Cornell University Press.

Radday, Y. T. (1990). Esther with Humor. In Y. T. R. a. A. Brener (ed.),

On Humor and the Comic in the Hebrew Bible (pp. 295–311). Sheffield: Almond Press.

Reardon, B. P. (1969). The Greek Novel. *Phoenix*, 23, 291–309.

—— (1971). *Courants littéraires grecs des IIe and IIIe siècles après J. C.* Paris.

—— (1991). *The Form of Greek Romance*. Princeton: Princeton University Press.

Reardon, B. P. (ed.). (1989). *Collected Ancient Greek Novels*. Berkeley: University of California Press.

Redford, D. B. (1970). *A Study of the Biblical Story of Joseph (Genesis 37–50).* (Vol. 20). Leiden: E. J. Brill.

Reed, C. A. (1992). Dirty Dancing: Salome, Herodias and El retablo de las maravillas. *Bulletin of the Comediantes* 44(1), 7–20.

Reid, J. D. (ed.). (1993). *The Oxford Guide to Classical Mythology in the Arts 1300–1900.* (Vol. 2). New York: Oxford University Press.

Richlin, A. (1992). *The Garden of Priapus: Sexuality and Aggression in Roman Humor.* (Revised edn). Oxford: Oxford University Press.

Rimmon, S. A. (1987). Comprehensive Theory of Narrative: Genette's Figures III and the Structuralist Study of Fiction. *PTL* 1, 33–62.

Robins, G. (1993). *Women in Ancient Egypt.* Cambridge, MA: Harvard University Press.

Roheim, G. (1934). *The Riddle of the Sphinx or Human Origins.* London: Leonard and Virginia Woolf at the Hogarth Press.

Romney-Wegner, J. (1988). *Chattel or Person?* New York: Oxford University Press.

Rosaldo, R. (1989). *Culture and Truth: The Remaking of Social Analysis.* Boston: Beacon Press.

Rose, J. (1986). *Sexuality in the Field of Vision.* London: Verso.

Rosen, P. (ed.). (1986). *Narrative, Apparatus, Ideology: A Film Theory Reader.* New York: Columbia University Press.

Rosenberg, J. (1986). *King and Kin: Political Allegory in the Hebrew Bible.* Bloomington: Indiana University Press.

Roux, G. (1992, c1964). *Ancient Iraq.* (3rd edn). London: Penguin Books.

Sancisi-Weerdenburg, H. (1995). Persian Food: Stereotypes and Political Identity. In D. H. M. D. John Wilkins (ed.), *Food in Antiquity*. Exeter: University of Exeter Press.

Sarna, N. (1989). *Genesis.* (Vol. One). Philadelphia. Jewish Publication Society.

Schafer, R. (1981). Narration in the Psychoanalytic Dialogue. In W. J. T. Mitchell (ed.), *On Narrative* (pp. 25–49). Chicago: University of Chicago Press.

Schneid-Ofseyer, M. (1989/90). The Concubine of Gibeah (Judges 19–21). *Jewish Biblical Quarterly* 18, 111–13.

Schwartz, R. (1990) (ed.) *The Book and the Text: the Bible and Literary Theory* Oxford, UK; Cambridge, MA: Basil Blackwell.

(1991). Adultery in the House of David: The Metanarrative of Biblical Scholarship and the Narratives of the Bible. *Semeia* 54, 35–55.

Scott, J. W. (1988). *Gender and the Politics of History.* New York: Columbia University Press.

Segal, C. (1986). *Language and Desire in Seneca's Phaedra.* Princeton: Princeton University Press.

Seneca. (1966). *Four Tragedies* (E. F. Watling, trans.). London: Penguin Books.

(1991). *Phaedra.* Cambridge: Cambridge University Press.

Serres, M. (1982). *Hermes: Literature, Science, Philosophy.* Baltimore, MD: The Johns Hopkins University Press.

Setel, D. (1985). Prophets and Pornography: Female Sexual Imagery in Hosea. In L. Russell (ed.) *Feminist Interpretation of the Bible.* Philadelphia: Westminster.

Showalter, E. (1990). *Sexual Anarchy: Gender and Culture at the Fin de Siècle.* New York: Viking Press.

Shulman, D. (1993). *The Hungry God: Hindu Tales of Filicide and Devotion.* Chicago: University of Chicago Press.

Silverman, D. L. (1989). *Art Nouveau in Fin-de-Siècle France: Politics, Psychology, and Style.* Berkeley: University of California Press.

Skinner, J. (1930). *A Critical and Exegetical Commentary on Genesis.* Edinburgh: Clark.

Sklar, R. (1994). *Movie-made America.* Rev. and updated. New York: Vintage Books.

Slesser, C. (1989). *The Art of Aubrey Beardsley.* London: Apple Press.

Slingerland, H. D. (1977). *The Testament of the Twelve Patriarchs: A Critical History of Research.* (Vol. 21). Missoula MT: Scholars Press.

Sly, D. (1990). *Philo's Perception of Women.* (Vol. 209). Atlanta GA: Scholars Press.

Smith, Barbara Herrnstein (1978). *On the Margins of Discourse: The Relation of Literature to Language.* Chicago: University of Chicago Press.

Smith, G. (ed.). (1989, c1983). *Benjamin: Philosophy, Aesthetics, History.* Chicago: University of Chicago Press.

Smith, J. Z. (1982). *Imagining Religion: From Babylon to Jonestown.* Chicago: University of Chicago Press.

Smith, M. (1973). *Clement of Alexandria and a Secret Gospel of Mark.* Cambridge, MA: Harvard University Press.

(1982). Clement of Alexandria and Secret Mark: The Score at the End of the First Decade. *HTR* 75, 440–61.

Snodgrass, C. (1990). Decadent Mythmaking: Arthur Symons on Aubrey Beardsley and Salomé. *Victorian Poetry* (Autumn/Winter).

Speiser, E. A. (1964). *Genesis AB 1.* Garden City, NY: Doubleday.

Spivak, G. C. (1993). *Outside in the Teaching Machine.* New York: Routledge.

Stacey, J. (1994). *Star Gazing: Hollywood Cinema and Female Scholarship.* London: Routledge.

Steiner, G. (1992, c1975). *After Babel: Aspects of Language and Translation.* (2nd edn). Oxford: Oxford University Press.

Stephens, S. A., and J. J. Winkler. (1995). *Ancient Greek Novels: The Fragments: Introduction, Text, Translation, and Commentary.* Princeton: Princeton University Press.

Sternberg, Meir. (1985). *The Poetics of Biblical Narrative.* Bloomington: Indiana University Press.

Strus, A. (1978). *Nomen-Omen.* Rome: Biblical Institute.

Suleiman, Susan Rubin (1990). *Subversive Intent: Gender, Politics, and the Avant-Garde.* Cambridge MA: Harvard University Press.

Symons, A. (1898). *Aubrey Beardsley.* London: At the Sign of the Unicorn.

Tatum, J. (ed.). (1994). *The Search for the Ancient Novel.* Baltimore: The Johns Hopkins University Press.

Tejirian, E. J. (1990). *Sexuality and the Devil: Symbols of Love, Power, and Fear in Male Psychology.* New York: Routledge.

Thompson, T. L. (1992). *Early History of the Israelite People.* Leiden: Brill.

Todorov, T. (ed.) (1982). *French Literary Theory Today: A Reader.* Translated by R. Carter. Cambridge UK & New York: Cambridge University Press.

Torgovnick, M. (ed.). (1994). *Eloquent Obsessions: Writing Cultural Criticism.* Durham, NC: Duke University Press.

Treuherz, J. (1993). *Victorian Painting.* London: Thames and Hudson.

Trible, P. (1973). Depatriarchalizing in Biblical Interpretation. *Journal of the American Academy of Religion* 41, 30–48.

⸻ (1978). *God and the Rhetoric of Sexuality.* Philadelphia: Fortress Press.

⸻ (1982). The Effect of Women's Studies on Biblical Studies. *JSOT* 22, 3–4.

⸻ (1984). *Texts of Terror.* Philadelphia: Fortress Press.

⸻ (1994). *Rhetorical Criticism: Context, Method, and the Book of Jonah.* Minneapolis, MN: Fortress Press.

Tyrrell, W. M. B. (1984). *Amazons: A Study in Athenian Mythmaking.* Baltimore: Johns Hopkins University Press.

van Seters, J. (1983). *In Search of History.* New Haven: Yale University Press.

Veeder, W., & Griffin, S. M. (eds.). (1986). *The Art of Criticism: Henry James on the Theory and the Practice of Fiction.* Chicago: University of Chicago Press.

Vernant, J.-P. (1979a). Naissance d'images, *Religions, histoires, raisons* (pp. 105–37). Paris: François Maspero.

⸻ (1979b). *Religions, histoires, raisons.* Paris: François Maspero.

(1980). *Mythe et pensée chez les Grecs: Etudes de psychologie historique.* Paris: François Maspero.

(1990, c1974). *Myth and Society in Ancient Greece.* New York: Zone Books.

(1991). *Mortal and Immortals: Collected Essays* (Trans. by Froma I. Zeitlin). Princeton: Princeton University Press.

Veyne, P. (1983). *Les Grecs ont-ils cru à leurs mythes?* Paris: Seuil.

(1990, c1976). *Bread and Circuses: Historical Sociology and Political Pluralism.* London: Allen Lane, Penguin Press.

von Rad, G. (1959). *Genesis.* Philadelphia: Westminster.

(1972). *Wisdom in Israel.* Nashville: Abingdon Press.

Walfish, B. D. (1993). *Esther in Medieval Garb: Jewish Interpretation of the Book of Esther in the Middle Ages.* Albany: SUNY Press.

Webb, R. L. (1991). *John the Baptizer and Prophet: A Socio-Historical Study.* Sheffield: Sheffield Academic Press.

Westermann, C. (1986). *Genesis 37–50.* (Trans. by John J. Scullion) Minneapolis, MN: Augsburg Publishing House.

White, H. (1972). The Forms of Wildness: Archaeology of an Idea. In E. Dudley & M. E. Novak (eds.), *The Wild Man Within.* Pittsburgh: University of Pittsburgh Press.

(1980). The Value of Narrativity in the Representation of Reality. *Critical Inquiry* 7(1).

White, S. A. (1992). In the Steps of Jael and Deborah: Judith as Heroine, *No One Spoke Ill of her: Essays on Judith.* Atlanta, GA: Scholars Press.

Whybray, R. N. (1968). *The Succession Narrative: A Study of 11 Samuel 9–20 and I Kings I and 2.* SBT 2.9; London: SCM Press.

(1989). *The Making Of The Pentateuch: A Methodological Study.* Sheffield: JSOT Press.

Wilde, O. (1894, reprinted 1957.) *Salomé, a Tragedy in One Act (pictures by Aubrey Beardsley).* London: E. Matthews & J. Lane; Copeland & Day. Reprinted by Heinemann.

Willemen, P. (1994). *Looks and Frictions: Essays in Cultural Studies and Film Theory.* London Indianapolis: British Film Institute. Indiana University Press.

Williams, B. (1993). *Shame and Necessity.* (Vol. 57). Berkeley: University of California Press.

Williams, J. G. (1985). *Women Recounted: Narrative Thinking and the God of Israel.* (Vol. 6). Sheffield: Almond Press.

Winkler, J. J. (1985). *Auctor & actor: A Narratological Reading of Apuleius' Golden Ass.* Berkeley: University of California Press.

(1990a). *The Constraints of Desire: The Anthropology of Sex and Gender in Ancient Greece.* New York and London: Routledge.

Winkler, J. J. and Froma Zeitlin (eds.) (1990b). *Nothing to do with Dionysos?:*

Athenian Drama in its Social Context. Princeton: Princeton University Press.

Winnington-Ingram, R. P. (1958). *Hippolytus: A Study in Causation*, Entretiens sur l'antiquité classique VI: Euripide. Geneva.

Wittig, M. (1981). One is Not Born A Woman. *Feminist Issues* 1–2.

Wright, A. (1966). The Literary Genre Midrash. *CBQ* 28, 418–22.

Wright, E. (1984). *Psychoanalytic Criticism: Theory in Practice*. London: Methuen.

Yee, G. (1989). "I Have Perfumed My Bed with Myrrh": The Foreign Woman in Proverbs 1–9. *JSOT* 43.

Yohanan, Y. D. (1968). *Joseph and Potiphar's Wife in World Literature: An Anthology of the Chaste Youth and the Lustful Stepmother*. Trans. by various hands and edited with commentary by John D. Yohannan. New York: New Directions.

Young-Bruehl, E. (ed.). (1990). *Freud on Women: A Reader*. New York: W. W. Norton & Company, Inc.

Zagona, H. G. (1960). *The Legend of Salomé and the Principle of Art for Art's Sake*. Paris: Librairie Minard.

Zatlin, L. G. (1990). *Aubrey Beardsley and Victorian Sexual Politics*. Oxford: Clarendon Press.

Index of references

General index

Abigail, 115, 118, 123, 134–36, 153–54
Abishag, 146
Absalom, 152–55
Ackerman, Susan, 170–73
Adam, 185
Ahasuerus, 187, 189, 192, 194–97
Albright, William Fox, 173–74
Alter, Robert: on Abigail, 136; on Esther, 187; on Genesis, 39, 45, 50; on narrator, 13–14, 21, 23–24
Amaru, Betsy 103
Amnon, 184–85
Aptowitzer, V. 108
aroma, 173–74; and Christianity, 176; and sacrifice, 170; and sexuality, 176–86
Arthur, Marilyn, 103
Aseneth, 95, 108–14, 126
Asherah, 173
audience: fictive, 23; as author, 160

Bakhtin, Mikhail, 16–17, 106, 148–50
Bal, Mieke: on Bathsheba, 134, 141; on binary opposition, 11; on Mut-em-enet, 61, 85–86; on narratorial embedding, 23–24; on narratorial focalization, 24–25; on visual interpretation, 158–60
banquets, 9–11, 187, 191; in *Esther*, 194–200; and fasting, 197, 203; in *Judith*, 203–04; in tale of Salomé, 220
Barthes, Roland, 57
Bathsheba: in Biblical interpretation, 132–34; in *David and his Wives*, 146–51; in feminist film version, 158–65; as matriarch, 142–44; as object of desire, 134–36

bayit (house), 45, 49
Beardsley, Aubrey, 241–48
Beer, G., 83
Berger, John, 132
Berlin, Adele, 56, 132–33
Bettelheim, Bruno, 206
Bickerman, Elias J., 107
Bloom, Harold, 17–18, 94–95
Braun, Martin, 73, 74, 100
Brenner, Athalya, 54, 56, 189
Brooks, Peter, 57–8, 85

Certeau, Michel de, 1–2
character, and reader, 2, 25–29, 38, 136, 186–87
characterization, process of, 235, 238
Chatman, Seymour, 132–33, 136
Circe, 185–86
Classen, Constance, 172, 176, 181
criticism: formalist, 40–42; rhetorical, 40–42; structuralist, 40–42
Culler, Jonathan, 13, 18, 39
Cultural Studies, 7–8

Daniel, 65, 67
David and Bathsheba (film), 159–60
David, 49, 115, 118, 122, 132–46; in *David and His Wives*, 146–51; sexual and political power, 141–54; in Talmudic interpretation, 147
de Lauretis, Teresa, 130
Deborah, 201, 203
Delilah, 49, 187, 190, 212–13
Detienne, Marcel, 171–72, 190
Doane, Mary Ann, 231, 249
doxa, 3, 5, 134, 187